ARMORED FIGHTING VEHICLES
OF GERMANY

World War II

Edited by Duncan Crow

Published by
ARCO PUBLISHING COMPANY, INC.
New York

Published 1978 by Arco Publishing Company, Inc.
219 Park Avenue South, New York, N.Y. 10003.

Library of Congress Cataloging in Publication Data

ARMORED FIGHTING VEHICLES OF GERMANY

Includes indexes
1. Tanks (Military science) 2. Armored vehicles,
Military. 3. Mechanization, Military – Germany.
I. Crow, Duncan.
UG446.5.A75 1978   358'.18   78-3546
ISBN 0-668-04641-4

CONTENTS

Coloured Illustrations by:

Tom Brittain, Uwe Feist, Terence Hadler, Martin Lee, Michael Roffe.

ACKNOWLEDGMENTS

The Editor, Authors, Artists and Publishers wish to acknowledge the kind assistance given by the Imperial War Museum, the Royal Armoured Corps Tank Museum, and the Bundesarchiv Koblenz, and by the publications and individuals whose help has been invaluable in the production of this book.

ERRATA

Page   6   Left-hand column, line 10: Delete 'in the Eastern Baltic States'.

Page   13   Amend the divisional sign on the PzKpfw I from 'Y' to 'X'.

Page   51   Left-hand column, bottom caption: The tank shown is in use with the Swedish Army not the Czech Army.

Page   55   Top caption: The cylindrical device is a 'Punkervärmare' fuel tank for the methylene spirit heater used for starting the engine during severe winter conditions.

Page   75   Right-hand column, line 24: Amend 'mm/sec' to 'm/sec'.

Page   88   Caption, line 2: Amend 'P2' to 'Pz'.

Page 129   Amend the turret marking '805' to 'S05'.

Panzer IV *in the Libyan Desert.*

Achtung! Panzer!
by Duncan Crow

THIS title is not original. It was used nearly forty years ago by the great German General Heinz Guderian for a book that he wrote telling how the German armoured forces had been developed up to that date and how he and his superior, General Lutz, believed that they should be built up in the future. But as Guderian's achievements with the panzer forces which he was so largely instrumental in creating are a continuing thread running through the present volume it seems apposite, legitimate, and indeed even obligatory, to borrow his title.

Although his name recurs frequently in the following pages, however, this book is not about Guderian. Far from it. In the German Army he was not a lone wolf in his enthusiasm for armour and mobility. Many others – strategists, tacticians, engineers, and the tank soldiers themselves – contributed to the great saga of the Panzers.

Walter Spielberger, author of the *Profiles* on the Panzers III and IV, the Mittlerer Schuetzenpanzer-wagen SdKfz 251, and the Elefant, who was himself a combatant in World War II after working as a design engineer with Professor Porsche, has written a book on the Panther in which he quotes from the regimental history of the British 23rd Hussars, one of the armoured regiments in the British 11th Armoured Division which fought in the North-West Europe campaign. The quotation describes Operation "Good-wood", south-east of Caen in July 1944, and highlights the actions between the Hussars' Shermans and the German Panthers that opposed them, in which the Panthers came off much the best. "It is left to the reader's imagination," comments Spielberger, "as to

what could have happened if the German Army would have possessed an adequate number of these armoured fighting vehicles, provided with adequate supplies and covered by a superior Air Force."

Although this comment savours a little of the old military axiom that if one's aunt had been differently equipped she would have been one's uncle, it is nonetheless a highly relevant conjecture. Having served throughout World War II and lived those years in the propaganda climate of the time I became accustomed to thinking of the German Army as being equipped with an unending supply of tanks and other weapons that always seemed to be available at any particular point in the conflict in greater numbers than our equipment. Clearly, we gathered, this was because the Germans had been planning the war for years and had been stocking up their armouries to be used against their unsuspecting victims. What about the Poles having to counter-attack with horsed cavalry charges against the thousands of heavy German tanks, for instance? And then the May 1940 campaign – thousands more heavy German tanks against the few hundred French and British light tanks. And the Russians in 1941 overwhelmed by dozens of Panzer Divisions. And Rommel driving the British back to El Alamein by sheer weight of numbers . . .

All that, and more, was part of the myth that grew up in the climate of war. It survived, as I recall, almost up to the Normandy landings. Somehow we thought of ourselves as the forlorn hope storming the impregnable Nazi fortress. And please note that I am not suggesting that we didn't think we had a chance or that we reckoned the German Army was any better than we were if the odds were reasonably even. The point is that we never thought the odds were anywhere near even. We were somehow conditioned into believing that the Germans always had more, if not better equipment, than we had.

It comes as a great shock, therefore, to anyone who was cozened throughout the war in this belief when he discovers the actual numbers involved. Take for example the accepted belief about the Battle of France – that the Germans overran the British, French and Belgians because they had so many more and so many bigger tanks than the Allies. In fact, the Germans had about the same number of tanks as the British and French had on the north-east front, and by far the greater number of the Germans' 2,574 tanks were the light Panzers I and II and the ex-Czech 38 and 35 Panzers. Or take the Rommel "weight of numbers" myth. By the time he had pushed his way to El Alamein and had tried to bounce the Eighth Army out of the Alamein Line the Afrika Korps on the morning of July 4, 1942 had only thirty-six tanks left in running order. The same is true of much of the Russian fighting. There were countless occasions when a handful of German tanks overwhelmed apparently insuperable odds. (In passing it must be noted that the reverse was also true. The exploits of a single Russian KV–1 against the supply echelons of 6th Panzer Division early in Operation "Barbarossa" are a case in point).

In fact the Germans built 23,487 tanks from the beginning of 1939 to the end of 1944. This was slightly less than the British, and just under one quarter of the American tank production, let alone the Russian output which was almost as large as the American. The output of British, American and Russian tanks during World War II totalled about 212,000.

The Germans also built 42,932 tracklaying self-propelled guns. But this was barely a third of American production alone.

Admittedly World War II was not won or lost by armour alone. But armour played a dominant part in the land battles. And the question therefore arises: given the enormous weight of armour against them, how did the Germans survive so long?

The answer, I think, is to be found in Brigadier Bryan Watkins' brilliant account of the achievements of German armour, *Only Movement Brings Victory,* which appears in Part II of this volume. "The story of German armour is a remarkable one," he says. "Years of study by dedicated professionals, superb leadership on the battlefield, sound training and high tactical skill, combined with a forceful and imaginative equipped policy, produced some notable achievements. Good though the German equipment was, however, it was above all the Germans' ability to achieve surprise, their great flexibility, . . . and the fighting spirit and determination of their soldiers, which were the telling factors in many of their successes." A bald, encapsulated account of the exploits of 40 Panzer Divisions (including the SS Panzer Divisions) completes the rest of Part II.

Both aspects of German armoured excellence in World War II – the equipment and its use on the battlefield – are covered in detail in this fifth volume of Profile's *Armoured Fighting Vehicles of the World.*

Part I consists of Profiles of the German AFVs, including the self-propelled guns that were mounted on the chassis of tanks and armoured cars, and which became an increasingly important part of AFV production as the trend of events in the war forced the Germans more and more on to the defensive. More

Sturmgeschuetz III *in Russia.*

Mittlerer Schuetzenpanzerwagen *SdKfz 251/10, the platoon commander's variant which mounted a 3·7 cm anti-tank gun.*

SPs were turned out in the last three months of 1944 than in 1943 as a whole.

The order in which the Profiles of the vehicles appear is as follows:

Panzerkampfwagen I and II: These were the vast majority of the tanks in the Panzer Divisions' *blitzkreig* against Poland in 1939, and to a lesser, though still dominant extent in the 1940 campaign against the Low Countries and France.

Panzerkampfwagen III: This was the tank which dominated the armoured battles of the early war years and which helped to start a new trend in the construction of armoured fighting vehicles.

Panzerkampfwagen 38(t) and 35(t): These were the most important of the foreign tanks taken into German service as standard equipment. These Czech vehicles fought in France and in the early part of the Russian campaign.

Panzerkampfwagen IV: While the Panther and the Tiger have tended to capture the limelight, it was in fact the Panzers III and IV which established the reputation of the German armoured forces. The Panzer IV, whose first prototype was built in 1934, eventually became the only German tank which remained in production and troop service throughout World War II, a fact which demonstrates its sound basic design and the brilliant foresight shown in its specification.

Panzerkampfwagen V Panther: This was probably the best German tank of World War II. It was built initially to meet the threat of the Russian T-34.

Panzerkampfwagen VI Tiger I and II: "Slow and heavy, large and cumbersome" the Tiger may have been, but it was a formidable tank to encounter and could stand tremendous punishment on its thick frontal armour. This Profile tells the story of the legendary Tiger – both the Tiger I (SdKfz 181) and

the Tiger II or King Tiger (SdKfz 182). Both had their drawbacks from the logistic and tactical points of view – faults, however, that were not always apparent to those who had to face them.

Panzerjaeger Tiger (P) Elefant: Elefant was the conversion of the original Porsche Tiger tank design into a self-propelled tank destroyer.

German Super-Heavy Tanks Maus and E-100: Maus, the largest armoured fighting vehicle ever built, was the culmination of Porsche's technical development in the Tiger field. E-100 was a rival design to the Maus.

Schuetzenpanzerwagen SdKfz 251 and SdKfz 250: In the German Army of World War II the tank found its classic partner in the armoured personnel carrier. There were two types – the *mittlerer Schuetzenpanzerwagen* SdKfz 251 (with 22 variants) and the *leichter Schuetzenpanzerwagen* SdKfz 250 (with 12 variants). Without all-arms support, notably from armoured infantry in their *Schuetzenpanzerwagen,* the great Panzer Division epic could never have happened. The vehicles in this Profile were no less important than the Panzers they supported.

German Armoured Cars: This Profile starts with the anti-balloon cars of the early years of the century. As light tanks became popular in the 1930s the importance of armoured cars declined – except in Germany and France. Germany attached great importance to armoured cars and they were the basic vehicles of the Panzer Divisions' reconnaissance units in World War II.

Illustrated Summary of German Self-Propelled Weapons (1939-1945): SPs were a highly important element of German armoured strength. This Profile illustrates 159 different types, all those for which photographs are known to be available.

A Glossary of German terms used appears at the beginning of this Profile on page 202.

Grosstraktor II, *the Rheinmetall prototype. There were two other* Grosstraktor *prototypes: I was built by Daimler-Benz, III by Krupp. All three were designed to the same basic specification and were similar in shape and size, though differing in suspension and details. I had a 105 mm gun as main armament, II and III had a 75 mm gun. Each had a machine-gun turret at the rear for enfilading enemy trenches as the tank crossed over them.*

Light Traktor *with 37 mm gun.*

Pz Kpfw I Ausführung (model) A distinguished from Ausf. B by the four suspension wheels and three return rollers.
(Photo: Imperial War Museum)

Panzerkampfwagen I and II

by Major-General N. W. Duncan

UNDER the Treaty of Versailles, signed after the First World War, Germany was restricted to an army of 100,000 men and was forbidden to have or to build any tanks. General von Seeckt, who was commander-in-chief of this force until 1926, was a firm believer in the value of flexibility and mobility, and in addition to publishing a book on the subject he lost no opportunity of driving these two virtues home to his command. Although he was not a great believer in the tank he appreciated the part that it could play in attaining his ideal and its potentialities were continually under review. Von Seeckt used the post-war German army as a gigantic training cadre to turn out a succession of junior leaders who would be required when the force was increased in size. He also instituted a series of war games and theoretical exercises to examine the conduct of operations and to determine the equipment needed to bring them to a successful conclusion.

For some years the official ban on tanks was reinforced in practice by the dislocation following the war. Reparations, requirements for civilian construction, and the ban on the manufacture of military equipment imposed by the Versailles Treaty, all meant that there was virtually no German heavy industry available or ready to undertake tank construction. However, in 1926 Rheinmetall built a tank in mild steel disguised under the description of a *Grosstraktor*. This so-called tractor had a turret-mounted 75-mm. gun, weighed about 20 tons, and resembled the Vickers Medium Mark II. In 1928 a light "tractor" was built mounting a 37-mm. gun. Then in the early '30s came the multi-turreted Neubaufahrzeug (new model vehicle) A which weighed 35 tons with a 75-mm. and coaxial 37-mm. in the main turret and machine-guns in each of two sub-

sidiary turrets fore and aft of the main turret. It had 70 mm. of armour and looked similar to the Vickers Medium Mark III or the Russian T-28, all three being influenced by the Independent A1E1. NbFz Type B had a 105-mm. gun in place of the 75-mm.

Forbidden to have tanks by the Versailles Treaty, the German army began its armoured training with canvas dummies pushed about by men on foot. In 1929 Guderian, who was tactical instructor at the Motor Transport Instructional Staff, Berlin, introduced motorized dummies of sheet metal.
(Photo: R.A.C. Tank Museum)

Despite the Versailles Treaty prohibition, Germany built some experimental tanks including these Neubaufahrzeuge.
(Photo: R.A.C. Tank Museum)

Guderian's dummy tanks. (Photo: R.A.C. Tank Museum)

Both types had a 500-h.p. engine and a speed of about 15 m.p.h. Excluding the Neubaufahrzeug, ten tanks in all were built—two each of two types of medium, and two each of three types of light. The light tanks all had 37-mm. guns and were the first gun-armed light tanks to be built; other nations were still making the machine-gun the main armament. These forbidden machines were tried out with Russian connivance at a tank testing centre established in 1926 at Kazan in the Eastern Baltic States.

Meanwhile a champion of armoured warfare had arisen in Lieut.-Col. Heinz Guderian who, in 1931, became Chief of Staff to General Lutz, Inspector of Motorized Troops. Lutz and Guderian were convinced that the future development of German armoured troops must be the formation of Panzer Divisions. As far as tanks were concerned they saw the requirement for two types: the first, a medium

tank in the 20-ton class, armed with a 75-mm. gun in the turret and two machine-guns, and capable of taking its place in the tank battle; and the second, a lighter machine intended primarily for reconnaissance, and armed with a 50-mm. armour-piercing gun and two machine-guns. These conclusions were accepted, except for the gun on the light tank which was to be 37-mm. because this was the size of gun with which the German infantry were already being equipped for the anti-tank rôle. The Chief of the Ordnance Office and the Inspector of Artillery favoured the 37-mm. gun and the desirability of production simplicity enhanced their argument. The change was reluctantly accepted by the armoured representatives.

None of the experimental models which had been built were considered adequate to fill the rôle required of these two types in the proposed Panzer Divisions. New models were necessary, and these eventually emerged in real life as the Pz Kpfw III and IV, but until they were ready, which would be several years, a training tank was needed. In the interests of speedy production and for the education of industry a light tank was the obvious answer. Light tanks were cheaper, they could be built easily—especially with the Carden-Loyd Mark VI chassis which had been bought in England ostensibly as a carrier for a 20-mm. anti-aircraft gun to serve as a design guide—and their potential would create no undue alarm in other countries.

In pursuance of this policy, the German Army Weapons Branch (Heereswaffenamt), on behalf of the General Staff, issued a requirement for a tank of approximately 5 tons weight with two machine-guns mounted in a turret with all-round traverse and protected by armour immune to attack by small arms fire. Five firms, an indication of the rapid recovery made by German heavy industry, were selected—Rheinmetall Borsig, Daimler-Benz, MAN, Henschel, and Krupp—and they were invited to submit their proposals for a machine to meet the requirement. Germany was lucky to have as many firms as this with the necessary engineering experience, design staff, and capacity to undertake work of this nature. Germany was more fortunate than other countries which on occasion have found civilian industry

Panzer I Ausf. As drawn up for inspection on peace-time manoeuvres. (Photo: Imperial War Museum)

Panzer I Ausf. As moving through a battered street in Granadella during the Nationalist offensive in Catalonia towards the end of the Spanish Civil War.
(Photo: Imperial War Museum)

reluctant to branch out into unknown fields, and it says a good deal for the resilience of German industry that it should have been able to undertake this task so relatively soon after the country's defeat.

LANDWIRTSCHAFTLICHER SCHLEPPER (La S)

After close and detailed examinations LKA1, a design submitted by Krupps and based on the Carden-Loyd Mk. VI chassis, was selected and Krupps were made responsible for the development of the chassis, while Daimler-Benz were to construct the turret and the hull. To ensure secrecy and to hide the project from the outside world, the machine was given the code name of "Landwirtschaftlicher Schlepper (La S)" or agricultural tractor. As the drawings and design reached completion in December 1933 Henschel were given orders to construct three prototypes. The first of these ran in February 1934, an extremely short time for constructional work of this nature even allowing for the fact that the tank was a very simple one.

Full-scale production began in 1934 with an order for 150 machines given to Henschel under the description IA La S Krupp and this was followed by another version known as IB La S May. About 1,800 in all were built and of these roughly 1,500 were the B model, longer and with a more powerful engine.

Panzer I Ausf. A showing twin MGs in turret.   (Photo: Imperial War Museum)

Panzer I Ausf. Bs entering Warsaw after it had been forced to capitulate on September 27, 1939. Note five suspension wheels and four return rollers.
(Photo: Imperial War Museum)

The La S designation was retained until 1938 when a standard code for tank designation was substituted. Experimental machines were given an identifying serial number—700 or 2000 or 3003, for example. The first number or pair of numbers indicated the weight class of the vehicle, e.g. 7 ton or 20 ton or 30 ton. The last two numbers were used to indicate the number of the prototype. A prefix VK indicated that the vehicle was fully tracked and where a multiple order had been given, the firms' initial letters followed in a bracket after the serial number, e.g. VK 2001 (H) and VK 2002 (DB) would have indicated tanks in the 20-ton class under experimental con-

struction by Henschel and Daimler-Benz respectively.

When a tank had been accepted for service it became known by its class name followed by the model number. Panzerkampfwagen abbreviated into Pz Kpfw or PzKw was used, e.g. Pz Kpfw I C indicating Model C of the first tank. On acceptance into the service a tank also received an Ordnance vocabulary number, e.g. Sonderkraftfahrzeug 101 abbreviated to SdKfz 101.

PZ KPFW I A (SD KFZ 101)

This tank was a straightforward machine with no unexpected characteristics or technical devices. It

Panzer I Ausf. A in Norway, April 1940, attacking a Norwegian position while German infantry take cover.
(Photo: Imperial War Museum)

was 13 ft. long and weighed 5·4 tons, with a crew of two men. It had welded turret mounting two coaxial 7·92-mm. MGs in an external mantlet and no special provision was made for observation by the commander who was perforce the gunner as well.

A 3·5 litre air-cooled Krupp M 305 four-cylinder engine was used which developed 57 h.p. at 2,500 r.p.m. and was housed in the engine compartment at the back of the tank together with a large oil cooler. The drive was taken forward to a five-speed sliding pinion gearbox and thence through cross shafts, carrying on each side a clutch and brake steering system, to the front driving sprockets. Several machines were fitted with the Krupp M 601 CI engine which developed 45 h.p. at 2,200 r.p.m., but the experiment proved unsuccessful and the Krupp petrol engine was used in all production models of the Pz Kpfw IA.

Krupps original prototype had four suspension wheels with a rear idler touching the ground: movement of the wheels was controlled by coil springs and three return rollers were mounted on the hull. The layout was changed in the production models which had an external girder covering the two rear suspension wheels. The ends of this girder were connected to the axle of the second suspension wheel and to the rear idler wheel axle by forked links carrying $\frac{1}{4}$ elliptic springs whose tips rested on the axles of the third and fourth suspension wheels. Movement of the leading suspension wheel was controlled by coil springs and three return rollers were mounted on the hull. The suspension was reasonably satisfactory at low speeds but pitched badly when the tank was moving faster, probably accentuated by the rear idler wheel which was in contact with the ground. The outside girder

appears in almost all original light tank designs whatever the country of origin. While it simplifies design to some extent it offers much additional drag in soft going and is vulnerable to hostile gun-fire. In practically every instance it disappears after the first batch of tanks, but in this instance it was used in the IA and IB and is included in the first two versions of Pz Kpfw II. Pz Kpfw I in all models used a single-pin skeletal track, having two guiding horns on each plate between which ran the suspension wheels: track plates were 10 in. wide.

PZ KPFW I B (SD KFZ 101)

This tank was evolved from Model A and appeared in 1935. Superficially the external appearance is the same but there are considerable differences in detail. A more powerful engine, a water-cooled Maybach NL 38 TR was installed and this required a longer and higher engine compartment. The tank was lengthened to provide the extra room and the sides of the superstructure were raised. The engine developed 100 h.p. at 3,000 r.p.m. and the extra power raised the speed of the tank from 23 to 25 m.p.h.

The armament remained the same as in the IA and despite the many disadvantages the two-man crew was retained. Armour thickness remained at 13 mm. and the turret showed no change except that an internal mantlet was used, a design feature that appeared on all German tanks until the introduction of the 50-mm. gun on the Pz Kpfw IIIs. A redesigned transmission incorporating a five-speed gearbox and a better final drive reduction gear was substituted for the IA pattern. The nose plate of the tank was redesigned to provide the necessary room for the final reduction gear which resulted in a complicated design pattern for casting.

Panzer Ausf. A in Norway. Soldier marching beside it gives good indication of its height. (Photo: Imperial War Museum)

Panzer I Ausf. B passing through a destroyed town during the campaign in the west, May 1940. The numbers 322 on the turret side are tactical markings. 3 indicates company in regiment, first 2 is Zug (platoon) in company, second 2 is vehicle in Zug.
(Photo: Imperial War Museum)

To allow for the extra room needed by the bigger engine the suspension was modified and an extra wheel, making five in all, was inserted: the rear idler wheel was raised clear of the ground which materially improved the ride, and the additional suspension wheel meant that the same amount of track as before was in contact with the ground. Four return rollers were used on the hull in place of the three of the earlier model.

The turret was set over on the right-hand side of the superstructure; the driver sat on the left-hand side of the hull in contrast to the general run of two-man tanks whose turret with the commander/gunner is usually directly behind the driver. There is no obvious reason for the German practice: it gives a wider hull with the tracks a little further apart and therefore the tank possesses a little more lateral stability and it may simplify mechanical layout; against these points must be put the extra size of the hull and the consequent weight increase.

KLEINER PANZER BEFEHLSWAGEN (SD KFZ 265)

This imposing title (abbreviated to Kl.Pz.Bef.Wg) was given to a command tank. The superstructure was considerably modified and the sides built up to form a rectangular non-rotating turret which carried a 7·92-mm MG in a ball mounting in the front plate for defensive purposes. An additional 17 mm. of armour plate was added to the turret face and the nose plate was also reinforced by an additional 10 mm.

Two hundred of the I B chassis were modified and three types were produced, 1KlB, 2KlB and 3KlB. Differences between them were slight, but one of them incorporated a rotating turret which was abandoned because the interior was too cramped. The crew of these tanks was increased to three men. Provision was made for a small table and for the display of maps, and two wireless sets, an FU2 and an FU6, were fitted. Additional dynamo capacity to keep the wireless batteries fully charged was also provided.

Great importance was attached to these tanks since they enabled a commander to be up with his leading

troops and also provided him with the means of controlling a battle and issuing the necessary orders. They were first used in the Polish campaign and 96 of them were available for use in the operations in the West in 1940.

PZ KPFW I C (VK 601)

In September 1939 a requirement was issued for a variation of the normal Pz Kpfw I to make it suitable for use as a fast reconnaissance vehicle, which could also be used for airborne operations. The project was given an experimental number VK 601, and two firms, Krauss Maffei and Daimler-Benz, were selected to build it. The order was for 40 machines which were to be completed by July 1942: it seems curious that so long a time should have been allowed for this contract when the speed of completion of other Mark Is is taken into consideration. Only one prototype is however believed to have been delivered and this is reinforced by the fact that this model never received an Ordnance vocabulary number.

Model C was to weigh about 8 tons and was to carry up to 30 mm. of armour. A 20-mm. gun and a 7·92-mm. MG were to be mounted coaxially in the turret which was to be angular in shape with an external mantlet and a form of cupola for the commander/gunner: the hull superstructure was lower than in the standard Mark Is. A six-cylinder Maybach HL 45 engine which developed 150 h.p. gave the tank a top speed of 40 m.p.h. despite the increased weight. No return rollers were fitted on the hull and the top run of the track was taken on the tops of two lines of overlapping suspension wheels, three on the inside and two on the outside. The track plates had a central guide and in contrast to earlier patterns were fitted with projecting grouser bars.

VK 1801 (PZ KPFW I D)

This heavily armoured version of Pz Kpfw I is most interesting because it represents a complete change of thought on the part of the General Staff. The aberration was short-lived and this tank was only produced in prototype form. It was intended for close co-operation with the infantry to provide them with

Panzer Is advancing through a burning village in Russia, 1942. Leading vehicle is an Ausf. B.

(Photo: Imperial War Museum)

Three Panzer I Ausf. As in Russia following an early model Panzer III (Ausf. B or C).　　　　(Photo: H. J. Nowarra)

immediate MG fire; this was in contrast to the normal practice of concentrating all armour in armoured divisions which were trained to exploit the mobility of the tank.

The requirement, issued in December 1939, called for a tank of between 18 and 19 tons weight: it was to carry 80 mm. of armour and was to have been armed with two 7·92-mm. MGs mounted in a heavily armoured external mantlet. The same type of suspension as in VK 601 but on much more robust lines was to have been used, but the track reverted to the earlier skeletal type with no projecting grousers. The Maybach HL 45 six-cylinder engine was again used and would have given a top speed of 15 m.p.h. The first machine ran in June 1940 but the project was then abandoned.

An interesting comparison can be drawn between this machine and the Infantry Tank Mark I which the British had in 1940. Armour thicknesses were approximately the same, the German had one more MG and if it had ever been used would have achieved the same results: immunity to current anti-tank guns and

Panzer I Ausf. A in the rôle of a flame-thrower. Vehicle was modified by the Afrika Korps for use against Tobruk fortifications. Right-hand MG was replaced by flame-gun. Fuel containers were carried in turret. The R on the turret side indicates that the vehicle belongs to Regimental H.Q., 15 being the identifying number of the tank at R.H.Q.　　　　(Photo: R.A.C. Tank Museum)

Pz Kpfw I Ausf. B showing the five suspension wheels, four return rollers, and raised idler wheel.   (Photo: R.A.C. Tank Museum)

insufficient gun power to achieve decisive results. The German machine had one great advantage—it was capable of nearly three times the speed the British tank could achieve.

PZ KPFW II—THE FIRST MODELS

For one reason and another, production of Pz Kpfw III and IV proceeded more slowly than forecast. To cover the delay in getting these tanks into the hands of troops it was decided to build a tank in the 10 ton class as a successor to Pz Kpfw I. The new tank was only to be a training machine stop-gap; paradoxically it fought in two wars, the Spanish Civil War and in the opening stages of World War II, and without it the early German successes could not have been achieved.

A specification for the new tank was issued in July 1934. Three prototypes were submitted, one of them being Krupps' LKA II which closely resembled their prototype LKA I for Pz Kpfw I. Machines

Three-quarter front view of Panzer I Ausf. B on a transporter showing driver's visor and entry hatch open.
(Photo: R.A.C. Tank Museum)

were also built by Henschel and MAN, both resembling the Krupp design except for radical differences in the suspension. Under the pseudonym La S 100 the MAN vehicle was selected for production.

Twenty-five tanks were issued during 1935 as 1/La S 100 and taken into service as Pz Kpfw II a1 (SdKfz 121). They weighed 7·2 tons and had a crew of three. They were armed with a 20 mm. KwK 30 gun and a 7·92-mm. MG, mounted coaxially in a turret with all-round traverse. They were powered by a Maybach HL 57 six-cylinder petrol engine developing 130 h.p. at 2,100 r.p.m. A plate clutch and a six-speed sliding pinion gearbox took the power to a cross shaft: this carried at either end the usual clutch and brake steering mechanism for each track and a driving sprocket. The suspension consisted of six small suspension wheels grouped in pairs in bogies which were sprung by leaf springs. An outside girder connected the outer ends of the bogie pivot pins, the inboard ends being housed in the hull which also carried three return rollers. The adjustable rear idler wheel was clear of the ground. The nose plate was a rounded casting, a distinct change from previous German tanks, and an internal mantlet was used in the turret.

These first 25 machines were followed, also in 1935, by a second batch of 25—Pz Kpfw II a2. Externally they were exactly the same as the a1s but had a better cooling system and more room had been found in the engine compartment. A further batch of 50 machines appeared in 1936—Pz Kpfw II a3. Further improvements had been effected in the cooling system and the tracks and suspension had been altered for the better in comparison with the earlier machines.

2/La S 100, or Pz Kpfw II·b, appeared in 1936. One hundred machines were built with frontal armour increased to 30 mm. and an all-up weight of 7·9 tons. The armament remained unchanged, but a Maybach HL 62 petrol engine was fitted which

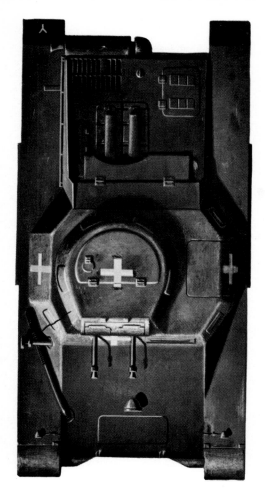

0   5 Feet

1 Metre

PzKpfw I Ausf. B of 1st Panzer Division at the time of the Polish campaign in September 1939. Plain white cross was national insignia for this campaign. Divisional signs of the first panzer divisions were changed in late 1940.

Panzer School training machine—Pz Kpfw I Ausf. B.
(Photo: Imperial War Museum)

other versions the superstructure sides tapered a little towards the front which meant that the driver's plate was narrower than the width of the hull. A radical change had been effected in the suspension. The outside girder and the small bogies disappeared and were replaced by five medium-sized suspension wheels each individually controlled by $\frac{1}{4}$ elliptic springs. Four return rollers were used on the hull. This suspension was used for all subsequent models of Pz Kpfw II.

PZ KPFW II A, B AND C

The early versions of Pz Kpfw II, together with Pz Kpfw Is, were tried out under operational conditions in the Spanish Civil War—an opportunity rarely given to tank builders during peace-time. The behaviour of the machines showed that though they were only intended as training machines they were soundly constructed and capable of playing their part in an armoured rôle provided that the opposition was not too strong, but even with the primitive anti-tank resources available in Spain the Pz Kpfw Is were virtually outclassed. It would appear that the vulnerability of the tanks under the conditions of war in Spain was misinterpreted by the German General Staff who at least acquiesced in the continued large-scale production of the Pz Kpfw II which by 1938-39 was on the way to becoming obsolescent. Even though its armour was increased it was barely proof against the current anti-tank guns in Europe. While the armament was adequate for taking on its own kind, the Panzer II was too undergunned to deal with heavier hostile tanks and had no HE capacity at all. However, despite these disadvantages which were well known to all armoured officers, production continued till 1942.

developed 140 h.p. Externally there was little change. These tanks had a new reduction gear in the cross drive and a new type of driving sprocket which incorporated a geared final drive. These sprockets, together with new pattern track plates that appeared with the machine, were adopted as standard fittings for all subsequent Pz Kpfw IIs.

In 1937 the third version, 3/La S 100 or Pz Kpfw IIc, appeared; slight alterations were made to the turret which still housed the same armament and the driver's front plate extended right across the tank: in

Panzer I Ausf. A and B chassis being used for training by the NSKK (National-Socialist Mechanized Corps)
(Photo: Imperial War Museum)

Panzer I on the Leningrad front.
(Photo: Imperial War Museum)

150-mm. infantry support gun (Infanteriegeschütz 33) on a Panzer I Ausf. B chassis. (Photo: Imperial War Museum)

Pz Kpfw II A, B and C appeared between 1937 and 1940. There is little difference between these models. The 1937 tanks which mark the real start of mass production show little change from Pz Kpfw II c. To improve protection the nose plate is changed and becomes angular and of welded construction instead of being round in shape and cast in construction. Gun mantlets are very slightly changed with flanges at the top and bottom of the internal moving shield, presumably to avoid lead splash. Otherwise the turret was unchanged except that provision was now made for the commander's observation—a periscope in model A and a cupola in B and in subsequent models.

The German Army had 955 Pz Kpfw IIs for the attack on France in May 1940, and 1,067 when the Russian campaign began in 1941. By the following April this figure had been reduced to 866 despite continued production, an indication of the casualties inflicted by the Soviet forces, and a further example of the folly of using undergunned and under-armoured tanks against an opponent with material superiority in armour.

PZ KPFW II D AND E

These machines, built by Daimler-Benz, were intended to be a faster version of the standard tanks. As far as the turret, superstructure, engine and transmission were concerned they showed no difference from the other Panzer IIs. However, the suspension was completely changed and used four large suspension wheels in Christie tank fashion but with their movement controlled by torsion bars. These tanks could reach 35 m.p.h. but their performance across country was considerably slower than the standard Pz Kpfw II.

Panzer Jäger I. Czech 4·7-cm. PAK (t) on Panzer I Ausf. B chassis. PAK=Panzerabwehr Kanone=anti-tank gun; (t)=(tscheche)= (Czech).
(Photo: Imperial War Museum)

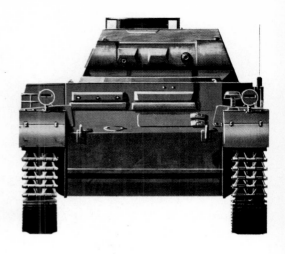

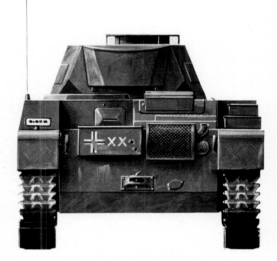

PzKpfw II Ausf. F of 6th Panzer Division. The national insignia was changed to a black cross after the Polish campaign and vehicles that had been in Poland had their white crosses modified as shown here.

Bottom right Wespe (the Wasp)—10.5 cm Pz FH 18/2 auf PzKpfw II (Sf), Sd Kfz 124. An AA MG34 is shown mounted above the superstructure. Three "kill" rings on the Wasp's gun barrel are tally of vehicles destroyed. Munition carriers were structurally similar except for a curved plate across the gun aperture.

Panzerjäger I. Germany's first self-propelled gun, converted from a
Panzer I B and mounting a captured Czech 4.7 cm PAK L/43.

Luchs (the Lynx)—Panzerspähwagen II (2 cm KwK 38), Sd Kfz 123.
Hadler/Brittain/Lee © *Profile Publications Ltd.*

Left side view of Kleiner Panzer Befehlswagen on Panzer I Ausf. B chassis.

(Photo: R.A.C. Tank Museum)

FLAMMPANZER II (SDKFZ 122)

Because the performance of Models D and E did not come up to expectation they were taken out of service and 95 were converted to a flame-throwing rôle. They were fitted with two flame-throwers each covering 180 degrees of arc with a flame range of about 40 yards, which is about the maximum that can be obtained with a pump-fed gun. To obtain greater range it is necessary to use a gas pressurized system which introduces problems over stowage. Sufficient fuel was stowed in internal tanks for about 80 shots each of 2-3 seconds duration.

PZ KPFW II F

The hollow charge anti-tank missile had by now become a menace to be reckoned with. After reference to Hitler and with his personal agreement, it was decided that all future AFVs were to be up-armoured by the addition of spaced plates to reduce the effect of the new missiles.

In pursuance of this decision the last of the Pz Kpfw II series appeared in late 1940. This was

Right side view of Kleiner Panzer Befehlswagen. Panzer I Command Tank with non-rotating turret and single MG.
(Photo: Imperial War Museum)

7/La S 100—Pz Kpfw II F. It weighed 9½ tons with 35 mm. of armour on the front and 20 mm. on the sides. Otherwise it was exactly the same as Model C in appearance with engine, transmission, armament and suspension remaining unchanged. The top speed was considerably reduced but this was a penalty that had been foreseen when the order authorizing additional armour was issued. Crew losses had been heavy, heavy enough to justify the reduction in performance in the hope of saving lives. Production of Model F was to have been at the rate of 45 per month but rarely reached this target.

In 1941 a new specification was issued which called for a ten-ton vehicle with increased armour over that of Model F and a higher speed. To meet this requirement MAN delivered a chassis in September which had a Maybach HL-P engine developing 200 h.p. and was capable of a top speed of 40 m.p.h. The tank was to have had 30 mm. of armour, a three-man crew, and was to have been armed with a 20 mm. type 38 gun of higher velocity than that used in the other models, together with a 7·92-mm. MG. Production was scheduled for July 1942 but by then the Pz Kpfw II was so obviously obsolete in its tank rôle that the order was cancelled.

PZ KPFW II L (SDKFZ 123) "LUCHS" (LYNX)

The final prototype Lynx (VK 1303) appeared in mild steel in 1942 but its development story goes back to 1938 when Daimler-Benz were given instructions to produce a new version of Pz Kpfw II "with principal emphasis on increased speed" under the development number VK 901.

A Maybach HL 45 six-cylinder petrol engine was used which gave 145 h.p. and a top speed for the tank of 32 m.p.h. The specified speed was 37½ m.p.h. but that was unattainable because no engine of the necessary power (200 h.p.) was available at the time. VK 901 had 30 mm. of front armour and weighed 9·2 tons. It was armed with a 20 mm. type 38 tank gun and a 7·92 MG which was mounted coaxially: both guns were installed in a stabilized mounting. The manufacture of 75 pre-production machines began in 1940. The third prototype VK 903 had a turret from VK 1303 which became the Lynx and which had been equipped with a range finder and locating instruments. This substitution of turrets gives some idea of the complexity of the German tank programme for at that time the Lynx chassis had been built by MAN: the interplay of one model on another is difficult to disentangle, but it is quite clear that development was on a most extensive scale which makes the continued retention of Pz Kpfw II difficult to understand.

To complicate matters even further, Daimler-Benz and MAN together received another contract in December 1939 for a very different type of machine. VK 1601 was to carry "the thickest possible armour" with a crew of three men. The Maybach HL 45 engine of 200 h.p. was used for the project giving a top speed of 20 m.p.h. with an all-up weight of 16½ tons. Frontal armour was 80 mm. thick and the side armour was 50 mm. Armament was the 20-mm. KwK 38 gun and an MG in a stabilized mount.

Both VK 901 and VK 1601 used a new type of suspension with five large overlapping suspension wheels with no return rollers. Torsion bar springing was used. This type of suspension, which had already been tried out on VK 601 (the Pz Kpfw I prototype of the 6-ton tank), ultimately led to the Panther and Tiger suspension where overlapping became interleaving—a necessary step to reduce ground pressure but one which brought many problems concerned with track jamming in its wake.

Early model Panzer II in action in Poland, September 1939. Probably Ausf. b, but possibly a1, a2 or a3.
(Photo: R.A.C. Tank Museum)

Out of these two models VK 1301, "Luchs," was born. VK 901 was considered too light for its proposed rôle and VK 1601 was much too heavy. The prototype VK 1301 in mild steel ran in April 1942, looking very like VK 901. Various alterations were made to this first prototype and VK 1303, the third prototype, was accepted for production at a weight of 11·8 tons, a reduction of a little over a ton on the first prototype VK 1301.

Intended primarily for reconnaissance the Lynx was also given the designation Panzerspähwagen II (2 cm. KwK 38) "Luchs," with the same Ordnance vocabulary number, Sd kfz 123. It weighed 11·8 tons and had a crew of four men: it was fitted with a Maybach HL 66P six-cylinder engine which developed 180 h.p. The drive was taken to the front driving sprocket through a Synchron SSG 46 six-speed gearbox and controlled differential steering on the cross shafts. The maximum speed was 38 m.p.h. Luchs used

Pz Kpfw II Ausf. c in November 1939. Note cast rounded nose plate and medium-sized suspension wheels which identify it. Compare angular welded nose plate of subsequent Ausf. A.
(Photo: Imperial War Museum)

Panzer divisional signs from late 1940. After their victory in France in 1940 the Germans doubled the number of their panzer divisions for the next campaign. Signs of the old divisions were changed and the new signs shown here were introduced. Panzer divisions from 21 onwards were formed after 1940. The Gross Deutschland was officially a panzer grenadier regiment but with its full tank regiment and armoured reconnaissance unit under command it was actually a panzer division.

1st Panzer

2nd Panzer

3rd Panzer

4th Panzer

6th Panzer

5th Panzer

7th Panzer

8th Panzer

9th Panzer

10th Panzer

11th Panzer

12th Panzer

Gross Deutschland

13th Panzer

14th Panzer

15th Panzer

16th Panzer

17th Panzer

18th Panzer

19th Panzer

20th Panzer

21st Panzer

22nd Panzer

23rd Panzer

24th Panzer

25th Panzer

Afrika Korps

116th Panzer

Afrika Korps (variation)

1st Panzer (variation)

4th Panzer (1943)

7th Panzer (1943–44)

19th Panzer (1943–44)

23rd Panzer (variation)

Panzer II Ausf. c in the attack on Warsaw, September 1939.

(Photo: Imperial War Museum)

the same five overlapping suspension wheel suspension that had been developed on VK 901 and VK 1601 with torsion bar springing. Frontal armour was 30 mm. and the side plates 20 mm. MAN at Nürnberg built the chassis, Daimler-Benz at Berlin-Marienfelde the hulls and turrets.

One hundred of these tanks were fitted with 20-mm. guns and a further 31 were fitted with 50-mm. KwK 39 L/60 guns. Admittedly the Lynx turret had been redesigned, but if it was possible to get a 50-mm. piece on the last L chassis it is curious that no effort was made to upgun earlier models, especially after the 20-mm. had proved inadequate during the campaign in France in 1940.

LEOPARD (VK 1602)

In 1941 the army Weapons Branch called for a vehicle capable of undertaking battle reconnaissance in contrast to the Lynx which was intended—and used—for general reconnaissance and was not intended to take part in the main battle. The new contract given to MAN and Daimler-Benz was for VK 1602 inspired by VK 1601 which has already been discussed as one of the forerunners of Lynx.

The new tank, Leopard—a favourite cognomen for German tanks—was to have 80 mm. of armour on the turret and the front and 60 mm. on the sides. It was to have a 550 h.p. engine to give it a top speed of 37 m.p.h. and it was to be armed with a 50 mm. type 39 L/60 gun and an MG coaxially mounted. It was to have a crew of four men, but their disposition in the tank is not known. There was no bow machine-gun so that the fourth man was not needed there: he could have been employed as wireless operator next to the driver, a common German practice; alternatively he might have been used in the turret as a loader and this is probably the more likely course. While it is interesting, the problem is actually only of academic interest because the tank never went into production although the turrets were used for the eight-wheeled armoured car Puma, Sd kfz 234/2.

PZ KPFW II—AMPHIBIOUS

In preparation for the invasion of England—Operation Sealion—a regiment's worth of Pz Kpfw IIs were converted to amphibious tanks. Extra flotation gear, pontoons of some sort, were attached to the return rollers on either side of the tank to provide the necessary buoyancy to make it float. As a further precaution the inside of the tank was divided into three watertight compartments. When afloat the tank was driven by a propeller off an extension shaft from the gearbox. It was said to float at track guard level and to be very seaworthy in seas Force 3-4; also to be capable of a speed of 5 knots in the water. In theory the guns could be fired from the turret when the tank was waterborne: in practice the tank was never used operationally and from experience with other amphibious tanks it is very unlikely that the quoted figure could have been reached.

Panzer II Ausf. A. Note horn-type periscope on turret top (centrally behind guns) which distinguishes Ausf. A from subsequent models; also absence of cupola. Background suggests tank is passing through Flemish square.

(Photo: Imperial War Museum)

Panzer II Ausf. B (note cupola and absence of horn-type periscope) knocked out in the Western Desert fighting.
(Photo: Imperial War Museum)

Panzer II Ausf. Bs in Russia.
(Photo: Imperial War Museum)

Panzer IIs Ausf. B or C on a desert road in North Africa spanned by one of the triumphal arches erected under Mussolini's rule.
(Photo: Imperial War Museum)

Flammpanzer II—Ausf. D or E modified as flame-thrower, showing location of flame-gun and rod of fuel which has apparently not ignited. Vehicle is in Russian hands having been captured on Leningrad front. (Photo: R.A.C. Tank Museum)

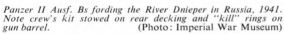

Panzer II Ausf. Bs fording the River Dnieper in Russia, 1941. Note crew's kit stowed on rear decking and "kill" rings on gun barrel. (Photo: Imperial War Museum)

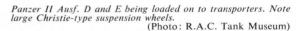

Panzer II Ausf. D and E being loaded on to transporters. Note large Christie-type suspension wheels. (Photo: R.A.C. Tank Museum)

PZ KPFW I AND II IN OTHER ROLES

When the Pz Kpfw Is were no longer required as tanks they were converted for other duties. Some were used for the carriage of ammunition while many of the IBs ended their days as tractors. Three hundred and fifty-eight IBs were converted into Pz Jäger I self-propelled guns armed with the Czech 4·7 cm. PAK L/43. They were used in the Western Desert and on the Russian front in later 1941 for a short period. Others mounted a 150-mm. gun for the close support of infantry in the attack: these guns were also used to give high angle covering fire for armoured attacks.

The Pz Kpfw II chassis was also used for various tasks. Models D and E, as mentioned previously, were early converted to flame-throwers following their lack of success as a fast version of the ordinary gun tanks. After the appearance of the Russian T-34 other Panzer II chassis, together with chassis of Pz Kpfw 38(t), were rapidly converted to anti-tank SP weapons using captured Russian 76·2 mm. anti-tank guns or field guns of the same calibre. Subsequently chassis were converted to anti-tank weapons using a 75-mm. PAK 40/2. In all, nearly 1,000 Panzer II chassis were converted either to the anti-tank rôle or else to an SP artillery weapon mounting a 105-mm. light field howitzer.

WESPE

In the latter rôle the vehicle was designated "Wespe" (Wasp): 10·5 cm. Pz FH 18/2 auf Pz Kpfw II (Sf)—Wespe Sd Kfz 124. Wespe had the Panzer II F chassis and the first vehicles were coming off the production line at the Famo assembly plant in Poland in December 1942. In February 1943 Hitler ordered that all Pz Kpfw II production capacity should be concentrated on Wespe, the anti-tank SP rôle being taken by the Pz Kpfw 38 (t) chassis. Wespe production continued until mid-1944 by which time 682 had been built and a further 158 completed as ammunition carriers without the gun.

Wespe was popular with the troops, being generally used in the divisional artillery of panzer and panzer grenadier divisions organized in batteries of six with up to five batteries in an abteilung (battalion).

THE PANZER DIVISIONS
by
DUNCAN CROW

Germany's first three panzer, or armoured, divisions ("panzer" is the German for "armour") were formed on October 15, 1935. The 1st Panzer Division, commanded by General Freiherr von Weichs, was at Weimar, the 2nd, under Colonel Guderian, was at Würzburg, and the 3rd, under General Fessman, was in Berlin. The main tank was the Panzer I.

Each panzer division had: one panzer brigade consisting of two panzer regiments, each with two tank battalions, each of four light tank companies; one motorized rifle brigade of three battalions, two of

Panzer II Ausf. F of a regimental H.Q. (indicated by R on turret side). Figures 06 identify the vehicle as part of reconnaissance Zug. Track on nose plate is for extra protection. Vehicle was captured in North Africa and is now in the Royal Armoured Corps Tank Museum at Bovington, England. Chassis number is 28434, Ausf. F having been allocated chassis number block from 28000 to 29400.
(Photo: R.A.C. Tank Museum)

Panzer II Ausf. F which was up-armoured on turret and nose. The visor beside the driver's true visor (under the 20-mm. gun) was a dummy, presumably to confuse enemy anti-tank gunners. To complete the illusion there was also a vision slit on the off-side super-structure to match the one seen here on the near-side. Conical idler wheel was also a feature of Ausf. F.

(Photo: R.A.C. Tank Museum)

them in a rifle regiment, the other a motor-cycle battalion (each rifle battalion had one motor-cycle company, two motorized rifle companies, one heavy machine-gun company, and one mixed company of engineer, anti-tank, and infantry gun platoons, while the motor-cycle battalion had three motor-cycle companies and one mixed company similarly organized); an armoured reconnaissance battalion consisting of two armoured car companies, one motor-cycle company, and one mixed company; an anti-tank battalion of three anti-tank companies; an artillery regiment of two battalions, each of three batteries of light field howitzers; a signals battalion of two companies, one equipped with telephones, the other with wireless; and a light engineer company.

The first public appearance of a German panzer division, which was in fact an improved copy of the British Experimental Armoured Force of 1927-28, was in 1937 at the autumn manoeuvres in Mecklenburg, when the show-piece was an attack by 800 tanks and 400 aircraft. For years the German General Staff—and especially Guderian, who was himself, as he admitted, a disciple of the type of warfare propounded by Liddell Hart, Fuller and Martel—had been considering three principles of tank fighting: the use of tanks in close co-operation with infantry; the independent use of tanks to break through and penetrate into the enemy's defensive position; and the best use of air co-operation. In order to decide on the type of tank to be built and the type of formation in which tanks should be organized it was necessary to choose between one or other of the first two principles: one sacrificed speed, the other armour protection.

Guderian had no doubt which principle should be chosen. In 1929 he had become convinced that "tanks working on their own or in conjunction with infantry could never achieve decisive importance. My historical studies," he wrote in his memoirs, "the exercises carried out in England and our own experiences with mock-ups had persuaded me that tanks would never be able to produce their full effect until the other weapons on whose support they must inevitably rely were brought up to their standard of speed and of cross-country performance. In such a formation of all arms, the tanks must play the primary rôle, the other weapons being subordinated to the requirements of the armour. It would be wrong to include tanks in infantry divisions: what was needed were armoured divisions which would include all the supporting arms needed to allow the tanks to fight with full effect."*

Guderian's view prevailed. The final decision favoured speed. The second principle was chosen; and to it was added the third—close support bombing would be used to give maximum striking power.

A number of Panzers I and II served with the Franco forces in the Spanish Civil War and gave valuable experience to the German army. Spain provided the dress rehearsal of blitzkrieg when, towards the end of the war, motorized columns pushed forward 25 miles a day in the Aragon battle and even faster during the drive through Catalonia; the enormous influence of air superiority was clear to all who saw it.

More experience was gained from the moves into

*General Heinz Guderian, *Panzer Leader,* Michael Joseph (London) 1952.

Austria and Czechoslovakia. Defects that were revealed in March 1938 were remedied before the occupation of the Sudetenland later in the year. The occupation of Czechoslovakia, carried out on March 15 and 16, 1939, in hard weather conditions, showed that panzer divisions could operate on frozen roads and in difficult country. For example, one panzer division on the first day of the march to Prague covered nearly one hundred miles over bad roads in a snowstorm without a single vehicle being disabled.

By September 1, 1939, when the Polish campaign began, there were six panzer divisions (1st, 2nd, 3rd, 4th, 5th and 10th), plus the Panzer Lehr Battalion, the Ordnance Department's own unit for tank testing and demonstrations, and the Reconnaissance Demonstration Battalion. All took part in the campaign, the two demonstration battalions as part of Guderian's XIX Army Corps. In addition there were four light divisions which also fought in Poland.* These light divisions were the cavalry's counterwork to the panzer divisions. Just as the cavalry in Britain strongly resisted any loss of identity or surrender of ground to the Royal Tank Corps, so the cavalry in Germany tried to remain independent of the panzers. They

*In Appendix III to *Panzer Leader* Guderian states that three light divisions took part in the Polish campaign. This appendix is a copy of a report he wrote as Inspector General of Armoured Forces in November 1944, five years after the campaign in which he was a corps commander. But the battle map earlier in the book (p.77) shows four light divisions engaged (just as it shows six panzer divisions) and the text on p.89 confirms this by implication. This error in Guderian's 1944 report has been repeated by most Wehrmacht historians.

formed light divisions, each of which had two motorized rifle regiments of two battalions each, a reconnaissance regiment, an artillery regiment, and a lorry-borne light tank battalion, as well as supporting units. Early in 1940, before the campaign in the west, the light divisions were converted to panzer divisions (6th, 7th, 8th and 9th).

By May 10, 1940, when the attack on the Low Countries and France began, the organization of a panzer division excluding its supply services was:

HQ

Armoured Recce Bn, consisting of:
two armoured car companies, each of ten armoured cars, *motor-cycle company, mixed company* of anti-tank, close support gun, mortar and engineer platoons.

Panzer Brigade, consisting of:
two panzer regiments, each of *two mixed tank battalions,* each of *two light and one medium companies.*

Motorized Rifle Brigade, consisting of:
one rifle regiment of *three battalions,* two of them each with *a motor-cycle company, two infantry companies, a machine-gun company, and a mixed company,* the third with *three infantry companies, a machine-gun company, and a mixed company,*
motorcycle battalion of *two motor-cycle companies, a machine-gun company, and a mixed company,*
heavy infantry gun company with six guns.

Anti-tank Bn, consisting of:
three companies each with 12 light anti-tank guns, *one company* with six heavy anti-tank guns.

Anti-aircraft Bn, consisting of:
one battery with nine heavy AA machine-cannons, *two batteries* each with 12 light AA guns.

Artillery Regiment, consisting of:
two battalions, each of *three batteries,* each of four field guns, signals etc., *one battalion* of *three batteries,* each of four howitzers, signals, etc.

Air Reconnaissance Squadron, consisting of:
nine recce aircraft.

Panzers I and II being prepared for embarkation. Apparatus for discharging smoke is fitted at tail. Note divisional sign on right-hand mudguard of right-hand tank and on tool chest of left-hand tank.
(Photo: Imperial War Museum)

Above: *150-mm. heavy infantry support gun (Infanterie-geschütz 33) on a lengthened Panzer II chassis.*
(Photo: Imperial War Museum)

Top left: *Wespe—10·5-cm. Panzerfeldhaubtize 18 on a Panzer II chassis.* (Photo: Imperial War Museum)

Bottom left: *Panzer II Ausf. F in the desert. This particular vehicle appears to have been fitted with a heavier gun than the 20-mm. weapon usual in this model.*
(Photo: Imperial War Museum)

Signals Bn, consisting of:
one wireless company, one telephone company.

Engineer Bn, consisting of:
two motorized engineer companies, one armoured engineer company, two bridging columns, light engineer column.
Bugle Platoon.
Supply Bn.
Administrative services.

This was the organization of the 1st-5th and 10th Panzer Divisions which were equipped entirely with German tanks. The 6th, 7th and 8th were equipped with captured Czech tanks and had only one panzer regiment of three battalions. The 9th, equipped with German tanks, had only one panzer regiment of two battalions.

At the opening of the Polish campaign the vast majority of the tanks in the six panzer divisions were Pz Kpfw I and II, most of the Pz Kpfw III and IV being allotted to the Panzer-Lehr. By May 10, 1940, the 35 tank battalions launched against the west had 523 Pz Kpfw I, 955 Pz Kpfw II, 349 Pz Kpfw III, 278 Pz Kpfw IV, 106 Pz Kpfw 35(t) (Czech), 228 Pz Kpfw 38(t) (Czech), 96 Kleine Panzer Befehlswagen (on Panzer IB chassis), and 39 Panzer Befehlswagen III (on Panzer III chassis)—a total of 2,574 tanks.

After their victory in the west the Germans doubled the number of their panzer divisions. But there were as yet insufficient tanks to equip all the divisions to the original scale, so that the doubling was only nominal. Each tank brigade was reduced to one regiment. Six divisions each had a three-battalion regiment, but the remainder had only two battalions. The battalions, however, were more powerful. Each had two light companies equipped with up-gunned Panzer IIIs and one medium company with 75-mm. Panzer IVs. The infantry brigade now had two two-battalion motorized rifle regiments and one motor-cycle battalion. Anti-aircraft artillery became a regiment equipped with 88-mm. guns.

Both the 5th (Light)—later re-designated the 21st

Panzer—and the 15th Panzer Divisions which arrived in the Western Desert in 1941 were on the reduced establishment of two tank battalions and three motorized rifle battalions; and this was basically the establishment of the panzer divisions which took part in the attack on Russia in June 1941. About 3,200 tanks were available at the start of the campaign in the east.

Three years later, on the eve of the battle of Normandy, the standard panzer division had two tank battalions (one generally equipped with Pz Kpfw IV, the other with Panthers). Only one of the three artillery battalions had SP guns, and only one out of the four infantry battalions had armoured personnel carriers. Tank battalions were now not mixed—each, in theory, had four companies of 22 tanks each. In practice it was usually three companies of 17 tanks each: by the end of the war it was 14. Some panzer divisions—especially the SS—were favoured and had three tank battalions; the Gross Deutschland, for example, had three battalions (one of Tigers) and six infantry battalions. Special Panzer-Lehr establishment when it became a division late in 1943 was two tank battalions, each of four companies, with a divisional HQ company of Tigers; its infantry battalions had half-tracks, and artillery units had SP guns.

In 1944 there were 25 army panzer divisions and seven SS panzer divisions, formed originally from panzer grenadiers. There was also the Hermann Goering Panzer Parachute Corps of two divisions formed of Luftwaffe personnel.

The army panzer divisions were numbered 1 to 27 inclusive, all formed before the end of 1942, plus 116 formed in spring 1944 and Panzer-Lehr. Of these the 10th, 18th, 22nd and 27th were destroyed or disbanded (the 18th) in 1943 and not re-formed. The 14th, 15th, 16th, 21st and 24th were destroyed in 1943 but all were re-formed—the 15th as a panzer grenadier division.

Type & Model Date	Weight tons	Crew	Length	Width	Height	Speed m.p.h.	Radius of action	Armament/Amn Main	Mgs	Armour max/min mm.	Engine BHP/r.p.m. BHP/ton	Transmission	Remarks
Pz Kpfw 1A Sd Kfz 101 1934	5·4	2	13'2"	6'10"	5'8"	25	90	—	2/ 3125	13/7	Krupp M.105 4-cyl. air cooled 60/2500 11·1 per ton	5 F I R clutch and brake steering	Four suspension wheels. External girder. Rear idler on ground. Three return rollers. External mantlet
Pz Kpfw IB Sd Kfz 101 1935	5·8	2	14'7"	6'10"	5'8"	25	90	—	2/ 3125	13/7	Maybach NL 38 TR 6-cyl. water cooled 100/3000 17·2 per ton	5 F I R clutch and brake steering	Five suspension wheels. External girder. Rear idler wheel raised. Four return rollers. Internal gun mantlet. Skeletal track
Kleine Panzer Befehlswagen (Kl.Pz.Bef.Wg.) Sd Kfz 265 1938	5·8	3	14'7"	6'10"	5'8"	25	90	—	1/ 900	30/23/ 7	Maybach NL 38 TR 6-cyl. water cooled 100/3000 17·2 per ton	5 F I R clutch and brake steering	Command tank. Two wireless sets
Pz Kpfw IC VK 601 1939	8·0	2	14'6"	6'10"	5'8"	40	90	1 × 20mm./ —	1/—	30/10	Maybach HL 45 6-cyl. 150/3000 18·8 per ton	5 F I R clutch and brake steering	Prototype only. Five overlapping suspension wheels of large diameter—no return rollers. Steel track with grouser bars. Commander's observation cupola
Pz Kpfw ID VK 1801 1939	18·5	2	14'4"	8'7"	6'9"	15	60		2/	82/20	Maybach HL 45 6-cyl. 150/3000 7 per ton	5 F I R clutch and brake steering	Prototype only. Intended for close co-operation with infantry. Five overlapping large diameter suspension wheels. No return rollers. External grouser bars on track Commander's observation periscope
Pz Kpfw II a1, a2, a3. (1, 2, 3 La S100) Sd Kfz 121 1934	7·2	3	15'10"	7'1"	6'8"	25	110	20mm. KwK 30/ 180	1/ 1425	14·5	Maybach HL 57 TR 6-cyl. 130/3000	6 F I R Synchromesh gearbox clutch and brake steering	Rounded nose plates. Minor variations between a1, a2, a3. Three pairs small suspension wheels each side. External girder. Raised rear idler. Three return rollers. Internal gun mantlet
Pz Kpfw IIb or 2 La S100b Sd Kfz 121 1934	7·9	3	15'10"	7'1"	6'8"	25	100	20mm./ 180	1/ 1425	14·5/	Maybach HL TR 6-cyl. 140/2600 17·7 per ton	6 F I R Synchromesh. Epicyclic steering	Similar to IIa but more powerful engine. Wider track
Pz Kpfw IIc or 3 La S100c 1934	8·8	3	15'10"	7'1"	6'8"	25	100	20mm./ 180	1/ 1425	30/10	Maybach HL TR 6-cyl. 140/2600 15·9 per ton	6 F I R Synchromesh. Epicyclic steering	Suspension—five large diameter suspension wheels each held on an arm with hull pivots. Movement controlled by ¼ elliptic springs. Four return rollers. Petrol tanks uparmoured to 10mm.
Pz Kpfw IIA Sd Kfz 121 1937	9·5	3	16'0'	7'7"	6'9"	25	100	20mm./ 180	1/ 1425	30/10	Maybach HL TR 6-cyl. 140/2600 14·7 per ton	6 F I R Synchromesh. Epicyclic steering	Angled nose plate replaced rounded pattern of earlier models. Suspension as for IIc. 15mm. extra fitted to nose plate and 20mm. on turret after 1941
Pz Kpfw IIB and C Sd Kfz 121 1938	9·5	3	16'0"	7'7"	6'9"	25	100	20mm./ 180	1/ 1425	30/10	Maybach HL TR 6-cyl. 140/2600 14·7 per ton	6 F I R Synchromesh. Epicyclic steering	
Pz Kpfw IID and E Sd Kfz 121 later	10·0	3	15'5"	7'5"	6'9"	35	125	20mm./ 180	1/ 1425	30/14	Maybach HL TR 6-cyl. 140/2600 14·0 per ton	6 F I R Synchromesh. SS 948 gearbox clutch, brake steering	Four large suspension wheels. No return rollers. Torsion bar springing. Converted to flame thrower 1940

TABLE OF TANK DETAILS—Pz Kpfw I and II

Type & Model Date	Weight tons	Crew	Length	Width	Height	Speed m.p.h.	Radius of action	Armament/Anm Main	Mgs	Armour max/min mm.	Engine BHP/r.p.m. BHP/ton	Transmission	Remarks
Flammpanzer II Sd Kfz 122	10·0	2	15'5"	7'5"	6'9"	35	125	Two Flame guns	1/2000	30/14	Maybach HL TR 6-cyl. 140/2600 14·0 per ton	6 F I R Synchro-mesh. SS 948 gearbox clutch, brake steering	Internal flame fuel tanks 225 gallon capacity. Flame range 40 yards
Pz Kpfw II F, (G, J) Sd Kfz 121	9·5	3	16'0"	7'8"	6'9"	25	125	20mm./180	1/2550	35/20	Maybach HL TR 6-cyl. 140/2600 14·7 per ton	6 F I R Synchro-mesh. SS 948 gearbox Epicyclic steering	35mm. on nose. 30 on glacis plate and 20 on hull sides. Redesigned hull. (Baggage box on turret back, Models G and J)
VK 901 1938	9·2	3	—	—	—	32	100	20mm. KwK 38/180	1/1425	30/10	Maybach HL 45 145/2800 15·7 per ton	—	75 pre-production machines begun in 1940. Guns in stabilized mounting. Five large overlapping suspension wheels: no return rollers
VK 1601 1939	16·5	3	—	—	—	20	100	20mm. KwK 38/180	1/1425	80/50/20	Maybach HL 45 200/3000	—	Prototype only. Guns in stabilized mount
VK 1301 1942	12·8	4	—	—	—						Maybach HL 66P 180/3200		First prototype for Luchs. Pz Kpfw II L. VK 1303 at 11·8 tons was accepted for production
"Luchs" Pz Kpfw II L, or Panzerspäh-wagen II (2cm. KwK 38) Sd Kfz 123 1942	11·8	4	15'5"	8'3"	7'1"	37½	155	20mm. KwK 38/180	1/1425	30/10	Maybach HL 66 P 180/3200 15·2 per ton	6 F I R Synchro-mesh. SS 948 gearbox con-trolled differ-ential steering	Suspension as for VK 901. Torsion bar springing. Fixed cupola. 100 of these tanks built with 20mm. guns: next 35 mounted 50mm. L/60 guns

Three-quarter front view of Panzerspähwagen II (or Pz Kpfw II L)—Luchs (Lynx) showing interleaved suspension wheels. Full side view of this vehicle, now in the R.A.C. Tank Museum, appears in colour on another page. (Photo: R.A.C. Tank Museum)

Panzer IIIs as far as the eye can see; an Ausf J with an H (left) leads a company of tanks forward during the victorious sweep into Russia, summer 1941. (Imp. War Mus.)

Panzerkampfwagen III

by Walter Spielberger

BY 1935, the tank-building industry in Germany had finally gained sufficient experience to incorporate ideas of its own in tank designs. The development of the Panzer I and II and the study of foreign tanks led to new ideas which turned out to be sometimes quite elaborate, complicated and costly. Consideration of the needs of mass production was generally neglected, for which mistake a high price had to be paid during later war years. General Guderian had initially envisaged two basic types to act as main equipment for the future German armoured force. The first vehicle was to be equipped with an armour piercing gun, in addition to two machine-guns, while the other type was to serve as a support vehicle, being equipped with a larger gun. The first one, later to become the Panzerkampfwagen III, was intended as the standard equipment for the three light companies of a tank battalion.

The selection of a suitable weapon caused some controversy between the Ordnance Department and the Inspector for Mechanized Troops. While Waffenamt (the Ordnance Department) seemed to be content with a 37 mm gun, the armoured troops demanded a gun of at least 5 cm calibre; however, since the infantry had already been equipped with the standard 37 mm anti-tank gun, this weapon also became the main armament for the Panzer III. Standardization and the fact that only one gun and its ammunition had to be procured, supported this decision. It was possible, however, to make the turret ring diameter big enough for subsequent up-gunning to 5 cm calibre without basic changes. Total weight was restricted to 24 metric tons to meet military bridging limitations inside

Germany. Top speed was to be 40 km per hour. The crew consisted of five men, with the commander, gunner and loader in the turret, and the driver and radio operator in the hull front. The commander had an elevated seat with a circular cupola mounted at the centre rear of the turret top. The tank commander communicated with the crew by intercom telephone using the same microphone and headsets employed with the vehicle's wireless. The commander, wireless operator and driver were all linked to the external wireless set. In the Model L onwards there was also a voice tube between the commander and gunner.

By the time of the invasion of Poland on September 1, 1939, however, the Panzer III was only in service in small numbers. At this time, the German Army had a total of six armoured divisions, all of which were engaged in the campaign. Supplemented by the Panzer-Lehr Regiment, the Ordnance Department's own testing unit, they were thrown against the poorly equipped Polish Army. With the added power of the German Air Force, this campaign was over within 18 days. The Polish Army fought bravely, but their forces proved to be completely inadequate. The campaign was the first full test of the German 'Blitzkrieg' tactics, close co-ordination in attack between dive-bombers and armoured forces. Though the Panzer III played only a minimal part in the invasion of Poland, the tactics evolved by General Guderian, in which the Panzer III was destined to figure more prominently later, were fully vindicated by the success of the campaign.

Preparation for the contemplated invasion of France brought a basic reorganization of the existing

First campaign involving the Panzer III, though only in relatively small numbers, was the invasion of Poland, September 1939. This is one of the Ausf D development models, distinguished by its front visor plate fittings (in this view), fording a river on the approach to Warsaw. Plain white cross was standard recognition mark for this campaign. (Chamberlain Collection.)

Panzer III Ausf E was the last model in the development series and had the torsion bar suspension adopted for all subsequent production models. Driver's visor cover and the machine-gun mount were also improved. This is an Ausf E in France, May 1940. It is evidently a vehicle brought from Poland since the cross shows evidence of being 'modified' from plain white. (Imp. War Mus.)

armoured force. The conversion of the four existing "Light Divisions" to 6th, 7th, 8th and 9th Panzer Divisions, planned before the war, was now carried out. Only six of the Panzer Divisions, 1st, 2nd, 3rd, 4th, 5th and 10th, had an armoured brigade* with a full establishment of four battalions, equipped with German armour. Three Panzer Divisions (6th, 7th and 8th) had a tank brigade with three battalions only. These were equipped with captured Czech vehicles (Panzer 35(t) and 38(t)). The 9th Panzer Division in

*British terminology—German equivalent to the British 'Brigade' was called 'Regiment'.

turn had only two battalions in its tank brigade, each equipped with German vehicles. A total of 349 Panzer III's, all mounting the 37 mm gun, were available at the beginning of the invasion of France and Flanders; they proved to be a decisive factor in German tank fortunes in this brilliantly conducted campaign.

Later, re-armed with a 50 mm gun, the Panzer III became the major equipment of German tank units

A Panzer III Ausf F or G with the Afrika Korps in late 1941. It has the early cupola but re-spaced return rollers, plus the short 5 cm. gun. (Imp. War Mus.)

suspension consisted of five large road wheels supported by coil springs. Front sprocket drive and rear idler wheels, together with two return rollers, completed the running gear. Armour 5 to 14·5 mm thick gave the vehicle a total weight of 15·4 metric tons. A Maybach "HL 108 TR" 12 cylinder gasoline (petrol) engine gave it a top speed of 32 km per hour (20 m.p.h.). Basic hull, turret, and superstructure remained unchanged throughout the Panzer III production life.

The second model in the series, Ausführung B, appeared in 1937. The only basic change was effected in the chassis design. Eight bogie wheels per side were now provided, two bogies each supported by one large horizontal leafspring. The number of return rollers was increased to three. Fifteen vehicles were produced (chassis numbers 60201-60215). Armour thickness was still 14·5 mm. The third model, the Ausführung C (chassis numbers 60301-60315) appeared at about the same time. Again, a total of 15 vehicles was produced. The Ausführung C differed from the B only by a modification to the suspension. Extra leafsprings each side were added bringing the number to four, allowing for an individual suspension of each bogie. The fourth development was the Ausführung D (Type 3b/ZW). The basic armour was increased to 30 mm, bringing the total weight to 19·8 metric tons. The suspension was almost identical to the Ausführung C, with the smaller leafsprings now arranged in an angle. Instead of the previous five-speed gearbox, a six-speed ZF transmission was

Above: Model N had the short L/24 75 mm. gun from the Panzer IV, and appeared in late 1942 and 1943 for the 'close support' role. It was sometimes called Sturmpanzer III. This is one of the Model Ns converted from a Model L. Others were built as Ns. (Imp. War Mus.)

In 1942 a total of 100 Panzer III Ausf M were converted to Flammenwerfer -Panzer III by replacing the 5 cm. long gun with a flame projector which resembled the gun barrel except for lack of taper. 1000 litres of flame fuel were carried in the hull in containers which replaced the ammunition racks, and on one loading 70–80 shots were possible. Range was 55–60 metres. Note the triple smoke dischargers on turret side. (Chamberlain Collection.)

installed (chassis numbers Ausführung D, 60221-60225 and 60316-60340).

Basic changes were incorporated with the introduction of the next model, the Ausführung E, which was the last of the development models. Built from 1939 until 1940, its Daimler-Benz designation was "ZW 38", its type "4/ZW" (chassis numbers 60401-60441). This vehicle had a new engine (Maybach HL 120 TR) and a new transmission (Maybach Variorex). The most drastic change, however, was reflected in the suspension system, which now incorporated transverse torsion bars with independent road wheels. This basic suspension remained in production, virtually unchanged, until the end of the entire model run. Though this system appears symmetrical, it was, in fact, offset by about five inches to allow the torsion bars to fit between each other. Detail changes on this model included an improved driver's visor and hull machine-gun mount.

By 1938 the Ordnance Department had themselves realised the error of insisting on a 37 mm gun for the Panzer III. They now authorized development of an up-gunned version. Krupp of Essen were asked to develop the turret and a 5 cm gun was specified, as first requested in vain by General Guderian in 1936.

The new gun mount was not ready, however, by the time the first major production version of the Panzer III, the Ausführung F (Type 5/ZW) appeared

Above: Ausf M had all the visible external features of the L but the pistol ports in the turret side were omitted as were the hull side escape hatches. Another prominent feature were the triple 90 mm. Nb.Kwg. smoke dischargers on the turret sides, replacing the tail smoke dischargers. (Chamberlain Collection.)

Below: Another Model M this time fitted with full skirt armour for hull and turret, a 1943 feature. (Chamberlain Collection.)

The Pz.Beob.Wg III (armoured observation post) had a dummy wooden gun barrel and a central ball-mounted machine gun in the mantlet to serve observation officers for motorized artillery units. This one is based on a Panzer III Ausf H. Turret was fixed. (Imp War Mus.)

Another Pz.Beob.Wg III, this time with armoured side skirts for turret and hull, Russian Front 1943. The early pattern cupola and superstructure front indicate that it is converted from a Model E or F. (Axel Duckert.)

in early 1940. This still had the 37 mm gun. Chassis, superstructure and turret remained unchanged and only improved ventilators on the turret distinguished it from the Ausführung E. Both models E and F and even early production Ausführung G's were fitted with the standard 37 mm gun, but starting late in 1940, they were all converted to take the 5 cm KwK L/42. This was against the wish of a determined Hitler, who immediately had demanded the fitting of the longer and more powerful L/60 5 cm gun.

The Panzer III Ausführung F had a modified version of the Maybach power-plant, the 12 cylinder "HL 120 TRM", of 300 h.p. Standard fitting on this model in the light of combat experience was a rack of five smoke generators on the hull remotely released by a rod from the turret. A stowage box was added to the rear of the turret in some vehicles. F series chassis numbers were 61001-65000.

The seventh model, the Ausführung G, appeared also in 1940, all except the very earliest already equipped with the 50 mm gun. The turret had a new commander's cupola with narrow twin covers that moved apart from each other instead of sliding shutters over its five vision ports and thicker armour. Vehicles destined for Africa received in production (or retrospectively) additional air filters and a different cooling fan reduction ratio. These were designated Ausführung G (Tp)*. A new driver's visor was fitted with a single shutter to offer better protection against "splash".

*Tp: Tropical.

Total Ausführung G production was 450, chassis numbers 65001-66000.

The appearance of the Panzer III, Ausführung H at the very end of 1940 brought a major change in the suspension system. The track width was increased from 360 mm to 400 mm. New final drive and idler wheels were used and the spacing of the return rollers was increased to give better support to the heavier track. New sprockets and idlers of simplified pattern were used and less complicated manual transmission was installed. Experience gained during previous battles resulted in a demand to increase the relatively thin armour of the Panzer III. As an interim solution, Ausführung H vehicles leaving the production lines in 1941 came equipped with additional 30 mm armour plates attached to the front faces of both hull and superstructure. The Ausführung H remained in production for the early part of 1941. Some vehicles of this type were later refitted with the longer L/60 50 mm gun. Chassis numbers of the H series were 66001-68000.

The first batch of the next version, the Ausführung J, (chassis numbers 68001-69100) were still equipped

Front view of a Panzerbefehlswagen III Ausf D (at first designated Pz.Bef.Wg Ausf A) converted from one of the old Model D development tanks. Note the old leaf spring suspension, the old type cupola, and the frame antenna on the rear deck which distinguished command tanks. (Chamberlain Collection.)

A Pz.Bef.Wg III Ausf E (originally called Pz.Bef.Wg III Ausf B) converted from a Panzer III Ausf E. Note rack for tail smoke dischargers and the frame antenna. (Chamberlain Collection.)

with the short-barrelled 5 cm gun. The basic armour, however, was increased from 30 mm to 50 mm. This necessitated a further change in the driver's visor and the ball mount for the radio operator's machine-gun. From vehicle 72001, the new 5 cm KwK 30 L/60 was used and was fitted in all future production vehicles until the end of the run of the Ausführung J version which terminated at chassis 74100. These later models had the right turret-front vision slot and the side vision slot omitted. With the long-barrelled gun, ammunition stowage was reduced from 99 to 84 rounds. These vehicles were built throughout 1941.

The Panzer Ausführung L was externally almost identical to its predecessor. However, a major change was the subsequent addition of a torsion bar compensator in the suspension to balance the nose-heaviness induced by the fitting of the 5 cm guns, plus the extra weight of the additional "spaced armour" now fitted over the superstructure and mantlet front. Coil springs were found insufficient to counteract the added weight. Only 78 rounds of ammunition were carried. With chassis numbers 74101-76000, Ausführung L was in production until 1942.

Also in 1942 the Ausführung M appeared, simplified by elimination of the vision slits and the hull escape door openings. With the introduction of skirting armour, some of these openings had become superfluous, and in any event, there was a continual quest for reducing production time. Some of the Ausführung M vehicles had a deep wading kit installed, allowing them to ford streams up to a depth of 4½ ft. Chassis numbers were in the range from 76001 to 78000.

The final version of the Panzer III, the Ausführung N came off the production line towards the end of 1942. It was simply a continuation of the Model M, equipped with the short-barrelled 75 mm gun, the previous main armament of the Panzer IV. Six hundred and sixty-six of these vehicles were manufactured when the production of the Panzer III was terminated in August 1943, and its production

Rare view of a Pz.Bef.Wg III Ausf H (formerly Ausf C) in service, with 9 metre aerial erected. (Axel Duckert.)

capacity given over to Sturmgeschütz III (Stug III) vehicles. Some Model L's were later refitted with the short KwK L/24 75 mm gun and re-designated Model (Ausführung) N accordingly. There was also a tropical version of the Ausführung L with the same modified fittings as the Ausführung G (Tp).

To conclude the Panzer III development story, a vehicle has to be mentioned which was intended to replace it. Developed by Daimler-Benz, its designation was "Panzerkampfwagen VK. 2001 (DB)". Daimler-Benz called it "ZW 40" in their production records. Two prototypes were built and thoroughly tested during 1939/1940. Equipped with a Daimler-Benz diesel engine, this 22-ton vehicle developed a top speed of 50 km/h. Leafspring suspension and various trans-

A Pz.Bef.Wg III Ausf E leading a company of Panzer II tanks during the invasion of France in May-June 1940. Note the extra aerials. (Imp. War Mus.)

A Panzer III Ausf G of the Afrika Korps. Note the excellent accessibility provided by the turret side doors, and the characteristic pile of stores on the hull rear. (Imp. War Mus.)

mission layouts characterized this development which was finally dropped in favour of heavier vehicles.

A Pz.Bef.Wg III fords a river during the initial stages of the invasion of Russia in 1941. Note the frame aerial, spare wheels, and tail smoke dischargers in a rack on the right rear. (Imp. War Mus.)

PRODUCTION

Since the Panzer III was intended to become the major equipment of the German tank force, ambitious production goals were immediately established. To cope with this production, several manufacturers received contracts. By 1939, the following companies were engaged in the manufacturing of "ZW" (i.e., Panzerkampfwagen III) vehicles:

Altmärkische Kettenfabrik GmbH (ALKETT) (Spandau works for assembly and Falkensee works for chassis construction)

Daimler-Benz AG (Berlin-Marienfelde)

Fahrzeug-und Motorenbau GmbH (FAMO) (Breslau)

Henschel & Sohn AG (Mittelfeld-Kassel, No. 111 plant)

Maschinenfabrik Augsburg-Nürnberg AG (Nürnberg)

Mühlenbau- und Industrie AG (MIAG) (Amme Braunschweig)

Waggonfabrik Wegmann AG (Kassel)

Maschinenfabrik Niedersachsen-Hannover (MNH) (Hannover-Linden)

Of all the manufacturers mentioned, Alkett produced the majority of Panzer III vehicles. Wegmann were engaged from 1937 to 1942. Henschel assembled most of its Panzer III output from 1939 to 1940. MIAG, starting late, completed approximately 1100 vehicles from 1941 to 1943. MNH's production goal

A British Universal Carrier passes a still burning Panzer III Ausf G which had been knocked out in the Alamein fighting, October 1942.

was 30 vehicles a month, while Daimler-Benz and FAMO both contributed 26 per month.

Most of the hulls, superstructures and turrets were supplied by Deutsche Edelstahlwerke AG. of Hannover. The main armament came from Karges-Hammer of Braunschweig and Franz Garny, Frankfurt. From November, 1940, a monthly production target of 108 vehicles per month was established; it was not always reached. In 1940 and 1941 total production reached 2,143 "ZW" vehicles, 1,924 of which were equipped with the 5 cm gun. Available to the armoured forces in July, 1941, were 327 Panzer III's with the 37 mm gun and 1,174 with the 50 mm armament. By April 1, 1942, the total of 37 mm armed vehicles was reduced to 131, while the 5 cm vehicles had been increased to 1,893. Total production figures for 5 cm L/60 armed Panzer III's were 40 in 1941, 1,907 in 1942, and 22 in 1943. A grand total of 5,644 Panzer III tanks was reached. The raw material consumption of a Panzer III was: Steel 39,000·00 kg. Tin 1·40 kg. Copper 60·10 kg. Aluminium 90·40 kg. Lead 71·10 kg. Zinc 49·10 kg. Rubber 125·00 kg.

For ease of production the Panzer III was divided into four pre-fabricated sub-assemblies—hull, turret, and front and rear superstructure. Most of the fittings were standardized with the Panzer IV. The use of sophisticated plant for pre-fabrication and assembly greatly speeded up production, even though mass-production was not foremost in the mind of the Ordnance Department when the Panzer III was first designed.

THE PANZER III DESCRIBED

The Panzer III hull, as stated above, consisted of three separate sub-assemblies, namely the main hull, the

Close up of a Panzer III Ausf F on the Russian Front, September 1941 shows the early type of cupola with prominent bolt heads and sliding shutters. (Imp. War Mus.)

front superstructure carrying the turret and the rear superstructure, covering the engine compartment. All these units were of single skin welded construction and the individual assemblies were bolted together. The hull section was divided into two compartments by means of a bulkhead; the front one housed the gearbox and steering mechanism. The driver's vision block was secured through an adjustable slot in the front plate of the superstructure. This plate also supported the ball-mounted machine-gun which was manned by the radio operator. Sideways vision for these two crew members was through visor blocks, protected by armoured flaps, mounted in the side-plate of the superstructure. Hinged escape doors were centrally located on both sides of the hull, though these were eliminated from the Model M. The top front plate of the main hull had hinged doors, giving access to the brake mechanism and providing means of escape for

Panzer IIIs of Panzer Group South cross the Don river during the advance on Stalingrad, summer 1942. Note the German national flag, commonly used as an aerial recognition sign. (Imp. War Mus.)

Panzer III. Ausf J. of the 3rd Panzer Division. Russian Front, 1941

A

C

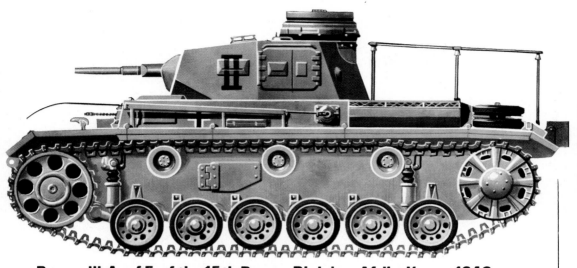

Terence Hadler © Profile Publications

Panzer III. Ausf E. of the 15th Panzer Division, Afrika Korps, 1942.
Battalion HQ vehicle.

A. Bear emblem of 3 rd Pz Div.
B. Alternative style seen on some vehicles.
C. Tactical marking of 3 rd Pz Div.
D. Insignia of the Afrika Korps.

0′   5′

the crew. All armour plates were made of high quality chromium-molybdenum steel.

The welded turret, similar to that of the Panzer IV, provided space for the other three crew members, namely the commander, the gunner and the loader. No rotating platform was provided, but the commander and the gunner had their seats suspended from the turret and thus traversed with it. The turret of Models H-M were fitted with a 50 mm cannon and one machine-gun which was mounted co-axial with the main armament. There were large hinged double doors on the turret sides, equipped with vision slots, and pistol ports provided for easy accessibility.

Additional observation ports were provided in each sidewall of the turret, together with two ports in the mantlet front. All well protected by armoured flaps. The 50 mm gun had an external mantlet, though the 37 mm gun of the early models was attached to an internal shield. The rear plate of the turret had two circular pistol ports. The turret roof itself provided openings for ventilators, signal ports, and the circular commander's cupola. Mounted centrally at the rear of the roof, it had five observation ports, equally spaced around its circumference; it was closed by a pair of semi-circular hatch covers. In early development models the cupola was of the "dustbin" type, and in models E and F it had armoured walls with projecting bolts. From Model G on a squatter type of cupola was fitted which had thicker (50-95 mm) armour and improved shutters.

The main armament of Models E-J was the 5 cm Kampfwagenkanone (KwK) L/42 with a barrel length of 2,103 mm. No muzzle brake was provided. Its maximum muzzle velocity with supercharge APC ammunition was 685 metres per second. It was capable of penetrating homogeneous armour of 47 mm thickness at a distance of 500 yards. The following different kinds of ammunition could be carried:

The first was the explosive loaded (supercharge) armour-piercing capped projectile previously mentioned. This was designated "Panzergranate 39". The second type was the "Panzergranate 40", which was a light-weight projectile with a tungsten carbide core. This ammunition, also called armour-piercing com-

Most important development on the Panzer III chassis was the Sturmgeschütz III (StuG III) which had the short 75 mm. L/24 gun in a limited traverse mount, originally based on the F chassis. This is a later production vehicle, the Ausf C. (Imp. War Mus.)

posite rigid, achieved a high muzzle velocity because of its light weight. However, this velocity and hence the penetration, decreased rapidly with increasing range, and it was less effective than APC over about 700 yards. At 100 yards however, its penetration was 97 mm compared to 55 mm for APC. The third type of ammunition carried was "Sprenggranate 38", or high explosive, for use against anti-tank guns and lightly-armoured vehicles. A total of 99 rounds of ammunition was provided in models with the L/42 gun, plus 2,700 rounds for the two MG 34 machine-guns. Turret traverse of 360° was by hand wheels, and elevation limits were −10° to +10°.

Another view, of a StuG III Ausf C with short 75 mm. gun, shows how the conversion was simply made on the basic Panzer III design by producing a completely new superstructure. Hull sub-assemblies did not require changing. Projection on left of superstructure (right) housed radio equipment. (Imp. War Mus.)

A Panzer III Ausf F passes a Soviet KVI tank it has just knocked out in the advance in the Ukraine, summer 1941. 'K' indicates that the vehicle is from Von Kleist's Panzer Group. (Imp. War Mus.)

From 1942 the StuG III had the potent long L/48 75 mm. gun. This official recognition shot shows the Ausf G model, complete with machine-gun shield on the roof, vision cupola, smoke dischargers and improved superstructure with increased 80 mm. armour maximum. (US Signal Corps.)

The main power plant, the HL 120 TRM in Model F onwards, was built by Maybach, and under licence by other manufacturers. It was a 12 cylinder "V", four-stroke gasoline petrol engine with a maximum output of 300 b.h.p. Cooling air entered through louvres in the front of the rear superstructure and also through wire mesh grids on the sides and passed over the engine to the two radiators placed one on either side of the engine compartment. The fans for the radiators were driven by long twin belts from a pulley mounted on an eccentric spindle. The pulley

A StuG III Ausf G negotiates an anti-tank ditch on the Orel Front, Russia, in support of advancing infantry. Note the machine-gun and shield, and the commander's binocular sight raised in the cupola. Skirt armour was a usual fitting by this period, July 1943. (Imp. War Mus.)

was coupled to the engine by a short universal joint shaft. Four oil bath air cleaners were mounted parallel to a manifold attached to the top face of the carburetters.

Power from the engine was transmitted via a swaged tubular cardan shaft. The clutch was situated in a casing mounted at the rear of the gearbox and transmitted the drive through various gears to the steering mechanism and final drive. Control of the transmission was effected through a vacuum-operated selector and gear change system, coupled with a hydraulically-operated gear synchromesh clutch. Gear selection was made by the hand pre-selector lever which in turn set cams to a pre-determined combination in a vacuum distribution box. To complete the gear change, the clutch pedal had to be depressed; this pedal was coupled to a hydraulic valve controlling the clutch and a vacuum valve to energize the distribution box. For engaging forward, neutral or reverse, a hand direction lever was provided, but once this lever had been set to forward, each of the ten forward speeds selected according to road conditions, could be engaged without further action. Speeds 1, 2, 3, and 4 were available only for reverse; however, only one reverse gear was commonly used. The Maybach "Variorex" 10-speed gearbox comprised four sets of constant mesh helical gears and one set of constant mesh spur gears mounted individually in line and on short shafts and roller bearings. The changes in ratio were effected through sliding dog clutches. Disengagement of the drive was by means of a multi-plate clutch on the primary shaft.

The steering mechanism was mounted at the front end of the gearbox forming an integral unit. The final drive and track brake were attached to the hull side plates. Very short propeller shafts connected these units. Output from the gearbox was transmitted to a

One in every nine StuG IIIs from 1942 onwards had the 10·5 cm. howitzer (and were classified 'Sturmhaubitze'). Otherwise they were identical to the StuG III Ausf G with the 75 mm. gun. This vehicle is shown in Northern Italy in July 1944. It is typical of very late StuG IIIs with Zimmerit anti-magnetic paste covering clearly visible. (Imp. War Mus.)

transverse shaft by means of spiral bevel gears, this shaft, in turn, driving the annulus of an epicyclic gear situated at either end. The outer wheel of this gear was extended outside the casing and carried the clutch brake drum. The drive itself continued via the planet wheel carrier to the final drive, which consisted of heavy spur gears. The Daimler-Benz/Wilson clutch braking system was operated hydraulically. Both right and left hand tracks were controlled independently by identical hydraulic systems, consisting of a steering control unit, a telescopic cylinder operating the clutch brake, and another one operating the track brake.

A total of 93 links, similar to the ones used on the Panzer IV, were needed to complete one track. Made of manganese steel and of the "skeleton" type, they were 360 mm wide. The track tensioning device was a robust ball crank lever to which was mounted the tensioning wheel. The lever, mounted on the rear portion of the hull side, was operated by a large diameter draw screw. The six independent road wheels per side were suspended by torsion bars. To allow these torsion bars to extend the full width of the hull, the corresponding right and left hand road wheels were staggered as previously noted, the anchor bracket on each side being constructed in one piece to form a housing for the suspension arm bearing and a location for the inner end of the opposite road wheel torsion bar. The four front and four rear torsion bars were larger in diameter than the four centre members. This was done to prevent undue pitching of the vehicle. In

addition, shock absorbers were fitted to the front and rear road wheels. Attached to the outer end of each torsion bar was a suspension arm, made of an alloy steel forging. The road wheel was mounted at its extremity on two substantial roller bearings. The road wheels were fabricated with the tyres vulcanized to the outer rim.

Electrical equipment consisted of a 600 watt Bosch GTLN generator, with a maximum output of 70 amps. Two starters were used, one the Bosch BNG 4/24 electric starter, and the other an AL/ZMA/R 4 hand-operated inertia starter. Two batteries were carried.

MARKS AND HYBRIDS

For the invasion of England (Operation Sea Lion), expected in 1940, a special amphibious tank battalion, called "Panzerabteilung A", was assembled in Putlos in northern Germany. Between September and October, 1940, two additional battalions were formed, named "Abteilung B" and "C". All the Panzer III and IV tanks in these units were made submersible. All existing openings on the vehicles were closed and sealed, and the air intake for the engine was completely eliminated. A rubber tube was inserted between the turret and superstructure, and rubber covers were placed over the main armament, the gun mounts and the commander's cupola to keep these assemblies water-tight. A detonator fuse, imbedded in these covers and activated after the vehicle had emerged from the water, was supposed to blow off the rubber shrouds and make the vehicles battle-ready. Fresh air supply was secured by means of a flexible tube 18 m long with a diameter of approximately 20 cm. It ended in a buoy to which a radio antenna was fitted.

The exhaust silencers were equipped with high pressure valves to keep water out. When submerged, seawater was used to cool the power plant. The diving depth was up to 15 m. Mode of operation was to submerge the vehicles from the landing craft before the English coast was reached. They were to land on the beaches by simply driving under water on the seabed to the shoreline. Extensive trials proved this theory to be feasible under actual conditions, but Operation Sea Lion never materialized. The vehicles, together with amphibious Panzer II's, later formed the 18th Panzer Regiment of 18th Panzer Division. They were used at the beginning of the Russian campaign to cross the River Bug in 1941.

For commanders of large armoured formations there was a special version of the Panzer III. As early as 1938, some Panzer III Ausführung D's had been adapted to make the so-called "Panzerbefehlswagen" (armoured command vehicle). Three different models, differentiated only by their radio equipment, were converted and designated Sd. Kfz. 266/267/268 respectively. They were almost identical in appearance to the standard model but their five-man crews consisted of the commander, adjutant, driver and two radio operators. The turret was fixed in position and a dummy gun barrel replaced the main armament. Two whip aerials (1·4 m and 2 m long), one retractable radio mast (9 m long) and the usual frame antenna mounted above the engine compartment completed the special equipment. The space left in the turret by

removal of the gun was utilized for map tables and the additional radio equipment. This vehicle was at first designated Panzerbefehlswagen Ausführung A. A few vehicles similarly converted from Panzer III Ausführung E's were originally designated Panzerbefehlswagen III Ausführung B, later E.

A modified version of the command vehicle was produced in 1940 based on the Panzer III Ausführung E. Chassis numbers were in the range 60501 to 60545. Production was completed in March, 1940. In November, 1940, a new version, the Panzerbefehlswagen III Ausführung H, appeared originally designated Ausführung C. The lack of a suitable main armament caused some concern, and the final vehicles of this type, the Panzerbefehlswagen III Ausführung K, were ordered from Daimler-Benz in January, 1941, with the 5 cm gun in a rotating turret. Only additional radio equipment distinguished these vehicles from the standard tank. Production of this later Panzerbefehlswagen continued until August, 1943. Totals of Panzerbefehlswagen III vehicles available for service at various times were as follows: July 1, 1941, 331; April 1, 1942, 273.

As an observation post vehicle for armoured artillery units, the "Panzerbeobachtungswagen III" (Pz Beob Wg III) was produced. This was originally considered only as an interim type until the specialized VK. 903 OP vehicle was ready. Equipped with substantial communication gear, the Pz Beob Wg III handled communication and fire direction between artillery units and served in this function until the end of the war. The VK. 903 in fact never materialized. Utilized for this conversion were mainly older chassis of the Panzer III Ausführung E, F and G series; the main armament was removed and a machine-gun substituted.

The Panzer III Ausführung F (5/ZW) also formed the basis for the production models of the "Sturm-

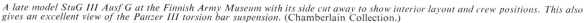

A late model StuG III Ausf G at the Finnish Army Museum with its side cut away to show interior layout and crew positions. This also gives an excellent view of the Panzer III torsion bar suspension. (Chamberlain Collection.)

Above: Driver's seat and steering controls; each lever controls steering of tracks.

Gunner's seat and sight. Note breech of the 75 mm. gun.

The political situation in Germany after 1933 when the National Socialists came to power led to much increased support for the original 10,000 man army of the former Weimar republic. An ambitious re-organization plan envisaged the conversion of most cavalry units to armoured or motorized battalions. In the meantime the basis for the Panzertruppe had been established and its nucleus created. The infantry, not content with a secondary role, also demanded motorized formations. To control these various trends, Hitler insisted on one command for all "Schnelle Truppen", and this wish was realized on November 24, 1938. Due to bureaucratic delays, however, the new command was not set up until September 19, 1939, when Germany was already at war. By this time the German armoured forces had already proved to the world that their concept of "Blitzkrieg" tactics could be realized. Within the armoured divisions, purpose-built vehicles played an important role, most important being the Panzer III, available only in limited numbers but bearing the distinctive stamp of its creator, General Guderian. Since most of the tank fighting in Poland was done by its smaller counter-parts, the Panzer I and II, the Panzer III was relegated to a supporting role, by virtue of the limited numbers available. The basic concept, however, was tested and found acceptable. Together with the captured Czech equipment, it proved much more important in France, in 1940. Improved tactics within sound strategic thinking made it the major equipment during the 1941 campaigns against Yugoslavia and Greece. Now equipping three out of four German tank companies, it fought all the major battles during the following

geschütz" (assault gun) series. These infantry support vehicles were demanded as soon as it became obvious that the newly-established armoured force was to be used within the framework of strategic warfare. An order, issued on June 15, 1936, awarded Daimler-Benz the contract for the construction of an armoured assault gun. Since they had been instrumental in creating the Panzer III, they also used its chassis components for the new vehicle. It carried the short 75 mm gun in a limited traverse mount and had 50 mm frontal armour. Neither the short 75 mm gun nor the thicker armour were incorporated in the standard Panzer III until 1943. At that time, the Sturmgeschütz already had the long-barrelled 75 mm gun and 80 mm frontal armour.

Thus, a trend was started to create a versatile vehicle which later proved to be invaluable in providing protection for infantry units. They were used in small numbers for the first time during the invasion of France in 1940, when they were designated "Gepanzerte Selbstfahrlafette für Sturmgeschütz 7·5 cm Kanone" (Sd. Kfz. 142). The official Speer report of January 27, 1945, gives the following production figures for Sturmgeschütz vehicles: 1940—184; 1941—550; 1942—828; 1943—3,319; and 1944—7,628. They were still in production when the war ended in 1945.

Breech and sight for the 50 mm. gun in the Panzer III Ausf L. Note the voice tube (upper left) from the commander's position in the cupola. (Imp. War Mus.)

Panzer IIIs under construction. These are E-G type chassis with the early pattern sprocket and idler wheels. Simple chassis layout is evident from this view. (Imp. War Mus.)

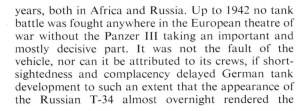

Close view of the Panzer III suspension, showing the side escape hatch from the fighting compartment. (Imp. War Mus.)

years, both in Africa and Russia. Up to 1942 no tank battle was fought anywhere in the European theatre of war without the Panzer III taking an important and mostly decisive part. It was not the fault of the vehicle, nor can it be attributed to its crews, if short-sightedness and complacency delayed German tank development to such an extent that the appearance of the Russian T-34 almost overnight rendered the

German tank force useless. This spelled doom for the Panzer III, which after 1943 was quickly phased out of front line service and its production capacity given over to more powerful vehicles. The necessity to protect infantry units against ever-increasing numbers of enemy tanks had hastened this decision, since both the long 5 cm and the short-barrelled 7·5 cm tank guns, the only weapons the Panzer III could carry, proved to be inadequate. The Panzer IV, with the 7·5 cm KwK 40 L/48, soon became the main arma-

A captured Afrika Korps Panzer III Ausf J seen on arrival in Britain where it was examined by British intelligence authorities. Note movable twin covers over vision ports in cupola. (Imp. War Mus.)

Above: The Krupp prototype for the ZW requirement. This vehicle was not adopted as the basis of the Panzer III but Krupp incorporated many of its features in the Panzer IV later. (Imp. War Mus.)

The Panzer III Ausf B differed from the A in having eight small bogie wheels. Note in particular the plain 'dustbin' type cupola with eight peep slots and the horn type periscope on the turret top. Model C was externally identical. (Imp. War Mus.)

Above: Panzer III Ausf D retained the small bogie wheels but had further modifications to the suspension, including large leaf-springs. This model was the first Panzer III with a cupola that incorporated shutters over the now only five vision ports. (Imp. War Mus.)

ment of the German tank regiments. The technical soundness of the Panzer III chassis, however, kept it in production for the StuG III role until the end of the war. The fact that a grand total of 15,350 "ZW" chassis was produced between 1935 and 1945 speaks for itself as an indication of its reliability and usefulness.

The Panzer III, without a doubt, wrote its own chapter in armoured warfare and dominated, like no other armoured vehicle, the tank battles of the early war years. It also helped to start a new trend in the construction of armoured fighting vehicles. Not least of its influences was its effect on future design in British and U.S. tanks. Prior to the appearance of the Panzer III and IV neither British nor U.S. tanks had been designed with much thought to standardization or to development potential. The Panzer III showed how a basic chassis could be progressively up-gunned, up-armoured, and used for several special purpose variants; contemporary British and U.S. tanks fell behind the Panzer III in all these respects, one of the reasons for German tank superiority in the Western Desert fighting. Ironically enough the Panzer III and its excellent fighting reputation in the early war years was one of the factors which led to the development of such medium tanks as the Shermans and Cromwells with which the Allies turned the tide of tank warfare in their favour in 1944-45. For this influence on tank development in World War 2, the Panzer III wins an important place in the history of the A.F.V.

Left: Excellent top view of a Panzer III Ausf E or F shows clearly the distinguishing features of the early models, including 37 mm. gun with internal mantlet, and flush fitting engine covers without raised louvres. Note also the early type of bow machine gun mount, and the hatches in the glacis plate for access to the drive mechanism which were also used as escape hatches. (Axel Duckert.)

Panzer III Ausf J with long 50 mm. gun, shown in Russia in 1942 with winter camouflage and trackshoes on nose and turret top for added protection. (Warpics.)

SPECIFICATION: PANZERKAMPFWAGEN III AUSFÜHRUNG F (TYPE 5/ZW)

General
Crew : Five—commander, gunner, loader, driver, radio operator.
Battle weight : 19·5 metric tons.
Dry weight : 18 metric tons.
Ground pressure : 0·99 Kg/cm².

Dimensions
Length overall : 5,380 mm.
Height : 2,435 mm.
Width : 2,910 mm.
Track centres : 360 mm.
Ground clearance : 385 mm.

Armament
Originally, one 3·7 cm KwK L/45, later up-gunned to 5 cm KwK 39 L/42.
One MG 34 7·92 mm, mounted co-axially.
One MG 34 7·92 mm, mounted in hull front, right.

Fire Control
Turret traverse, 360°, by hand wheel, elevation by hand 10°, depression 10°. Electric primer operated by trigger. Co-axial MG fired by rod and pedal from gunner's right foot. Hull MG fired by trigger.

Ammunition
3·7 cm KwK : 120 rds. mixed HE and APC.
5 cm KwK : 99 rds. mixed.
7·92 mm : 3,750 rds.

Sighting and Vision
Main armament : 1 TZFa, vorl. 5 cm telescope.
Hull machine gun : 1 telescope.
Commander : 5 vision slots in cupola.
Gunner : 1 vision slit each in turret front and side
Loader : 1 vision slit each in turret front and side.
Hull gunner/RO : 1 vision slit on right hand hull side.
Driver : Fahrerblende 30 and vision slit on left hand hull side.

Communications
W/T Set (2 receivers, 1 transmitter) L/T Set.

Armour
Machinable quality armour plate, austenitic welded.
Hull : nose 30 mm/20°, vertical front plate 30 mm/9°. Lower sides 30 mm/90°, upper sides 30 mm/90°. Top 17 mm/horizontal, bottom 16 mm horizontal.
Turret : mantlet 30 mm/curved, front 30 mm/15°. Sides 30 mm/25°,

rear 30 mm/12°, roof 12 mm. Some series with 30 mm spaced armour on front portions of hull and superstructure.

Engine
Maybach HL 120 TRM : petrol.
12 cylinders, 60° "V", water cooled.
Capacity 11867 cc.
300 bhp at 3000 r.p.m.
Fuel : 320 litres in one tank in engine compartment.

Transmission
Maybach "SRG 328145" Variorex pre-selector.
Type : 10 forward speeds, 1 reverse (4 possible).
Final drive ratio : 4 :1.
Steering : Daimler-Benz/Wilson clutch brake, hydraulically assisted.

Suspension
Six independently sprung rubber-tyred road wheels (size, 520×95—398) per side, mounted on transverse torsion bars. Torsion bars are staggered approximately 5 in.
Three return rollers per side (size 310×70—203).
Track : Cast manganese steel, skeleton type. Width : 260 mm, pitch 120 mm. 93 links per track.

Electrical System
One 12 V generator.
Two 12 V batteries.
One 4 hp starter motor.

Performance
Maximum road speed : 40 Km/h.
Maximum gradient : 30°.
Trench crossing : 2,300 mm.
Wading depth : 800 mm.
Range : Road 165km/cross country 95 Km.
Fuel consumption : 187 litres/100 Km.

Conversion Table
1 millimetre	=0·0394 in.
1 centimetre	=0·3937 in.
1 metre	=39·3708 in. (approx. 3 ft. 3 in.).
1 kilometre (Km)	=0·6214 mile. (8 Km=5 miles approx.).
1 litre	=1·76 pints.
50 litres	=11 gallons.
1 kilogram (Kg)	=2·2046 pounds.
1 metric ton	=2204·6 pounds.
1 ton	=2240 pounds.

Above: A Panzer III Ausf D pictured in Norway in April 1940 at the time of the German occupation. Note crew in berets, discarded after 1940.

Below: A fine view of one of the Panzer III Ausf A development vehicles on test, showing the large bogie wheels used in this first model. (Chamberlain Collection.)

Skoda LT-35 in German service as PzKpfw 35(t).

Panzerkampfwagen 38(t) & 35(t)

By John Milsom

INTRODUCTION

SEVERAL armaments firms in Czechoslovakia, prior to the occupation by Germany, were concerned with the design, development and production of tanks and other armoured fighting vehicles—both for use by the Czech Army and many foreign armies. Many of these foreign armies still employ these same Czech tanks or modifications of them. In these pages, however, we are concerned only with the influence of Czech tank development on the German Army, and are therefore concerned primarily with two basic tank models; the Skoda LT-35 and the CKD (Ceskomoravska Kolben Danek) TNHP, which the Germans took into service as the PzKpfw 35(t) and the PzKpfw 38(t) respectively, the (t) being an abbreviation of (tscheche), the German for Czech.

DEVELOPMENT OF THE TNHP

In 1933 the CKD firm in Prague began the design of a new light tank series for export. This series received the factory designation LT (Light Tank) L. The first completed model was called the LTL-H and, when tested by the MOD (Ministry of Defence), the TNHB. For export purposes it was often referred to as the LT-34.

During October 1937 the Czech MOD formed a tank evaluation committee to conduct thorough testing of all available Czech tank designs. A new tank evaluation centre was established outside the factory during January 1938. Several factories submitted vehicles for tests apart from CKD; among these being the famous Skoda firm and the lesser known Adamov firm. By

this time the CKD LTL-H series had resulted in the LTL-P (TNHS) model with improved armament, armour and inboard facilities. Results of the trials showed the TNHS to be the most exceptional model of those submitted and after a gruelling 3,000 mile test, some 1,000 miles of which was across country, the tank showed virtually no mechanical defects. Throughout its life this tank chassis earned great respect for its reliability and durability. The maintenance and servicing of the tank was found to be minimal and could be carried out in the field.

Following a report on these tests the Czech MOD specified that the TNHS should enter production and become the standard tank of the Army. Orders were issued for 150 vehicles. After alteration the new tank received the designation TNHP.

Prior to, and during the course of, the tests by the Czech Army, CKD had received orders for most of the developed models for foreign governments. These included Sweden, Switzerland, Peru, Latvia, Yugoslavia and Afghanistan. A total of 196 tanks of this series were exported. One vehicle was purchased by the War Mechanisation Board (WMB) in Great Britain, who tested it extensively.

TECHNICAL DESCRIPTION OF THE ORIGINAL TNHP

This originally 8-ton tank mounted a 37·2 mm. tank gun (Model Skoda A7) L/47·8 and a coaxial 7·92 mm. Besa machine-gun in a turret with all-round traverse. The bulge at the rear of the turret was fitted for ammunition stowage. A further 7·92 mm. Besa

49

The LTL-H Light Tank (otherwise known as the TNHB or LT-34).　　(Chamberlain Collection)

machine-gun was stationed in a spherical mounting at the front of the hull. The elevation gear of the 37 mm. gun could be locked for firing and it was intended to fire only when the vehicle was stationary. The coaxial 7·92 mm. machine-gun was provided with independent action when required, by means of its spherical mounting. The traversing gear, which was fast and light in action, was operated by a wheel on the left-hand side of the gunner. It could be thrown out of action and the turret could then be pushed round by the gunner. The turret ring was 47·5 inches internal diameter and there was no turntable. The cupola, which was fixed, was replaceable with 4 periscopes—each having replaceable mirrors and protective glasses. The forward machine-gun could be operated if necessary by the driver, via a

Bowden cable attached to one of the steering levers.

All main construction was rivetted with the exception of the top of the superstructure which was bolted. Protection was 25 mm. basis at the front, 19 mm. on the sides, and 15 mm. on the rear.

Four rubber-tyred single wheels 31 inches diameter were provided on each side, each wheel being mounted on a cranked stub-axle and each pair of wheels being controlled by a semi-elliptic spring freely pivoted. There were two return rollers on each side, mounted well forward. Front sprocket drive was employed, the sprocket being mounted high off the ground and 22·25 inches in diameter. The tracks were engaged by twin sprockets with 19 teeth, and each sprocket was driven through an internally toothed gear by a pinion

Below and right: The LTL-P Light Tank (otherwise known as the TNHS).　　(Chamberlain Collection)

First prototype of the TNHP; note the new dish-shaped wheels, reduction in return rollers to two, and replacement of the two water-cooled machine-guns by air-cooled types. The tank also had an experimental gun arresting gear. (Milsom Collection)

One of the first production TNHP vehicles (chassis Nos. 0001–0150) which was tested by the War Mechanization Board. This is the vehicle described in the text. (Model A).
(Chamberlain Collection)

attached to the cross-shaft. The cross-shaft carried two steering units comprising epicyclic and clutch elements giving two steering ratios and driven by a bevel gear from an epicyclic Praga-Wilson pre-selector 5-speed gearbox situated between the driver on the right and the machine-gunner on the left. The forward end of the vehicle was in consequence extremely congested.

The propeller shaft passed through the centre of the fighting compartment, and a 6-cylinder, water-cooled, Praga TNHP OHV lorry petrol engine—developing about 125 h.p. at 2,200 r.p.m.—was mounted vertically on the centre-line of the vehicle in the rear compartment. A single dry-plate clutch was installed. The engine had a dry sump and was cooled by a finned cylinder incorporating an Auto-Klean filter. Bosch

magneto ignition was employed and all the sparking plugs were screened. A 12 volt Scintilla dynamo was belt-driven from the crankshaft and charged a 9-cell NIFE battery of 190 amp. hours capacity. Cooling was effected by a centrifugal fan driven through a Rzeppa universal joint from the crankshaft. The air was drawn partly through the bulkhead, but mainly through a mushroom type louvre over the engine compartment and thence through a radiator of the continuous fin and tube type. The air was ejected through an opening in the rear top plate protected by armour-steel slats covered by expanded metal. The fuel tanks of tern plate were situated on either side of the engine compartment and the total capacity was 49 gallons (Imperial). The floor plates immediately below the

Second production model TNHP (Model B) in use with the Czech Army prior to the Nazi occupation.
(Milsom Collection)

Close-up of the engine installation in a first production model TNHP (Model A). (Chamberlain Collection)

Third production model TNHP (Model C) was identical to the Model B but had an inverted recuperator (i.e. the recuperator was moved to the top of the gun). This feature was retained in all further production models.

Photo showing the armament installation of a production TNHP-S tank. (Chamberlain Collection)

1

2

3

Above and below: *Fourth production model TNHP (Model D) with new aerial installation. Note the variation in armament in these photos 1-3 have the German 3·7-cm. KwK L/40 or 45.*
(Chamberlain Collection)

fuel tanks were secured by a few small-diameter bolts, the idea being that in the event of an explosion resulting from damage to the fuel tanks the floor plates immediately would be blown out and so reduce the possibility of damage within the vehicle.

The track was made up of cast steel shoes 4·09 inches pitch and 11·55 inches wide, and the pins were each secured by a circlip. Detachable spuds were provided to increase track grip in snow and ice. These were located on the extremities of the pins, which projected beyond the faces of the lugs.

After testing one of these vehicles during 1939, the War Mechanisation Board passed the following comments:—

"......*It is extremely difficult for the tank commander to load the turret machine-gun or to get at it to clear stoppages; on the other hand if the third man is used for this purpose his position is remarkably cramped. A convenient action position is provided for a case of 8 rounds of ammunition for the 37-mm. gun ...... The belt of the turret machine-gun obstructs the driver when the turret is trained forward or to the left front. The workmanship and detail design appear to be generally good, but not extravagant, and the cost/ton should be less than British tanks. Comfort of the crew and ease of evacuation of wounded are inferior ......*"

Above and below: *Fifth production model TNHP (Model E) with new stowage arrangements (note the long stowage boxes placed along the sides) and internal modifications.*
(Milsom Collection)

GERMAN INFLUENCE ON DEVELOPMENT

Following the German occupation of Czechoslovakia, from March 15, 1939, all tanks in service with the Czech Army—as well as those in production under export contracts—were taken over by the Wehrmacht. The Germans designated the TNHP the PzKpfw 38(t) (3·7 cm.) and continued its production until early 1942, when Czech tank production was suspended. Production of the vehicle under German guidance was also carried out by the Skoda firm. In 1940 the CKD firm became redesignated BMM (Böhmisch Mährische Maschinenfabrik AG.) The Germans initially requested a monthly production figure of 40 vehicles, although this fluctuated greatly according to the availability of

Close-up of the rear idler and track on the Model E.
(Chamberlain Collection)

Rear view of the Model E; compare the exhaust pipe arrangement with the Model F. (Chamberlain Collection)

Rear view of the sixth production model TNHP (Model F). Note the straight exhaust pipe and modified stowage boxes.
(Chamberlain Collection)

Below: *Model C in German service.*

materials and man-power. A total of 1,168 tanks of this type were built for the Wehrmacht: 275 in 1940, 698 in 1941 and 195 in 1942. In 1940 228 were in service with the 7th and 8th Panzer Divisions. By July 1, 1941 there were 763, but this figure dropped to 522 by April 1, 1942.

The original gun-tank saw service with the Wehrmacht in Poland, France, Yugoslavia, Greece and Russia. Among others, the PzKpfw 38(t) formed a major part of the tank strength of Rommel's 7th Panzer Division during its rapid drive across Northern France in the 1940 campaign. During 1940–41 the PzKpfw 38(t) formed 25% of the total German tank force. As late as 1944 the vehicle was still being used as an artillery observation vehicle.

Shortly after gaining control of the Czech facilities, the Germans ordered the manufacturers to increase the frontal armour to 50 mm. and that on the sides to 30 mm. As the result, the turret front had a basic thickness of 25 mm. with an additional 25 mm. plate. The front vertical hull plate was similarly armoured; the side superstructure armour was 30 mm. thick. (In some vehicles the Germans substituted the 37 mm. KwK L/45 for the original Czech gun). The tank's weight correspondingly increased to 11 tons. This new model became the TNHP-S (S meaning "Schwer", or heavy). The Germans had 9 models of this tank in service (Models A to H and S). The chassis numbers of the models were as follows:—

Model	Chassis No.	No. Produced
A	0001-0150	150
B	0151-0260	110
C	0261-0370	110
D	0371-0475	105
E	0476-0750	275
F	0751-1000	250
S	1001-1090	90
G	1101-1600	500
H	1601 (onwards)	

All models up to chassis No. 1600 (Model G) were powered by a 125 h.p. (at 2,200 r.p.m.) 6-cylinder engine (single carburettor) EPA Models I-III. The model H was powered by a 150 h.p. (at 2,600 r.p.m.) 6-

The seventh production model TNHP (Model S), originally built for Sweden. Note the cylindrical device (function unknown) on the RHS behind the driver's episcope. Photos are of the Swedish vehicle (Strv m/41).

(1 Milsom Collection. 2 Chamberlain Collection)

cylinder engine (double carburettor) Model epa/AC Model IV. The final engine model, the AC/1800, which was mounted in the Hetzer, was 160 h.p.

During 1940/41 90 PzKpfw 38(t)s which had been built for Sweden were impounded by the Wehrmacht and were designated the Model S by German armoured units. With additional radio equipment a commander's model was adopted, designated the Panzerbefehlswagen 38(t).

THE T-15 AND T-25 TANKS

When Skoda was instructed to participate in the PzKpfw 38(t) programme, the OKH requested them to undertake the design and development of two new tanks utilising its basic automotive components. In 1942/43 the Heereswaffenamt (Wa.Prüf.6) laid down specifications for a 10·5 ton light reconnaissance tank (T-15) and a 22-ton medium tank (T-25). Both

vehicles were to employ lengthened, widened and automotively modified chassis of the TNHP-S tank. Their maximum speeds were to be up to 38 m.p.h. —facilitated through the development of a new Skoda steering system.

The T-15 was a fast, fully-tracked reconnaissance tank with a 220 h.p. air-cooled diesel engine. It had a rear drive sprocket and a mechanical-shift transmission. The mock-up mounted a simulated 37 mm. gun in a turret very similar to that of the PzKpfw 38(t), although intentions were made clear to mount a 50 mm. tank gun. The armour was to be 50 mm. on the front, 20 mm. on the sides and 15 mm. on the rear. Modification to the hull design resulted in the mounting of the glacis plate at an angle of considerably more inclination. In both the T-15 and T-25 tanks the protection was increased through appropriate shaping of the

The eighth production model TNHP (Model G). Very similar to the Model F in appearance but note the smaller stowage boxes on the track guards.

(Chamberlain Collection)

Above and right: *The final production model of the TNHP (Model H). This vehicle has the increased armour thickness and other minor alterations.* (Milsom Collection)

armour walls (believed to have been inspired by the Soviet T–34 design). This was normally accomplished by inclining the plates towards the direction of fire. Skoda laid much stress on the proper covering of the cooling air inlets and outlets. In both vehicles Skoda utilised welded armour. The T–25 existed only in the blue-print form and the construction of a prototype was never authorised. The main armament was to be a 75 mm. tank gun having a muzzle-velocity of 2,920 ft./second. This gun had automatic ammunition feed from a revolving drum magazine located beneath the floor plate. It was semi-automatic operation. Smoke was to be removed from the barrel by compressed-air. Removal of empty cartridge cases was to be achieved

via openings in the floor plate. The turret was to be traversed hydro-electrically.

A project was under consideration to arm the T–25 with the le.F.H.43 (sfl) Skoda 10·5 cm. L/30 gun with coaxial machine-gun. This vehicle, which was designated the Heuschrecke (Grasshopper) 10 was only completed in mock-up form. The gun was to be mounted in a fully rotating turret and to be removable for field use. This vehicle was estimated to weigh 24 tons and carry 60 rounds of ammunition for the main armament. The armour was to be 30 mm. on the front, 20 mm. on the sides and 10 mm. on the rear. That on the turret was to range from 10 to 30 mm. The crew was to consist of 5 men.

THE PANZER JÄGER 38(D) (PzJg 38(d).) SERIES

This series—which was to enter service with the Wehrmacht after 1945 as a short-term stop-gap prior to the introduction of the E-10 light tank—was intended to provide the light standard chassis for a whole new armoured vehicle family. The original drawings were dated February 1945. With a few modifications it was to be used as an air-defence weapon (with two 7·62 mm. MGs and two 2 cm. cannons in a closed revolving turret, similar to that of the Kugelblitz), a reconnaissance tank, a full-tracked

Three pictures show various views of PzKpfw 38(t) commanders' tanks. (Panzerbefehlswagen 38(t)). (Chamberlain Collection)

Jagdpanzer 38(t) Hetzer was developed during 1943 on the widened chassis of the TNHP-S. Compact, simple and reliable, "Hetzers" were used on the Russian front and then in the West, especially during the Ardennes offensive. Post-1945 Hetzers served with the Czechoslovak army and in the Swiss army. The Swiss designated them Pz Jg G13. Remotely controlled machine-gun on the roof was for close defence.

Martin Lee © Profile Publications Ltd.

A unit modified PzKpfw 38(t) commander's model with the hull machine-gun removed and the aperture covered by armour plate.
(Chamberlain Collection)

A similar vehicle used by the Rumanians.
(Chamberlain Collection)

Wooden model of the Skoda T-15 light reconnaissance tank.
(Milsom Collection)

armoured personnel carrier and an armoured weapons carrier for the artillery arm. The basis chassis differed from that of the PzKpfw 38(t) mainly in the installation of an air-cooled Tatra III 12-cylinder diesel engine developing 210 h.p. at 1,800 r.p.m. and was to weigh 16 tons. Two hull configurations were to be built; Model W.1807 with the engine at the rear, and Model W.1806 with the engine mounted centrally. Both vehicles were to have armour ranging from 6-30 mm., and the smaller vehicle was to have 4 wheels per side, as against 6 on the larger model. One version was to have the 75 mm. KwK 42 or Pak L/70 in a rigid mounting, but the Germans considered replacing the 75 mm. gun by an 88 mm. in the tank-destroyer version. Development of the 75 mm. SP received top priority during 1944/45. It was to be a limited traverse mount and was to weigh about 14 tons. Some studies were carried out on the feasibility of providing all-round traverse and high-angle elevation. German engineers were also working on a 150 mm. recoilless gun, 105 mm. howitzer and a 128 mm. rifle mounting. (see the Waffenträger section later).

All firms originally producing the PzKpfw IV tank and the more advanced III/IV chassis were scheduled to turn over to the production of the PzJg 38(d)

series. Production was planned to be 2,000 vehicles per month, including 300-350 Waffenträgers, and reconnaissance vehicles. Due to the termination of the war, however, production was never undertaken.

GERMAN CONVERSIONS OF THE PzKpfw 38(t) CHASSIS

These fall into two main categories; firstly, normal supporting vehicles, and secondly, self-propelled weapons.

Aufklärungspanzer 38(t) Sd.Kfz.140/1

In October 1943 a new light reconnaissance tank was developed using the chassis and components of the 38(t). It was designed for the Russian Front since the normal semi-tracked and wheeled vehicles used for this rôle proved poor in respect of maintenance, mobility and armour protection. Seventy such vehicles

General arrangement drawings of the T-25 tank.

(Milsom Collection)

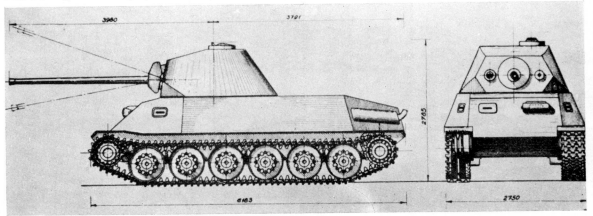

were built by BMM during 1943 and entered service during early 1944. The chassis and hull of the basic tank were practically unaltered, rather resembling those of the SP Flak 30 or 38 version, but the turret was removed and the turret ring altered to accept the turret of the Sd.Kfz.222 light armoured car with its organic 2 cm. KwK 38 and MG-34 armament.

Panzerkampfwagen 38(t) mit Nebel Ausrüstung

In 1943 a number of vehicles were converted as smoke dispenser vehicles. These had the turret removed and smoke dispensers built on behind the engine.

Schützenpanzerwagen auf 38(t)

During late 1944/early 1945 plans were laid for a fully-tracked troop carrier based on an elongated PzKpfw 38(t) chassis. This vehicle was never completed.

Munitionspanzer 38(t) Sd.Kfz.138/1 (Munitionspanzer auf Geschützwagen 38(t))

Ammunition carrier converted from PzKpfw 38(t). 102 built during 1943 to accompany armoured

Aufklärungspanzer 38(t) Sd.Kfz.140/1.
(Chamberlain Collection)

Panzerkampfwagen 38(t) mit Nebel Ausrüstung.
(Chamberlain Collection)

General arrangement drawings of the two Panzerjäger 38(d) variants.
(Milsom Collection)

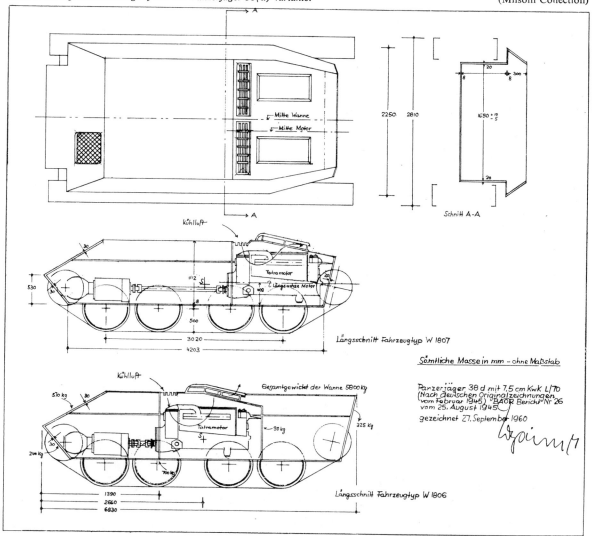

Right: PzKpfw 38(t) which took part in the invasion of France, May 1940. 7th and 8th Panzer Divisions were equipped with these former Czech TNHP tanks.

Left above and centre: PzKpfw 35(t)— Czech LTM-35— of 6th Panzer Division May 1940.

Below: Flakpanzer 38(t) (2 cm.) equipped with 2-cm. FLAK 38. It weighed 9·8 tons and had a crew of four.

FT

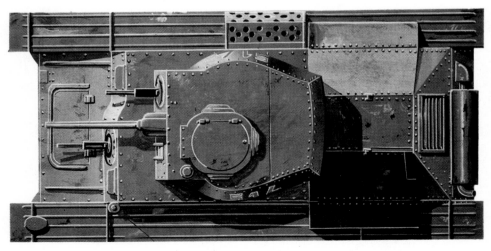

Martin Lee © Profile Publications Ltd.

Munitionspanzer 38(t) Sd.Kfz.138/1 (Munitionspanzer auf Geschützwagen 38 (t)). (Milsom Collection)

Hybrid conversion of the PzKpfw 38(t) for use as a tractor in both military and civil capacities. (Chamberlain Collection)

artillery units on the Russian Front. Each vehicle could carry 40 rounds.

Munitionsfahrzeug auf Fahrgestell PzKpfw 38(t)
1943 conversion; gutted PzKpfw 38(t)s used as ammunition carriers and artillery tractors.

Up-Gunned Versions
When operations began in Russia the 37 mm. armament was found to be ineffective against the new Soviet tank models. For this reason several attempts were made to provide the PzKpfw 38(t) with more powerful armament. Krupp endeavoured to install the PzKpfwIV turret mounting the 75 mm. KwK 40 L/48 gun on this chassis during 1944. The project proved technically impossible and the project was dropped. A similar project was undertaken during November 1944 to mount the 75 mm. L/70 KwK 42 gun of the Panther tank. This mounting was to have 30° traverse and elevate from −8°+15°. It was never built.

SELF-PROPELLED WEAPONS
All of the early SP mountings on the PzKpfw 38(t) chassis—prior to the introduction of the Hetzer—were makeshift or improvised conversions.

(1) Early Conversions
The first SP development on the PzKpfw 38(t) was the "s.I.G.33 on PzKw 38(t) Model H, Sd.Kfz.138/1, Bison". This vehicle was designed by Alkett and built by BMM. The armament, a 15 cm. s.I.G. 33 L/11, was designed by Rheinmetall-Borsig. An improved version, designated "s.I.G.33/1 on Selbstfahrlafette 38(t) sf Ausf M, Sd.Kfz.138/1", or Geschützwagen 38 (Bison), appeared in September 1942 and had a rear-located fighting compartment. 370 vehicles were built before production ceased in 1944. Following this, there appeared the "Panzerselbstfahrlafette 2 für 7·62 cm. Pak 36r (Sd.Kfz.139) Marder III". This vehicle was intended to provide the German infantry with an effective vehicle for the Russian Front. Production began on March 24, 1942 at BMM at 17 vehicles per month. The original OKH order had been for 30 vehicles per month. A total of 344 were built. The gun was rechambered to take the German Pak 40 cartridge case and was fitted with a muzzle brake. Another early conversion was the "7·5 cm. Pak 40/3 (L/46) auf Pz.Jag 38(t), Marder 38(t), Sd.Kfz.138. There were two models: firstly the Model H with rear engine, which appeared during 1942, secondly the Model M with front engine, appearing in March 1943. Production orders were issued in May 1942 and the first vehicle appeared in June. 418 of the first type and 381 of the second were built by BMM before production ceased in May 1944.

s.I.G.33 on PzKpfw 38(t) Model H, Sd.Kfz.138/1 "Bison". Side view is centre picture on next page. (Chamberlain Collection

s.I.G.33/1 on Selbstfahrlafette 38(t) sf Ausf M, Sd.Kfz.138/1, or Geschützwagen 38 "Bison".   (Chamberlain Collection)

s.I.G.33 on PzKpfw 38(t) Ausf H, Sd.Kfz 138/1 "Bison".

A Flak version of the PzKpfw 38(t) was built during 1943 by BMM and 162 were in service by October 1943. The vehicle was designated "2 cm. Flak 30 or 38 L/55 on PzKpfw 38(t), Sd.Kfz.140".

(2) Later Conversions

The first of the more successful SPs based on the PzKpfw 38(t) was the Hetzer. "7·5 cm. A/Tk. gun 39(L/48) on redesigned Czech LTH light tank chassis

'Baiter'. Pz.Jag. 38(t) Hetzer, or Jagd Panzer 38(t)". This vehicle was developed during 1943 using the original PzKpfw 38(t) chassis widened to accommodate the 75 mm. gun. It mounted the same armament as the Jagdpanzer IV. The track was strengthened and the width between centres increased from 6·16 to 6·98 feet. The engine was uprated to 160 h.p. at 2,800 r.p.m. which gave the vehicle a maximum speed of 25 m.p.h.

The fuel tank capacity was increased from 48 to 73 gallons. Manufacture of the vehicle, beginning in December 1943, was carried out by BMM and Skoda of Königgrätz. The armour was supplied by Poldihütte of Komotau, BMM, Linke-Hoffmann-Werke of Breslau and Skoda of Pilsen. Later models had a better shaped mantlet and later pattern road wheels. A total of 1,577 vehicles were built up to May 1945. (Production continued after the war by Skoda of Königgrätz for the Czech and Swiss armies). Plans were drawn up for a projected 15 cm. s.I.G. mounting on the Hetzer, but no prototype was built. The Hetzer was also experimentally fitted with a recoilless "Panzerwurfkanone" or light gun. It too did not pass the experimental stage. During late 1944 a number of

Below and right: Panzerselbstfahrlafette 2 für 7·62-cm. Pak 36r Sd.Kfz.139, Marder III.   (Milsom Collection)

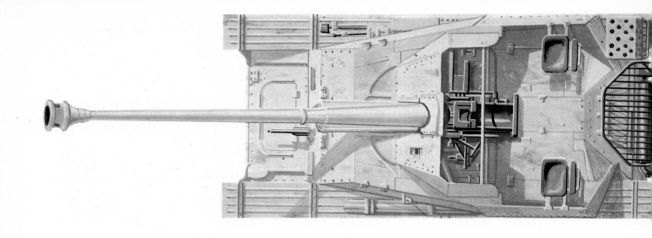

Panzer Jaeger 38(t) für 7·62-cm. PAK 36(r)— Marder III. (Panzerselbstlafette 2 für 7·62-cm. Pak 36r (Sd. Kfz 139).) Many of the 344 weapons built served in North Africa with the Afrika Korps. The guns were captured from the Russians, re-chambered to take the PAK 40 cartridge, and fitted with a muzzle brake. Marder III had a four-man crew.

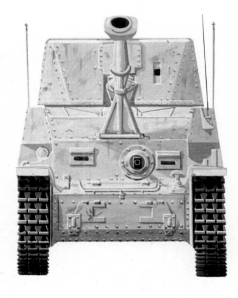

Above and below: *7·5-cm. Pak 40/3 (L/46) auf Pz.Jag. 38(t) Marder 38(t), Sd.Kfz.138, Model H.*   (Milsom Collection)

7·5-cm. Pak 40/3 (L/46) auf Pz.Jag. 38(t) Marder 38(t), Sd.Kfz.138, Model M.   (Chamberlain Collection)

2-cm. Flak 30 or 38 L/55 on PzKpfw 38(t), Sd.Kfz.140.   (Chamberlain Collection)

Below and top left opposite: *7·5-cm. A/Tk. gun 39 (L/48) on redesigned Czech LTH light tank chassis "Baiter", Pz.Jag. 38(t) Hetzer, or Jagd Panzer 38(t).*
(Chamberlain Collection)

8·8-cm. Pak 43/3 auf Panzerjäger 38(t). (Milsom Collection)

flame-throwing tanks were built using the Hetzer chassis and hull; these was designated Pz.Jag. 38(t) Flammenwerferpanzer 38(t). There was also an armoured recovery version designated the Bergepanzer 38(t) Hetzer.

Other SP mountings under consideration for the 38(t) and 38(d) programmes were as follows:—

(a) *8·8 cm. Pak 43/3 auf Panzer-Jäger 38(t)*—original prototype for series of Panzer-jägers, with new Tatra III 12-cylinder air-cooled engine of 210 h.p. (1945).

(b) *8·8 cm. Panzerjägerkanone 43 auf Sfl. 38(d)*—Rheinmetall-Borsig/Ardelt prototype for 38(d) Waffenträger series (1945).

(c) *8·8 cm. Panzerjägerkanone 43/3 auf Krupp/Steyr Sfl. 38(d)*—based on redesigned PzKpfw 38(t) chassis (1945).

THE WAFFENTRÄGER PROGRAMME

During 1943 it was decided to begin the development of a gun carriage to specifications laid down by the artillery branch. The limited traverse fairly-heavily armoured gun mountings then in use were evidently considered unsuitable.

The requirements laid down at the time were as follows:—

(a) Fully tracked running gear.

(b) Gun must be quickly removable from vehicle, power-driven mechanism for that purpose to be an integral part of the vehicle.

(c) Provision to be made that the gun can be mounted on the ground and fired separately from the vehicle. Parts required for their operation to be carried on the vehicle.

(d) The gun must have 360 degrees traverse, both on the vehicle and on the ground mount.

(e) The gun should be mobile when separated from the vehicle and set on its own field carriage.

(f) Armour protection for the crew need only be light splinter protection, approximately 8–10 mm. plates but all round protection for the gun crew is desirable.

On this basis a number of designs were laid down and several samples built by the firms of Krupp, Steyr, and Rheinmetall-Borsig. Some of these were on the PzKpfw 38(t) chassis. This initial series were found unsatisfactory. Another series of designs were begun by the same firms with the addition of Ardelt in Eberswalde. All these proposals were based on the use of the 38(t) components. After sample vehicles had been demonstrated to the army, the one by Ardelt was accepted for production. Krupp was charged with

Bergepanzer 38(t)—Hetzer. (Chamberlain Collection)

Above and below: *LTM-35 (S IIa) light tank in original Czech camouflage before German internment.*
(Milsom Collection)

Mock-up of Waffenträger based on PzKpfw 38(t) components.
(Milsom Collection)

the responsibility for final design and co-ordination of the various manufacturers concerned in the production programme. It was decided at this stage to build two sizes of weapon carrier—one for smaller, the other for larger calibre guns. Detailed drawings for both units had been furnished in March 1945 and preparations for production were underway. The lighter vehicle was to have 4 wheels/side and be powered by a Tatra 6-cylinder 100 h.p. engine. The heavier to have 6 wheels/side and be powered by a Tatra 12-cylinder 100 h.p. air-cooled engine. The lighter vehicle was to mount either a 88 mm. K-43 or 10·5 cm. light howitzer or 37 mm. flak or a Kugelblitz turret. It was to weigh approximately 14 tons (metric). The heavier vehicle was to mount the 12·8 cm. K-44 or a 15 cm. howitzer.

It was intended that these vehicles no longer have a removable gun and that the gun cover protection extend for less than 180 degrees. The only ones of the original requirements retained were fully tracked running gear and 360 degree traverse on the lighter model. The elevation on the guns was to be very high (42° for the 88 mm. gun).

Ammunition stowage was under the floor of the gun platform. Separate ammunition carriers on the same chassis were also requested by the army. Production was to start in the spring of 1945 and was to reach 300-350 vehicles per month. Components were to be taken out of the 38(t) and 38(d) programmes, and manufacture to be handled by some of the firms

which had previously built gun carriages on the Pz.IV chassis.

DEVELOPMENT OF THE LT-35

During 1934, based on the experiences gained by the Skoda firm with a prototype tank, the MU4/T1, a larger machine was considered. This was designated the Skoda 10·5 ton tank, Model T-11 and has often been referred to as the LTM-35 (S II a).

Particular care was taken in the design of this vehicle to enable it to travel long distances under its own power. In addition to achieving a high degree of manoeuvrability great care was taken in securing suitable crew comfort and durability of power train. The general design requirements of this vehicle were as follows:—

(1) A rear sprocket drive so as to have the fighting compartment as free as possible from all power train elements.

(2) The engine design was as short as possible so as to have a large fighting compartment.

(3) A 6-stage transmission with an air-shift was to be used.

(4) Power steering through the use of compressed air was to be used so as to permit long driving hours without excessive driver fatigue.

(5) The suspension was of such a design as to obtain equal pressures on all bogie wheels.

Above and below: *PzKpfw 35(t) in German unit service.*
(Chamberlain Collection)

8·8-cm. Panzerjägerkanone 43/3 auf Krupp/Steyr Sfl. 38(d).
(Milsom Collection)

(6) The main accessories were to have double installations so as to ensure a high degree of reliability
and performance.

Satisfactory results were achieved with the prototype
and hence the vehicle was set up for production during
1935.

TECHNICAL DESCRIPTION OF THE LTM-35

The vehicle, which weighed 10·5 tons, was armoured
with plate up to 35 mm. thick. Its armament consisted
of a 37 mm. gun in a rotating turret (in 1934 this was
the first Skoda tank to be fitted with a rotating turret).
The gun had a monobloc barrel, was semi-automatic
and used a dial sight. The elevation range of the
installation was from –10 to +25 degrees. Horizontal
movement of the piece was secured through traverse
of the entire turret. Rough adjustment of the piece

was obtained through traverse of the whole turret while fine sighting adjustment was secured by traverse through a handwheel. This arrangement proved successful with light tanks in as much as a counterweight at the rear of the turret balanced the gun's weight. Elevation of the piece would be secured not only through direction action of the gunner's shoulder, but also through an elevating mechanism. At the moment of firing, however, the gun was arrested by an hydraulic installation.

A coaxial machine-gun was used as a secondary weapon. Both weapons could be fired simultaneously or individually. For this purpose the dial sight of the gun was fitted with reticule scales having two different scales. In addition each machine-gun had its own sighting telescope. A further machine-gun was mounted in the hull, and fired, in a similar fashion to that on the TNHP tank. The A3 gun was further modified to adapt itself to the narrow turret by shortening the recoil and modifying the elevation wheel so that it was unnecessary for the gunner to release it for firing. The gun was improved by increasing the muzzle velocity to 2,620 fps. The general internal layout was similar to that of the PzKpfw 38(t).

The particular advantage in the design of this tank was the operating efficiency which reduced driver fatigue. The vehicle was very fast and easy to steer thanks to its 12-speed gearbox and pneumatic-servo-mechanical steering unit. Trips of 125 miles per day at average speeds of 12-16 m.p.h. could be achieved,

although the maximum speed of the vehicle was only 25 m.p.h. The suspension durability of the design was also remarkable in that track and bogie-wheel life ranged from 4,000-8,000 kilometres.

GERMAN EMPLOYMENT OF THE LTM-35

This tank was adopted by the Wehrmacht as the PzKpfw 35(t) during 1939, and was issued to the 6th Panzer Division. Originally the Germans had 106 of these tanks but by June 1, 1942 there was a total of 167 in service (total production unknown). During experiences in Russia it was found that the steering system froze, and consequently a heater was installed.

When these vehicles were phased out of service they were used for towing purposes—e.g. the Mörserzugmittel 35(t), mortar tractor 35(t), and the Zugkraftwagen 35(t), tractor 35(t), with a towing capacity of 12 tons. They were sometimes employed for tank recovery purposes. Such vehicles had crews of 2 men each. No self-propelled mountings are known to have been produced by the Germans on this chassis, although one such vehicle was produced by the Hungarians. (The latter produced an extensively modified version of this tank, designated the Turan II, as well as the Turan III based on a similar vehicle (the T-21) produced by CKD. Hungarian units equipped with these vehicles fought alongside the Wehrmacht during operations in Russia.)

Transmission lay-out of PzKpfw 38(t).

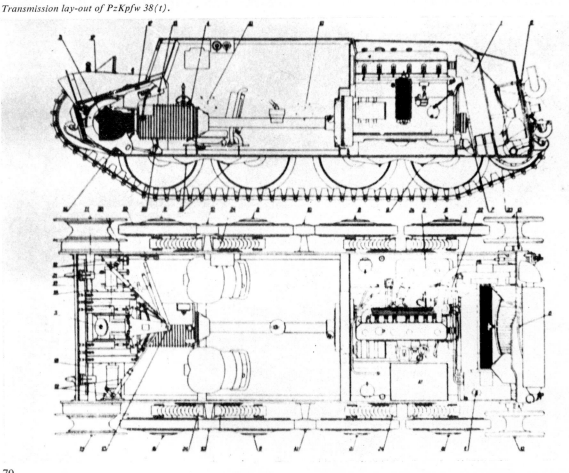

PzKpfw 35(t) of 6th Panzer Division in Champagne, June 1940.

SPECIFICATIONS

	Panzerkampfwagen 38(t) (3·7 cm) TNHP-S	Panzerkampfwagen 35(t) LTM-35
General:		
Crew:	4—commander, gunner, loader/radio-operator, driver.	4—commander, gunner, loader/radio-operator, driver.
Battle weight (tons):	8·5*/9·7	10·5
Dry weight (tons):	7·7*/8·9	9·9
Ground pressure (p.s.i.):	7·8*/10·2	7·55
Dimensions:		
Length overall (ft.):	14·91	14·88
Height overall (ft.):	7·76	7·21
Width overall (ft.):	6·62*/6·74	7·03
Track centres (ft.):	6·16	5·41
Ground clearance (ft.):	1·32	1·15
Ground contact length (ft.):	9·56	10·7
Armament:		
Main:	Skoda A7, 37·2 mm.L/47·8**	Skoda A3, 37·2 mm. L/40
Coaxial:	7·92 mm. 7165 CZ Type 37 machine-gun.	7·92 mm. 7165 CZ Type 37 machine-gun
Hull:	7·92 mm. 7165 CZ Type 37 machine-gun.	7·92 mm. 7165 CZ Type 37 machine-gun
Fire Control:		
Turret traverse:	360° (by hand-wheel or free-wheeling)	360° (by hand-wheel or free-wheeling)
Elevation:	−6° +12° (by hand)	−10° +25° (by hand)
Sighting equipment:	Various German sighting telescopes fitted.	Dial sight (some German modifications)
Special features:	Hull MG fired by driver via Bowden cable attached to steering lever. Fixed cupola with 4 episcopes.	Gun hydraulically arrested during firing, shoulder controlled in elevation.
Ammunition:		
Main Armament:	37 mm. gun: 90 rounds (HE and AP)	37 mm. gun: 90 rounds (HE and AP)
Secondary Armament:	7·92 mm. MG: 2,550 rounds.	7·92 mm. MG: 2,550 rounds.
Communications:		
External:	W/T set (various German models)	W/T set (various German models) and flag.
Internal:	Internal system of coloured lights	Internal system of coloured lights
Armour:		
Type:	Machinable quality armour plate, rivetted and bolted.	Machinable quality armour plate, rivetted and bolted.
Hull—Nose (mm.):	25*/25 + 25	35
Vertical front plate (mm.):	25*/25 + 25	23
Glacis plate (mm.):	25	28
Lower sides (mm.):	15*/30	16
Upper sides (mm.):	19*/30	24
Roof (mm.):	10 (Some variations in armour	20
Floor (mm.):	8 according to model)	12
Rear (mm.):	12	20
Turret—Mantlet (mm.):	25	35
Front (mm.):	25*/25 + 25	23
Sides (mm.):	15*/30	16
Rear (mm.):	15*/22	16
Roof (mm.):	10*/15	16

Engine:		
Type:	6-cylinder, water-cooled in-line O H.V. Models A-G: 125 H.P. at 2,200 r.p.m. (single Solex 48 FNVP I carburettor) EPA Models I-III. Model H: 150 H.P. at 2,600 r.p.m. (twin Solex 46 FNVP carburettors) epa/AC Model IV.	6-cylinder, water-cooled in-line O.H.V. Skoda model T-11, 8·5L developing 120 H.P. at 1,800 r.p.m. (Twin Zenith UDD carburettors)
Fuel capacity (galls.):	49	34
Transmission:		
Make and Type:	Praga-Wilson TN-100 epicyclic pre-selector (2-stage).	Praga-Wilson-Skoda pneumatic-servo assisted.
Gears:	5 forward, 1 reverse (with transfer).	6 forward, 6 reverse (provided by mechanical servo).
Steering:	Praga-Wilson epicylic clutch and brake.	Clutch and brake (servo-pneumatic assisted).
Suspension:		
Type:	4 rubber-tyred wheels per side, each mounted on a cranked stub-axle and each pair of wheels being controlled by a semi-elliptic spring freely pivoted. (Wheel diameter: 2·58 ft.). 2 return rollers per side.	8 small bogie wheels per side, coupled in pairs and mounted on hull in fours on rocker arm with inverted semi-elliptic leaf springs. Small guide wheel between front idler and first bodgie wheel. 4 return rollers/side.
Tracks:		
Type:	Cast manganese steel, skeleton type.	Cast manganese steel, dry pin.
Width (ins.):	11·5	10·5
Pitch (ins.):	4·09/4·17***	4·15
No. links per track:	87-90*/93	105
Electrical system:	9-cell NIFE battery, 100Ah, charged by 12V Scintilla dynamo, Bosch magneto ignition.	9-cell NIFE battery. 100Ah, charged by 12V Scintilla dynamo, Twin Vertex-Scintilla magneto ignition.
Performance:		
Maximum speed (m.p.h.):	35*/26	25
Maximum gradient (degrees):	30*/26	28·6
Trench crossing (feet):	6·1	6·6
Wading depth (feet):	3·0	2·6
Vertical step (feet):	2·6	2·6
Range—road (miles):	125*/94	120
c.c. (miles):	89*/64	72
Fuel consumption (m.p.g.):	2·6*/1·92 (road)	3·5
Turning circle diameter (feet.):	14·9	16

NOTES:
*Before/after chassis No. 1601.
**Some vehicles had 37 mm. KwK L/45 or L/40
***w/o or with detachable spuds.

Mörser Zugmittel 35(t).　　　　　　　　　　　　　　　　　　　(Chamberlain Collection)

Panzer IV in action.

Panzerkampfwagen IV

by Walter Spielberger

MOST postwar publications on German armour of the Second World War tend to over-emphasise the importance of the well-known Tiger and Panther. These vehicles, while undoubtedly making quite an impression on their opponents during their somewhat limited appearance on the battlefield, should be considered above all as derivatives of the Panzerkampfwagen III and IV. It was these two tanks which established the reputation of the German armoured forces, and demonstrated the most advanced technical and tactical features of their time.

While the PzKpfw III was intended to equip three out of four German tank companies, the PzKpfw IV was originally given a limited rôle as a support vehicle equipping the fourth company of a standard tank battalion. This vehicle, conceived in 1934 but neglected through the years by inadequate production schedules, eventually became the only German tank which remained in production and troop service until the end of the war. This is an indication of its sound basic design, supplemented by remarkable foresight in the specification. Most of the other armoured vehicles originally designed during the same period

progressively disappeared under the stress of war from 1939 onward.

One man most instrumental in the design of the Panzer IV was the creator of the German *Panzertruppe*, Colonel-General Heinz Guderian, who had laid down the basic prerequisites for armoured fighting vehicles as early as 1933–34. These were mobility, fire-power, armour protection and communication, specified in that order. A five-man crew was also considered essential. The latter allowed for a distinct allocation of duties between the crew, an advantage both in training and in battle, which gave German tanks their marked tactical superiority over their Allied counterparts despite other shortcomings. Guderian's insistence on supplying the crews with communication systems, usable not only between tanks but also on intercom., was another key factor enabling these vehicles to be used as practical and effective units of the newly-created armoured force, trained in the disciplined and co-ordinated art of armoured warfare. However, despite these major advantages, most German tanks of the development period could not be considered superior in Guderian's

Panzer IV Ausf. A of 1st Panzer Division, only 35 of this model were built. Ausf. A had stepped front plate with driver's position protruding at left, round bow machine-gun mount at right. Driver had single centre vision slit and rectangular side view opening in front plate.

Another recognition feature of Ausf. A was the drum-shaped commander's cupola protruding through rear plate of turret. Engine was Maybach HL 108. Weight 17·3 tons.

first three requirements of mobility, fire-power and armour protection. In fact many of the French tanks opposing the German attack of 1940 had heavier armour, while the British cruisers were superior in manoeuvrability. What the Allied armour lacked most was the administrative backing of supply and maintenance required by modern mechanised forces, and the fighting efficiency afforded by well-designed crew compartments.

German armour had a further weakness which became apparent during the Russian campaign in 1941. The German General Staff had foreseen the future deployment of armoured fighting vehicles primarily in Western Europe. The capacity of European bridges and railroad profiles, and the existence of a dense road network determined to a large degree the specifications for ground pressure and power/weight ratio, thus limiting basic dimensions and cross-country performance. These factors became obvious handicaps among the vast plains, swamps and forests of Russia. The challenge set by the T-34—tailor-made for its environment with its wide tracks, high speed, effective armour and powerful gun—could only be met fully by completely new designs with their inevitably lengthy development time. But immediate solutions were found which up-dated especially the Panzer IV to such an extent that it was still a usable weapon when the war ended. Its modification was continuous, if often makeshift. Much was left to the tactical ability and determination of Panzer crews to make up for deficiencies in their vehicles. Tanks returned for overhaul were, in principle, brought up to the latest standards, considerably complicating the recognition of later marks.

The outstanding basic vehicle of this wartime development period, created to restore the balance of power in favour of German armour, was PzKpfw IV Ausf. F2.

DEVELOPMENT HISTORY

The story of Panzer IV began at a policy meeting called at the Army Ordnance Department on January 11, 1934. The agenda was to settle some final problems concerning a proper balance of armoured fighting vehicle equipment for a 63-division German Army. As a result of this discussion, final specifications for a "medium tractor" were agreed and orders for

prototypes were issued to industry. The armament required was a short 7·5 cm. assault gun; this was thought necessary to support the new Panzer army's standard vehicle, PzKpfw III which was to be equipped with a 3·7 cm. gun. The limit for its battle weight, imposed by the capacity of standard bridges, was 24 tons. Rheinmetall-Borsig AG. immediately started their design and completed a wooden mock-up by the end of the year. Their first prototype, called "VK 2001", went to Kummersdorf for trials in 1935. Both M.A.N. of Augsburg and Friedr. Krupp AG. of Essen submitted their proposals to the *Waffenamt* (War Office) during 1935. Intensive trials of all prototypes resulted in the acceptance of the Krupp design in 1936.

In order to disguise these vehicles the code name *"Bataillonsführerwagen"* or "BW" was established, a designation which served for identification throughout the entire model run. While development and construction of prototypes took place at Krupp's Essen factory, the production line was established at Krupp-Grusonwerke AG. at Magdeburg. Now called *"Versuchskraftfahrzeug 622"* (VsKfz 622), a few examples of the first version, or Ausführung A, came off the production line in 1936. The second, Ausf. B, appeared in 1937, again in very limited numbers. Ausf. C was produced in 1938, as was Ausf. D.

The campaign against Poland in September 1939 saw only 211 Panzer IV in action, since production had been curtailed after all existing units had received their allotted number of vehicles. Encouraged by the results of this first battle, Panzer IV was accepted as standard issue on September 27, 1939, and now received the Ordnance Number *Sonderkraftfahrzeug 161* (SdKfz. 161). In December 1939 production began of Ausf. E, bringing the total of Panzer IV available for the impending campaign against France up to 278. In fact only 280 Panzer IV were built during 1940. It was not until a *"Führerbefehl"*—Hitler's order—of August 20, 1940 finally put more urgency into tank production that both Panzer III and IV were placed in production class "SS", a high priority classification.

AUSFUHRUNG F APPEARS

The Panzer IV model profiting most from the accumulated experience of the Polish campaign was the "6/BW" or Ausf. F. Altogether 393 PzKpfw IV

Ausf. B and C were very similar to each other in appearance. Both had a straight frontal plate with double driver's visor and pistol port and peep slot instead of bow machine-gun. Commander's cupola was no longer drum-shaped. Ausf. C had its turret machine-gun partially protected by an armoured sleeve. Engine in Ausf. B and first C vehicles was Maybach HL 120 TR; in later C vehicles and subsequent models Maybach HL 120 TRM engine was installed. Thickness of turret armour was increased in Ausf. C. Only 42 Ausf. B were built. Note also cone-shaped signal port flap on turret roof, which appeared on Ausf. B, C, and D.

Ausf. F were built in 1940 and 1941, with the first batch of 20 leaving the factory in February 1940. Compared to previous models, the basic armour was increased from 30 to 50 mm. The front of the superstructure was now in the form of a single plate extending straight across the tank. The front revolver port was omitted altogether and a *"Kugelblende 50"* for the radio-operator/hull gunner, together with a *"Fahrersehklappe 50"* for the driver were now provided. Modifications to the two hinged maintenance hatches in the glacis plate included the incorporation of air intake apertures on each door. These were protected by a cast cowl welded to the cover. Another change affected the access doors to the turret; the single door previously fitted was superseded by double doors similar to those fitted on Panzer III. The forward door on each side incorporated a vision port, while revolver ports were provided in each rear door. The additional armour increased the weight from 21 to a total of 22·3 metric tons and required a modification of the chassis. Track width was increased from 380 to 400 mm. (Track type Kgs. 61/400/120) to lower ground pressure. These new tracks also had the sole and outer webs of each shoe slotted to fit ice sprags.

The front driving sprocket of Panzer IV Ausf. F, while similar to previous models, had its spokes bent outwards from the hub, giving the outside a dished appearance. The rear idler wheel was completely changed. Constructed of 2¼ in. welded tube, both outside and inside sections were secured together by flat plates welded to their respective spokes. Thus modified the vehicle was ready to accept the final major modification, which again made it an even match for the Russian T-34.

THE NEW 7·5 cm. GUN

The surprise created by the Soviet's T-34 when it was encountered for the first time at the end of July 1941 could have been avoided. Guderian indicates in his book *"Erinnerungen eines Soldaten"* that a group of Russian officers received Hitler's personal permission to inspect German tank factories as late as the spring of 1941. The Russians, confronted with the Panzer IV, would not believe that this was supposedly the heaviest German tank. They protested so strongly that they should be shown everything as promised by Hitler that it was deduced that they must have something much better. They actually had. In the event, no German weapon other than the 8·8 cm. gun, available only in limited numbers, was able to defeat the new Russian tanks in an open encounter. To compensate for this, the Ordnance Department issued Order No. 917/41 gKdos Wa. Pruef. 4 of November 18, 1941 to Friedrich Krupp AG. of Essen to design in co-operation with Rheinmetall-Borsig AG. a replacement for the short-barrelled 7·5 cm. Panzer IV tank gun. Originally called *Kampfwagenkanone* 44 (later KwK 40), the weapon was to have a barrel length of 3,218 mm. (L/43). Muzzle velocity was to be increased from 450 to 990 mm./sec. and range from 6,500 m. to 8,100 m. Mass production was ordered in March 1942. Installed for the first time in the F version of the Panzer IV, it received the official nomenclature F2, while vehicles with the short-barrelled weapon were renamed Ausf. F1. Serial numbers of Ausf. F1 run from 82001 to 82393; those for F2 from 82394 to 83700. The fighting weight of the F2 version increased to 23·6 metric tons; 87 rounds of ammunition were carried. The price per unit (without weapons) amount-

This three-quarter rear view of Ausf. B or C in France shows the single hatch door on the turret sides. Double doors were not substituted until Ausf. F. Exhaust configuration and track tensioning device are typical of all Panzer IV vehicles. Weight of Ausf. B was 17·7 tons, of Ausf. C 20 tons.

ed to RM 103,462. These vehicles remained in production until 1942 when they were succeeded by the Ausf. G.

PRODUCTION

Panzer IV production was originally intended to be on a limited scale. Only one prime contractor, Krupp-Gruson AG., was engaged, while Panzer III production was divided among eight major companies. This limited production and the effects of losses left the following numbers of Panzer IV on Army strength during the first three years of the war: end of 1939: 174; end of 1940: 386; end of 1941: 769. In fact, the total Panzer IV production during 1941 amounted to only 480 units, despite an order dated July 18, 1941 which requested production of 2,160 to equip the planned 36 armoured divisions. A monthly production goal of 40 units per month was set for 1941. In January 1942 a monthly output of 57 units was anticipated. In the event this target was exceeded and a total of 964 urgently needed Panzer IV were produced during 1942. Originally the main assembly was by Krupp-Gruson, with hulls and turrets supplied by Krupp of Essen and Eisen-und-Huettenwerke of Bochum. This picture changed considerably during 1942 under the influence of Allied air raids. The relocation of key war industry to areas not readily accessible to the bombers was begun in 1940 and established several new tank factories. One of these was "Nibelungenwerke" at St. Valentin (Lower Austria), managed by Steyr-Daimler-Puch AG. Initially intended for the production of a replacement vehicle for Panzer IV—the Porsche "Leopard" (Porsche Type 100)—it became operational just in time to take on the expanded Panzer IV production. From 1943, Panzer IV was assembled almost exclusively at this factory and remained in production there until the end of the war. Its proximity to the Hermann Goering steel mills at Linz established a new source for hulls and turrets including Gebr. Koehler & Co of Kapfenberg and Eisenwerke Oberdonau of Linz. The raw material consumption of one Panzer

IV (without weapons, optical instruments or radio equipment) was as follows: Steel (Fe), 39,000·00 kg.; Tin (Sn), 1·20 kg.; Copper (Cu), 195·10 kg.; Aluminium (Al), 238·00 kg.; Lead (Pb), 63·30 kg.; Zinc (Zn), 66·40 kg.; Magnesium (Mg), 0·15 kg.; Rubber, 116·30 kg. These totals illustrate the profound strain on the blockaded and stretched German industry of tank production and go far to explain its limitation even in the early days of the war and by comparison with the achievements of Allied industry in this field.

Concluding Panzer IV production were Ausf. H and J, both mounting the final version of the 7·5 cm. gun with a length of L/48. A total of approximately 9,000 Panzer IV was produced.

PANZER IV F2 DESCRIBED

The hull was a comparatively simple design, incorporating various sizes of steel plates. All joints were austenitic steel welds and the plates were high-quality chromium-molybdenum steel made by the electric furnace process. Two bulkheads separated the hull into three compartments—driving, fighting and engine. The front driving compartment housed the transmission and final drive assemblies in addition to seats for both driver and radio operator/hull gunner. Three petrol tanks with a capacity of approximately 105 gallons were located beneath the floor of the centre fighting compartment. A most noticeable and characteristic feature of Panzer IV was the superstructure, of welded construction, bolted to the top flange of the hull. To accommodate the rather large turret race, it projected well beyond each side wall of the hull. One bolted and two hinged maintenance hatches were provided in the front glacis plate; access hatches for driver and radio operator were provided in the roof plate.

THE TURRET

The welded turret provided seats for three crew members—commander, gunner and loader. The sides were sloped so that the overall width was appreciably greater than the internal diameter of the turret ring. The 7·5 cm. gun was mounted on a trunnion axis. The forward end of the recoil mechanism projected through the mantlet to afford additional protection. The commander's cupola, set well back on the turret roof, had five observation ports equally spaced around its circumference with the front port pointing

Panzer IV in action in Russia supporting infantry: Ausf. B, C, or D. Note fuel cans on side.

Ausf. D again had a stepped front plate like Ausf. A, but the bow machine-gun for the radio operator was now in a square shaped mount with internal ball. The driver had a side opening for a sub-machine-gun. The mantlet for the main armament was external, as opposed to the internal mantlet on all earlier models.

directly forward in line with the gun. It was closed by a pair of semi-circular hatch covers. An observation port was provided in each side wall of the turret, in front of the side access hatches. Additional observation ports appeared on Panzer IV turrets at either side of the gun mantlet, although official documents indicated that the right side port should be omitted on the F2 version. Not all turrets were so modified, since even the later Ausf. G sometimes carried both ports. Only one signal port appeared on the turret roof, similar to the ones mounted on both driving compartment crew access hatches. There were also two revolver and carbine ports at the rear of the turret. The fighting compartment was ventilated by a roof-mounted extractor fan.

The new gun KwK 40, of Panzer IV Ausf. F2 was easily distinguishable by its increased barrel length and muzzle brake. While the first production model was fitted with a single-baffle globular muzzle brake, later vehicles had a double brake. The gun itself was capable of penetrating homogeneous armour of 77 mm. thickness at 2,000 yards using PzGr.39 at normal impact. It could fire at least six different kinds of ammunition: *Panzergranate* 40 (A.P.C.R.), PzGr. 39 (A.P.C.B.C.), *Sprenggranate* 38*A* and *B* (H.E.A.T.), *Sprenggranate* 34 (H.E.) and *Nebelgranate* (Smoke shell). A total of 87 rounds were carried, plus 2,250

rounds of 7·92 mm. ammunition for both MG 34 machine-guns, one of which was mounted co-axially on the right side of the gun. The second machine-gun was mounted on the right side of the front vertical plate and operated by the radio operator. It had a ball mounting with a hemispherical fixed external mantlet, the ball being inserted from the outside. Turret traverse was effected by both hand and electric power gears supplied from a generator, driven by a DKW two-cylinder two-cycle 10 h.p. 500 c.c. petrol engine.

POWER AND TRANSMISSION

The main power plant was the standard medium tank engine of World War II, the Maybach "HL 120 TRM", a 12-cylinder, 11,867 c.c. liquid-cooled petrol engine built under licence by Norddeutsche Motorenbau GmbH. of Berlin-Niederschoeneweide. Normally developing an output of 300 b.h.p. at 3,000 r.p.m., the engine was in most instances restricted to 2,600 r.p.m. giving a rating of 265 b.h.p. The engine used only 74 octane petrol. Cooling air entered through louvres on the left hand side of the engine compartment, was drawn through two radiators and over the engine by two ten-bladed fans. An exceptionally large filter provided clean air for the power plant. Engine output was transmitted by a propeller shaft and a three-plate

Front and side views of an Ausf. D of the Afrika Korps. Bow machine-gun has been removed. Note that although this Panzer IV can be identified as Ausf. D from its stepped front plate and the shape of the driver's visor and the bow machine-gun mount it does not have the cone-shaped signal port flap on the turret roof. This was removed from Ausf. D vehicles when they were uparmoured.

Three-quarter rear view of Ausf. D shows clearly the shape of the commander's cupola compared with that on Ausf. A. The four return rollers identify all Panzer IV vehicles.

Four of the five-man crew of a Panzer IV can be seen in this picture of an Ausf. D cruising along. 250 of this model were built, their chassis numbers running from 80501 to 80750.

Top view of Ausf. D. Note round pistol ports at rear of turret; in Ausf. A these were square. To the right of the cone-shaped signal port flap the rectangular ventilator flap can be seen slightly open. In later models the flap was replaced by a fan ventilator.

dry clutch to the Zahnradfabrik Friedrichshafen AG. synchro-mesh six-speed gearbox. Small multi-disc synchronising clutches were used for 2nd, 3rd, 4th, 5th and 6th gears. A Krupp-Wilson "Clutch-Brake" final drive and steering mechanism was used. In this, the input gear drove the annulus of an epicyclic train. The sunwheel was coupled to a steering brake drum, which was held stationary by an external band and compression spring while the vehicle was in motion. The drive from the epicyclic annulus was transmitted through the planet carrier to the spur reduction gears, which drove the track sprockets. The six-speed gearbox and the final drive units had one common oil circulation system.

Each track consisted of 98 links, each one 400 mm. wide with 120 mm. pitch. Manganese steel was used for this "skeleton" type of track which weighed approximately 1,400 lb. Track tension was adjusted by means of a large diameter idler wheel mounted on an eccentric axle at the rear of the vehicle. The suspension system consisted of four bogie units per side, each one of which was fitted with two $18\frac{1}{2}$ in. diameter rubber-tyred wheels. Quarter elliptic springs were mounted on the underside of the leading axle arm of each bogie. The other end of the spring rested on a shackle pin and roller, carried on an extension of the trailing axle arm. Four support rollers per side completed the suspension.

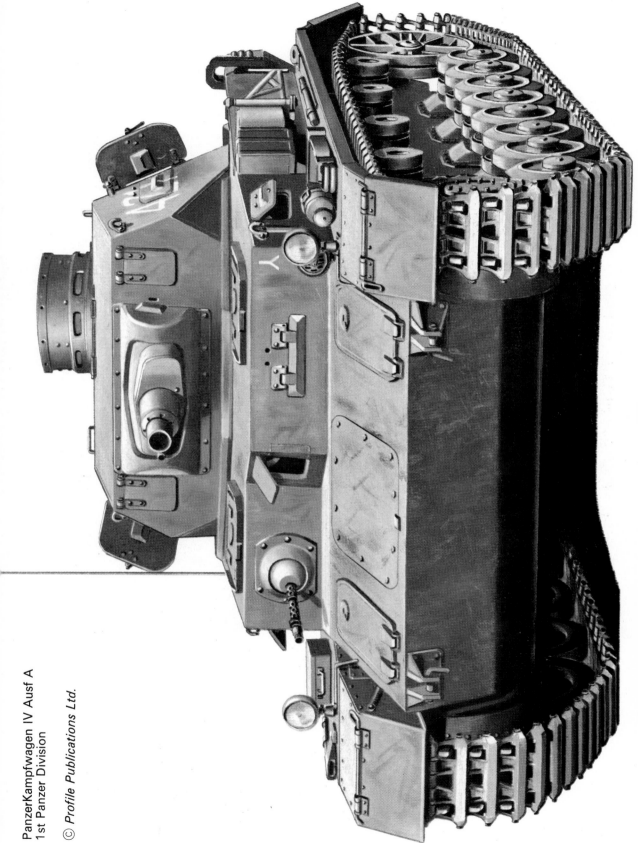

PanzerKampfwagen IV Ausf A
1st Panzer Division

© *Profile Publications Ltd.*

Ausf. E of 13th Panzer Division early in the Russian campaign, 1941. This model still had the stepped front plate, although with modifications to the driver's visor and the bow machine-gun mount. Other changes included: modified commander's cupola installed further forward so that it no longer protruded from the back plate of the turret which was now unbroken; increased armour on nose plate, bolted on armour for hull to improve fighting compartment protection (see picture), spaced armour in front of bow machine-gun and sometimes in front of driver's position; replacement of rectangular ventilator flap on turret roof by fan ventilator, and removal of cone-shaped single port flap which was replaced by a flat lid (see picture: the new ventilator is half-way along the turret roof in front of the cupola).

Close up of front plate of Ausf. E showing the new driver's visor with single hinged flap and the modified bow machine-gun mount.

Ausf. E moving up for action in North Africa. Chassis numbers of this model were 80801 to 82000. Weight was 21 tons.

VARIANTS

Before deciding to install the long-barrelled 7·5 cm. gun on the Ausf. F, Krupp carried out extensive research into utilising the 5 cm. Pak 38 for the Panzer IV. Krupp maintained that if a decision was reached by August 1941, "Nibelungenwerke" would be able to produce 80 Panzer IV with the 5 cm. Pak by the following spring. An order was issued resulting in one prototype, which was demonstrated on November 15, 1941. Events in Russia, however, had already rendered this project obsolete, and it was dropped.

Vehicles returning to the factories or home maintenance depots for major overhaul received, after March 1943, standard armour skirts. This additional 5 mm. armour was loosely attached to the sides and the turret of the vehicle and provided extra protection against the very efficient Russian anti-tank rifle; it was also intended to defeat the effect of hollow-charge projectiles.

Chassis of Panzer IV Ausf. Fs were utilised for Panzerjäger IV, a tank destroyer vehicle built by

Vomag of Plauen. Shown as a wooden mock-up for the first time on May 14, 1943 the vehicle mounted the 7·5 cm. Pak 39 L/48 with limited traverse. It entered troop service in January 1944 under the designation *Jagdpanzer IV Ausf. F* (SdKfz.162). Battle weight was 24 metric tons, with 79 rounds of ammunition and a crew of four. Early versions of the 15 cm. *Sturmpanzer IV Brummbär* (SdKfz.166) were also based on PzKpfw IV Ausf. F.

The introduction of super-heavy artillery units in 1941 necessitated the conversion of several Panzer IV Ausf. F to ammunition carriers. To supply the 60 cm. "Karl" mortars with shells weighing 2,200 kg. each, Krupp created a limited number of *"Munitions-träger für Karlgerät"*. Equipped with a special superstructure and a three ton crane, these vehicles supported the gigantic guns during the siege of Sevastopol.

GESCHÜTZWAGEN III/IV

One of the most useful and numerous of the many makeshift chassis developed after 1940–41 was the

In the foreground a Panzer IV Ausf. E with turret pointing almost at nine o'clock among other German tanks knocked out in Russia.

The turret, mounting the short 7·5 cm. gun of PzKpfw IV Ausf. FI

The insignia of the Afrika Korps; varying in detail, the basic palm-and-swastika motif was widely used on vehicles of all types.

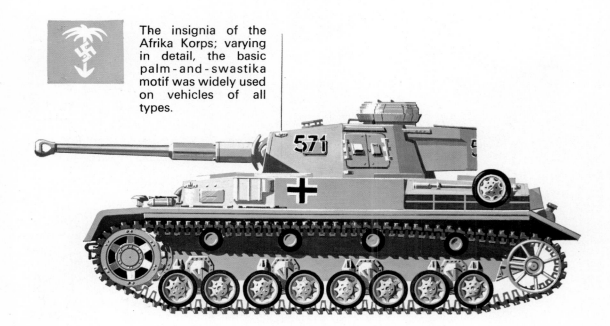

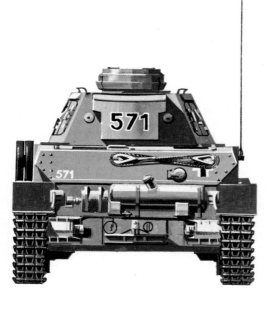 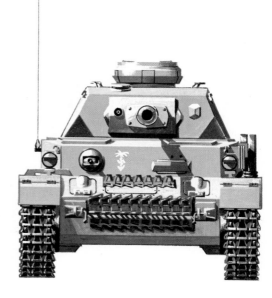

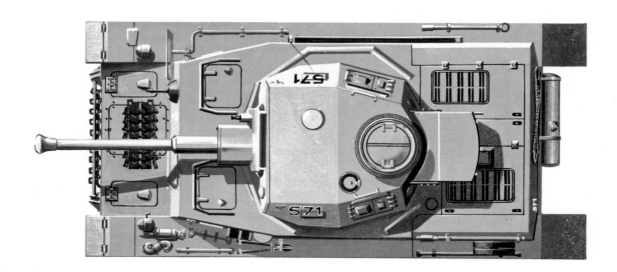

PANZERKAMPFWAGEN IV Ausführung F2
This up-gunned version of Germany's famed Panzer IV, armed with the long 7·5 cm. K L/43, appeared from March 1942 as a hurried answer to the Soviet T-34. It gave the Panzer IV a new lease of life which, with the L/48, saw it through to the end of the war; this version was known to the Allies as the ''Mark IV Special''. Some of these tanks were operated by the 15th and 21st Panzer Divisions in North Africa, and they played an important part in the German operations at Alam Halfa and El Alamein in September and October 1942.

M. Roffe © Profile Publications Ltd.

Ausf. F had a straight front plate. Basic armour was increased from 30 mm. to 50 mm. and the track width was increased by 20 mm. to 400 mm. Turret hatch doors were changed from single to double. The first 393 vehicles of this model still had the short-barrelled 7·5 cm. gun as their main armament. Later vehicles had the new long-barrelled KwK 40 L/43. Those with the short-barrelled gun were re-designated Ausf. F1, those with the long-barrelled 7·5 cm. gun were designated Ausf. F2.

Ausf. F1. As well as reverting to the straight front plate Ausf. F had the driver's visor and bow machine-gun mount modified yet again.

Geschützwagen III/IV based on components of both Panzer III and IV by Altmaerkische Ketten-Fabrik GmbH. (ALKETT) of Berlin. The vehicle used PzKpfw IV Ausf. F bogie units, return rollers and idler wheels with PzKpfw III Ausf. J final drive assemblies, tracks and transmission components. Principal types built on this chassis were the 8·8 cm. Pak *"Nashorn"* (SdKfz.164) of which 473 were produced by Deutsche Eisenwerke, Teplitz-Schoenau works; and the 15 cm. heavy field howitzer 18/1 *"Hummel"* (SdKfz.165) of which 666 were built in 1943–44. There were also 150 ammunition carriers constructed on the chassis.

TACTICAL EMPLOYMENT

Painted in the usual dark blue-grey of the German Army, the Panzer IV backed up the occupation of Czechoslovakia in 1939 and the attack on Poland on September 1 of the same year. Equipping the heavy support companies of the tank battalions, the only opposition encountered came from Polish anti-tank guns. Losses were light here and in the invasion of

France in 1940. Here the superior deployment of German armour proved decisive. Battle experience modified the tactical application of armour considerably but technical improvements were negligible. Neither the protection nor the fire power was greatly improved. The same story was repeated during the Balkan campaign of 1941 and the first appearance of the Panzer IV in North Africa. During all this time, Panzer III had replaced the obsolete Panzer I and II and fought, already up-gunned with a 5 cm. gun, most of the tank battles. The Panzer IV, still restricted by its limited availability, acted only as a back-up unit.

The reorientation in German tank design after the appearance of the Russian T-34 in 1941 resulted in a gradual phase-out of Panzer III by 1943. Therefore the only vehicle in mass production and suited for carrying improved armour and armament was Panzer IV. It had to close the gap and did so most effectively. The new designs, such as Tiger and Panther, required time to be developed and made battle-ready, and it was left to Panzer IV to carry the main load.

Panzer IV F2s were delivered to the Russian Front in small numbers for the spring campaign of 1942. They also appeared in North Africa in the summer of that year. They were identified by the British as the "Mark IV Special" and accounted the most formidable

Hitler, surrounded by a ring of SS men with a single Army officer in attendance, inspects the first prototype PzKpfw IV F2, with the long-barrelled 7·5 cm. gun, at Krupp's Magdeburg factory early in 1942: note the ball-shaped, single-baffle muzzle brake of the early version.

Three-quarter rear view of
P2 KpfW IV Ausf F2. P2 Division
Grossdeutschland

© Profile Publications Ltd.

Ausf. F2 destroyed by its own crew in the Libyan desert; numbers of tanks had to be abandoned as fuel and spare parts shortages increased under British blockade. Note the raised glacis plate access doors; these were changed from earlier models, each door having an air intake cowl.

The increased track width of 400 mm. demanded new idler wheels, which were constructed of metal tube by a unique welding process.

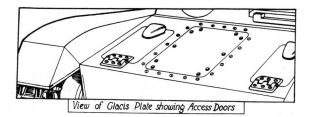

View of Glacis Plate showing Access Doors

ACCESS DOOR
and HINGE
SHOWING AIR INTAKE
COWL

Glacis plate access door of Ausf. F and later Panzer IV models.

tank they had yet met. F2s led Rommel's push for Alexandria in August 1942, until they were halted by British 6-pdrs. at El Alamein. Their effect on the 8th Army far outweighed their numbers. British Intelligence was astonished to discover later from captured Deutsches Afrika Korps records that on June 11, 1942 the total number of Panzer IV on strength was only 14 of which six were "specials" and by August 30, on the eve of the Battle of Alam Halfa, the strengths were 37 and 27 respectively.

On March 9, 1943 General Guderian read an important paper at Hitler's HQ presenting his ideas about the future of the German armoured forces. He

A snow-camouflaged Panzer IV F2 in Russia during the winter of 1942–43. This was the only tank then available to the Wehrmacht capable of defeating the Russian T–34.

The turret on Ausf. F and later Panzer IV models was equipped with double doors similar to those of Panzer III. Note the flat lid of the signal port beside the cupola and the turret ventilator in front of it; these first appeared in Ausf. E.

Side view of Ausf. F2 with ball-shaped muzzle brake on the KwK 40 L/43.

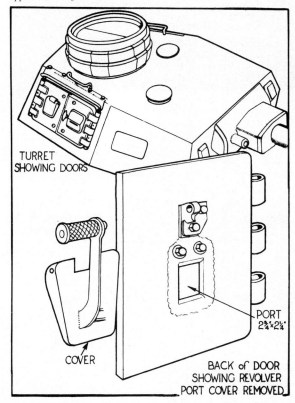

TURRET SHOWING DOORS

COVER

PORT 2¾″×2¼″

BACK of DOOR SHOWING REVOLVER PORT COVER REMOVED

Ausf. G had a double-baffle muzzle brake on its KwK 40 L/43. In other respects it was similar in appearance to Ausf. F2. Its side armour, however, was 30 mm. compared with 20 mm. + 20 mm.

Red Army infantry attacking past a disabled Panzer IV Ausf. F1.

Three-quarter left front view of Ausf. G. Note track links added for extra protection on nose and glacis plates.

To give protection against Russian anti-tank rifles and hollow-charge projectiles side armour plates called Schürzen were attached to German AFVs. Those on the hull sides were removable, being hung loosely from rails, and were often lost in the turmoil of battle; those round the turret were a permanent fixture.

Ausf. H, the penultimate Panzer IV model, had the L/48 7·5 cm. gun as its main armament, as did Ausf. J, the last model. The cupola lid which had been divided in two in earlier models now became a circular one piece lid. Driving sprocket and idler wheel were changed. Front armour was increased to 80 mm. In Ausf. J the power traverse was replaced by a two-speed hand gear to provide room for increased fuel capacity. A new gearbox in later Ausf. H vehicles and in Ausf. J gave improved cross country performance. Mesh Schürzen instead of plates were sometimes used on Ausf. J vehicles. Weight of Ausf. J was 25 tons, slightly less than Ausf. H. These two models together accounted for about two-thirds of the total number of Panzer IVs produced. In appearance they were very similar. Note rail on side from which Schürzen were suspended.

emphasised the fact that the basic equipment of the armoured divisions now consisted exclusively of Panzer IV. All efforts, therefore, would have to be made to ensure its continuous production throughout 1944 and 1945. His recommendation was relayed to industry in the form of an Order. Personal quarrels within the ranking hierarchy of the Ordnance Department led to constant attempts to disregard this directive and divert Panzer IV production from battle tanks to assault guns. These attempts reflected an

ever-increasing tendency to adjust the thinking of the armoured forces to defensive tactics in the closing stages of the war.

In 1943, tremendous losses during the campaigns around Bjelgorod, Kursk, and Orel depleted further the already overtaxed tank units. Some armoured divisions were reduced to a strength of 12 to 18 tanks. During this time, an allocation of ten new Panzer IV to a division was considered an outstanding event. In 1942, a tank battalion still consisted of light and

Fuel shortage in Germany made it necessary for tanks to be test-driven on bottled gas: a turretless Panzer IV.

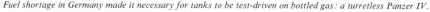

Chassis of Ausf. F were converted to ammunition carriers for super-heavy artillery; the crane had a load capacity of 3 tons.

Top view of Ausf. H showing fixed plates round turret (those protecting the turret hatch doors were hinged to allow access), and the one piece cupola lid that appeared on Ausf. H and J. Cylinder between Schürzen *and superstructure on right hand side is additional air filter.*

Nashorn *in action, with nine "kill rings" on its 8·8 cm. gun barrel showing the number of tanks destroyed. Another name for it was* Hornisse *(Hornet).*

To improve the mobility of the famous 8·8 cm. gun, chassis components of Panzer IV Ausf. F were used for the Nashorn (Rhinoceros) tank destroyer, of which 473 were built.

Firing a 95·7lb. shell to a maximum range of 14,550 yds. the 15 cm. s.FH 18/1 on the Hummel *was in service until the end of the war. This* Hummel *is shown under camouflage in Russia.*

Panzer IV Ausf. F chassis were used for fully enclosed Jagdpanzer IV tank destroyers which mounted a 7·5 cm. PaK 39 L/48. Late models of SdKfz 162, one of which is shown here with Zimmerit *anti-magnetic mine paste, had no port on left hand side of front plate and no muzzle brake.*

Jagdpanzer IV was sometimes called Guderian Ente *(Guderian Duck). Late versions of SdKfz 162 mounted a 7·5 cm. StuK 42 (L/70) and were given the number SdKfz 162/1. At first these had four return rollers, later three, as shown here. Other modifications included first two bogie wheels steel-tyred instead of rubber-tyred because of heavy gun weight.*

medium tank companies having the 5 cm. Panzer III as standard equipment. 1943 brought more and more of the up-gunned Panzer IV F2s to the forefront and by the end of that year, the Panzer III had almost disappeared. Only command and observation vehicles based on this chassis were retained in service into 1944.

Panzer IV equipped with the long-barrelled 7·5 cm. L/43 and L/48 guns had taken over since the defence against enemy tanks was now their main task. This eliminated the necessity for light and medium tank companies. The equipment of the German tank force thus became for the first time in its history uniform in both organisation and armament.

The climax in the history of Panzer IV came in

1944 when it was continuously thrown into the battle against Allied tank forces. In the East and, after the Normandy landings, also in the West and on impossible terrain in Italy, Panzer IV fought against overwhelming odds. A proposal by the General Staff to cancel its production by the beginning of 1943 and to rely completely upon the Tiger would have had disastrous consequences. An early collapse of the German Army would have been a foregone conclusion. Panzer IV proved to be the most reliable German armoured fighting vehicle. And after the installation of the improved armament in 1942, it was equal to most of its Allied counterparts.

Late production Sturmpanzer IV Brummbär *(Grizzly Bear). Brummbärs were built on Panzer IV Ausf. F through J chassis. Early versions had Tiger fahrerblende 80 with visor for the driver, and short collar on gun. Later versions, on Ausf. H and J chassis, had periscopes for driver, longer collar on gun, and different roof layout. Finally, as shown here, a machine-gun in ball mount was added in front for self-defence. Panzer IV chassis were also used for anti-aircraft S.P.s and tanks (Panzer flak and Flakpanzer).*

Built on a similar chassis to the Nashorn, *the self-propelled 15 cm. howitzer* Hummel *(Bumble-bee) was a highly successful piece of* Panzerartillerie.

(Picture sources for this Profile are Spielberger Collection, Chamberlain Collection, Bundesarchiv, Imperial War Museum, E.C.A., and H. Nowarra).

SPECIFICATION—PANZERKAMPFWAGEN IV AUSF. F2

General
Designation and Ordnance No.: PzKpfw IV (7·5 cm.), Ausführung F2 (Sd. Kfz. 161). Krupp type: 7/BW.
Crew: 5—commander, gunner, loader, driver and radio operator.
Battle weight: 23·2 tons.
Dry weight: 22 tons.
Power/weight ratio: 13·6 b.h.p./ton.
Ground Pressure: 2·86 lb./sq. in.
Bridge classification: A.

Dimensions
Length overall, gun front: 21 ft. 9 in.
Hull length, overall: 17 ft. 9 in.
Height: 8 ft. $9\frac{1}{2}$ in.
Width: 9 ft. $5\frac{1}{2}$ in.
Track centres: 8 ft. $\frac{1}{2}$ in.
Track width: $15\frac{3}{4}$ in.

Armament
Main armament: One 7·5 cm. Tank Gun 40 (KwK 40) L/43, centre turret, 360° traverse, +20° and −1·0° elevation.
Auxiliary armament: Two 7·92 mm. 34 MG machine-guns, one coaxial right of main armament, one in gun mount in front hull plate for radio operator.

Fire Control
Graduated target position indicator ring inside of cupola for commander. Turret position indicator with two dials for gunner.

Ammunition
87 rounds for 7·5 mm. gun.
3,192 rounds for 7·92 mm. machine-guns.
6 hand grenades.
24 signal cartridges.

Sighting and Vision
Commander: Five observation ports in cupola.
Gunner: Sighting telescope TZF 5 f vorl. 13 (T).
Radio operator: *Kugelblende* 50 with sighting periscope KzF 2 1,8 x 18°.
Driver: *Fahrerblende* 50.

Communication
Two receivers, one transmitter—gunner, driver and commander connected with one intercommunication circuit.

Armour
Chromium-molybdenum homogeneous steel, welded. Brinell No. 10/3000.
Hull: Front 50 mm. 10° Brinell 460–490; Glacis 25 mm. 73° Brinell 460–490; Sides 20 + 20 mm. 0° Brinell 500–520; Rear 20 mm. 12°; Roof 15 mm. 90°; Floor 10 mm. 90°.
Turret: Mantlet 50 mm. curved Brinell 490–510; Front 50 mm. 11° Brinell 490–510; Sides 30 mm. 26°, Rear 30 mm. 16°; Roof 10 mm. 90°.

Engine
Main: Maybach "HL 120 TRM" V-12 cyl. petrol. 11,867 cc. 300 b.h.p. at 3,000 r.p.m.
Auxiliary: DKW/Auto-Union "ZW 500" 2 cyl. inline. 497 cc. 10 b.h.p. at 2,800 r.p.m.
Fuel capacity: 105 gallons in three tanks underneath fighting compartment.

Transmission
Zahnradfabrik Friedrichshafen "ZF SSG 76 Aphon", Synchromesh, six forward and one reverse speeds. Krupp-Wilson clutch steering brakes.

Suspension
Running gear per side: One final drive wheel, one idler wheel. Four bogies with eight roadwheels (470/90–359) on quarter-elliptic springs. Four return rollers (250/65–134). Steel "skeleton" track, dry pin, type "Kgs 61/400/120", each one having 98 links. Pitch $4\frac{1}{4}$ in.

Electrical System
Bosch generator, type GQL 12 volt, 300 watt. Four batteries 12 volt 105 Ah.

Performance
Max. road speed: 24·8 m.p.h.
Gradient: 30°.
Vertical: 2 ft.
Trench: 7 ft.
Wading: 3 ft. 3 in.
Range: Road—130 miles; cross country—71 miles.

Special Features
Additional 5 mm. armour skirts attached to turret and sides as retrospective modification to all vehicles returning to base maintenance after March 1943.

View of a later production Panther Ausf D (the Ausf D proper) which was known as the D₂.   (Chamberlain Collection)

Panzerkampfwagen V Panther

by Chris Ellis and Peter Chamberlain

"NUMEROUS Russian T-34s went into action and inflicted heavy losses on the German tanks at Mzensk in 1941. Up to this time we had enjoyed tank superiority, but from now on the situation was reversed. The prospect of rapid decisive victories was fading in consequence. I made a report on this situation, which was for us a new one, and sent it to the Army Group; in this report I described in plain terms the marked superiority of the T-34 to our PzKpfw IV and drew the relevant conclusion as that must affect our future tank production. I concluded by urging a commission be sent immediately to my sector of the front, and that it consist of representatives of the Army Ordnance, the Armaments Ministry, the tank designers, and the firms that built tanks. If this commission was on the spot it could not only examine the destroyed tanks on the battlefield, but could also be advised by the men who had used them as to what should be included in

The Panther that never was; a wooden project model of the VK.3002(DB) prototype which was abandoned in favour of the MAN design. Its close resemblance to the T-34 is obvious but as finalized the VK.3002(DB) was to have twin wheels like the T-34 rather than the interleaved wheels shown.
(Chamberlain Collection)

the design for our new tanks. I also requested the rapid production of a heavy anti-tank gun with sufficient penetrating power to knock out the T-34. The commission appeared on the Second Panzer Army's front on November 20, 1941''.

General Heinz Guderian, in his book *Panzer Leader*.

THE sudden decline in German panzer fortunes brought about by the unexpected appearance of the revolutionary T-34 tank in Soviet hands, jolted the German Army Staff out of a complacency which had been caused entirely by the excellence and versatility of the PzKpfw IV. Work on a successor to the PzKpfw IV had started as early as 1937 when the firm of Henschel and others had been asked to produce designs in the 30-35 ton class. However, progress on these was slow, due partly to changing ideas and requirements. By 1941, prototypes by Henschel, VK.3001(H), and Porsche, VK.3001(P), had been completed but, at the time of the invasion of Russia, when the T-34 was met, requirements were changed yet again in favour of a larger design with a 8·8 cm. gun in the 45 ton class, the VK.4501. This eventually became the Tiger heavy tank, whose development is described separately in this Series. Because the VK.4501 design was needed urgently, however, it largely incorporated features from the earlier development prototypes and the Tiger thus owed nothing to the T-34 design. The 8·8 cm. gun and the heavy (100 mm.) armour specified for the VK.4501 design were, however, influenced by the T-34's appearance for it was considered essential to have a tank with these features in production as a safeguard against any eventual Soviet development of an up-gunned and up-armoured version of the T-34.

One of the uncompleted VK.3002(DB) prototypes. Unlike the T-34, this vehicle had return rollers. Resemblance to the T-34 is particularly striking in this front view.

(Chamberlain Collection)

One of the first 20 Panthers produced, originally designated Ausf A, later classed as Ausf D, and known as the D₁. Major distinguishing feature is the cupola protruding through the turret side, but the single baffle muzzle brake and smoke dischargers on the turret side are other early features to note.

(IWM)

Meanwhile, as Guderian recounts, the commission appointed by the Armaments Ministry acted swiftly. They made an "on the spot" investigation on November 20, 1941, to assess the key features of the T-34 design. The three main characteristics of this vehicle which rendered all existing German tanks technically obsolete were (1) the sloped armour which gave optimum shot deflection all round (2) the large road wheels which gave a stable and steady ride, and (3) the overhanging gun, a feature previously avoided by the Germans as impracticable. Of these the first was the most revolutionary. The Armaments Ministry acted promptly and on November 25, 1941, contracted with two principal armament firms, Daimler-Benz and MAN, to produce designs for a new medium tank in the 30-35 ton class, under the ordnance designation VK.3002. To be ready the following spring, the specifications called for a vehicle with 60 mm. frontal armour and 40 mm. side armour, the front and sides to be sloped as in the T-34. A maximum speed of 55 km. per hour was to be achieved.

In April 1942, the two designs, VK.3002 (DB)—DB: Daimler-Benz—and VK.3002 (MAN), were submitted to a committee of Waffenprüfamt 6, the section of the Army Weapons Department (Heeres-waffenamt) responsible for AFV design and procurement. The designs afforded an interesting contrast. The Daimler-Benz proposal was an almost unashamed copy of the T-34 in layout, with the addition of a few typical teutonic refinements. It had a hull shape similar to the T-34's with turret mounted well forward, so far forward in fact that the driver sat within the turret cage, with remote control hydraulic steering. A MB507 diesel engine was fitted with transmission to the rear sprockets again exactly duplicating the T-34 layout. Paired steel bogies (without rubber tyres) were suspended by leaf springs, and other features included escape hatches in the hull sides and jettisonable fuel tanks on the hull rear in the T-34 fashion. The VK.3002 (DB) was in fact a remarkably "clean" design with much potential. Leaf springs, for example, were cheaper and easier to produce than torsion bars, and the use of all-steel wheels recognized the problem of rubber shortage from the start. The compact engine and transmission at the rear left the fighting compartment unencumbered for future up-gunning or structural change, while the diesel engine itself would have been an advantage in later years when petrol supply became acutely restricted.

By comparison, the VK.3002 (MAN) displayed

An early production Panther Ausf D with single baffle muzzle brake and smoke dischargers on turret side.   (Chamberlain Collection)

Late production Panther Ds had the improved pattern cupola with periscopes and MG ring. It was also fitted retrospectively to some earlier models. This Ausf D, knocked out in Italy in 1944, also has Zimmerit anti-magnetic coating and side skirts. A 75mm shell can be seen on the glacis plate. (IWM)

Panther Ausf A had a ball mount for the hull machine-gun and the later type of cupola which featured a ring mount for an AA machine-gun. (IWM)

original German (rather than Russian) thinking; it was sophisticated rather than simple. It had a higher, wider hull than either the VK.3002 (DB) or the T-34, with a large turret placed well back to offset as much as possible the overhang of the long 7·5 cm. gun which was called for as the main armament. Torsion bar suspension was used with interleaved road wheels, while a Maybach HL 210 petrol (gasoline) V-12 engine was proposed, with drive to the front sprockets. The internal layout followed conventional German practice with stations for the driver and hull gunner/wireless operator in the front compartment.

Hitler always took a personal interest in AFV design and was on several occasions instrumental in ordering policy changes or design improvements. When the respective Daimler-Benz and MAN designs were submitted to the Waffenprüfamt 6 committee in April 1942, Hitler was most impressed with the Daimler-Benz "T-34 type" proposal, though he suggested that the gun be changed from the 7·5 cm. L/48 model to the longer and more powerful L/70 weapon. Hitler's intervention in the proceedings at this stage led to an order for 200 VK.3002 (DB) vehicles being placed, and prototypes actually went into production. However, the committee set up by Waffenprüfamt 6—which was already being called unofficially the "Panther Committee"—preferred the VK.3002 (MAN) design, because it was far more conventional by existing German engineering standards. MAN's proposal was accepted in May 1942 and they were asked to go ahead and produce a mild steel prototype as fast as possible. Subsequently, later in 1942, the order for the 200 Daimler-Benz vehicles was discreetly rescinded.

Meanwhile Ing. Kniepkampf, chief engineer and designer of Waffenprüfamt 6, took personal charge of detail design work on the MAN vehicle. This reflected the priority given to the Panther project. Kniepkampf was a key figure in German AFV design at this time, having been with Waffenprüfamt 6 since 1936 and remaining as chief engineer almost until the war's end in 1945. Among other things he was principally

responsible for German half-track development and introduced features like interleaved road wheels, torsion bar suspension, and the Maybach-Olvar gearbox to German tanks.

In September 1942 the first pilot model of the VK.3002(MAN) was completed and tested in the MAN factory grounds at Nuremburg. This was closely followed by the second pilot model which was transported to the Heereswaffenamt test ground at Kummersdorf for official army trials. By this time, incidentally, the Tiger was already just in production, but its shortcomings—including excessive weight, low

The Panther Ausf A showing its later pattern cupola. Note that all turret side openings are deleted except for the rear escape hatch. (IWM)

A close view of the cupola in the Panther Ausf A, showing the armoured periscopes (one has been shot away), the gun ring, and the horizontally opening hatch. (IWM)

Inside the Panther turret, showing loader's seat (right) and the elevating and traversing handwheels (left, centre). (IWM)

speed, and poor ballistic shape—were already recognized. The new vehicle was ordered into immediate production as the PzKpfw V Panther, under the ordnance designation Sd Kfz 171, with absolute top priority rating. The first vehicle was turned out by MAN in November 1942. It was planned to build at a rate of 250 vehicles a month as soon as possible, but at the end of 1942 this target was increased to 600 a month. To reach such an ambitious target it was necessary to form a large Panther production group. Daimler-Benz were quickly switched from work on their now-discarded design (prototypes of which had by then been almost completed) and in November 1942 they, too, began tooling up to build Panthers, the first vehicles coming from Daimler early in 1943. Also in January 1943, Maschinenfabrik Niedersachsen of Hanover, and Henschel, began tooling up to build Panthers—production started in February/March—and scores of sub-contractors were soon involved in what became one of the most concentrated German armaments programmes of the war. In fact, even aircraft production was cut back, partly to conserve fuel for use in tanks but partly, also, to free manufacturing facilities for Panther engines and components.

The monthly target of 600 vehicles was never achieved, however. By May 1943 output had reached a total of 324 completed vehicles and the monthly production average over the year was 154. In 1944 a monthly production average of 330 vehicles was achieved. By February 1945, when production tailed off, 4,814 Panthers had been built. Panthers were first used in action in the great Kursk Offensive of July 5, 1943, but the haste with which the design had been evolved, and the speed with which it had been put into production led to many "teething" troubles. In particular the complicated track and suspension gave trouble, with frequent breakages, while the engine presented cooling problems and this led to frequent engine fires. In the early months of service, indeed, more Panthers were put out of service by mechanical faults than by Soviet anti-tank guns. There were three basic production models of the Panther, Ausführung D, A, and G, in that order. The differences between them are explained later.

THE PANTHER DESCRIBED

The Panther conformed to the usual layout of German tanks. It had the driving and transmission compartment forward, the fighting compartment and turret in the centre, and the engine compartment at the rear. The driver sat on the left hand side forward with a vision port in front of him in the glacis plate. This was fitted with a laminated glass screen and had an armoured hinged flap on the outside which was

Unlike the roughly made T-34, the Panther was a sophisticated design demanding high precision engineering. This official German picture shows Panthers being assembled. (IWM)

closed under combat conditions. Forward vision was then given by two fixed episcopes in the compartment roof, one facing directly forward while the other faced half left in the "10.30" position. This restricted vision considerably and in the later Ausf G a rotating periscope was fitted in place of the fixed forward episcope, and the half left episcope and the vision port were completely dispensed with. The Ausf G was thus easily recognized from the front since it had an unpierced glacis plate. The wireless operator, who was also the hull machine-gunner, sat on the right side forward. In the early Ausf D models, he was provided with a vertical opening flap in the glacis plate—rather similar to a vertical letterbox flap—through which he fired a standard MG 34 machine-gun in action. In the Ausf A and G, however, this arrangement was replaced by an integral ball-mount which took the MG 34 in the standard type of tank mounting. The radio equipment was fitted to the operator/gunner's right and was located in the sponson which overhung the tracks. Episcopes were fitted, duplicating the driver's side.

Between the driver and wireless operator was located the gearbox, with final drive led each side to the front sprockets. The gearbox was specially evolved for the Panther as this vehicle was bulkier and heavier than previous designs and developed considerably more power. Known as the AK 7-200, the gearbox was an all syncromesh unit with seven speeds. Argus hydraulic disc brakes were used for steering in the conventional manner by braking the tracks. However, the epicyclic gears could also be used to assist steering by driving one or other of the sprockets against the main drive, so retarding the track on that side and

allowing sharper radius turns.

In the turret the gunner sat on the left hand side of the gun and was originally provided with an articulated binocular sight; this was later changed to a monocular sight. He fired the gun electrically by a trigger fitted on the elevating handwheel. The co-axial machine-gun, fitted in the mantlet, was fired by the gunner from a foot switch. Traverse was by hydraulic power or hand, the same handwheel being used for either method.

The vehicle commander's station was at the left rear of the turret, the offset location being necessitated by the length of the breech which virtually divided the turret into two. A prominent cupola was provided which was of the "dustbin" type with six vision slits in the Ausf D. In the Panther Ausf A and G, however, an improved cupola was fitted which had seven equally-spaced periscopes. This had a hatch which lifted and opened horizontally. Above the cupola was fitted a ring mount for a MG 34 which could be used for air defence, though this mount was sometimes removed.

The remaining crew member was the loader who occupied the right side of the turret. The turret itself had sloped walls and a rounded front covered by a curved cast mantlet. The cage had a full floor which rotated with the turret. Drive for the hydraulic traverse was taken through the centre of the floor to a gearbox, and thence to an oil motor. Turret openings were kept to a minimum and included a large circular hatch on the rear face which was an access/escape hatch for the loader and was also used for ammunitioning. On the left side beneath the cupola was a circular hatch for ejecting expended cartridge cases

Below and Following Page: The Panther Ausf G, the final production type, had several improvements. Notable is the simplified hull shape with a continuous sloping line to the lower sponson edges, the deletion of the driver's vision ports and episcopes, and the substitution of a rotating periscope, clearly seen in the top view. This view also shows the aperture for the bomb thrower in the turret roof, fitted in place of the smoke dischargers carried in the Ausf D. (IWM)

and re-ammunitioning, but this was eliminated in the Ausf A and G, Similarly eliminated were three small pistol ports, one in each face, which were normally plugged by a steel bung and chain.

The engine, housed in the rear compartment, was a Maybach HL 230 P30, a V-12 23 litres unit of 700 h.p. at 3,000 r.p.m. This was a bored out version of the HL 210 engine originally planned. The earliest production vehicles had this unit, but like most AFV designs, the Panther had increased in weight considerably during the development stage with a heavier gun and heavier armour (among other things) bringing its weight up from the 35 tons originally envisaged to about 43 (metric) tons. The easy way to increase the power to compensate for the added weight was to enlarge the engine. Access to the engine for maintenance was via a large inspection hatch in the centre of the rear decking. Cooling grilles and fans occupied most of the remainder of the rear decking. Exhaust was taken away through manifolds on the squared off hull rear. Most Panthers had stowage boxes flanking the rear exhaust pipes, but these were not always fitted.

The actual hull and superstructure was a single built-up unit of machinable quality homogeneous armour plate of welded construction but with all main edges strengthened by mortised interlocking. The heaviest armour, 80 mm., was on the glacis plate which was sloped at 33° to the horizontal, an angle specifically selected to deflect shells striking the glacis upwards clear of the mantlet.

The suspension consisted of eight double inter-leaved bogie wheels on each side, the wheels being dished discs with solid rubber tyres. Some very late production vehicles, however, had all-steel wheels of the type fitted to the Tiger II (Royal Tiger), as described later. The first, third, fifth, and seventh wheels from the front were double while the intervening axles carried spaced wheels overlapping the others on the inside and outside. Each bogie axle was joined by a radius arm to a torsion bar coupled in series to a second bar lying parallel to it. The torsion

bars were carried across the floor and the bogie wheels on the right hand side of the vehicle were set behind their respective torsion bars while those on the left were set in front. Thus the wheel layout was not symmetrical. Though this suspension was technically advanced and gave the vehicle superb flotation, maintenance was complicated due to the size of the wheels and consequent inaccessibility of the axles and torsion bars. In addition wheel replacement was a heavy and lengthy task.

The 7·5 cm. L/70 gun mounted in the Panther was developed by Rheinmetall-Borsig who had been asked in July 1941 to design a high velocity version of the 7·5 cm. weapon which could penetrate 140 mm. of armour plate at 1,000 metres. Soon after this the firm were asked to design the turret and mount to hold this gun for installation in the VK.3002 design. The prototype gun was ready in early 1942, a weapon 60 calibres long. Test firing indicated that performance was a little below the requested minimum, so the barrel was lengthened to 70 calibres, the improved

prototype being ready for tests in June 1942. In this lengthened form the gun went into production. Initially it had a single baffle muzzle brake—and was so used on the earliest Panthers—but later a double baffle muzzle brake was adopted.

PANTHER PRODUCTION MODELS

The first Panther models which came off the MAN line from November 1942 were designated in standard German fashion as PzKpfw V Ausf A. The designation PzKpfw V Ausf B was earmarked for a proposed version of the vehicle which was to have the Maybach-Olvar gearbox in place of the specially developed AK 7-200 unit. However, the Maybach gearbox was considered unsuitable for installation in the Panther and the Ausf B never materialized. The first twenty Panthers which originally had the Ausf A designation were really "pre-production" vehicles in modern terms. They had the 60 mm. thick front armour as originally called for, the Maybach HL 210 engine, also as originally specified, a ZF 7 gearbox with clutch and brake steering, the earliest form of the L/70 gun, and a cupola bulge in the side of the turret. From January 1943, however, Panthers appeared with all the design improvements suggested from trials with the pilot model. The glacis plate thickness was increased to 80 mm., the bored out HL 230 engine was fitted together with the new AK 7-200 gearbox, as already described, which allowed single radius turns (i.e., a definite fixed radius of turn depending on the gear engaged) and also made a neutral turn possible with the vehicle stationary. To simplify turret production, the cupola was shifted slightly to the right, thus eliminating the bulged housing.

This first full production type was designated PzKpfw V Ausf D. No record has been unearthed of an Ausf C model, but it seems almost certain that this was a "paper project", like the Ausf B with some other proposed mechanical change. Much confusion has always existed over the designations of these early Panthers, mainly because the Germans themselves

The Panther's biggest adversary in the Normandy fighting was the rocket-firing fighter, (notably the Typhoon) which more than made up for the Allies lack of tanks able to meet the German tanks on equal terms. This Panther A is shown soon after a rocket attack. (IWM)

Determined stalking could pay off, even for the infantry. Here a platoon of US infantrymen rush forward to capture a Panther which has just been immobilized by two quick shots at point-blank range from the bazooka crew in the foreground. Normandy, July 26, 1944. (IWM)

later classed the early Ausf A vehicles with the full production Ausf Ds for record purposes. Early in 1943 they confused the record further by identifying the original Ausf A as the "Ausf D_1" and the Ausf D as the "Ausf D_2".

Characteristics of the Ausf D were the "dustbin" cupola, the vision port and machine-gun port on the glacis, smoke dischargers on the turret sides, and a straight edge to the lower sponson sides with separate stowage compartments fabricated beneath the rear ends. On later Ausf Ds the improved type of cupola was fitted and the smoke dischargers were dropped in favour of a bomb thrower installed in the turret roof and operated by the loader. Later Ausf Ds also had the skirt armour, which was adopted as standard to protect the top run of the tracks from "bazooka" hits, and Zimmerit anti-magnetic paste covering to prevent the attachment of mines. All except the earliest vehicles had the L/70 gun with double baffle.

Next production model of the Panther was designated Ausf A, an anomaly which has not been fully explained. It has been suggested that this out-of-sequence designation was deliberately adopted to

A remarkable view of a burning Panther Ausf A, photographed through the driver's visor of the approaching SU-85 which had just knocked it out, Russian Front, winter 1944. (IWM)

US infantry cautiously approach a burning Panther which has just been savaged by a rocket attack from fighters, Normandy, June 1944.
(US Official)

confuse the Allies but this seems most unlikely. It may conceivably have resulted from an early administrative, phonetic, or clerical error, since the logical designation was Ausf E. Be that as it may, the Ausf A appeared in the latter half of 1943 and featured several detail improvements. Chief among these was the adoption of the new cupola with armoured periscopes, and the provision of a proper ball-mount for the hull machine-gun. Side skirts of 5 mm. armour and a Zimmerit finish were standard. The side skirts, incidentally, were only loosely fixed by bolts and they were frequently removed, either by the crew or by adjacent foliage in combat conditions. The gunner's binocular sight was replaced by a monocular one, though this was not noticeable externally. To further simplify turret production, however, the pistol ports and the small loading hatch featured in the Ausf D were eliminated completely, leaving just the big loading/escape hatch in the turret rear. The Panther Ausf A was the main type encountered by the Allies in the Normandy fighting.

The final production model of the Panther in its original form was also in action in Normandy in June 1944. This was the Ausf G. By this time, incidentally, the designation PzKpfw V had been dropped following a personal directive from Hitler on February 27, 1944, and the vehicle was simply known as the Panther Ausf G. Considerable modifications featured in this vehicle. The superstructure sides were altered, mainly to simplify production, so that the rear stowage compartments were now integral with the hull instead of separate additions. This gave a sloping lower edge to the sponsons. The hull sides were at the same time increased in thickness from 40 mm. to 50 mm. with the angle of slope altered from 30° to 40°. The driver's vision port was eliminated from the glacis plate and his vision was greatly improved by provision of a rotating periscope in place of the episcopes. New hinged hatches with spring-assisted opening replaced the original hatches provided in the hull roof for the driver and wireless operator. The earlier models had pivoted hatches which were found

The Beobachtungspanzer Panther (Sd Kfz 172) was an old Panther D converted as an OP vehicle or command vehicle for SP artillery battalions. The "gun" was a wooden dummy and main armament (for self-defence) was the ball-mounted machine-gun.
(IWM)

The Befehlspanzer Panther was a standard vehicle (in this case an Ausf D) fitted with extra radio for the use of unit commanders. It was distinguished by the extra aerials.
(IWM)

This Panther Ausf G ("Cuckoo") was captured by 4th Tank Battalion, Coldstream Guards, and used in action by them in January 1945. (IWM)

to jam easily. Internally, armoured ammunition bins were fitted inside each sponson with sliding armoured doors to reduce fire risk. The 7·5 cm. ammunition stowage was also slightly increased in this model from 79 to 82 rounds.

Some amendments were made to external stowage, including the provision of a stronger method of attaching the skirt armour. In very late production vehicles the cylindrical stowage box for the gun pull-

through and cleaning gear was removed from the left side of the hull and mounted across the hull at the rear of the engine compartment.

THE PANTHER II

With Tiger and Panther production under way, a new generation of tanks was planned which was to incorporate the lessons from existing designs. In particular,

"Battle of the Bulge" in December 1944 was the last big armour offensive by the Germans on the Western Front. This Panther Ausf G was successfully stalked and "brewed up" by a flank shot from a Sherman on the road between Wirtzfeld and Krinkel. (US Official)

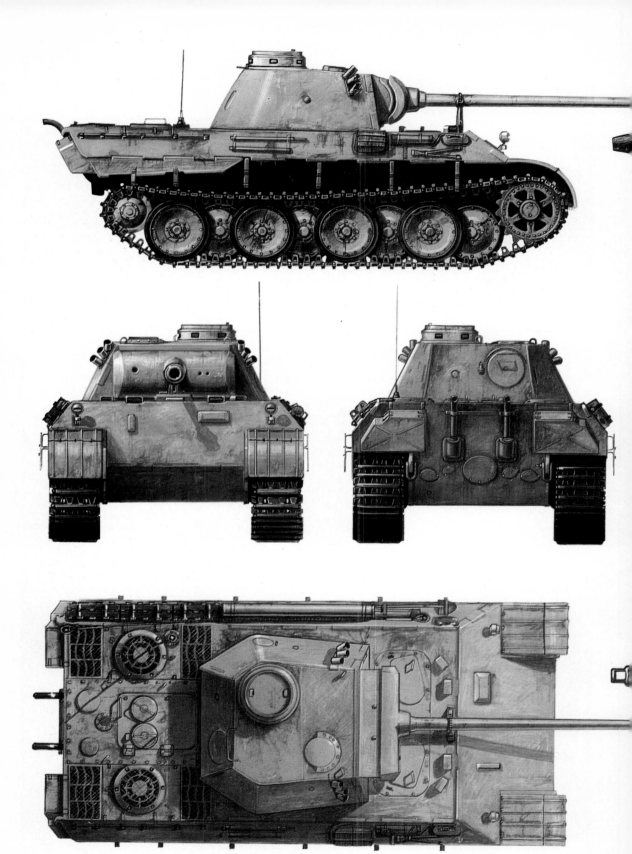

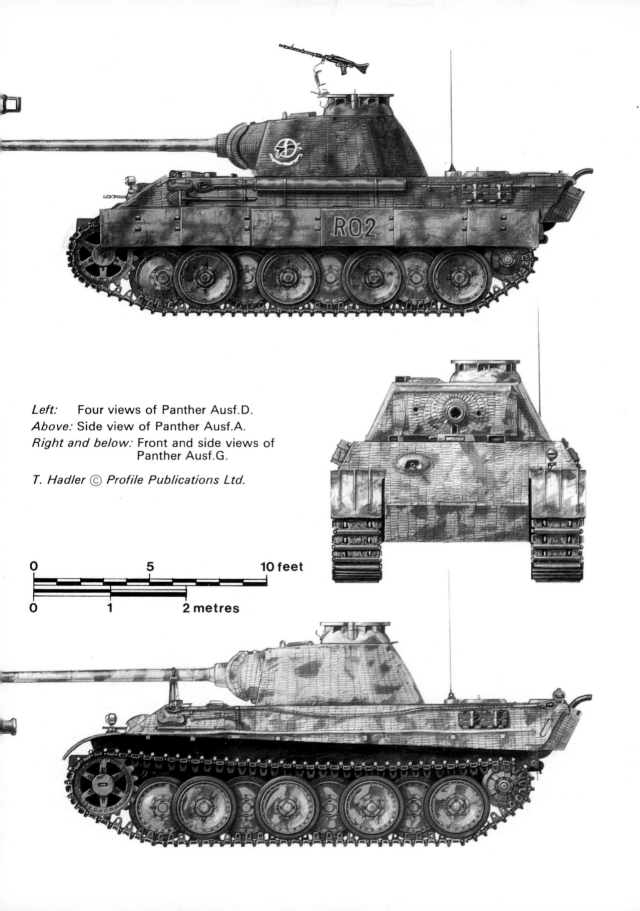

Left: Four views of Panther Ausf.D.
Above: Side view of Panther Ausf.A.
Right and below: Front and side views of
Panther Ausf.G.

T. Hadler © *Profile Publications Ltd.*

0   5   10 feet
0   1   2 metres

Above and Right: *The Bergepanzer Panther (Panther ARV) was an important special purpose type with winch and recovery gear. The earth anchor was raised and lowered from the winch. The light jib could be erected either side for lifting components.* (IWM)

attention was to be given to simplifying production, economizing on materials, reducing maintenance, and standardizing components as far as possible. In February 1943 Waffenprüfamt 6 asked MAN and Henschel to produce improved designs for the Panther and Tiger respectively, ensuring maximum interchangeability of parts. Henschel produced the Tiger II which went into production at the end of 1943 since a replacement for the somewhat unsatisfactory Tiger was urgently needed. The improved Panther, the Panther II, officially designated Panther Ausf F, was to have a hull similar to the existing Panther but with the same form of interleaved all-steel resilient wheels as the Tiger II. Other changes were to be the adoption of an improved gearbox and transmission, the AK 7-400, and mechanical parts such as brakes identical to those in the Tiger II. The armour on the hull top was to be doubled to 25 mm. and the ball-mount was to be altered to take the MG 42. The

major change, however, was to be a new design of turret, known as the Panzerturm Schmal (small), which, as its name implies, was much smaller than the original Panther turret. The object was to reduce weight, simplify production, reduce frontal area, eliminate shot traps beneath the mantlet (a weakness in the original Panther turret) and enable a larger gun to be fitted. It was to have a built-in stereoscopic rangefinder, and a gyrostabilizer for both the sight and the gun based on that fitted in American tanks. As part of the experimental work for this a standard Panther was fitted with a gyrostabilizer for firing trials and proved to have its accuracy and effectiveness doubled.

The new small turret was developed as a separate project by Daimler-Benz under the direction of Dr. Wunderlich, assisted by Col. Henrici, a gunnery expert from Waffenprüfamt 6. Kniepkampf was in overall charge of both the Tiger II and Panther II

Not all Bergepanthers were fitted with earth spades. They were used as towing vehicles only. Others had the winch removed and were used as munitions carriers. (IWM)

A very early production Jagdpanther (possibly, indeed, the prototype) showing the one-piece 8·8 cm. barrel which characterized early models. The unusual twin vision port for the driver supports the view that this is the prototype vehicle.
(Chamberlain Collection)

projects. The new turret proved a most successful design. It had the same ring diameter as the old turret, but took 30% less time to make and had 30% more armour plate all within the same weight limit. It could take the L/70 gun and was also designed to accommodate a proposed lengthened L/100 version of the same weapon. It could take the same 8·8 cm. gun as the Tiger II as yet another alternative. The wide mantlet, difficult to manufacture, which characterized the old turret, was replaced by a relatively simple Saukopf (pig's head) mantlet, of conical shape as its description implies. The turret was ready before the Panther II, but though running prototypes of this vehicle were produced in 1944, the rapidly deteriorating conditions of the war with facilities curtailed and the need for continued supply of types already proven meant that the Panther II, or Ausf F, never went into production and there was thus no chance for this fine design, virtually a perfected version of the original Panther, to prove its mettle. It would have undoubtedly been a much more useful and potent weapon than the very heavy and bulky Tiger II.

Final production models of the Panther Ausf G did, in fact, incorporate one feature intended for the Ausf F. This was the all-steel resilient road wheel which replaced the rubber tyred type and became standard for late-production Tigers as well as the Tiger II. It is apposite also to mention here the engine improvements which were gradually introduced for the Maybach HL 230 motor. Over-heating had been

a problem at the start, as previously mentioned. This was overcome by fitting a second cooling pump, modifying the coolant distribution, and improving the bearings and cylinder head seal. Later Panthers, therefore, proved very much more reliable than the early vehicles involved in the Kursk debacle. To increase the power of the HL 230 for the Tiger II and Panther II it was proposed to increase the compression ratio and incorporate fuel injection and, later, superchargers. Though modified prototypes were built and tested, the war had ended before the up-rated engine could go into production.

OTHER PANTHER PROJECTS

By late 1944, several advanced projects based on the Panther chassis were in the design stage. Of these the most important were an AA tank, a Waffentrager, a minesweeper tank, and a dozer tank. For the Panther II chassis a Panzerjager SP variant was proposed incorporating a 12·8 cm. gun, the largest possible weapon which could be fitted on the chassis. Because of the war situation, however, few of these projects got beyond the mock-up stage, though the Waffentrager existed as a single prototype. A further development associated with the Panther which did see service was infra-red night-fighting equipment. A number of Panthers were actually fitted experimentally with infra-red sights and these operated in conjunction with a 60 cm. infra-red searchlight carried on an

Below and Right: Views of a standard early production Jagdpanther with narrow cast collar round mantlet and one-piece gun barrel. Note the moving arc on the roof and slot for the sighting telescope. (IWM)

accompanying half-track vehicle called the Uhu (Eagle Owl). The Uhu could "illuminate" targets at 1000 metres and the Panther could pick out this target on closing to 500 metres.

PANTHER VARIANTS

There were several special purpose conversions of the Panther, two of these for the command rôle. For unit commanders the Befehlspanzer Panther was produced. These were simply versions of either the Ausf D, A or G fitted with extra radio equipment and the associated aerials. A second wireless receiver and transmitter were fitted to the inside right wall of the turret and the loader acted as operator. There were two externally similar models, differing only in the radio installation. The Sd Kfz 267 had Fu 5 and Fu 8 equipment, while the Sd Kfz 268 had Fu 5 and Fu 7.* In each case ammunition stowage was reduced to 64 7·5 cm. rounds. Befehlspanzer Panthers were used by regimental and battalion command and staff officers and could only be distinguished externally by the extra aerials (or the call sign number when this was visible).

* Fu 5 was the standard German tank wireless for short-range communication within tank regiments and battalions on RT or MCW transmission. Fu 7 was the standard air co-operation set and Fu 8 was the set used for main divisional nets. (Fu = Funk = radio.)

Close up of a Panther Ausf D glacis plate shows the driver's vision port (closed), the machine-gun flap, the episcope housings on the front decking, the mortised welded joints and the chassis number painted above the right dustguard. (IWM)

The Beobachtungspanzer Panther (Sd Kfz 172) was an old Ausf D converted as an OP vehicle for observation officers, commanders, and staff officers of SP artillery regiments. The gun was replaced by a short wooden dummy, the turret was fixed in place, extra

First used in action in the Kursk Offensive, many Panther Ausf D were lost through mechanical failure. Here Soviet troops examine one such abandoned vehicle. (IWM)

Engine installation in a Panther and a close view of the V-12 Maybach HL 230 engine. (IWM)

The radius arms from the axles were attached to the torsion bars running across the hull floor. In this view can also be seen the anchorage points for the alternate torsion bars from the opposite axles. (IWM)

wireless was fitted, and a map table was added inside the turret. A ball-mounted MG 34 in the turret front was the only armament.

Finally there was the Bergepanzer Panther (also known as the Bergepanther), designated Sd Kfz 179, which was a recovery vehicle specially for work with tanks in the 45 ton class. The Bergepanther replaced the 18 ton half-track in the heavy recovery rôle, since it took up to three of these vehicles to move heavy tanks like the Tiger or Panther. The Bergepanther was an old Ausf D model converted by the removal of the turret and the fighting equipment. A movable winch and winch motor were installed in the fighting compartment. A limited superstructure was provided round the former turret opening consisting of heavy wood cladding over mild steel framing. A canvas tilt could cover the complete compartment in inclement weather. An "A" frame was fitted over the

rear decking and this supported a towing eye and towing rollers. A heavy earth spade was hinged on the hull rear and was raised and lowered from the vehicle's winch. There was a light demountable jib which could be erected either side for lifting work and there was either a MG 34 or 2 cm. cannon for air defence, mounted as required. Design and conversion of the Bergepanther was carried out by Demag and 297 vehicles were so altered. Not all of these were fitted with earth spades, however, and these were used as towing vehicles. Some of the Bergepanthers without spades later had their winches removed and were used as munitions carriers. Some other old Panthers simply had their turrets removed and were also used as munitions carriers.

THE JAGDPANTHER

The most important derivative of the Panther, however, was the famous Jagdpanther, one of the best-known AFVs to appear in World War II. The Germans built several important items of self-propelled artillery equipment as assault gun or tank destroyers but invariably these were makeshift adaptations on obsolescent, if not obsolete, chassis.

This front view of a final production type Panther Ausf G shows clearly the simplified hull shape with a continuous sloping line to the lower sponson edges and the rotating periscope.

(IWM)

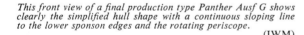

The need for a fast, up-to-date tank destroyer on a modern chassis was met by adapting the Panther. Previous attempts to produce a heavy tank destroyer had been largely unsuccessful. The 8·8 cm. Pak had been mounted on the Porsche Tiger chassis (to make the Ferdinand) and on the PzKpfw III/IV chassis as the Nashorn, but both of these improvisations proved unsatisfactory as the Ferdinand was too heavy and the Nashorn too small and underpowered. By 1943, however, there was an urgent need for tank destroyers in quantity so it was decided to utilize the best available chassis, that of the Panther. MIAG were asked to work out the design and the prototype was first demonstrated, in the presence of Hitler, on October 20, 1943. The Panther chassis was used unaltered, but the front and upper side plates were extended upwards to make a well-sloped enclosed superstructure. The mantlet was fitted in the centre of the hull front with a limited traverse for the 8·8 cm. Pak 43/3 L/71 gun of 11° each side. Armour was 80 mm. in front and 60 mm. at the sides. A ball-mounted MG 34 was fitted in the right front and the

driver sat in the usual position in the left front. Sighting equipment consisted of a rangefinder and periscope telescope. The telescope protruded through

These three illustrations show the later production Jagdpanther *with the two-piece barrel of the later 8·8 cm. gun. This simplified barrel changing. Note the Zimmerit anti-magnetic paste and the side skirts.* (Chamberlain Collection)

8·8 cm. gun breech, driver's seat (left), *and telescope sight* (top left) *inside a* Jagdpanther. (IWM)

A later production Panther Ausf D which shows the dustbin-type cupola and the vision port and machine-gun port on the glacis.
(Chamberlain Collection)

a slot in the roof within an armoured quadrant arc linked to the gun mount.

The new SP version of the Panther was at first designated 8·8 cm. Pak 43/3 auf Panzerjager Panther (Sd Kfz 173) but at Hitler's personal suggestion in February 1944 it was redesignated simply as the Jagdpanther (Hunting Panther).

Top facing page, and below: *Panther Ausf D's on the Russian Front in 1944. Note how the spare bogie wheels are carried on the hull side. Panthers on the other fronts rarely carried these since they were not subject to such a vast amount of long-distance running as those in Russia.*
(IWM)

The Panther II was to be an improved design with as many parts as possible standardized with the Tiger II. It did not go into production, but the new turret—Panzerturm Schmal—was built in prototype form. It was smaller and lighter than the original Panther turret and could take an 8·8 cm. gun.
(IWM)

MIAG commenced building Jagdpanthers in February 1944, using the Ausf G chassis which had by then become the current production type. By the war's end 382 had been completed. The only mechanical change compared with the Panther tank was the provision of the AK 7-400 gearbox as was also earmarked for use in the Panther II. First production Jagdpanthers had a one-piece barrel, but later a two-piece barrel was used on the 8·8 cm. weapon to ease barrel changing (the barrel did not wear uniformly and it was economical to make it in two corresponding parts). Very late Jagdpanthers had a simplified collar round the mantlet which was of thicker bolted construction. As already mentioned, a project existed for a Panzerjager version of the Panther II with 12·8 cm. gun, this being drawn up in late 1944 but built only as a wooden mock-up.

Crew of the Jagdpanther consisted of a commander, gunner, two loaders, wireless operator/machine-gunner and driver. The vehicle carried 60 8·8 cm. rounds. The Jagdpanther was the best and most potent of all the German tank destroyers. It was well-shaped, low, fast, and heavily armoured. It was intended to build Jagdpanthers at a rate of 150 per month, but disrupted production facilities in the last year of the war made this target quite impossible to achieve.

Had the war dragged on (and had Germany been able to maintain its planned production programme unhindered), the Panther, Panther II, and Jagdpanther would have become the backbone of the German panzer divisions (together with the Tiger II and Jagdtiger in lesser numbers), and from late 1944 a rationalization programme was introduced (Richtwert-Programm IV) which terminated production of all earlier types in favour of the "new generation"

A rear view of an early production Jagdpanther *which shows the large escape hatch and the small hatch for re-ammunitioning and discarding empty cases.* (IWM)

The visit of Colonel Ishide and the Japanese Military Attachés to examine a Panther and Tiger. Japan later bought one of each as recounted in the text. (IWM)

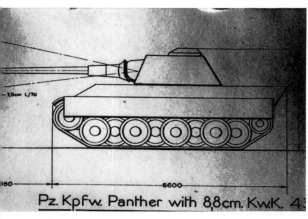

The project drawing for the Panther II design which was to mount the small turret with either a 7·5 cm. or 8·8 cm. gun. Suspension and other components were interchangeable with the Tiger II. (IWM)

Project drawing dated November 17, 1944, for the proposed Panzerjager Panther with 12·8 cm. gun. This would have been on the Panther II chassis. Only a wooden mock-up was completed before hostilities ceased. (IWM)

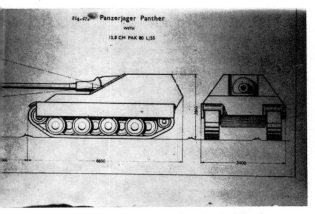

Final production model of the Jagdpanther had a wider, squarer collar which was bolted in place to simplify production. (IWM)

vehicles. The other type to be included in the new programme was a family of Waffentragers and SP types developed on a light chassis adapted from the Czech-built PzKpfw 38(t) (and its German-developed derivative, the 38(d)). However, cessation of hostilities in May 1945 brought the Panther story to a swift and premature close with much of the potential of the design still unrealized. A few Panthers served on for a number of years post-war, however, but in the French Army which equipped some units with captured vehicles. The other victorious nations each took a few Panthers for trials. The British actually built at least one Panther in 1946, using spare and cannibalized parts to assemble a "new" vehicle which was used in comparative trials with the Black Prince and Centurion.

An interesting "clandestine" use of the Panther took place during the last desperate German offensive in the West, the so-called "Battle of the Bulge." Here at least ten, probably more, Panthers were effectively disguised and marked to resemble U.S. Army M-10 tank destroyers. The cupola was removed, together with the external stowage boxes on the hull. The turret and nose were then disguised with thin sheet metal to resemble the shape of the M-10, including the distinctive rear overhang of that vehicle's turret counterweight. Despite being finished in very convincing U.S. markings, the phoney M-10s enjoyed little success largely because the subtlety of the idea was nullified by the general confusion prevailing at the time.

One final little-known aspect of the Panther story is that Japan actually purchased one of these vehicles with a view to producing licence-built versions for use in the Pacific. Colonel Ishide, an AFV specialist with the Japanese Military Mission to Germany, witnessed a demonstration of both a Tiger I and a Panther at the Henschel works on July 30, 1943. As a result the Japanese purchased one sample of each vehicle with the intention of shipping them to Japan for further trials and probable production of their own versions. This transaction took place in November 1944 when a Tiger and Panther were formally handed over to the Japanese Mission in Germany. However, by this time there was no means of getting these vehicles safely to Japan and as far as is known they never actually left Germany. Had the war been prolonged, the Nipponese Panther might well have been yet another chapter in the history of this classic tank, and surely no less interesting.

Data	Model D (Ausf D)	Model A (Ausf A)	Model G (Ausf G)	A.R.V. (Bergepanther)	O.P. Tank (Beob. Panther)
General					
Weight (in action): tons		44 tons 15½ cwt.		42	
Crew	5	5	5	4	4
Armament					
Main		7·5 cm. Kw. K.42 (L/70)		2 cm. Kw. K.38	—
7·92 mm. M.G.34 (No.):	1	3	3	1	2
Ammunition (Main armt.): (rounds)	79	79	79	—	—
Ammunition (7·92 mm.): (rounds)	2,500	4,500	4,500		4,500
Armour					
Turret front: (mm.)	110 at 10°	110 at 10°	110 at 10°	—	
Turret sides: (mm.)	45 at 25°	45 at 25°	45 at 28°	—	
Turret rear: (mm.)	45 at 28°	45 at 28°	45 at 28°	—	
Turret roof: (mm.)	15 at 83° and 88°	15 at 83° and 88°	15 at 83° and 88°	—	
Superstructure:					
Front: (mm.)	80 at 55°	80 at 55°	80 at 55°	80 at 50°	80 at 55°
Sides: (mm.)	40 at 40°	40 at 40°	50 at 30°	40 at 40°	40 at 40°
Rear: (mm.)	40 at 30°	40 at 30°	40 at 30°	40 at 30°	40 at 30°
Roof: (mm.)	15 horizontal	15 horizontal	40 horizontal	15 horizontal	15 horizontal
Hull front: (mm.)	80 at 55°	80 at 55°	80 at 55°	80 at 55°	80 at 55°
Hull sides: (mm.)	40 vertical	40 vertical	40 vertical	40 vertical	40 vertical
Hull rear: (mm.)	40 at 30°	40 at 30°	40 at 30°	40 at 30°	40 at 30°
Hull belly: (mm.)	20 + 13 horizontal	20 + 13 horizontal	20 + 13 horizontal	20 + 13 horizontal	20 + 13 horizontal
Engine:					
Type	Maybach HL210 P.30*	Maybach HL230 P.30	Maybach HL230 P.30	Maybach HL210 P.30 or HL230 P.30	Maybach HL210 P.30
Output at 3,000 r.p.m.: (b.h.p.)	642	690	690	642 or 690	642
Gearbox (Z.F.)					
Type:		AK 7–200		AK 7–200	AK 7–200
Number of speeds:		7 forward, 1 reverse		7 F. 1 R.	7 F. 1 R.
Steering:		Discontinuous regenerative type giving one radius of turn for each gear engaged.			
Drive:		All models front sprocket.			
Suspension:		8 stations per side, each consisting of 2 large bogie wheels and independently sprung on 2 torsion bars connected in series. Wheels overlapped and interleaved. One small return roller behind sprocket.			
Tracks:		Single link single pin type, recessed construction 4 wheel paths and twin guide horns.			
Dimensions:					
Overall length: (ft. and in.) (incl. Gun)	29' 1"	29' 1"	29' 1"	26' 9"	22' 7"
Overall width: (ft. and in.)	11' 3"	11' 3"	11' 3"	10' 9"	11' 3"
Overall height: (ft. and in.)	9' 9"	9' 9"	9' 9"	9' 0"	
Ground clearance: (ft. and in.)	1' 10"	1' 10"	1' 10"	1' 10"	1' 10"
Track centres: (ft. and in.)	8' 7⅛"	8' 7⅛"	8' 7⅛"	8' 7⅛"	8' 7⅛"
Track width: (ft. and in.)	2' 1¾"	2' 1¾"	2' 1¾"	2' 1¾"	2' 1¾"
Track on ground: (ft. and in.)	12' 10"	12' 10"	12' 10"	12' 10"	12' 10"
Performance:					
Max. speed (roads): (m.p.h.)	34	34	34	20	34
Max. speed (cross country): (m.p.h.)	15	15	15	10–15	15
Radius of action (roads): (miles)	105	110	110	105	105
Radius of action (cross country): (miles)	53	55	55	53	53
Gradient:	35°	35°	35°	35°	35°
Trench: (ft. and in.)	6' 3"	6' 3"	6' 3"	6' 3"	6' 3"
Step: (ft. and in.)	3' 0"	3' 0"	3' 0"	3' 0"	3' 0"
Fording depth:	4' 7"	4' 7"	4' 7"	4' 7"	4' 7"
Observation:					
Sight—main armament	T.Z.F. 12	T.Z.F. 12a	T.Z.F. 12a	—	—
Sight—subsidiary armament	—	K.Z.F. 2	K.Z.F. 2	K.Z.F. 2 (Model A)	K.Z.F. 2 (in turret)
R/F:	—	—	—	—	Em. 1·25 m. R (Pz)
Observation periscopes:	—	—	T.S.R. 1	—	T.B.F. 2 and T.S.R. 1 or S.F.14Z
Odometer:	—	—	—	—	Blockstelle "O"
Cupola:	6 slits with glass blocks	7 episcopes		—	7 episcopes
Driver:		2 episcopes and 1 periscope			2 episcopes
Loader:	—		Episcope		
W/T operator:	2 episcopes and rectangular port		1 periscope	2 episcopes and 1 rectangular port	
Communication:		Fu.5 and Fu.2 OR Fu.2 only		—	Fu. Sprech. "f" and receiver M. W.E. "e"

*Model D₁ (original Ausf A) only; D₂ had HL 230 engine.

Tiger company in the Tarnopol area of the Ukraine, spring 1944. Note reserve fuel drums roped to the hull of each tank. (Imperial War Museum)

Panzerkampfwagen VI Tiger Ausf. H (E) and Tiger Ausf. B

by Peter Chamberlain and Chris Ellis

PART ONE

Tiger I (Ausf. H later Ausf. E)

"At half-past five the next morning the advance continued through Briquessard and Amaye-sur-Seulles. Villers Bocage was entered without incident, although the 11th Hussars and 8th Hussars had both contacted the enemy on either side of the centre-line. 'A' Squadron of the 4th County of London Yeomanry and 'A' Coy. of the 1st Rifle Brigade then pushed on according to plan towards the high ground to the north-east of the town. In order to clear the traffic on the roads behind, the column had to move out comparatively closed up, and it was this that gave a Mk. VI tank, which suddenly appeared from a side road, its opportunity. Its first shot destroyed one of the Rifle Brigade half-tracks, thus blocking the road; and then at its own convenience it destroyed the remainder of the half-tracks, some Honey tanks of the Recce Troop, four tanks of the Regimental Headquarters troop and the two OP tanks accompanying the squadron. Escape for the tanks, carriers and half-tracks was impossible; the road was embanked, obscured by flames and smoke from the burning vehicles whose crews could only seek what shelter they could from the machine-gun fire, and our own tanks were powerless against the armour of the Tiger, with limitless cover at its disposal. Meanwhile 'A' Squadron, in the lead with the Commanding Officer, were cut off. Their last radio message, received at half-past ten, reported that they were completely surrounded by tanks and infantry, that the position was untenable and withdrawal impossible. Relief was equally impossible as, in addition to the burning tanks and vehicles, the road was blocked by the same Mk. VI which commanded all approaches."

(A Short History of 7th Armoured Division; Sept. 1945.)

A late production Tiger Ausf. E on the Russian front, summer 1944; note episcope-fitted cupola and "Zimmerit" anti-magnetic plaster ripple coating.
(Chamberlain Collection)

THUS wrote the official historian of one of the most outstanding individual tank actions of the Second World War, an exploit which almost made a legend of the man who held up an entire armoured division—the famous "Desert Rats"—and contributed not insignificantly to the events which followed. Obersturmführer-SS Michel Wittmann was the commander of the Tiger tank which caused the carnage at Hill 213 on the road from Villers Bocage during the battle for Normandy. The date was June 13, 1944. The British 7th Armoured Division, having outflanked Bayerlein's *Panzer Lehr* Division which had been thrown into the offensive towards Bayeux, was running for Caen as part of an overall plan to take the city by a "right hook" round the defenders when the leading echelon ran into No. 2 Company of 501 *Waffen-SS* Heavy Tank Battalion, commanded by Wittmann. At the moment of contact Wittmann's Tigers were concealed in a wood on Hill 213, with his own vehicle nearest the road and thus best able to bear on the approaching British column. In the engagement which followed and which has been described above, Wittmann knocked out 25 vehicles to add to his massive score of 119 Soviet tanks destroyed during his service on the Russian Front.

Though this was but one short action, it stands as a classic; and immortalises the Tiger I as one of the milestones in the evolution of the tank. Few would claim it as the best tank of all time, nor for the

Germans was it the right tank at the right time; but it showed the way to the Panther and Tiger II which went a long way towards making up in firepower and effectiveness for the numerical deficiency in armour with which the *Wehrmacht* had to face the Allies in the closing stages of the Second World War.

THE TIGER PEDIGREE

The Tiger series had its origins in a number of tank developments initiated in 1937. In that year the firm of *Henschel u. Sohn GmbH* of Kassel were instructed to design and construct a 30–33 ton tank intended to replace the early Panzer IV tanks, the vehicle being known as the DW.1 (DW was an abbreviation of *Durchbruchswagen* or "breakthrough vehicle"). However, after one chassis with interleaved road wheel suspension had been built and testing had commenced, the trials were suspended in 1938 to allow work to be carried out on a further design for a 65 ton tank, the VK.6501* (*Vollkettenkraftfahrzeug*—"fully tracked experimental vehicle, 65 tons, first design"). The VK.6501 was itself a further development of the PzKpfw VI (NbFz PzKpfw VI; NbFz for *Neubaufahrzeug*—"new construction vehicle" of 1934, a multi-turret design of which only a few were pro-

---

*Also known as the SW (Sturmwagen "assault vehicle") or PzKpfw VII.

duced). Two prototypes of the VK.6501 were built and were undergoing trials when this project was cancelled and development resumed on the DW.1. By 1940, Henschel had so improved the original design that it was renamed DW.2; in this form it weighed 32 tons and accommodated a crew of five. The planned armament was the short 7·5 cm. gun with two Model 34 machine-guns. Trials were carried out with a prototype chassis until 1941, by which time Henschel had received an order for a new design in the same class and weight as the DW.2, the development code for the new vehicle being VK.3001. This order was also given to Henschel's competitors, Porsche, MAN and Daimler-Benz. The Henschel version, VK.3001(H), was a development of the DW.2; four prototypes were built, differing only in detail from one another, two in March 1941 and two the following October. The superstructure of the VK.3001(H) resembled the PzKpfw IV, and the suspension consisted of seven interleaved road wheels and three return rollers per side. It was planned to mount the 7·5 cm. L/48 gun in this vehicle; but due to the appearance of the Russian T34 with its 76 mm. gun, the vehicle became obsolete and development was discontinued. Two of the VK.3001(H) chassis were, however, converted to self-propelled guns by lengthening and fitting a lightly armoured superstructure, and mounting a 12·8 cm. K.40 gun. These two vehicles were used in Russia in 1942. The Porsche version, VK.3001(P), was also known to its designers as the Leopard or *Typ 100*. This turretless prototype incorporated several new design features such as petrol-electric drive and longitudinal torsion bar suspension. MAN and Daimler-Benz also constructed prototypes to this design but like the Henschel project they had become obsolete.

Concurrently with the order for the VK.3001 an additional order had also been placed in 1941 for a 36 ton tank designated VK.3601. The specification for this design had been proposed by Hitler; it included a powerful high velocity gun, heavy armour, and a maximum speed of at least 40 km./h. A prototype of this project was built by Henschel in March 1942, but experimental work on both the VK.3001 and VK.3601 was stopped when a further order for a 45 ton tank was received in May 1941. Designated VK.4501, the vehicle was proposed to mount a tank version of the 8·8 cm. gun. With the order came a stipulation that the prototype was to be ready in time for Hitler's birthday on April 20, 1942, when a full demonstration of its capabilities was to be staged. As design time was limited, Henschel's decided to incorporate the best features of their VK.3001(H) and VK.3601(H) projects into a vehicle of the weight and class required. Henschel planned to build two models, the type H1 mounting an 8·8 cm. 36 L/56 and the type H2 a 7·5 cm. KwK L/70, although the H2 existed only as a wooden mock-up at that time. Porsche had also received the order for the VK.4501 and like Henschel they decided to use the experience and features from their previous model, the VK.3001(P), which had performed well on trials.

The demonstration of the two competing prototypes, the VK.4501(H) and VK.4501(P) type 101, duly took place before Hitler at Rastenburg on April 20. The Henschel design was judged to be superior. An order for production to commence in August 1942 was given and the vehicle was designated *Panzerkampfwagen VI Tiger Ausf. H*; the *Sonderkraftfahrzeug,* or Ordnance Number was SdKfz 181. In February 1944 the designation was changed to *PzKpfw Tiger Ausf. E,* SdKfz 181.

Several production modifications—a new cupola, new-type wheels, and simplified fittings—appeared to

(Top right) Early progenitor of Henschel's Tiger Ausf. E (originally Ausf. H) was the 30-ton VK.3001 project. This is one of four prototypes built by Henschel in 1941. (Chamberlain Collection/Col. R. J. Icks)

(Bottom right) Porsche's rival prototype for the VK.4501 requirement seen on test at Rastenburg. Only two vehicles were completed with turrets. (Chamberlain Collection/Col. R. J. Icks)

(Below) Henschel's VK.3601(H) prototype for a 36-ton tank specified by Hitler in 1941. It was followed by VK.4501(H), the Tiger prototype demonstrated to Hitler on April 20, 1942.
(Chamberlain Collection/Col. R. J. Icks)

"Feifel" air cleaning system at rear, plain cylindrical cupola, and rubber-tyred road wheels are hallmarks of the early production Tiger Ausf. H. These three views show the standard equipment stowage for this vehicle including tow-cables each side, gun cleaning rods each side of turret, tools, and turret bin. The holes just ahead of the vertical front plate are for camouflage support stanchions; the tube on the right side aft is for radio aerial stowage. This vehicle has brackets for "S"-mine dischargers at each corner of the hull top and immediately ahead of the engine decking. (Chamberlain Collection)

coincide with the change of designation to Tiger Ausf. E, though no official confirmation of this has been found.

The Tiger was in production for two years, from August 1942 until August 1944, and in this period a total of 1,350 vehicles were delivered out of 1,376 ordered. Chassis numbers ran in a continuous series from 250001 to 251350. Maximum monthly production was achieved in April 1944, when 104 Tigers were built. It is interesting to note that the specified weight of 45 tons was exceeded in production by as much as 11 tons.

THE PORSCHE MODEL

Production of the Porsche VK.4501 design had been ordered before the trials as a safeguard against the failure of the Henschel design. As 90 vehicles were already in hand when the result of the trials was announced, it was decided to utilise the chassis as the basis of a self-propelled carriage for the 8·8 cm. L/71 gun. This equipment was designated *Panzerjäger Tiger (P) Ferdinand* SdKfz 184; it was subsequently re-designated *8·8 cm. 43/2 L/71 Ausf. Pz Jäg Tiger (P) Elefant früher Ferdinand.* The original name "Ferdinand" had been adopted in honour of the designer, Dr. Ferdinand Porsche. Only two of the VK.4501 Porsche vehicles had actually been completed as tanks and in this form they had been designated *PzKpfw VI VK.4501(P), Tiger(P).* Two other variants of the Porsche Tiger were projected but never materialised. These were a *Ramm-Tiger,* or "dozer-tank", ordered for production by Hitler and visualised for street-fighting and ramming enemy tanks; and a converted Porsche chassis designed to mount a 21 cm. mortar.

THE HENSCHEL TIGER DESCRIBED

At the time of its arrival in service in late 1942, the *PzKpfw VI Tiger I Ausf. H* was an outstanding design among its contemporaries by virtue of its powerful gun and armour protection up to 100 mm. thick. These factors made the 56 ton Tiger the most formidable fighting vehicle then in service. It was, however, relatively costly to produce in terms of man-hours and difficult to adapt for mass production. In January 1944 the heavier and generally superior *Tiger II Ausf. B* went into production with the result that successively fewer E models were produced until they were finally phased out of production completely in August 1944.

Tiger I was the first German combat tank to be fitted with overlapping road wheel suspension, arranged with triple overlapping and interleaved wheels of a steel disc type with solid rubber tyres (although after chassis number 250822 these discs were steel-tyred and internally sprung). The overlapping wheel system was adopted for optimum weight distribution. There were eight independently sprung torsion bar axles on each side. In order to carry all the axles inside the hull envelope it was necessary to stagger them on the floor so that the right hand axles trailed aft and the left hand axles led forward. It was thus possible to incorporate the maximum number within the vehicle's length, and this resulted in an extremely soft and stable ride for a tank of this weight and size. Two types of track were used; a wide type

measuring 28½ inches was fitted for combat and narrow, 20½ inches wide, for travel and transportation. When the narrow tracks were fitted the outer wheels were removed from each suspension unit. Though this type of suspension gave a superior ride, it also had its drawbacks; one being that the inter-leaved road wheels were liable to become packed with mud and snow during winter fighting, and if ignored until frozen this could jam the wheels. The Russians discovered this and took advantage of the situation by timing their attacks for dawn when the vehicles were likely to have become immobilised.

The Tiger was originally fitted with a Maybach V-12 petrol engine, the HL 210 P45 of 21 litres capacity, but it was soon realised that the vehicle was underpowered and, from December 1943, the HL 230 P45 of 24 litres was substituted. The Tigers used in North Africa were fitted with an air cleaner system called *Feifel.* This was attached to the rear of the hull and linked to the engine by means of the engine cover plate. These tropical Tigers were known as the *Tiger (Tp).* The *Feifel* air system was discontinued on vehicles built after the cessation of fighting in Tunisia in early 1943.

While all earlier designs of German tank had the simple clutch-and-brake type of steering, the Tiger's greatly increased weight necessitated a more refined system. Henschel therefore developed and adopted a special steering unit, similar to the British Merritt-Brown type, which was fully regenerative and continuous. It had the added feature of a twin radius of turn in each gear. The gearbox, which was based on earlier Maybach types, gave no less than eight forward gear ratios and, with its pre-selector, made the Tiger very light and easy to handle for a vehicle of its size. The Tiger's mechanical layout followed that of previous operational German designs in that the transmission shaft led forward beneath the turret cage to the gearbox set alongside the driver. The steering unit was mounted transversely in the nose of the tank, a bevel drive leading to a final reduction gear in each front sprocket. Power take-off for the hydraulic turret traverse unit, mounted in the turret floor, was taken from the rear of the gearbox, and it is typical of the Tiger's well-thought out design that the hydraulic unit could be disconnected from the power drive shaft by releasing a dog-clutch, thus allowing the turret to be lifted from the vehicle without the complications of disconnecting any other joints or pipes.

Arrangements for wading and total submersion to a depth of 13 feet with Snorkel breathing were introduced on the first 495 Tigers produced, and then abandoned on all subsequent vehicles leaving them capable of wading only to a depth of about 4 feet. The method used for total submersion of the first 495 vehicles was very ingenious. All hatches and doors were rubber sealed and the turret ring was sealed by means of an inflatable rubber tube. The gun mantlet was sealed by a sliding frame, with a rubber sealing ring, and the machine-gun ports were provided with expandable rubber plugs which were inserted when the machine-guns were dismounted. The main air supply for the crew and engine was obtained through a three-piece Snorkel pipe that was mounted on the engine compartment roof when wading.

During submersion the fan drives were disconnected and the radiator compartments sealed off and flooded.

Factory view of early production model Tiger Ausf. H showing a second pistol port in place of the loading and escape hatch. (Chamberlain Collection)

Driver's compartment of Tiger Ausf. H (Ausf. E) showing steering wheel, visor, and instrument panel. (Imperial War Museum)

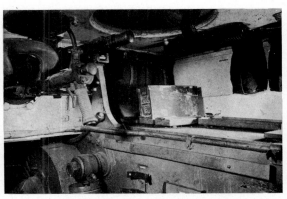

Hull gunner's position, showing 7·92 mm. machine-gun. This was fired by hand trigger and sighted by telescope. The wireless sets were carried on a shelf to the right of the hull gunner. (Imperial War Museum)

A bilge pump, mounted on the fighting compartment floor and driven by the power take-off from the main gearbox which also drove the power traverse oil pump, was used to pump out any water that penetrated the sealing devices. This bilge pump was retained in the later production vehicles. These vehicles could stay under water for $2\frac{1}{2}$ hours.

CONSTRUCTION

One of the Tiger's biggest advances over any previous design was in its method of construction. In order to simplify assembly as much as possible and allow the use of heavy armour plate, flat sections were used throughout the hull. Machinable quality armour plate was employed. Hull and superstructure were welded throughout, in contrast to previous German tanks where a bolted joint was used between hull and superstructure. The Tiger front and rear superstructure was in one unit, and interlocking stepped joints, secured by welding, were used in the construction of both the lower hull and the superstructure. A pannier was, in effect, formed over each track by extending the super-

structure sideways to full width and the complete length of the vehicle was so shaped from front vertical plate to tail plate. The top front plate of the hull covered the full width of the vehicle and it was this extreme width which permitted a turret ring of 6 ft. 1 in. internal diameter to be fitted which was of ample size to accommodate the breech and mounting of the 8·8 cm. gun. The belly was also in one piece, being a plate 26 mm. thick and 15 ft. $10\frac{1}{4}$ in. long by 5 ft. 11 in. wide.

Internally the hull was divided into four compartments; a forward pair housing the driver and the bow gunner/wireless operator, a centre fighting compartment and rear engine compartment. The driver sat on the left and steered by means of a steering wheel which acted hydraulically on the Tiger's controlled differential steering unit. Emergency steering was provided for by two steering levers on either side of the driver operating disc brakes. These brakes were also used for vehicle parking and were connected to a foot pedal and parking brake lever. A visor was provided for the driver and this was opened and closed by a sliding shutter worked from a handwheel on the front vertical plate. Fixed episcopes were

Interior of turret, showing breech of 8·8 cm. gun, commander's seat, and traverse handwheel. (Imperial War Museum)

Looking down at the turret floor. Six 8·8 cm. rounds were accessible with the turret traversed to the twelve o'clock position.

(Imperial War Museum)

Tiger suspension showing wide battle track. (Imperial War Museum)

Tiger suspension showing narrow track. When this was fitted the outer row of wheels was removed. (Imperial War Museum)

provided in both the driver's and the wireless operator's escape hatches. A standard German gyro direction indicator and instrument panel were situated to the left and right of the driver's seat respectively. The gearbox separated the two forward crew members' compartments. The machine-gunner/wireless operator seated on the right manned a standard 7·92 mm. MG 34 in a ball mounting in the front vertical plate; this was fired by a hand trigger and sighted by a KZF cranked telescope. The wireless sets were mounted on a shelf to the operator's left.

The centre fighting compartment was separated from the front compartments by an arched cross member and from the engine compartment in the rear by a solid bulkhead. The floor of the fighting compartment was suspended from the turret by three steel tubes and rotated with the turret. The breech mechanism of the 8·8 cm. gun reached almost to the inside rear turret wall, dividing the fighting compartment virtually in two.

MAIN ARMAMENT

The 8·8 cm. KwK 36 gun which formed the Tiger's main armament had ballistic characteristics similar to those of the famous Flak 18 and Flak 36 8·8 cm. guns

from which it was derived. The principal modifications were the addition of a muzzle brake and electric firing by a trigger-operated primer on the elevating handwheel. A 7·92 mm. MG 34 was co-axially mounted in the left side of the mantlet and was fired by mechanical linkage from a foot pedal operated by the gunner. The 8·8 cm. had a breech of the semi-automatic falling wedge type scaled up from the conventional type used on smaller German tank guns. The great weight of the barrel was balanced by a large coil spring housed in a cylinder on the left-hand front of the turret. Elevation and hand traverse were controlled by handwheels to the right and left of the gunner respectively and an additional traverse handwheel was provided for the commander's use in an emergency. The hydraulic power traverse was controlled by a rocking footplate operated by the gunner's right foot. Because of the turret's great weight, traverse was necessarily lowgeared both in hand and power. It took 720 turns of the gunner's handwheel, for instance, to move the turret through 360 degrees and power traverse through any large arc demanded a good deal of footwork (and concentration) by the gunner. "Stalking" Allied tanks—more lightly armoured—were often able to take advantage of this limitation to get in the first shot

Rear view of Tiger Ausf. E showing an "S"-mine discharger on the superstructure. (Chamberlain Collection)

Side view of mid-production Tiger Ausf. E shows clearly the loading and escape hatch that was omitted on the early production models. (Chamberlain Collection)

An early production Tiger Ausf. H captured in Tunisia in 1943. (Imperial War Museum)

when surprising a Tiger from the side or rear. For sighting purposes the gunner was provided with a binocular telescope TZF 9b, a clinometer for use in HE shoots, and a turret position indicator dial. Ammunition for the 8·8 cm. gun was stowed partly in bins each side of the fighting compartment and partly alongside the driver and under the turret floor.

Some early production Tigers were fitted with "S"-mine dischargers on top of the superstructure, a total of five being mounted in various positions on the front, sides and rear. These devices were installed for protection against infantry attacking with such anti-tank weapons as magnetic mines or pole charges. The "S"-mine was an anti-personnel bomb shaped like a jam jar and about 5 in. deep by 4 in. wide; it was shot some three to five feet into the air where it was set to explode and scatter its contents—360 three-eighths inch steel balls.

TURRET

Like the hull, the turret was a simple structure; the sides and rear were formed from a single 82 mm. plate curved horseshoe fashion. The front was joined by two rectangular bars, 100 mm. thick, which were

dovetailed and welded to the main turret front plate. The upper and lower edges of the turret sides converged towards the front to allow for movement of the mantlet when the gun was elevated or depressed. The turret roof was a single shaped plate 26 mm. thick, bent slightly forward of the centre line to match the taper of the sides at the front. This roof was recessed and welded into the turret sides. Two types of cupola could be seen fitted to Tigers; the original type had five vision slits and was of plain cylindrical appearance, while the later type had six episcopes and was exactly similar to the type fitted to the Panther. In fact, the adoption of this later type of cupola was yet another instance of production simplification; by late 1943 Panther production was under way and it was decided to standardise on the Panther cupola once stocks of the original Tiger cupola were exhausted. Other external turret fittings were three NbK 39 90 mm. smoke generators on either side towards the front and two stowage bins either side of the centre line at the rear. The bins were used to stow the bedding, rations, packs and other personal effects of the crew. Again, in later production Tigers, the bins were often omitted or reduced to one, not always at the rear.

PzKpfw VI Tiger Ausf.E (Tiger I) SdKfz 181
© U. Feist/Profile Publications Ltd.

Late production Tiger Ausf. E with Panther type cupola which has fitting for anti-aircraft machine-gun (Fliegerbeschuss-gerät). Tank has steel-tyred wheels. Note absence of Feifel on this late model.
(Chamberlain Collection)

Early production Tiger Ausf. H (Ausf. E) rigged for deep wading.
(Chamberlain Collection)

Late production Tiger Ausf. E on the Russian front.
(Chamberlain Collection)

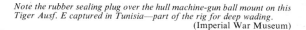

British troops erecting the three-piece Snorkel tube on an early production Tiger Ausf. E captured by the British in Tunisia, 1943.
(Imperial War Museum)

Note the rubber sealing plug over the hull machine-gun ball mount on this Tiger Ausf. E captured in Tunisia—part of the rig for deep wading.
(Imperial War Museum)

TACTICAL EMPLOYMENT

It was intended to use the Tiger as a heavy infantry or assault tank and Tiger battalions were organised as independent units under GHQ troops. Armoured divisions engaged in a major operation would receive an allotment of Tigers to spearhead an attack, but owing to the Tiger's basic lack of manoeuvrability, due to its bulk and relatively low speed, it was always considered necessary to employ lighter tanks in supporting platoons on the flanks. Normally PzKpfw IIIs or IVs fulfilled this function. It was later decided to include Tigers in the basic organisation of armoured divisions but, due to attrition which depleted the number of serviceable Tigers at any one time, it was never possible to put this plan into operation except in *Waffen-SS* armoured formations. These divisions were among the first units to receive Tigers and these went into service with such famous formations as the 1st SS Panzer Division *Leibstandarte SS "Adolf Hitler"*, and the 2nd SS Panzer Division *"Das Reich"*. The fact that there were never sufficient Tigers to go round was probably the greatest comfort that opposing forces could take from their appearance.

In the earliest Tiger actions of the war, on the Russian Front before Leningrad and in Tunisia, the employment of these formidable and sinister-looking vehicles was restricted to such limited numbers that resolute action by anti-tank gunners taking full advantage of the situation was more than enough to counter their impact. The first attack by Tigers in Russia in 1942 took place on terrain unsuitable for any successful tank action and, restricted to single-file progress on forest tracks through the swamps, the Tigers proved easy targets for the Soviet gunners posted to cover the tracks.

The British first encountered the Tiger in February 1943, near Pont du Fahs in Tunisia. Having received advance warning of the impending attack, the British anti-tank gunners were concealed with their 6-pounders with instructions to hold their fire until signalled. Two Tigers, flanked by nine PzKpfw IIIs and PzKpfw

IVs, advanced with artillery support and were not engaged until the range had closed to 500 yards on each flank. Fire from the 6-pounder anti-tank battery knocked out both Tigers. Tiger I's epitaph was written in France in 1944 where it finally proved its best not in attack but in defence.

TIGER VARIANTS

Three Tiger Ausf. E variants are known to have been in service.

(1) Tiger Command Tank (Panzerbefehlswagen)

Designated Pz.Bef.Wg Tiger Ausf. E, this version was the normal fighting tank adapted for the fitting of additional wireless equipment. Two sub-variants existed of this Command Tank, SdKfz 267 and SdKfz 268, the difference between these two models being solely in the wireless equipment fitted. The SdKfz 267 carried combinations of the Fu 5 and Fu 8 radio and the SdKfz 268 was fitted with combinations of the Fu 5 and Fu 7.

To accommodate the extra wireless equipment, the co-axial machine-gun together with its ammunition, spares and tools were dispensed with and the ammunition for the 8·8 cm. gun was reduced by 26 rounds. The crew of five consisted of, Commander, Wireless Officer (Gunner), W/T Operator I (Loader), W/T Operator II (Hull Gunner) and Driver.
Fu (Funkgerät=Wireless Equipment).
Fu 5: the standard tank set.
Fu 7: standard ground-air co-operation equipment.
Fu 8: standard set for main divisional links; it had a range of about 6 miles.

(2) Pz.Kpfw Tiger Recovery Vehicle (Berge Pz.Wg. Tiger)

This was not standard equipment but is believed to have been a field workshop modification, a specimen of which was captured in Italy. It was intended as a towing vehicle for assisting crippled AFVs back to an area where repairs could be effected. It consisted of a normal Tiger modified by the removal of the 8·8 cm.

PanzerKampfwagen VI Tiger Ausf.H (SdKfz 181), commanded by Untersturmfuehrer Michel Wittman, of the 1st SS Panzer Division "Leibstandarte Adolf Hitler" in Russia. Wittman and his crew fought in the Kharkov area during the winter of 1942-43, destroying 88 enemy tanks as the tally on the gun barrel indicates. Wittman was killed in Normandy shortly after his conflict against the British 7th Armoured Division on June 13, 1944.

M. Roffe © Profile Publications Ltd.

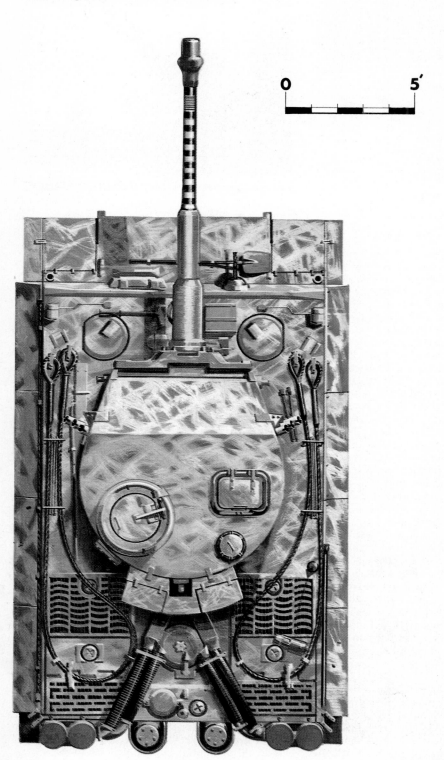

0

5′

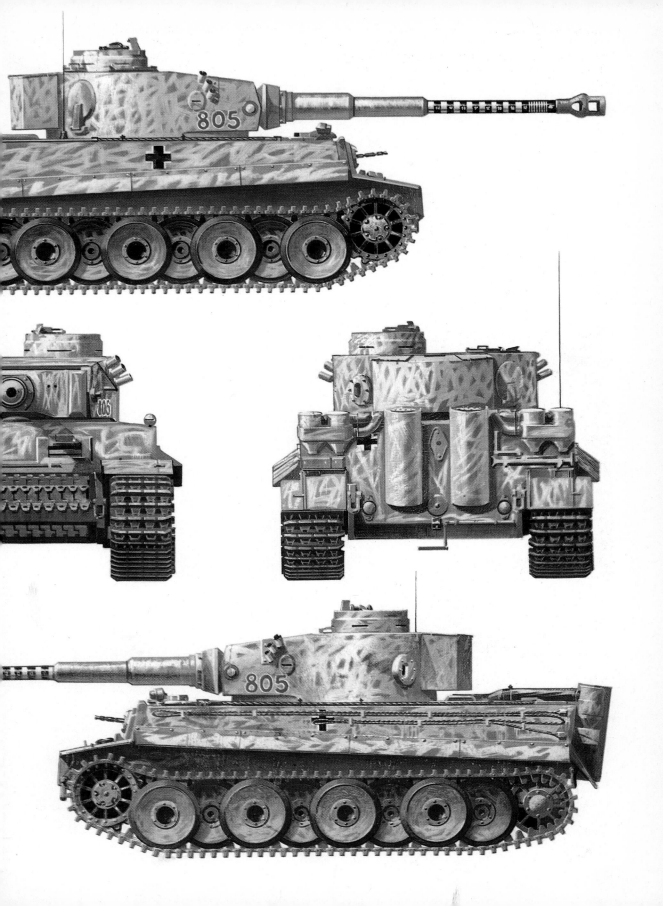

Side view of Tiger recovery vehicle (Berge PzWg Tiger), showing hand-operated winch and wire rope guide. The wire rope can be seen lying on the side of the vehicle. (Imperial War Museum)

Close up of the Sturmtiger's loading crane and ammunition stowage hatch. A smoke projector with 360° traverse is mounted in the hatch door. (U.S. Official)

gun and the mounting of a hand-operated winch at the rear of the turret with a wire rope guide at the front. Although the gun and barrel sleeve were removed the mantlet was retained, the opening in its centre being covered by a circular plate with a central aperture for the use of a machine-gun.

(3) 38 cm. Raketenwerfer 61 auf Sturmmörser Tiger

Also known as Sturmtiger, Sturmpanzer VI, or Sturmmörser, this weapon was developed to requirements from the German Army engaged in the heavy street fighting at Stalingrad and other similar places in Russia. The fighting troops had requested a self-propelled 21 cm. howitzer capable of following up the advancing troops and able to engage difficult targets with high angle fire. When development work was started on this project it was decided that the Tiger E chassis would be used, but it was found that no suitable gun of 21 cm. calibre was available. It was finally proposed to use the Raketenwerfer 61 L/54, a 38 cm. rocket projector that had been developed by the firm of Rheinmetall-Borsig as an anti-submarine weapon for the German Navy. A model of the Sturmtiger was first shown on October 20, 1943 and

Sturmtiger, showing the 38 cm. rocket projector. Note the perforated ring which allowed the escape of propellant gases. Also visible on the front superstructure plate is, (left) the hull ball mounted machine-gun, and (right) the driver's episcope slit above which is a large sight aperture for the projector layer's sighting instrument. (Imperial War Museum)

Three-quarter right front view of Sturmtiger showing the ammunition loading crane. On the off-side front of the roof plate is the electric fan extractor.
(Imperial War Museum)

Interior view of the Sturmtiger showing breech, collapsible loading tray, and ammunition cradles. (Chamberlain Collection)

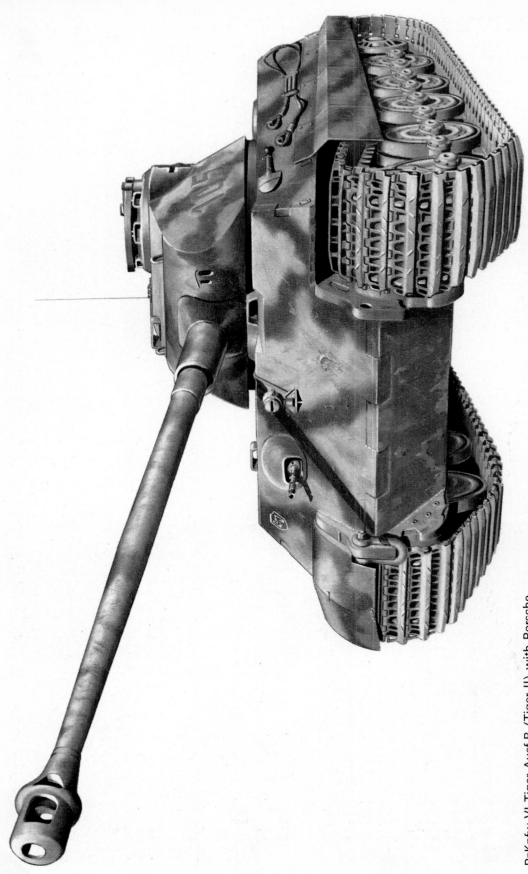

PzKpfw VI Tiger Ausf.B (Tiger II) with Porsche turret. Tiger Ausf.B (SdKfz 182) was also known as Koenigstiger (King Tiger, or Royal Tiger).

© U. Feist/Profile Publications Ltd.

limited production began in August 1944, a total of 10 Tigers being converted by the Berlin firm of Alkett.

The hull of the Sturmtiger was similar to that of the Tiger E but a fixed turret was superimposed on the hull with a single plate extending upwards from the rear edge of the standard Tiger glacis plate and sloped at 45 degrees to the vertical. The sides extended upwards at 20 degrees to the vertical from the top edges of the normal tank superstructure sides, which they overlapped slightly. The rear plate started at the forward edge of the engine compartment top and was sloped at about 10 degrees. The fighting compartment was roofed in by 40 mm. thick plate. The rocket projector which was breech loaded, was mounted offset to the right of centre in the 6-inch front plate, and fired a 5 foot long projectile weighing 761 lb. to a maximum range of 6,200 yards. A hand operated ammunition stowage crane was mounted at the off side of the superstructure rear plate; this was used to lift the rockets from the supply vehicle and lower them through the roof ammunition hatch into the fighting compartment. There were stowage arrangements for 12 rockets inside the vehicle, six on either side of the compartment; the rockets were stowed horizontally and held in position by collapsible cradles. The roof inside the compartment was fitted with overhead rails to carry a hand operated winch that could be run from side to side to place rockets on the loading tray and also assist in the stowage of ammunition. The rocket was loaded by hand, with the projector set at 0° elevation, from a loading tray fitted with six rollers. This could be folded into the floor when not in use. Additional armament consisted of a ball-mounted machine-gun MG34 set into the front plate on the right side.

The Sturmtiger when combat loaded weighed 70 tons and carried a crew of seven comprising a commander, observer, and five men to operate the vehicle and projector.

Overall Length: 20 ft. 8½ in.
Overall Width: 12 ft. 3 in.
Overall Height: 11 ft. 4 in. including crane.
Speed: 15-25 m.p.h.
Range: Road 87 miles.
Cross Country 55 miles.

SPECIFICATION: PANZERKAMPFWAGEN VI TIGER 1 (H)

(Desig. from February 1944: PzKpfw VI ausf E.)
Crew: 5—commander, gunner, loader, driver, hull gunner/wireless operator.
Battle weight: 56 tons.
Dry transport weight (narrow tracks): 50 tons 5 cwt.
Ground pressure: 14·7 lb./sq. in. (20·4 lb./sq. in. narrow tracks).

Dimensions
Length overall, gun to front: 27 ft. 9 in.
Hull length: 20 ft. 8½ in.
Height: 9 ft. 4¾ in.
Width: 12 ft. 3 in. (10 ft. 4 in. narrow tracks).
Track centres: 9 ft. 3½ in. (8 ft. 11½ in. narrow tracks).
Track width: 28½ in. (20½ in. narrow tracks).
Ground clearance: 1 ft. 5 in.

Armament
One 8·8 cm. gun, KwK 36 mounted in turret; length 56·1 calibres.
One MG 34 7·92 mm. machine-gun mounted co-axially, belt fed.
One MG 34 7·92 mm. machine-gun mounted in hull front, right.
One 9 mm. machine pistol MP 38 stowed in turret.
One Walther 27 mm. signal and grenade pistol stowed in turret.
Six NbK Wg smoke dischargers (2 ×3) mounted on turret sides firing 90 mm.

Fire control
One dial target position indicator fitted in turret ring to left of gunner, driven off turret rack by pinion and universal jointed shaft.
Sighting vane in front episcope of commander's cupola.
One EM 34 coincidence-type rangefinder for mounting on turret roof; ranges from 200 to 10,000 metres.
One portable SF 14Z scissors-type telescope for mounting in cupola (stowed in roof of turret).
Turret traverse: 360° by hand or hydraulic power; hand traverse by gunner; auxiliary control provided for commander; power traverse controlled by gunner only, by foot pedal.
Elevation: by hand only, controlled by gunner; elevating gear of sector and pinion type.
Maximum workable elevation: 11°.
Maximum workable depression: 4°.
Firing system: electric primer operated by trigger behind elevating hand wheel; power from vehicle batteries (12 volt).
Co-axial machine-gun: fired by rod and pedal from gunner's right foot.
Hull machine-gun: fired by trigger.

Ammunition
8·8 cm.: 92 rounds of mixed HE and APCBC in required proportions.
7·92 mm.: 5,700 rounds in 38 belts of 150 rounds each (maximum stowage).
NbK 39 smoke generators: six rounds (no reloads).
27 mm. signal cartridges: 24 rounds.
9 mm. machine pistol: variable nos.

Sighting and vision
Main armament: one TZF 9b binocular telescope.
Hull machine gun: one KZF 2 telescope.
Commander: seven vision slits in cupola. (Later model H and model E with Panther cupola, seven vision blocks.) Pistol port in left-hand rear of turret.
Gunner: one vision slit in left-hand side of turret.
Loader: one vision slit in right-hand side of turret; episcope in roof hatch (model E only). Loading and escape hatch in right-hand rear of turret.
Hull gunner: one episcope in escape hatch.
Driver: visor in vertical front plant with sliding double shutter; episcope in escape hatch.

Communications
W/T set (transmitter/receiver/intercom.): Fu 5 and Fu 2 or Fu 5 only.
L/T set.

Armour
Machineable quality armour plate. All-welded construction with stepped inter-locking joints. Austenitic welding.
Hull: nose 100 mm./66°, vertical front plate 100 mm./80°, lower sides 60 mm./90°, upper sides 80 mm./90°, vertical back plate 82 mm./82°, top 26 mm., bottom 26 mm.
Turret: mantlet 110 mm., front 100 mm./80°, sides 80 mm./90°, back 80 mm./90°, roof 26 mm./9°.

Engine
Early model H: Maybach HL 210 P 45. Petrol. 60° V-12 cyl. Water-cooled. 21·35 litres. 650 b.h.p. at 3,000 r.p.m.
Later model H and model E: Maybach HL 230 P45. Petrol. 60° V-12 cyl. Water-cooled. 23·88 litres. 700 b.h.p. at 3,000 r.p.m.
Fuel: 125 gallons in four tanks, two each side of engine compartment.

Transmission
Gearbox: Maybach Olvar pre-selector type; 8 forward speeds, 4 reverse.
Ratios: (1) 15·4:1, (2) 10·2:1, (3) 7·15:1, (4) 4·86:1, (5) 3·16:1, (6) 2·11:1, (7) 1·14:1, (8) 0·98:1.
Steering: Regenerative controlled differential type. Epicyclic train to each sprocket. Annulus driven by gearbox output, sun wheels driven from gearbox input. Planet carriers forming output to final drives. Speed and direction was imposed on sun wheels by controlled gearing via hydraulic clutches, giving two radii of turn in each direction in each gear. Steering wheel controlled clutches, hydraulically operated.
Emergency steering: by steering levers controlling disc brakes on each output shaft.

Suspension
Triple overlapping road wheels independently sprung by torsion bars. Outer row of road wheels removable for fitting of narrow tracks. Right-hand side axles trailed; left-hand side axles led forward.
Wheels: steel disc type with solid rubber tyres (model H). Internally-sprung all-steel disc type (model E).
Track: (wide type) cast manganese steel, 96 links each side; width 28½ in., pitch 5·125 in.; (narrow type) as above, width 20½ in.

Electrical system
One 12 volt dynamo.
Two 12 volt wet cells in parallel (for starting and auxiliary services).

Performance
Max. road speed: 23 m.p.h. Cross-country speed: 12·4 m.p.h.
Max. gradient: 35°. Trench crossing: 13 ft.
Wading depth: 13 ft. (prepared), 4 ft. (unprepared).
Road range: 73 miles. Cross-country range: 42 miles.

A battalion of Royal or King Tigers (Koenigstiger, Tiger Ausf. B, also known as Tiger II) drawn up for inspection.

PART TWO

Tiger II (Ausf. B) "Koenigstiger"

DEVELOPMENT AND PRODUCTION

THE last important German tank development to go into service was the Tiger Ausf "B" or Koenigstiger, known to the Allies as the Tiger II or King Tiger or Royal Tiger. This vehicle was put into production in late 1943 and was first engaged in action on the Russian front in May 1944 and was later encountered by the Allies in France in August of that year. The Royal Tiger had resulted from the need to create a tank capable of dealing with any new tank development that the Russians could possibly produce.

In August 1942, the Heereswaffenamt (Ordnance Department) issued specifications for a redesigned Tiger incorporating thicker armour, sloped plates as on the Panther and Russian T34, and armed with the 8.8cm L/71 gun. Both Porsche and Henschel were asked to submit designs to these specifications.

Porsche re-designed his Tiger (P) to conform to this specification, this design being known as the Type 180. This was projected with a turret forward and an engine at the rear, mounting a 15cm L/37 or 10.5cm L/70 gun. The design was rejected, however, and then Porsche submitted a second type, VK.4502 (P), with a rear turret armed with the 8.8cm L/71 gun, and a forward

engine in a reshaped hull. At first this design was considered for production and the construction of turrets for this vehicle was begun by Wegman AG, but due to the shortage of copper required for the parts in the electrical transmission this tank project was later cancelled.

The first design from Henschel was also rejected, being a modified version of the Tiger I, but the second design offered by Henschel, the VK.4503 (H), was accepted and the first prototype was delivered in October 1943. That this was three months behind schedule was due to the insistence of Waffen Prufamt 6 (Section of Ordnance Department responsible for combat vehicle design) that for simplification of production the vehicle should incorporate several components and design features of the experimental M.A.N. Panther II that had also been projected as an improved Panther tank, thereby achieving a degree of standardisation between the two vehicles.

Production of the Tiger Ausf "B" began in December 1943 when the pilot vehicle was produced. Production models started coming off the lines in February 1944, parallel with the Tiger Model "E", in which month eight Model "B" were produced as compared with approximately 95 of the Model "E" in the same period. By September 1944 Tiger Ausf "E" production had completely ceased in favour of the new vehicle. By this time production of the Model "B" was scheduled to reach a rate of approximately 100 tanks per month, increasing to 145 per month by December and then continuing at this rate until August 1945. In practice, however, disruption by enemy bombing and shortage of materials reduced the best ever monthly output to 84 in August 1944. By March 1945 this total had fallen to 25. Final total of Tiger Ausf Bs produced was 484.

The first 50 Royal Tigers to be completed were fitted with the spare turrets originally intended for the Porsche Tiger, VK.4502 (P). The remaining production vehicles had a modified turret, specially designed for the Tiger "B", having thicker armour and eliminating the re-entrant angle under the trunnion axis. The introduction of this new turret was accompanied by a change in the gun barrel from monobloc to two piece construction. This new barrel was also fitted to some of the Porsche turret vehicles.

GENERAL DESCRIPTION

The Tiger Model "B" was a logical development of the Tiger Model "E", incorporating all the good points of the Panther tank and armed with a new main armament, the 8.8cm KwK 43 L/71 which was almost 21ft long. This gun represented the largest calibre and calibre length to be employed operationally by the Germans in a tank mounting during the war. On the early production types the gun was supported on two trunnion supporting arms, bolted to prepared surfaces on the sides of the forward floor of the turret, and the trunnions were bolted to brackets welded to each side of the cradle through which the piece recoiled. On the later production vehicles, the gun was supported on trunnion brackets bolted to prepared blocks 11 inches apart on the forward floor of the turret. The breech mechanism, recoil system and muzzle brake conformed generally to standard German tank gun design, except that the recoil cylinders were mounted side by side above the gun. A hydro-pneumatic balancing cylinder was fitted between the recoil mechanism cradle and the gun mounting. The gun was offset 3.1 inches to the right of the turret centre line. To assist in loading, 22 rounds were carried in a large bulge at the rear of the turret with the nose of the round facing the gun breech so that the round required the minimum of handling in loading. These rounds were stowed 11 per side, thereby providing a clear passage for the ejection of the empty cartridge cases through the hatch at the rear of the turret. 48 additional rounds were stowed

Early production Tiger Ausf. B with the Porsche turret which was distinguished by the bulged commander's cupola on the left side.

Three-quarter right front view of Koenigstiger with Porsche turret, showing the curved front gun mantlet and monobloc gun barrel.

Early Royal Tiger, knocked out in Normandy in 1944, being examined by British troops.

Henschel-turret Tiger Ausf. B with battle tracks and armoured skirting. The tank is covered with Zimmerit to prevent the attachment of magnetic mines.

Royal Tiger with Henschel turret and two-piece gun barrel. This vehicle is equipped with transport tracks.

Rear view of King Tiger, showing drop hatch flap at rear of turret. Part of the armoured skirting has been inserted between the hull and the twin exhaust pipes. This Tiger II has a Porsche turret.

horizontally in panniers on each side of the vehicle's hull. Power traverse was the same as for the Panther and Tiger "E". Two machine-guns, M.G. 34, were carried, one coaxially mounted in the turret and the other in a ball mounting in the front glacis plate. There was also a fitting on the cupola for an A/A M.G. mounting (Fliegerbeschussgerät).

Internally this vehicle followed the usual German layout with the engine at the rear, the driver and bow gunner in the hull, commander, gunner and loader in the turret. The vehicle was well provided with escape hatches and as there was no turret basket it was comparatively easy for the driver and bow gunner to escape through the fighting compartment, or alternatively for the members of the gun crew to escape through the hatches provided for the driver and bow gunner; these consisted of two irregular shaped spring-balanced hatches, one each side above the driver and hull MG operator respectively.

A periscope was provided close to the front edge of the superstructure roof to enable the driver to see. This could be traversed from about 11 o'clock to about 1 o'clock. Part of the top of the glacis plate was cut away to afford better vision. The driver could also drive with his head protruding through his escape hatch, and for this purpose the driver's seat, the accelerator pedal and the steering controls were adjustable. An episcope set at 12.30 o'clock was provided for the hull gunner close to the forward edge of the superstructure roof, part of the glacis plate being cut away to provide better vision. For the gunner there was a monocular gunsight on the left of the gun, and for the loader there was an episcope facing forward situated on the right hand side of the sloping front section of the turret roof. This was protected by an armoured shield.

There were installations for the normal German

Close-up of the commander's seven episcope all-round vision cupola. Clearly shown is the rail and attachment for the mounting of the anti-aircraft machine-gun (Fliegerbeschuss-gerät). Seen also is the turret ventilator.

Driver's position. Note the roof stiffener, which was carried into the panniers and attached to the pannier floor.

Centre ammunition rack in nearside pannier. Note the bulkhead and the spaced joints between it and the armour.

Hull machine-gunner's position with ball mount. Operating gear for the roof hatch is on the right.

Nearside rear corner of turret showing ammunition racks. The roller on the turret floor (left) was to carry the gun when it was withdrawn from the mounting.

tank wireless equipment, one transmitter and one or two receivers. The equipment was stowed above the gearbox to the left of the hull MG operator. Intercom facilities were also provided for the commander, gunner, driver and hull operator. An aerial was mounted on the offside of the superstructure roof at the rear.

ARMOUR

The armour, particularly that carried on the front of the vehicle, was the thickest to be employed on a tank that was due for large scale production. The front glacis of 150mm was set at 40 degrees to the vertical, and the nose plate of 100mm set at 55 degrees, resembling in design the Panther rather than the earlier Tiger "E". The side plates of the superstructure, including the turret wall, were 80mm thick and set at an angle of 25 degrees, with the exception of the hull sides which were vertical and the turret front which was rounded. Top and belly plates were 42mm thick and the tail plate 80mm thick. The armour consisted of rolled plates interlocked with the main joints step welded.

TURRET

Two types of turret appeared on this vehicle, the first, the Porsche type was some 11ft 6 inches long and incorporated extensive use of bent plates in its manufacture. The front was rounded while the left side was bent vertically to receive the commanders cupola. The second type, which was the main production type, was modified primarily to facilitate production; the turret was made wider and the cupola set in the roof so as to obviate the use of the special bent plate on the left side of the turret. The turret front now consisted of a single flat piece of armour 180mm thick sloped at an angle of 10 degrees to the vertical; the turret front of the Porsche design had consisted of an 80mm plate bent round from the roof to the base. This modification not only made production easier but actually increased the armour protection.

The gun mantlet was also redesigned. Both types were substantially bell-shaped, but whereas the earlier version had a square skirt and was fitted for movement over the cylindrical front surface of the turret, the later type had a circular skirt and was fitted as a socket member over a ball protuberance welded to the turret front plate. The hole for the coaxial M.G. in the early

Koenigstiger carrying paratroops as "tank marines" in the opening phase of the Battle of the Bulge in the Ardennes forest, December 16, 1944.

version was a vertical slot in the turret front to the right of the mantlet, while in the late version it passed through the mantlet skirt.

There was only one hatch in the turret wall, a rectangular one at the rear which opened outwards and downwards; this also incorporated a conical pistol port that was closed by a plug attached to a chain. The hatch measured $20\frac{1}{2}$ by $18\frac{3}{4}$ inches on the late version of the turret as against 20 by 14 inches on the early version. The commander's cupola was similar to the type that were used on the late production Panthers and Tiger "E" models. It was fitted with seven episcopes to give the commander all-round vision, and a dished lid that swivelled to the left. A rail for the mounting of a machine-gun for anti-aircraft defence was also fitted.

A smoke projecting device with 360° traverse was mounted on the offside portion of the turret roof, and an electric extractor fan in the centre rear.

Jagdtiger, showing the hull and suspension of the Royal Tiger. At 70 tons this was the heaviest armoured vehicle to see service in World War II.

SUSPENSION AND TRACK

Suspension followed the well-known German arrangement of employing torsion bars as the springing medium. The general assembly of the suspension units was similar to that used by the Tiger Model "E", the only important departure being the use of overlapping bogie wheels as distinct from the overlapped and interleaved system that was used on the Panther and Tiger "E". This change was adapted to simplify the maintenance problems which had been inherent with the interleaved road wheels. Similarly the tendency for the wheels to jam in shingle, or to freeze solid with packed snow was obviated to some extent.

The suspension consisted of overlapping bogie wheels mounted on torsion bars. There were nine axles each side, each carrying double bogie wheels set together; on the first, third, fifth seventh and ninth axles, the wheels were on the outside overlapping those on the intermediate axles. The bogie wheels had steel tyres mounted on rubber cushions. A single torsion bar was attached to each wheel axle by means of a radius arm, shock absorbers being fitted to the front ones. The normal front driving sprocket and rear idler wheel were used.

A new type of track was fitted. This was 2ft 7in wide and consisted of a double pin main link with a connector. The main link consisted of two spuds, each with a chevron pattern set in relief to provide a better grip. The track was provided with two sets of guide horns, the bogie wheels that were fitted on the inside running either side of the inner set, and the outer bogie wheels running either side of the outer set. A narrow loading track (2ft 2in wide) was used for the transportation of the Tiger "B" on rail flats.

VARIANTS OF THE ROYAL TIGER

PANZERBEFEHLSWAGEN TIGER AUSF "B"

A few of the Royal Tiger vehicles were adapted to the role of command tanks (Pz.Bef.Wg.). This was achieved by reducing the ammunition stowage in the rear of the turret and installing the appropriate radio equipment. The command version was also equipped with an additional mast aerial at the rear of the hull. The normal crew was retained, but the loader acted as second radio operator.

THE JAGDTIGER

Following the Heereswaffenamt policy of the time, a limited traverse tank destroyer version of the Royal Tiger was also produced. This vehicle, the heaviest armoured fighting vehicle to go into service, was designated Jagdpanzer VI, Panzerjäger Tiger Ausf B (Sd Kfz 186), or Jagdtiger. It was first shown as a full scale iron model in October 1943 and a total of 150 vehicles was ordered, but due to shortages of components and disruption by bombing only 70 machines were built, 48 of them in 1944.

One of the Jagdtigers was experimentally equipped with the torsion bar suspension designed by Dr Porsche who claimed that his design simplified manufacture, but this design was rejected. It had eight axles each side as against nine in the Henschel design.

The Jagdtiger consisted of the normal Tiger "B" hull with a lengthened suspension and a built-up superstructure to form a fixed turret or barbette. The front plate of the turret was 250mm thick and sloped back at 15 degrees to the vertical; it was made of one piece of solid cast steel. The sides of the hull were combined into one piece with the sides of the turret and like the Tiger "B" were 80mm thick and sloped at 25 degrees. The rear plate of the superstructure was also 80mm thick and was sloped at 10 degrees; this

contained an entry hatch fitted with double doors. The turret was enclosed with a 40mm armoured roof that was secured by bolts. Fitments in the roof included a hatch, ventilator, smoke discharger and sighting devices.

The 12.8cm Pak 80 (L/55) (the most powerful anti-tank gun to be used during the war) was mounted centrally in the front plate within a cast bell-shaped gun shield similar in design to that of the 8.8cm KwK 43 on the Tiger "B". Early production vehicles were armed with the 12.8cm Pak 44 and some of them, because of the shortage of these weapons, were armed with the 8.8cm Pak 43/3 as mounted on the Jagdpanther.

The 12.8cm rounds consisted of a projectile and charge of which there were 38 of each. These were stowed in separate racks inside the fighting compartment. In addition to the normal ball-mounted hull M.G. 34, a simple monopod A.A. mounting for an M.G. 42 was welded to the engine compartment roof. This incorporated a rack and ratchet mechanism by means of which its height could be extended from 44 inches to 68 inches above the engine compartment roof. The vehicle commander, at the right front of the fighting compartment, was provided with a periscope mounted on a circular plate in the roof, with 360° traverse. The plate also contained a rectangular hatch permitting the use of a scissors type telescope.

Weight in action: 70 tons 12 cwt.
Crew: 6, Commander, gunner, two loaders, driver, W/T operator.
Length overall: 34 ft 11½ in.
Width (Battle Track): 11 ft. 10¾ in.
      (Transport Track): 10 ft. 8¾ in.
Height: 9 ft. 3 in.
Gun overhang: 9 ft. 5¾ in.
Road speed (max): 23·6 mph.
Cross-country speed (max): 9 to 12 mph.
Radius of action (Road): 100 miles.
Radius of action (Cross-country): 75 miles.
Trench ability: 8 ft. 2 in.
Gradient: 35 degrees.
Vertical step: 2 ft. 9½ in.

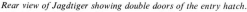

Top view of Jagdtiger, showing rotating hatch, and four episcopes located one at each corner of the turret roof. A further periscope with 360° traverse is mounted in the left centre. On the hull front the driver's and hull gunner's periscopes can be seen.

Rear view of Jagdtiger showing double doors of the entry hatch.

Side view of the Jagdtiger that was equipped with Porsche torsion bar suspension. This was distinguished from the Henschel design by its different wheels, different wheel assembly, and by having one less wheel each side—eight instead of nine.

SPECIFICATION – PANZERKAMPFWAGEN VI, TIGER AUSFUEHRUNG "B" (Sd Kfz.182)

Crew: 5, Commander, gunner, loader, driver, gunner/wireless operator.

Battle Weight: Original turret, 67 tons 7 cwt.
Production turret, 68 tons 13 cwt.

Dimensions
Overall length (including gun): 33 ft. 8 in.
Overall width (wide tracks): 12 ft. 3⅝ in.
Overall width (narrow tracks): 10 ft. 8¾ in.
Overall height: 10 ft. 1⅝ in.
Ground clearance: 1 ft. 7½ in.
Track centres (wide tracks): 9 ft. 1⅞ in.
Track centres (narrow tracks): 8 ft. 6¾ in.
Track width (wide tracks): 2 ft. 7 in.
Track width (narrow tracks): 2 ft. 2 in.
Track on ground: 13 ft. 6½ in.

Armament
One 8·8 cm gun, KwK 43. L/71.
One MG 34 (7·92 mm) mounted co-axially.
One MG 34 (7·92 mm) mounted in hull front.
One MG 42 (7·92 mm) mounted on cupola for A/A defence.
One breech loaded smoke mortar inset in turret roof with 360° traverse.

Ammunition
8·8 cm: 80 rounds, (40 APCBC, 40 HE) 22 rounds were stowed horizontally in rear of turret, protected by an 8 mm armour plate spaced about ¾ in. from the turret wall. 48 rounds were stowed horizontally in panniers on each side of the hull; these were stowed in three groups on each side, and were divided by 20 mm gusset plates. A further 10 rounds were carried loose.
MG: 5850 (7·92 mm) rounds (39 belts, each 150).

Observation
Cupola with 7 episcopes, and sighting vane on turret roof, opening for episcope in turret front, and monocular sight to left of gun. Traversing periscope for driver and episcope for hull machine gunner.

Communication
Fu 5 (Transmitter and receiver) and/or Fu 2 (receiver). Bord (intercom) for commander, gunner, driver and hull MG operator.

Armour
Homogeneous machinable quality rolled plate except for mantlet and exhaust brackets (cast) and hull MG mount (forged).
Turret Front: 185 mm at 10° (Porsche Turret 100 mm rounded).
Turret Sides: 80 mm at 21° (Porsche Turret 80 mm at 30°).
Turret Rear: 80 mm at 20° (Porsche Turret 80 mm at 30°).
Turret Roof: 44 mm at 80°/90°/80° (Porsche Turret 40 mm at 78°/90°/20°).

Superstructure
Front: 150 mm at 50°.
Sides: 80 mm at 25°.
Rear: 80 mm at 30°.
Roof: 40 mm Horizontal.
Hull Front: 100 mm at 50°.
Hull Glacis: —.
Hull Sides: 80 mm Vertical.
Hull Rear: 80 mm at 30°.
Hull Belly: 40 mm and 25 mm Horizontal.
Thin skirting plates of mild steel extended from the bottom of the superstructure sides to the top of the track and were spaced 2 ft. 11 in. from the hull sides.

Engine
Type: Maybach HL230 P30.
Output (r.p.m./b.h.p.): 2,600/600.
Gearbox type: Maybach-Olvar 401-216.
No. of speeds: 8 forward, 4 reverse.
Steering: Henschel L801 giving 2 radii of turn in each gear.
Drive: Front sprocket.

Suspension
Torsion bar, with overlapped resilient steel disc wheels, nine axles each side. Internal shock absorbers on outer (1st and 9th) axles. Wheels 2 ft. 7 in. diameter, 3⁵⁄₁₆ in. thick.

Performance
Max. speed (roads) (m.p.h.): 25·7
Max. speed (cross-country) (m.p.h.): 9–12.
Radius of action (road): 106 miles.
Radius of action (cross-country): 75 miles.
Gradient: 35°.
Trench: 8 ft. 2⅜ in.
Step: 2 ft. 9½ in.
Fording depth: 5 ft. 3 in.
Fuel (gallons): 189.
(Fuel disposed in 7 tanks, 2 each side of engine, one behind engine, one each side of fighting compartment).
Chassis numbers for the Royal Tiger were as follows:
Late 1943 early 1944 280001–280050 with Porsche turret, 280051–280066 with production turret.
Mid-late 1944 280067–280400 with production turret.
Early 1945 280401–280484 with production turret.

The Porsche Jagdtiger on trials.

Professor Porsche's first attempt to create an armoured fighting vehicle resulted in two prototypes of the Porsche Type 100 or, as it was internally called, the "Leopard".

Panzerjäger Tiger (P) Elefant

by Walter J. Spielberger

DURING the battle north of Orel, Russia, in 1943, a Russian tank column marched far out of reach of conventional German anti-tank fire on a northerly course towards Karatschew. The tanks were barely visible at a distance of more than three miles and the Germans seemed unable to interfere with this troop movement, which was threatening their exposed flank.

Then, at this critical moment, a company of German self-propelled anti-tank equipment, using a vehicle called "Ferdinand" was called up to intervene. Fire was opened against the Russian vehicles in spite of the distance and soon eight of them were destroyed. Another victory for the incredible German 88 mm. gun was ready for the history book. This long-barrelled 88 mm. anti-tank gun, or "8,8 cm. Pak 43/2 L/71", as the Germans called it, was one of the most outstanding weapons of World War II. Intended originally for anti-aircraft purposes, it was soon recognised as a potent anti-tank weapon and was eventually mounted, slightly modified, in the turret of Tiger II.

An earlier version of the gun, the Flak 36, with a barrel length of L/56, had already been modified and mounted in the turret of the original Tiger I model as early as 1941. In the meantime, Heeresflak units, unprotected and towed by soft-skinned, half-track tractors, had attempted to protect infantry and other units against the numerous Russian tank attacks. They had suffered unbearable losses. Only if able to engage their enemies at the proper distance could their success be assured. But the towed gun with its awkward and time-consuming positioning problems was no solution and soon attempts were made to provide the weapon with a self-propelled mount. The

only chassis readily available at this time were Panzer III and IV. Since neither of them was originally intended and suitable for SP use, a composite chassis was designed, utilising chassis and hull components of both vehicles. An anti-tank version, called "Nashorn", mounted the 8,8 cm. Pak 43/1 L/71. Despite their open and only thinly-armoured superstructure, these vehicles were quite successful. They were replaced by an excellent vehicle, the fully-enclosed and adequately-armoured "Jagdpanther" in 1944. This unit was beyond a doubt one of the most versatile and effective tank destroyer vehicles of its time. It remained in production until the war came to a close.

The vehicle described in this *Profile* also mounted the same weapon. It was a direct outgrowth of the "Tiger" development. Never intended originally as a self-propelled mount for the long-barrelled 88 mm. gun, it turned out to be a technically most complicated and unreliable vehicle. It came into existence almost by a freak of nature and it should only serve as an example so far as its unique chassis design is concerned. As a complete unit, the "Elefant" must be considered a failure. This is said despite the fact that your author was engaged as design engineer on this project and that he participated actively in the action in Russia, described at the beginning of this *Profile*.

DEVELOPMENT HISTORY

Professor Porsche's first attempt to create a military vehicle dates back as far as the days of World War I. Then working for the Austrian Daimler factory, he motorised the heavy Austrian artillery with four-wheel

This unit was intended to replace the Panzer IV and was equipped with two air-cooled V-10 engines which drove electrically the two front sprockets.

During intensive field trials the Porsche Type 100 was also used to supply the Porsche Type 101 with electric current during the initial field testing of the Porsche Tiger.

tractors capable of pulling enormous loads. They incorporated mixed petrol-electric drive systems, a solution which later became the trade mark of Porsche armoured fighting vehicles. His independent company, created in 1930 in Stuttgart, acted as a design office for various international automotive concerns. Among others, he received, in 1939, an order from the Ordnance Department to participate in an attempt to find a successor vehicle for the standard Panzer IV. A vehicle was required which, having a total weight of 25 to 30 metric tons, had to be capable of carrying either the 75 mm. tank gun or a 105 mm. high velocity weapon. Porsche's solution produced a vehicle with two parallel installed air-cooled petrol engines, coupled to an electric dynamo supplying electric motors driving the front sprockets. Steering and gear-shifting were effected electrically. The suspension incorporated torsion bars in a new and unique way. Two prototypes were built at the Nibelungenwerke of St. Valentin in Lower Austria. They carried the internal designation "Leopard", or Porsche Type 100, (Ordnance designation VK 3001 (P)).

The appearance of the Russian T-34 rendered most of these attempts useless and forced Porsche to abandon this project in favour of a heavier vehicle, capable of mounting the 88 mm. gun. This was done in anticipation of even heavier vehicles expected to appear from the arsenals of both the Russians and the Western Allies. The outdated tank weaponry used by the Germans at the beginning of the Russian campaign called for a drastic reappraisal, with a demand for an armour penetration of at least 100 mm. from a distance of 1,500 metres. The selection of gun calibre was left to the manufacturer. But, meanwhile, the 88 mm. gun had established itself, to such an extent that it appeared most likely to be considered as the standard tank weapon for new German tank designs.

The Waffenamt insisted, however, that lesser calibres of 6 cm. or 7,5 cm. should be afforded the same opportunity, provided they achieved the same performance. The thinking behind this order was based upon the fact that such weapons could be installed within smaller turret rings, thus allowing for a reduced overall weight. Given frontal armour of 80 mm. and side armour of 60 mm., a reduction in turret ring diameter from 1,850 mm. (73 in.) to 1,650 mm. (65 in.) would have lowered the weight of the turret by almost 2·2 tons. Equal armour penetration with smaller weapons, however, called for utilisation of tapered bore designs using tungsten steel ammunition. These were in too short supply and could not be considered. Conventional weapons had to be used. Thus, Krupp of Essen received an order from the Ordnance Department, in July 1941, to develop a tank gun derived from the 88 mm. anti-aircraft gun with a barrel length of 4,930 mm. (L/56). This was originally intended only for the Porsche vehicle VK 4501 which was ordered as a parallel design to the Henschel VK 3601 on 26th May 1941. It appeared for a time that two distinct vehicles would emerge from these orders—passed down from Hitler himself—both with production beginning May-June 1942, namely a Porsche type (VK 4501 P) with an 8,8 cm. gun and the Henschel vehicle (VK 3601), with the tapered bore weapon 0725. But, since tungsten steel was no longer available, the Krupp turret, originally intended for the Porsche vehicle only, had to be used for the Henschel, the pressing timetable allowing no other solution. Thus, the Henschel vehicle was also developed as a 45 ton unit (VK 4501 H) and eventually became the Panzerkampfwagen VI Tiger I (H)—later (E).

Porsche relied to a large extent upon his experience gained during the development of the VK 3001, the Type 100. Additional new ideas were incorporated, but petrol-electric drive was retained. The design of the air-cooled power plants created almost insurmountable difficulties. Hitler, however, had insisted that both vehicles were to be developed side by side, a common practice of the Waffenamt. Pronounced controversies developed between Dr. Porsche and the Ordnance Department over these years, and were never entirely resolved. Interesting as Porsche's technical solution for such a heavy vehicle may have appeared, the actual vehicle turned out to be most complicated. And, because it had to be put in production without the benefit of extensive trials, it could only be put into service with combat units after costly re-development and basic changes. In fact, only a few of the 90 vehicles originally authorised and put in production were actually completed as battle tanks. They were designated Panzerkampfwagen VI, VK 4501 (P), Tiger (P).

Because of the difficulties with the air-cooled engine and in order to meet set deadlines for presentation of the Porsche Tiger to Hitler field trials were conducted of the electric components without the main engines installed. Power was supplied from a Type 100 unit.

THE PROTOTYPE TRIALS

On 19th March 1942, Armament Minister Speer reported to Hitler that, commencing in October 1942, 60 Porsche and 25 Henschel Tiger tanks would be completed. Prototypes of both vehicles were demonstrated before Hitler on 20th April 1942. Only twelve months had gone by from the moment the order was received to the date of completion of the prototypes. It was an extremely short time in the development of such a sophisticated weapon, and it is perhaps not surprising that the simpler, more conventional Henschel vehicle was chosen as the basis of the new battle tank.

Dr. Porsche never believed in the reliability of a mechanical transmission for such a heavy vehicle. Two alternative transmissions were therefore envisaged, one electric and the other hydraulic. The hydraulic unit was rather large and had a poor efficiency compared with a mechanical transmission although it was expected to equal the electric alternative. It was to be built by Voith of Heidenheim. However, serious troubles with the air-cooled engines delayed installation and caused a complete lack of interest in this unit by the time it was actually completed.

The production of the Henschel Tiger was already in full swing at this time. The unit designed by Porsche had a fighting weight of 57 metric tons, after its belly armour had been increased to 100 mm. Its main armament, originally the 8,8 cm. KwK 36, was changed to a 15 cm. KwK L/37 or a 10 cm. KwK L/70. But both developments never materialised and the Porsche Type 101 never saw action as a battle tank.

Eighty-five of the 90 chassis assembled at the Nibelung-enwerke were shipped in 1942 to the Altmaerkische Kettenfabrik GmbH (Alkett) of Berlin-Spandau. There they received new superstructures and additional armour and were equipped with the long-barrelled 88 mm. anti-tank gun mounted in limited traverse. A new tank destroyer vehicle was thus created. It was demonstrated for the first time on 19th March 1943 at Ruegenwalde. Instead of the two air-cooled Porsche engines, two standard Maybach HL 120 TRM tank engines were installed. The new unit received the official designation Panzerjäger Tiger (P) Elefant (SdKfz 184). Originally called "Ferdinand" after its designer, Dr. Ferdinand Porsche, its official designation was "Elefant". These vehicles proved to be more of a liability rather than an asset to the units finally receiving them.

PRODUCTION

Only a grand total of 90 vehicles were produced. Professor Porsche's association with the Steyr-Daimler-Puch AG., which owned and operated Nibelungen-werke, put the production of all of his designs and prototypes in this location. Originally intended for mass production of the Porsche Type 100, this factory served until the end of the war as the main source of Panzer IV. It carried out extensive research work and built, among other fighting vehicles, the Jagdtiger. Component parts and hull assemblies were supplied by Eisenwerke Oberdonau of Linz and assembly of the chassis continued at Ni-Werke until a final order relocated the production line to Alkett, in Berlin-Spandau. Serial Numbers ranged from 150001 through 150090. Only five recovery vehicles were completed at Ni-Werke.

ELEFANT DESCRIBED

Elefant was nothing but a conversion of the original Porsche Tiger tank design. The hull, consisting of various-sized armour plates, was welded on all joints. Only high quality chromium-molybdenum steel was used. The original layout of the battle tank was changed at Alkett by separating the driver's compartment completely from the fighting area. The engine compartment was inserted in between. The tank version had the usual layout, with the fighting compartment in the front

A model of the Porsche Tiger with the Krupp turret which was later put into production for the Henschel Tiger E.

A wooden mock-up of the Porsche Tiger hull with a spacious driver compartment showing the air tanks for the hydro-pneumatic steering system.

The rear-driven vehicle allowed for a more spacious driver compartment. This wooden mock-up also indicates the hull machine gun and the tensioning devices for the tracks.

Two of these air-cooled engines were coupled with an electric generator and installed in the limited-spaced engine compartment of the Tiger tank. Clearly visible are the two air fans for the engine.

and the power plants located in the rear section. The space for the driver and radio operator was relatively uncluttered, since the rear drive allowed freedom of movement in this section. Only the air-tanks for the hydro-pneumatic steering were located forward, together with radio equipment. The original fighting compartment was used after the conversion to a tank destroyer vehicle as the engine compartment, accommodating two Maybach engines and the cooling system. Because the engines were the same as those already described in detail in the Panzer IV *Profile* the engine described here is the original Porsche tank engine. Two of these were coupled together to produce, through an

electric transmission, an output of approximately 600 net h.p. This particular design was chosen to allow for high power output from the relatively small space available in the Tiger engine compartment. The crankshaft of each unit was coupled directly to the generator concerned and blowers for cooling the cylinders of the engines were mounted on the generator. Some of these engines, which gave satisfactory results during trials, were actually mounted in some of the electrically-operated Tiger tanks, but production of the engine was never started, since official opinion in Berlin favoured a 16-cylinder X Diesel engine.

The Porsche Type 101 engine was an air-cooled, four-stroke petrol engine, with carburettors and magneto-ignition. The cylinders were arranged in "V" form, and the engine was fitted with overhead valves actuated through push rods. Its maximum output was 320 b.h.p., at 2,500 r.p.m. With a bore of 115 mm. and a stroke of 145 mm., total displacement amounted to 15,060 cc. A total of ten cylinders was provided. The five-throw crankshaft was supported in six lead-bronze bearings. The forked connecting rods ran on a common, interchangeable bearing shell. A divided oil sump was incorporated. Engine cooling was effected through a double rotary blower driven from a pinion on the generator shaft through a jointed shaft. An oil cooler was installed. Solex down-draught carburettors of the type 50 JFF II were mounted. Fuel was stored in one tank of 115 gallons (520 litre) capacity, mounted above the generator. It was supplied through two feed pumps directly to the carburettors.

The hull of the tank-destroyer vehicle consisted, after re-arrangement, of a driver compartment, providing seats for both the driver and radio operator, an engine compartment, housing two parallel Maybach engines of 300 h.p. each, and a fighting compartment, where the commander, gunner and two loaders were situated. A separate transmission compartment contained two electric motors, one for each driving sprocket. Both sides of the engine compartment held the two fuel tanks with a total capacity of 240 gallons.

Siemens-Schuckert of Berlin supplied the electrical components, namely the generator and the two electric drive motors. Each track was driven independently. Each of the electric motors was linked to the rear driving sprocket through a geared drive. Steering, while hydro-pneumatic assisted, was effected electrically by means of controls installed in the driver compartment. A reduction ratio for the final drive of 16·75:1 was obtained, allowing for a top speed of 12·5 m.p.h. The gearbox was electrically operated and three speed ratios were available in either direction.

PORSCHE SUSPENSION

The most interesting feature of the vehicle was, without a doubt, the suspension. It consisted of a rear drive sprocket, six bogie wheels, and a front idler wheel on each side. The Porsche bogie unit embodied some unique features in the application of torsion bars as a flexible medium. The conception of the design was based on the practice of having adjacent wheels straddling the track guide and on the use of steel-rimmed wheels. A short cantilever spindle supported each bogie unit in such a manner that all loads were overhanging in relationship to it. The bearing load at the bogie oscillation point was, therefore, of enormous proportion. A secondary arm, which carried the torsion bar, was placed under the spindle of the leading wheel, which, in fact, limited the height of the track guides. Difficulties in finding a workable means for mounting a conventional type of track support roller forced the designers to adopt a makeshift track support in the form of a curved spring steel friction plate. One of the main arguments claimed in favour of the Porsche design was the fact that fewer road wheels (six per side against eight per side on the Henschel vehicle) were required. Smaller diameter wheels gave room for larger wheel movement. All these advantages were based on the fact that the road wheels had steel wearing surfaces and could, therefore, carry higher loads than larger wheels with rubber tyres.

Each bogie unit consisted basically of a carrying bracket and a primary and secondary arm, each of which carried one road wheel. The bracket, which was fixed to the tank hull, was integral with a spindle on which the primary arm oscillated. The primary arm carried a fixed shaft, the outer end of which formed the spindle for the leading wheel and the inner end of which was a hinged pin for the secondary arm. This secondary arm was made of a hollow steel casting in which the torsion bar was carried. This torsion bar was splined on both ends. It was anchored to the trailing end of the secondary pin. The forward end of the torsion bar was connected with a torsion cam unit which consisted of a relatively long tubular member of which the load carrying cam was an integral part. This cam unit was free to oscillate in plain bearings, located in the forward end of the secondary arm. The cam reacted against the arm which was splined to a shaft. A tension helical spring was used for holding the bearing surfaces to a reaction arm and the cam. A substantial rubber bumper was mounted on the trailing end of the primary arm.

The steel tracks of a skeleton type (track type Kgs 62/640/130) were in their final form 25 in. wide. The track pitch was 5 in. and 109 links per track were used. Originally, narrower tracks of 20 in. and 23·5 in. width were tested but the ever-increasing total weight demanded a lower ground pressure. It was still too high, since the Elefant had to be content with 3·44 lb./sq. in., a very high figure.

Instead of a rotating turret, the vehicle had a box-like superstructure, with slightly inclined plates. The common practice of interlocking armour plates was utilised. Six escape hatches were provided, two of which were situated on top of the driving compartment. Three appeared on the superstructure roof, serving as entrance and exit for the rest of the crew. One circular hatch cover of approximately 32 in. diameter was located in the rear inclined plate of the body, facilitating the removal and installation of the main armament, while a much smaller opening within the large hatch allowed for ejection of spent cartridges. The basic armour of the Porsche Tiger was increased, and an additional 100 mm. plate was added by means of conical bolts to the front portion of the hull. The superstructure received a frontal armour of 200 mm. thickness. The rest of the vehicle carried 80 mm. plates throughout.

Visibility from the fighting compartment was poor, only forward vision being provided.

THE 8,8 cm. GUN

The 8,8 cm. Pak 43/2 L/71 was the only armament the vehicle carried. It was mounted in limited traverse.

Elevation was from +14° to —8°, while traverse extended to 14° on either side. Fifty rounds of ammunition were carried in the fighting compartment.

The 88 mm. Pak 43/2 mounted on this vehicle was, at that time, the latest in the series of anti-tank guns developed from the 88 mm. anti-aircraft guns. As mentioned earlier, the 88 mm. KwK 36 mounted in the Tiger Model E was adapted from the Flak 36. In order to improve the performance of the anti-aircraft guns of the Flak 36 class, a higher velocity weapon was developed and introduced as Flak 41. This weapon had the muzzle velocity increased to 3,280 feet per second, giving the shorter projectile flight time desirable in an anti-aircraft gun. However, by the time it was introduced, a heavier projectile with a larger explosive content was desirable for anti-aircraft use and interest in this weapon centred on its possible employment as an anti-tank weapon. The original Flak 41 was successfully used in the anti-tank rôle. However, it was designed with a long, narrow cartridge case, which was somewhat awkward to handle and would have been impossible to use inside a vehicle. Development of the anti-tank weapon continued with the appearance of the Pak 43/41, and the Pak 43. These weapons had the same ballistic performance as the Flak 41, but were redesigned with a shorter, fatter cartridge

A Porsche Tiger during field trials in Austria in 1942. This is the front of the vehicle, with the turret pointing toward 6 o'clock.

The same vehicle from the rear, showing the layout of the engine compartment and other stowage.

Two of the Porsche Tiger units during the test period in 1942. The turrets are reversed.

case to improve the ammunition handling characteristics. The Pak 43/41 was mounted on a split trail carriage, while the Pak 43 was fitted to a low silhouette, cruciform mount. The shorter ammunition of these weapons made them particularly suitable for vehicle mounts, and several were developed. Of these, the Pak 43/1 was fitted to the Nashorn. The Pak 43/2 was mounted in the Elefant and the Pak 43/3 in the Jagdpanther. A similar weapon adapted to Tiger B was designated the KwK 43. These vehicle weapons were slightly longer than the ground mounted anti-tank guns Pak 43 and 43/41. Although they were designated L/71, they were, in fact, 71·6 calibres in length. This weapon was undoubtedly the finest anti-tank gun produced by either side during World War II. With its explosive loaded APCBC ammunition, it could penetrate 137 mm. of 30° slope homogeneous armour at 2,000 yards.

Although APCR ammunition was designed for this weapon, tungsten shortages prevented its use. However, it must be pointed out that such ammunition was neither necessary nor particularly desirable in view of the high performance and greater destructive power of the explosive loaded APCBC. The 8,8 cm. L/71 gun could destroy any armoured vehicle it was likely to encounter at almost any normal combat range, using this standard ammunition. It not only could penetrate its target, but the projectile exploded inside the vehicle, almost always ensuring the destruction of both vehicle and crew.

For self-protection, the crew had only personal arms —one machine gun 34 and two sub-machine guns 38. Since this arrangement rendered the early vehicles almost helpless against close range attacks, remaining units were subsequently equipped with a ball-mounted machine gun 34 in the bow, crewed by the radio operator.

Radio equipment consisted of a receiver and a transmitter (Fu 5 and Fu 2). Internal communication was provided.

PORSCHE VARIANTS

Nibelungenwerke, in setting up production schedules for the Porsche Tiger tank, envisaged also the necessity of creating armoured tank retrievers for such a heavy vehicle. From the first production batch, five chassis were set aside for this purpose. While the rest of the production, after the chassis had been assembled, was moved to Alkett for completion, these units remained in St. Valentin and were fitted with a small but fully-enclosed armoured superstructure. A Kugelblende 80 (ball-mounted machine gun 34) was installed in the front plate of the superstructure, providing necessary close-range protection. The basic armour of the tank with 100 mm. frontal plates was retained. No reinforcement was added. The recovery vehicles were issued to the two Elefant battalions and saw action both in Russia and in Italy.

A 21 cm. heavy mortar mounting on the chassis of the Porsche Tiger was also contemplated. But, since a similar attempt failed with the Henschel chassis, the project was dropped before it reached the prototype stage.

As a result of the experience gained during the savage street fighting in Stalingrad, Hitler ordered the production of so-called "Ramm" vehicles. They were supposed to wreck buildings which were heavily defended. In order to increase their radius of action, armoured fuel trailers were to be coupled to these units. Porsche investigated this requirement, preparing blueprints and models of a vehicle which was supposed to be called "Ramm-Tiger". Using the Type 101 chassis, they were fitted with a turtle-like superstructure sporting a pointed, shovel-like frontal section. Visibility for the driver was provided by means of a large opening in the glacis plate. Since grave doubts existed about the practicability of such an approach, the design never progressed beyond the blueprint stage.

This picture shows the installation of the two power plants parallel to each other, occupying the engine compartment almost completely.

A side view of the Elefant shows the armoured superstructure which replaced the rotating turret of the Porsche Tiger. The circular indentation on the side of the hull was originally an escape hatch for the driver. Later it was eliminated completely.

The additional armour bolted to the Elefant's hull is clearly visible in this picture.

This unit was intended to become the main German tank engine starting in 1945. It never reached the stage of mass production however.

Continuous failures experienced with the 10-cylinder air-cooled tank engines prompted Porsche to create a 16-cylinder diesel engine designed to replace the Maybach water-cooled Tiger power plant. Only a few engines of this kind were built by Graz-Simmering-Pauker.

Type 102 in the Porsche design programme was the already-mentioned Tiger with hydraulic instead of electric drive. One prototype of this series was equipped with a Voith "NITA" transmission and had, unlike previous models, two radial engine blowers to provide necessary cooling air for the transmission. This test vehicle had the designation Type 103. Tests were also conducted to investigate the feasibility of using half a Volkswagen engine with two cylinders only as a starting motor for the air-cooled tank engines.

The redesign of the Tiger tank, ordered by the Ordnance Department in the autumn of 1942, initiated at Porsche both Types 180 and 181. The Ordnance designation was VK 4502 (P). The designs now had inclined armour plates, following the trend of the time. Both models again appeared as drawings only. However, the turret, as in the case of the Tiger I development, was put in production. It was used for the first 50 units of the Henschel version of Tiger II, the so-called "King Tiger". Type 180 had a proposed petrol-electric drive, while its counterpart, Type 181, was intended to receive a hydraulic drive train. Two basic layout versions appeared on the drawing boards: one had the conventional arrangement with the fighting compartment in the front section of the vehicle, while the second placed the turret towards the rear. No changes were contemplated in the engines of these two types. Two parallel power plants were envisaged, however, and a diesel version was investigated. Fuel injection for the Otto engine was also examined.

The disadvantages of the dual engine arrangement were obvious and eventually led to the design of a brand new power plant which incorporated the combined experience of all previous attempts. Designed by both Porsche and Graz-Simmering-Pauker of Vienna, a 16-cylinder air-cooled diesel engine was conceived, which was supposed to deliver approximately 700 b.h.p. With a total displacement of 37 litres, it was intended to become the standard tank engine of the German armoured forces. Only a few trial engines were completed when the war came to an end. Under the designation "SLa 16" (Porsche Type 212), one was installed in a Jagdtiger, where it performed rather promisingly. Unfortunately, the new engine demanded a modification of the Tiger hull, thus delaying even further this much-

Three new Elefants of the first production run during test trials at the Alkett factory in Berlin. The gun mantlet is without the additional protection applied later on.

A rear view of the Elefant preserved at the Aberdeen Proving Grounds, shows the interlocking armour plates of the superstructure used on most German vehicles from 1943. The concentric hatches in the rear plate of the superstructure served for the ejection of empty cartridges during combat, and also (the larger one) for the removal of the gun.

needed innovation. As an 18-cylinder unit with an output of 780 b.h.p., the engine was also intended to be used for the Panzerkampfwagen "Maus" (Porsche Type 205). With that the story of the Porsche Tiger development ends.

TACTICAL EMPLOYMENT

The appearance of superior Russian tank and anti-tank weapons shortly after the beginning of the German campaign in 1941 forced the German High Command into many a makeshift solution. Emergency orders to the German armament industry and the use of captured enemy equipment stabilised to a certain extent conditions on the front and again established a balance of power. Two categories of new anti-tank weapons emerged from this situation. One was the lightly armoured self-propelled gun mounted on an almost obsolete tank chassis. Most of these vehicles had their fighting compartment open on the top. The other solution provided for well-thought out, well-armoured and fully-enclosed full-tracked vehicles, eliminating the rotating turret, and

The Elefant armoured recovery vehicle lacked the supplementary armour of the tank destroyer version.

Two Elefants knocked out during the summer offensive in Russia in July 1943. Assigned to Army Group Model, the northern arm of the pincer movement against the Kursk salient they were unable to provide enough momentum for the German attack. Determined Russian resistance stopped the offensive and forced the Germans on to the defensive.

with their guns mounted in limited traverse. Both categories existed side by side for almost two years before the latter became predominant. Eventually these vehicles replaced to a large extent the conventional battle tank as German tactics responded to the defensive nature of warfare toward the end of the European conflict. The Ferdinand or, as it was later called, the Elefant, was something in between. The necessity of having to use all conceivable means to balance the situation forced the Germans to utilise all available equipment. Ninety chassis were around; they had to be used. They became equipment for two battalions of an armoured regiment (Panzer Abteilung 654). Each battalion had three companies plus a headquarters and supply section. Each company consisted of three platoons with four Elefants each. The headquarters company had two Elefants, one Panzer III and a number of soft-skinned vehicles. With reserve units allocated to these outfits, the total number of tank destroyer vehicles per battalion amounted to 44. They were intended to be used for break-through of defensive lines and for engagement against enemy tanks, anti-tank guns and artillery. Normally, two companies attacked in two front echelons, while the third company acted as a back-up unit.

JULY OFFENSIVE, 1943

On 5th July 1943 the great German offensive, Operation Citadel, started in the area of Bjelgorod in Russia. A total of 17 armoured, three armoured infantry and 16 infantry divisions attacked in a pincer movement north and south of Kursk, against heavily fortified Russian positions in an attempt to change the course of the war. All the Elefants assigned to Army Group Model in the north participated. But they could not fulfill their obligation. Mechanically unreliable because of the complicated technical layout, short of ammunition because of limited storage, and unable to defend themselves against determined close-range attacks, they were never able to utilise the potential of their powerful gun. The attack bogged down after six miles and most of the vehicles which could not be retrieved fell into Russian hands during the ensuing counter-attacks. Removal of incapacitated equipment from the battlefield was a trying task, since the 18 t. half-track tractors normally

Battle experience in Stalingrad prompted Hitler to demand a vehicle equipped with a superstructure capable of ramming and destroying buildings. An order to Porsche resulted in this wooden mock-up of the "Ramm-Tiger".

used for this purpose proved unable to move these heavy vehicles. However the bulk of them were somehow recovered, reconditioned and re-used on other parts of the front. They disappeared rather rapidly from the scene because of spare-part shortages, and the fact that copper for the electrical components was in too short supply. Removed from the Eastern Front, some of them saw action in Italy in 1944, where road conditions soon made it impossible for these vehicles to operate. They were either abandoned, captured or destroyed by their own crews.

To sum up, it should be emphasised that the prototype Porsche vehicles served a definite technical purpose, namely to explore all possibilities of a petrol-electric drive train. This development found its climax in the adaptation of its features during the construction of the largest armoured fighting vehicle ever built, the 187 ton PzKpfw Maus. It was proven beyond any doubt, however, that a strictly technical solution, without consideration for military necessities, could only be a compromise at the best, and these findings were rather drastically demonstrated during the brief battlefield appearance of the Elefant.

Thus, we can conclude that we have been introduced to an interesting armoured fighting vehicle, reflecting in its own way the genius of its designer, Professor Dr. F. Porsche, who had proved yet again that he could master any conceivable area of mechanical design.

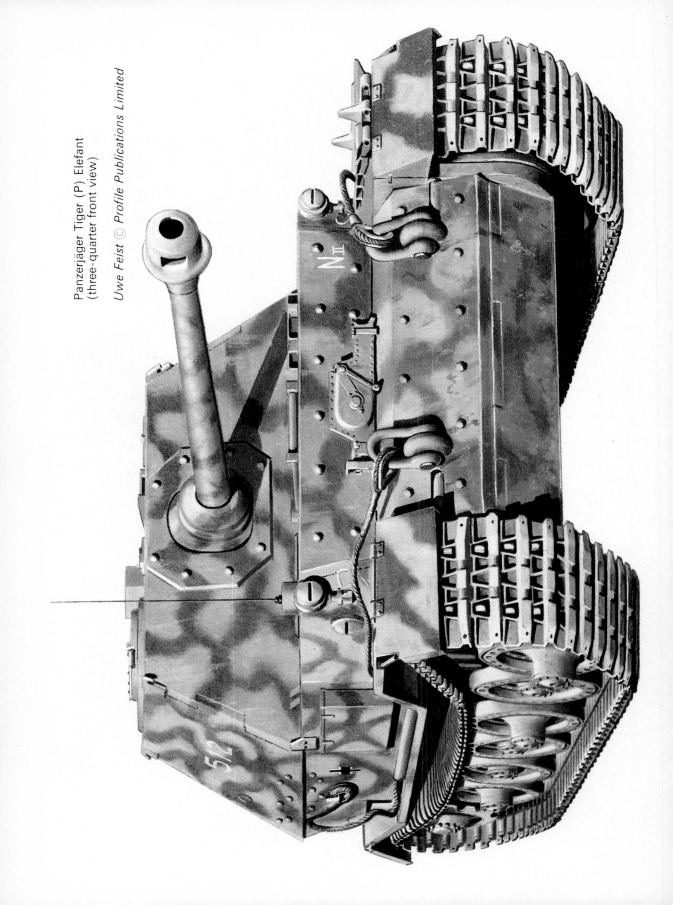

Panzerjäger Tiger (P) Elefant
(three-quarter front view)

Uwe Feist © *Profile Publications Limited*

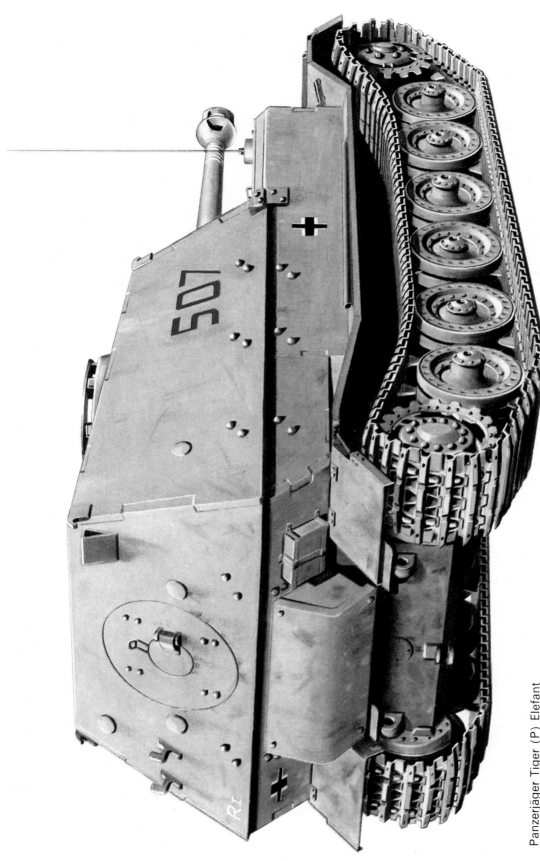

Panzerjäger Tiger (P) Elefant
(three-quarter rear view)

Maus I with its turret fitted complete with armament.

German Super-Heavy Tanks Maus and E-100

by John F. Milsom

DURING the course of the war the Germans directed a large amount of resources to the development of super-heavy armoured fighting vehicles, ranging in weight from 100 to 1500 tons. Apart from a super-heavy gun carriage called Grille and a heavy self-propelled mortar Karl (which was actually used in operations), only two vehicles, both tanks, were actually built. These were the Maus (Mouse) and the E-100.

It is uncertain just how much the men in the German tank industry generally believed in the future of heavy tanks. At the end of the war, all the engineers interrogated claimed that they were always opposed to such vehicles as impractical in combat and uneconomical of production resources. It is quite possible that their stories were coloured by later experience. At any rate, in 1942, many men must have felt differently because two Mouse vehicles were started at that time, together with one E-100. Both types were to use a turret mounting a 128 mm. gun (one layout showed a 150 mm. gun) as main armament with a coaxial 75 mm. gun. The armour was about 30% heavier than on the Tiger II. The weight of the Maus was about 200 tons and that of the E-100 about 150 tons. For the Maus, Porsche was developing all his own components, and the E-100 was to use Tiger II components until larger power plants were developed. Both developments were progressing quite slowly and there is no doubt that at the end of the war interest had ceased completely.

THE MAUS—DEVELOPMENT HISTORY

On June 8th 1942 Porsche was interviewed in Berlin by Hitler and Speer. The question of fitting the 8,8 cm. L/71

gun in the Tiger (P) was discussed, and then Porsche was asked to start work on a chassis to mount a 12,8 cm. or 15 cm. gun in a revolving turret, or, as an alternative, an 18 cm. gun as a piece of SP equipment. A coaxial 7,5 cm. gun was also to be incorporated.

At this time, Porsche was still President of the Panzer Kommission, and very influential due to his close relationship with Hitler. He pushed the design of super-heavy tanks. Heydekampf, Kniepkampf and Guderian were, on the other hand, of the opinion that tanks of this size did not have much future. When the project was first suggested, the vehicle was referred to as Mammut (Mammoth). They were intended to operate in pairs with the support of smaller AFVs. Basic armour requirements were to be:

> Front: 200 mm.
> Sides: 180 mm.
> Track guards: 100 mm.
> Turret front: 220 mm.
> Turret sides and rear: 200 mm.

The Porsche organisation was primarily responsible for designing the machinery of this vehicle, which was given the Porsche type number 205. They also, of course, had certain responsibilities in connection with the hull.

Porsche suggested that he should design an air-cooled diesel engine for the vehicle but was over-ruled by Speer on the grounds of insufficient time. A Daimler-Benz aircraft engine was to be used instead. No stipulations were made as to the size, weight or performance of the tank, and the extreme latitude given to Porsche is even more striking here than in the case of the Tiger. The tank was, from here on, to be known as Maus (Mouse).

Five views of the Maus during its trials, with a 55-ton weight set on the superstructure towards the rear of the vehicle to simulate the turret which was not yet completed. It was over 30 ft. long.

The Maus was an effort to give a relatively large armament protection and 360 degrees traverse, together with the most adequate mobility. It was Porsche's opinion that the vehicle should not be classed as a tank in the strict sense of the word, but as a heavily-armoured mobile pill-box.

As with his Tiger design, Porsche decided to use electric transmission again but this was, of course, before the use of copper was given as one of the official reasons for the rejection of Tiger (P). He states, however, that he would have used it in any case as he considered

it by far the most practical method of obtaining light steering of an ultra-heavy vehicle. It was decided, however, to redesign the system.

Towards the end of 1942 the Heereswaffenamt appointed a Col. Haenel to act in the capacity as chaser to all firms who were involved in the construction of the Mouse. His directive was to pay continual visits to all such firms, threatening them with serious penalties if they fell behind schedule in their work. Haenel's first visit to Stuttgart was on December 18th 1942 when he issued orders that the Mouse was to be completed and

Assembly of the E-100 prototype was not complete when the war ended in May 1945. The partially finished vehicle was captured by the Allies. It was 869 cm long (without barrel overhang)

ready for trials on May 5th 1943. This was naturally considered as being more humorous than anything else and no notice was taken.

Slightly before this, at the end of November, a hitch occurred as Daimler-Benz intimated that they could not supply the diesel engine which Porsche had proposed to use. The only other possible engine was the MB 509, an I.C. engine, which therefore had to be used in spite of Porsche's desire for a C.I. engine. It was found that this engine could only be installed in an inverted position necessitating the provision of a vertical gear train to bring the drive down to the level of the generator shaft.

The next event of any interest was on January 4th 1943 when Porsche was ordered to Berlin for the purpose of showing Hitler a model of the Mouse. Hitler showed considerable interest but no concrete comments or suggestions were made.

On January 12th members of the Heereswaffenamt came to Stuttgart and the allotment of the construction was put on an official basis as follows:

Design and production of vehicle as a whole—
    Porsche KG
Hull and turret responsibility—Krupp
Engine development—Daimler-Benz
Electrical apparatus—Siemens-Schuckert
Suspension, tracks and gearing—Skoda, (Prague)
Assembly—Altmaerkische Kettenfabrik (Alkett)
Design and specification of tracks—Alkett.

There followed a very large conference at Berlin on

January 21st at which all outstanding major points were discussed, and it was decided to push on with the project as fast as possible. The only discordant voice appears to have been that of Kniepkampf (representing Wa. Prüf.6) who was positive that the vehicle would prove to be quite unsteerable.

Porsche was again summoned to Berlin on February 2nd 1943 and was informed by Haenel that he must incorporate a flame-thrower carrying 1,000 litres of fuel. He said that it could not be done but was over-ruled and was told that the flame-thrower was considered to be essential.

At this time it appears that the earliest possible completion of the Mouse was considered a matter of great urgency and there was a further "pressure" meeting between the Heereswaffenamt and representatives of the contracting firms at Stuttgart on February 10th. All the manufacturers protested against the inclusion of the flame-thrower on grounds that it would cause considerable delay in delivery dates, but it was again insisted upon. At the end of the meeting it was agreed that all firms would do their utmost but no actual dates were set.

The necessity for fitting the flame-thrower was the direct cause of a major change in design, i.e. a change from torsion-bar to volute-spring suspension. This was necessitated by the fact that a new suspension system had not been designed, the intention being to use Tiger (P) suspension units. The first detailed weight estimate

The partially completed prototype of the E-100 has been hoisted on to a low recovery trailer for removal by its captors.

had come out at 179·3 metric tons but this had increased slightly and with the addition of the flame-thrower (4900Kg) the total increase amounted to slightly more than $5\frac{1}{2}\%$. This could only be catered for by the inclusion of two additional suspension units (one on each side) but as there was not enough room to accommodate them this solution was not practicable. In collaboration with Skoda it was therefore decided to adopt a simple volute spring suspension as time was all-important and Porsche did not wish to design a new torsion-bar layout in a hurry and without time for proper mechanical testing. This appears to be the complete explanation for Porsche's departure from his favourite form of suspension.

At the end of February 1943 extensive tests of the somewhat complex engine cooling arrangements were carried out at the Technical Institute of Stuttgart under the supervision of Professor Kamm. These were found to be quite satisfactory.

Speer paid an unexpected visit to the Stuttgart offices on April 6th 1943 and remained for half-an-hour inspecting a full-size wooden model of the Mouse.

On April 10th orders were received to take the model to Berchtesgaden, doubtless as a result of Speer's inspection. It was accordingly dismantled and packed up but on April 16th the order was cancelled so it was re-assembled again. On May 6th the order came through for the second time and the model was finally inspected by Hitler at the Führerhauptquartier at Rastenburg on May 14th 1943. Complaints were made that the size of the tank made the 12,8 cm. gun like a child's toy and accordingly Krupp was ordered to prepare a new turret mounting a 15 cm. gun, the coaxial 7,5 cm. to be retained. It seems hardly probable that Hitler would have ordered a larger gun on purely aesthetic grounds but in point of fact it does appear that this is what actually occurred.

The Heereswaffenamt now began to complain about the amount of copper being used, so Rabe (Porsche's chief engineer) was sent to Zahnradfabrik of Friedrichs-hafen to discuss plans for using the well-known ZF electro-magnetic gearbox, developed by this firm before the war and by now further developed to provide seven ratios. Wiedman, a director of ZF, refused to do anything without an OKH contract and as this was not forthcoming the matter was dropped and the manufacture of the electric drive was continued without alteration.

On July 16th, the MB 509 engine arrived at Stuttgart and was sent to the Technical Institute for further trials both of itself and of the cooling system, under Professor Kamm. The only modifications necessary to convert the engine from aircraft to tank use had been minor detail to permit operation in an inverted position and a lowering of compression-ratio and boost pressure in order to allow for lower grade fuel. No troubles were experienced on these tests.

At the beginning of August it was decided to construct a second prototype tank as Daimler-Benz could now supply a diesel engine modified from the MB 517 motor boat engine.

Alkett had begun assembly of the first tank on August 1st when Krupp intimated that they could not keep their delivery dates on account of interruption by air-raids.

A very significant date is October 27th 1943 when Porsche and Rabe met Speer in Berlin and were told that no arrangements were going to be made for the eventual production of the Mouse. However, the construction of Mouse I (with MB 509 petrol engine) and Mouse II (with MB 517 diesel engine) was to be continued. (Speer and Saur stated that this project helped to clarify their ideas on the optimum size of heavy tanks. In Saur's opinion 80 tons was the economic limit in weight).

Krupp supplied the hull in the middle of September

Rear view of the partially assembled E-100 prototype. The tank was 448 cm wide.

and Mouse made its first trial run at Alkett on December 23rd 1943 with a 55-ton weight in place of the turret. This trial was satisfactory as far as it went and on January 10th 1944 the tank was sent to Böblingen near Stuttgart for extensive trials on the tank-testing ground there. Herr Zadnik was the driver on these trials.

The trials were very trouble-free except for several cases of spring failure and it is stated that these would have been stiffened slightly had the tank gone into production. There was also a bearing failure in the auxiliary gearbox which could not be accounted for, as no trouble had been experienced with this assembly on the test-rig. The tracks gave no trouble nor did the two-stage epicyclic reduction—about both of which Porsche had expressed concern earlier.

Herr Zadnik reported that the steering was excellent, it being possible to turn the tank on its own axis, with, of course, contra-rotation of the tracks. Manoeuvrability and cross-country performance were tested on snow, ice, grass, mud and hard surfaces, and independent observers, who had witnessed earlier tests of different vehicles, are reputed to have told Zadnik that the Mouse did everything that the Panther did. This indicates very exceptional resistance to bellying and is explained by the phenomenally high ratio of track width to belly width. The maximum speed on a hard surface with full motor speed was 13 k.p.h., and on weakening the field to a minimum a speed of 22 k.p.h. was recorded.

At about this time instructions were given to Porsche by Hitler that the complete tank, with turret and guns, was to be ready by June.

Mouse II, to be fitted with the MB 517 engine, arrived at Böblingen on March 20th 1944, and was put on one side until such time as the engine was delivered.

On May 3rd the first turret arrived from Krupp in a bare condition. A few days later the guns arrived (12,8 cm. L/55 and 7,5 cm. L/36·5) together with the powered traverse and all other turret fittings. By June 9th the turret had been assembled and fitted to the tank (by Krupp engineers) and further trials were started. These were very satisfactory and performance was slightly up, doubtless due to the fact that the turret weighed rather less than 55 tons (the weight previously fitted). At the beginning of October orders were received to send the tank to Kummersdorf.

Immediately after this, the MB 517 engine arrived at

Böblingen. During tests in September 1944, this engine had shown itself to be superior to the MB 509, and, in addition, special manifold cooling arrangements had been made in order to overcome the trouble experienced with the petrol engine.

The engine was installed and Mouse II was sent straight to Kummersdorf without trials. This was at the beginning of November and was on instructions from the OKH, the reason for these instructions not being known. On arrival at Kummersdorf the engine was started and immediately broke its crankshaft, this being traced to faulty alignment of engine and generator.

In the middle of March 1945 another engine was delivered to Kummersdorf and Porsche sent a team of fitters to install it. These returned to Stuttgart on April 3rd having completed their job and successfully run the engine, but they state that the tank had not been driven up to the moment of their departure.

Thus the Mouse situation at the end of the war in May 1945 was:

a) Mouse I, with MB 509 petrol engine and 12,8 cm. L/55 and 7,5 cm. L/36·5 guns, completed and fully tested;

b) Mouse II, with MB 517 diesel engine but no turret, untested.

A further nine prototypes were in various stages of construction, and production plans had been made for 150. The vehicles at Kummersdorf were blown up by the Germans.

THE E-100—DEVELOPMENT HISTORY

Since the development of the E-100 tank was less spectacular than that of the Maus, and since it was never completed to the running stage, not a great deal is available on this vehicle. For this reason, a full technical description of the Maus is given, but only a partial one of the E-100.

The Heereswaffenamt knew that, should Hitler ever decide to build very many super-heavy tanks, they would have to supervise the construction, and as a result they wanted a design which could be most easily built. Such a vehicle was needed to offset Dr. Porsche's Mouse. Originally, Henschel was given an order to build a super-heavy version of the Royal Tiger, called the VK 7001 Tiger-Maus. This was, however, cancelled in favour of the E-100. As the result, the engineering staff of Adler, under the direction of Dr. Jenschke, were loaned to the Heereswaffenamt to design the new tank, the design of which was commenced at Friedberg on June 30th 1943. The E-100 was one of a whole range of new armoured fighting vehicles designated the "E" (Entwicklung=Development) series.* By the end of the war its parts were under assembly near Paderborn.

The Germans were seeking to gain more room in the fighting compartments of their tanks, necessitated by the stowage requirements of larger-calibre ammunition, without increasing the exterior dimensions appreciably. This unwillingness to increase the exterior dimensions was prompted by (1): realisation of the fact that armour is the larger percentage of total vehicle weight; therefore the size of the exposed space should be a minimum, and (2): the fact that there were limitations in size for

*The others were: E-5 (5 tons); E-10 (10–15 tons); E-25 (25–30 tons); E-50 (50 tons—Panther replacement); E-75 (75 tons—Tiger I and II replacement).

Close up of left side of E-100 hull showing the lugs used for securing massive armoured side skirts.

strategic mobility. To achieve maximum use of space in the fighting compartment and to increase the fighting ability of the tank, it was decided to do away with torsion-bar suspension and to eliminate the power-train from the crew compartment. The result was a new exterior-fitted suspension and a combined transmission, steering and final drive system packed into as small a space as possible for mounting in the rear of the engine. The positioning of the power-train in the engine compartment was expected to improve accessibility to a considerable degree, in addition to saving weight and space. In the design of this new vehicle the maintenance factor was to play a much more important part than had been the case in previous models. Another reason given for the elimination of the torsion-bar suspension was the desire to install a floor escape hatch in tanks, heretofore impossible with the interleaved wheel and torsion-bar suspension. Belleville washer springing was used instead and fitted externally, in an interleaved arrangement. The suspension system was developed by Dr. Lehr of M.A.N. at Augsburg. As regards the design of the new suspension units, a low spring rate was desirable to aid in reducing the pitch rate of the vehicle as low as possible.

Dr. Jenschke stated that the vehicle as a tank was obsolete as soon as the drawings were finished, due to inability to load the weapons in a turret mount.

E-100 used the same engine as the E 50/75 models,

based on the Maybach HL-230 P30. This 12-cylinder V engine developed 700 h.p. at 3000 r.p.m., which would have resulted in the low power/weight ratio of about 5 h.p./ton. A modified HL 234 engine with Bosch fuel injection developing 900 h.p. was completed. With super-charging this engine was to have developed between 1000 and 1200 h.p., which would have raised the power/weight ratio to 8·5 h.p./ton.

The gearbox was a Maybach 8-speed OG 40 1216B. The steering system (the same as used on the Tiger) was built by Henschel Werke at Kassel. The tracks were built by Adler. The M.A.N. suspension consisted of two-wheeled single springs in overlapping arrangement with two guide lugs, suspended by double spiral springs outside the hull. There were shock-absorbers on the inside. In combat a 1-metre steel track was to be used, which would have given a ground-pressure of 19·9 p.s.i. For rail transport a special new track was to be mounted.

Frontal armour was 200 mm. at 30° and side armour 120 mm. All armour was interlocked. A crane was fitted for lifting protection skirts and ammunition.

The turret was made by Fried. Krupp, Essen, and was very similar to that of the Mouse. As its completion was delayed, an equally heavy trial turret was to have been mounted for driving tests. The final turret was to have had a gun of calibre 17,4 or 15 cm. When the hull was completed, however, it was determined that the vehicle did not have sufficient space to carry a 50 ton turret as

Top view of partially assembled E-100 being examined by American troops. The tank was to be 332 cm high.

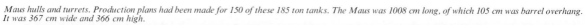

Maus hulls and turrets. Production plans had been made for 150 of these 185 ton tanks. The Maus was 1008 cm long, of which 105 cm was barrel overhang. It was 367 cm wide and 366 cm high.

originally planned. After some time, therefore, it was decided to alter the vehicle to an SP mounting.

Although the vehicle was produced at Adler Werke, assembly of the one prototype was half-complete at Henschel proving grounds (Haustenbeck near Paderborn) when the war ended. The project had been officially discontinued in June 1944.

MAUS DESCRIPTION

The general impression given by the interior of the Maus, in spite of its size, is that it is filled almost completely with a mass of complicated machinery. The production difficulties facing the designer were mainly as follows:

a) Overall size and weight—185 tons
b) A 12,8 cm. gun with 38 in. recoil and 60 in. ammunition. This necessitated an overall turret-ring diameter of 9 ft. 7 in.
c) Armour plate thickness up to 350 mm. (horizontal across the driver's front) and strong frontal floor armour against mines
d) Performance—top speed of $12\frac{1}{2}$ m.p.h.
e) Power unit—to provide 1200 h.p.
f) Transmission
g) Suspension—incorporating small vertical movements
h) Transportation.

The hull of the vehicle was designed as an armoured box, spanning the entire width of the chassis. The track and suspension arrangements caused two sponsons which ran the length of the vehicle and were large since the tracks were more than 43 inches wide. There was thus a central well also running the length of the tank filled with the complicated power and drive train. The front portion of the tank had the fuel tanks in each sponson, and in the compartment which contained the driver and the wireless operator in the central well between them. Behind this was the compartment containing the engine, cooling fans, radiators etc. Again, behind this, the main generator was placed centrally, and

in this transverse section all the nearside sponson was occupied by ammunition stowage, and the offside partly so, and partly by batteries and the auxiliary power plant. The rear part housed the propulsive motors in the sponsons, the output from these being inwards into the well through transfer cases to the final drives and sprockets which were, of course, in the suspension tunnels. The crew in the fighting compartment were situated above the main generator and thus, being cut off from the forward compartment by the engine and its cooling apparatus, had no access to it. The air intake was situated centrally above the engine and just behind the driver and wireless operator. The wireless and inter-communication equipment was situated on the operator's right-hand side in the forward compartment. The centre of gravity of the vehicle was further to the rear than usual. This was due to the location of the turret. The armour was all rolled with the exception of the turret front and mantlet. A 100 mm. thick front belly plate was incorporated as an anti-mine precaution. One access door was provided for the driver and operator and two for the crew in the turret. Some of the periscopes were of conventional design, but others were specially prepared for submersion. The driver's seat had two positions; one for driving in action (closed down) and the other for driving with the escape hatch open and the driver's head exposed. His controls were fixed relative to the seat position, so that he was given the maximum of comfort in both positions.

Two types of engine were considered—compression-ignition (MB 517) or air-cooled petrol (DB 603). Porsche was in favour of the compression-ignition type. The two engines used in the Maus I and II were developments of the Daimler-Benz 603 inverted 12-cylinder V petrol aircraft engine. That in the Maus I was called the Mercedes-Benz 509 and retained the petrol-injection characteristics, while that in the Maus II was called the Mercedes-Benz 517 being installed in the upright position and converted to C.I. There was a 2-cylinder 8 h.p. auxiliary petrol engine which was used to give pressurization to the crew compartment for air-con-

Maus turret. It weighed 50 tons and was almost identical to the turret intended for the E-100.

ditioning purposes and snorkelling. It was also used for heating, poison-gas filtration and battery charging.

The electric transmission provided the tank with an infinitely variable range of ratios. It also provided a means of self-starting and was used for propulsion during submersion, the power being provided through cables by a second tank. The electric motors developed a speed of 20 k.p.h. at 3100 r.p.m. They drove simple reduction gears that could be shifted for either road or cross-country operation. The final drives and sprockets were in the suspension tunnels.

A schematic design utilising bogey type torsion-bar suspension (the type used on the experimental Porsche Jagdtiger) was considered, but abandoned due to space considerations. Later a new unconventional volute-spring type was used. This consisted of 24 identical double rollers assembled in 12 bogies, 6 on each side. The bogies were attached to a cross-beam which in turn was secured to the hull and apron. Each pair of bogies was attached to a double crank-arm, and was sprung by double coil springs. The road wheels were similar to those on the Tiger II and had steel rims with rubber inner liners. The tracks were produced by Altmaerkische Kettenfabrik and were 44 inches wide.

The turret was practically identical to that intended for the E-100. The front was rounded and consisted of a single plate. Three bare hulls and turrets were found on the Krupp proving ground at Meppen. Two turrets were without armament but a mounting for a 12,8 cm. KwK 82 L/55 (originally referred to as 12,8 cm. KwK 44 (Maus)) and a coaxial 7,5 cm. KwK 44 L/36·5 was under construction. The cradle in which the guns were mounted was referred to as Mauswiege (Mouse cradle). The gun was sent to Meppen in November 1943 for firing trials. It was intended eventually to mount a 15 cm. weapon of lower velocity 38 calibres long. An AAMG was also to be installed in the turret roof, as well as a light mortar.

The turret was fitted with a shock-absorption device to distort and absorb the horizontal energy components of violent blows given to it. It was of welded construction, massive interlocks being used. Total weight of the turret with armament and ready-to-use ammunition was 50 tons. It was rotationally out of balance. Assisted manual loading was used for the main armament. Both guns were fired electrically. The guns originally used fixed ammunition, although provisions were made later to use separate ammunition for the main armament.

The Maus was submersible to 26 feet. Tanks were to work in pairs, power being supplied to one, whilst submerged, by the other, stationed on the river bank. Lowering of the turret into the sealing ring was achieved by means of eccentrically located bearings of the six turret ring rollers. Two trunks were to be used initially, the forward one as an air-intake, and the rear as an exit. In this scheme each tank was to propel itself by its own petrol-electric machinery. This was, however, abandoned on account of the fact that full power from the engines could not be developed, that difficulties existed with cooling air and exhaust gas disposal, and that it appeared unlikely that these tanks would operate singly. The successor scheme incorporated one trunk only. The electric transmission of the tank was used but power was supplied to it by cable from another vehicle stationed on the river bank. By operating in pairs the tanks could thus push and pull each other across. This latter operation (including sealing) would have taken about three-quarters of an hour. On reaching the far bank the crew would dismount to remove the trunk etc.

A special war flat was designed to carry this vehicle and at least one was made and used.

SPECIFICATION PANZERJÄGER TIGER (P) ELEFANT

General
Designation: 8,8 cm. Panzerjager 43/2 (L/71) Tiger P (SdKfz 184)
Crew: Six—commander, gunner, two loaders, radio operator, driver
Battle weight: 65 metric tons.
Power/weight ratio 8,16 b.h.p./ton.
Ground pressure: 3·44 lb./sq. in.

Dimensions
Length overall: 26 ft. 8 in.
Height: 9 ft. 10 in.
Width: 11 ft. 1 in.
Track centres: 8 ft. 9 in.
Track width: 25 in.

Armament
Main armament: One 8,8 cm. StuK 43/2 L/71 in limited traverse, centre fighting compartment.
Auxiliary armament: One machine gun 34 (loosely stowed inside vehicle), two sub-machine guns 38. (Later vehicles with ball-mounted machine gun 34 in the bow.)

Fire Control
Maximum elevation +14° to −8°.
Maximum traverse to 14°.
Traverse and elevation by hand wheels through gunner.
Firing system: Electric primer operated by trigger.

Ammunition
50 rounds for 88 mm. gun.
600 rounds for 7,9 mm. machine gun.
384 rounds for 9 mm. sub-machine gun.

Sighting and Vision
Main armament: One SF1. Zf 1a binocular telescope.
Commander: Telescope.
Driver: Telescope.

Communication
W/T set (transmitter/receiver/intercom): Fu 5 and Fu 2.

Armour
Machinable chromium—molybdenum armour.
Plate: All-welded construction, superstructure partially interlocked. Austentic welding.
Hull: Nose 100 + 100 mm. 31°, front plate 100 + 100 mm. 11°, lower sides 80 mm. vertical, upper sides 80 mm. vertical, rear 80 mm., 45°, top 30 mm. horizontal, bottom 20 + 30 mm. horizontal.
Superstructure: Front 200 mm. 22°, sides 80 mm. 31°, rear 80 mm. 19°, roof 30 mm. 87°.
Engines: Two Maybach "HL 120 TRM", gasoline 60° V-12 cylinder, water-cooled 11,867 cm., together 530 b.h.p. at 3,000 r.p.m.
Fuel: 240 gallons in two tanks on each side of the engine compartment.
Transmission: Porsche/Siemens-Schuckert petrol-electric drive with one generator and two electrical drive motors. Final drive ratio 16,75:1, three speeds. Electrical steering, hydro-pneumatic assisted.
Suspension: Three bogies each with two bogie wheels each per side, mounted on primary and secondary arms, incorporating longitudinal torsion bars.
Steel-rimmed road wheels. 31 in. diameter.
Track: Type Kgs 62/640/130, cast manganese steel, 109 links per track, 24 in. wide, track pitch 5 in.

Electrical System
12 V. dynamo. Two 12 V. batteries—120 Ah. Bosch BNG 4/24, 4 h.p. starter motors.

Performance
Maximum road speed: 12·5 m.p.h.
Cross-country speed: 6 m.p.h.
Maximum gradient: 22°.
Trench crossing: 10 ft. 6 in.
Wading depth: 4 ft.
Road range street: 95 miles. Cross-country: 55 miles.

Dating back to 1927, this Krauss Maffei MZ 10 four-wheel drive tractor could be converted into a half-tracked vehicle. It was one of the very first prototypes for a series of half-tracked vehicles used for towing purposes and equipped with armoured superstructures as armoured personnel carriers.
(Spielberger Collection)

Mittlerer Schützenpanzerwagen SdKfz 251

by Walter J. L. Spielberger

ONE of the first attempts to provide an armoured vehicle for infantry was made by the British as early as 1918 when the Mark IX, capable of carrying 50 men and a crew of four, was introduced. The years after World War I saw additional efforts in this direction, restricted at first only by economic conditions. The principal aim in attempting to motorize infantry units and their support elements, was to provide maximum mobility for these units and particularly to assure their compatibility with the expanding tank force. Mechanization, although strongly resisted, was inevitable. France and Britain appeared to lead the field in those early days and carried out numerous experiments, using soft-skinned wheeled, half-tracked and even full-tracked vehicles. But, while armour protection for these units was contemplated, it was never applied in mass production.

During this period Capt. B. H. Liddell Hart had already concluded, by comparing Genghiz Khan's attack of 1241 with the potentialities of a modern tank force, that "fully motorized armed forces have to be able to perform similar feats to the marauding hordes of the Mongol army." He considered it entirely possible for armoured groups to achieve strategic breakthroughs by eliminating enemy supply routes and maintenance bases in deep thrusts behind enemy lines.

He found it essential to support such an armoured force with mobile infantry, artillery, and engineers to enable them to operate completely independently. But such progressive thinking was not accepted and the lessons to be drawn from experimental vehicles and tactical exercises were not appreciated. By the early 'thirties, the tanks were again largely envisaged as infantry support weapons and slowed to their walking pace. The lead which the pioneers of armour in Britain and France had gained was now irrevocably lost. In Germany, on the other hand, where integrated, mobile, armoured forces found more favour, the creation of large armoured formations in division strength after 1933 was pushed ahead so fast that it taxed the already overburdened automotive industry virtually to breaking point. Spearhead armoured fighting vehicles had to be procured quickly and in substantial numbers and were given first priority, while the infantry remained largely foot-bound. This compromise was gradually overcome within the Light and Panzer divisions by the use of soft-skinned four or six-wheeled troop transport vehicles, mostly of commercial origin.

While such a solution assured reasonable mobility, given a good road network, the more forward-looking studies of future war conditions showed that units

The production version of the Leichter Zugkraftwagen SdKfz 11, a three ton tractor used mainly to tow the 10·5 cm. light howitzer. Its chassis was utilized almost unchanged as the basis of the medium armoured personnel carrier. (Spielberger Collection)

Some of the development prototypes were equipped with rear engines. They were designed as turreted armoured combat vehicles for cavalry units. The model shown is Hanomag type H8 (H). (Imperial War Museum)

Ausf. A and B of the medium MTW during the attack in France in 1940. Vehicles belong to 1st Panzer Division, with the Panzer Group of General Guderian, which spear-headed the drive into central France. At the left is one of the very early Sturmgeschütz units. (Spielberger Collection)

thus equipped would have no certainty of success. Wheeled vehicles could never match the cross-country ability of their fully-tracked counterparts. At the same time, a fully-tracked and armoured vehicle for transporting infantry was not officially considered to be feasible and was not seriously contemplated.

THE HALF-TRACK SOLUTION

As early as 1927–28, a highly-specialized industry already existed, turning out military half-track vehicles of extraordinarily high quality. They were in great demand by all units needing tractors to tow their equipment. But the usual production bottlenecks hampered efforts to meet this demand. Beginning in 1935, attempts were made to provide armour protection for some of these vehicles, resulting in proto-types with various drive-train layouts.

The most suitable chassis to carry a fully-equipped infantry squad under light armour protection which emerged from these trials was the standard 3-ton half-track tractor. Only minor modifications to the chassis were necessary, and prototypes of an armoured personnel carrier or *Gepanzerter Mannschafts Trans-*

portwagen (MTW) appeared in 1938. A company of the infantry regiment of the 1st Panzer Division, stationed at Weimar, received their first complement of these vehicles in the spring of 1939, and used them successfully in Poland.

The versatility of these vehicles was quickly appreciated and an ever-increasing number of armoured half-tracks left the production lines of various manufacturers throughout the War. They saw service in all theatres and almost every arm of the German forces used them in substantial numbers. Because of their application, generally in support or transport rôles, they never made headlines. But they became indispensable and served with such distinction that they are now seen in perspective as part of the history of German armour.

DEVELOPMENT HISTORY

The history of the half-track tractor from which the armoured vehicle was subsequently derived can be traced back to a parent development company, the Hansa-Lloyd-Goliath Werke AG. of Bremen which was charged in 1933 with the development of a tractor capable of towing loads of up to 3 tons weight. Design work was started in that year and the first prototype of the so-called "3 t. half-track and HK. 600 series" was completed by 1934. Equipped with a 3·5 litre Borgward six-cylinder petrol engine, the vehicle received the designation "HL kl 2". During 1936 a second prototype, the "HL kl 3", replaced the original vehicle. Production started in 1936 with the next development, the "HL kl 5", still equipped with the same engine, and 505 vehicles were built. During this period several other prototypes were built for development and trials with armoured superstructures. They all had the engine located at the rear and originally carried the designations "HL kl 3 (H)" and, in 1936, "HL kl 4 (H)" (H=hinter=rear). This development period was concluded in 1938, when models of the type "H 8 (H)" appeared. This year also saw the introduction of the final version of the half-track tractor, the type "H kl 6". Equipped now with a Maybach engine, it remained in production until the end of 1944. By the end of 1942 the German Army already had a total of 4,209 of these vehicles in use. Thus a chassis was developed and available in numbers which could be utilized as a basis for an armoured troop carrier capable of carrying a squad of nine men, a driver, and a commander. Armour protection was specified to 12 mm. thickness in front and 8 mm. on the flanks. This final solution was still a compromise, but time was short and only existing vehicle components could be considered.

The armoured personnel carrier was in fact never developed into a fully fledged fighting vehicle, as Guderian had originally envisaged. Like the soft-skinned vehicles pressed into this specialized rôle, it was intended merely to carry infantry units to the battle area, where they were expected to dismount and fight on foot. It was not sufficiently realized during the vital early development period that conditions later on would force Panzergrenadier units to fight from their vehicles as they swept forward with the tanks. But the development of a basically new infantry fighting vehicle was by this time no longer possible. It can be said that in Germany, at least, where the requirement was foreseen, its realization was largely thwarted by the higher priorities given to other projects pressing on the fully extended German war industries.

The Ordnance number given to the vehicle finally developed was *Sonderkraftfahrzeug* 251 and the official designation: *Mittlerer Gepanzerter Mannschaftskraftwagen*. The Hanomag company of Hanover was charged with the development of the chassis to make it suitable for use with the armoured superstructure designed by Buessing-NAG of Berlin-Oberschoeneweide. The first prototypes underwent trials at Kummersdorf at the end of 1938 and the issue to troops commenced in the spring of 1939. A few companies were actually equipped with these vehicles for the campaign against Poland. They were intended to be used for many purposes. Among the rôles envisaged were the transport of machine-gun squads, engineer squads and towing the light, 75 mm. infantry howitzer. A special version was intended as an ambulance.

Three basic vehicle models, *Ausführung* A, B and C, had appeared by 1940, differentiated only by minor variations from each other.

Intensive training and exploitation of the battle experience gained in Poland resulted in much improved tactical use of these vehicles during the *blitzkrieg* against France. This campaign in turn produced valuable lessons which resulted in yet further improvements for the initial phase of the campaign against Russia in 1941. Now officially designated *Schützenpanzerwagen* (SPW) (=Armoured

Personnel Carrier (APC)), the basic vehicle was armed with machine-guns behind armoured gun shields. Platoon leader vehicles carried the 37 mm. anti-tank gun.

FIREPOWER

These vehicles wrote an entirely new chapter in armoured warfare. The tank at last had found a tactical partner. Of course, the half-tracks were handicapped by the shortcomings of an interim solution and particularly by their limited cross-country ability. The open top, while allowing for good observation and freedom of movement, also made them vulnerable to enemy defences. The relatively thin armour afforded protection only against small arms fire and shell fragments. Nevertheless, as the German armies plunged into the vast wilderness of Russia and extended their lines ever further across the Western Desert towards Egypt, the ubiquitous half-tracks, armed to fight with the Panzer spearheads, became the most numerous and valued vehicle of all arms.

Additional manufacturers joined in the production programme which was increased to such an extent that all Panzer divisions could at last be equipped with an SPW battalion. Even more important was the increase in fire power achieved by these battalions which were now able to carry the following weaponry: 30 light machine-guns, four heavy machine-guns, two medium 81 mm. mortars, three 37 mm. anti-tank guns and two 75 mm. L/24 tank guns. In addition, each regiment received a platoon of flame thrower SPWs, while some

A radio communication vehicle, SdKfz 251/3, during the French campaign, 1940.   *(Spielberger Collection)*

French prisoners of war passing SdKfz 251 MTWs during the French campaign in 1940. Note the canvas to cover the open tops of the vehicles.
(Spielberger Collection)

Illustration shows the large double door and hinging mechanism in the rear used on all but the late Ausf. D. vehicles. Also clearly indicated is the pivot for the second machine-gun. This an Ausf. B. captured from the Afrika Korps.
(Imperial War Museum)

This picture shows clearly the front end arrangement and the drive sprocket of the same Afrika Korps vehicle. Exhaust system was located on both sides of the vehicle. Engine cooling was provided through the flap on the bonnet, which could be remotely-controlled from the driver's seat.
(Imperial War Museum)

This unit, SdKfz 251/10, is equipped with the 3·7 cm. anti-tank gun and was issued to platoon leaders in 1940. It acted as a support vehicle until the 7·5 cm. gun became standard equipment. The chassis is that of an Ausf. A.
(H. Nowarra)

A standard Ausf. C equipped with full armament including the armoured shield of the forward machine-gun. Earlier vehicles were modified to carry this shield. The rear machine-gun was demountable as part of the armament of the dismounted squad. Note the enlarged, flat, front armoured plate and protected air intakes on the sides of the engine compartment.
(Spielberger Collection)

Rommel's command vehicle SdKfz 251/6 crossing a bridge in France, followed by motorcycle riders and an eight-wheeled armoured radio vehicle.
(Col. Robert Icks)

Panzer divisions had SPWs equipped with launching platforms for heavy rockets.

In 1943 the SdKfz 251 *Ausf.* D appeared with a considerably modified superstructure. It had cleaner lines and was designed to accept the most modern mass production procedures. Matching of hull components was simplified and the ballistic properties improved. At least 20 different versions were now anticipated not only for the Panzergrenadier but also for artillery, engineer, anti-aircraft, medical and communication units. These vehicles remained in action until the very last days of the War. Unit price (without armament and radio equipment) was RM 22,560.

OTHER DEVELOPMENTS

Attempts to standardize production within the so-called "Schnell-Program" in 1939 resulted in new prototypes for the three-ton half-track series, named H 7 and built by Hanomag. Also in 1939 both Hanomag and Demag of Wetter-Ruhr worked on a successor vehicle for all three-ton half-track vehicles. While Hanomag developed a standard tractor version, Demag designed an armoured vehicle called HKp 602. Hanomag also developed yet another vehicle, the HKp 603, directly intended to replace the SdKfz 251. Weighing eight tons, all these vehicles were equipped with a Maybach HL 45 Z engine, delivering 120 b.h.p. The development cycle was concluded in 1941–42, when Demag designed the type HKp 606, which again was supposed to replace all existing SPW versions. With a total weight of seven metric tons, these prototypes had the Maybach HL 50 engine installed, coupled with a Maybach pre-selective transmission. They had Argus disc brakes. All these developments, as interesting as they might appear technically, never went beyond the prototype stage. Finally, evidence exists of attempts to utilize components of the Czechoslovak

Praga Panzer 38 (t) to create a fully-enclosed, full-tracked Armoured Personnel Carrier—a development which materialized only 20 years later with the introduction of the new HS 30 APC to the Bundeswehr.

PRODUCTION

Mass production of three-ton half-tracks was started by Hanomag in 1937. Only ten tractor chassis were built during this year. Since the chassis was developed for either the tractor or the SPW production figures were not separated. Hanomag thus built 6,270 chassis by the end of 1944, while Borgward (formerly Hansa-Lloyd-Goliath) had produced 2,572 units by the end of 1943. The official Speer Report—Nr. M 1362/45 g. Rs.—published on January 27th, 1945, mentions the following production figures for the 3 t. *Mannschafts-transportwagen:* 1940—348, 1941—947, 1942—1,190, 1943—4,250, 1944—7,800. Production figures for 1945 are no longer available.

Based on these figures, there can be no doubt that this unit was by far the most numerous armoured vehicle of the German Wehrmacht. To handle production on this scale, various other manufacturers had to be engaged and in addition to the aforementioned two companies, Weserhuette of Bad Oeynhausen, Wumag of Goerlitz and F. Schichau of Elbing were involved. Chassis were supplied by Adler of Frankfurt, Auto-Union of Chemnitz and Skoda of Pilsen. The latter company, being located in Czechoslovakia, continued producing the same vehicle for the new Czech army until the mid-fifties. The superstructures for these vehicles were manufactured by the following companies: Ferrum of Laurahuette, Schoeller & Bleckmann of Muerzzuschlag, Boehmisch-Leipa of Bohemia and Steinmueller of Gummersbach. Production priority was indicated by a group "SS" classification, the highest priority available.

SdKfz 251 DESCRIBED

The standard half-tracked vehicle of the German Army had the front end of a conventional wheeled vehicle, with a front axle carrying a pair of pneumatic tyred, Ackerman-steered front wheels. Most of the weight of the vehicle, however, was borne on two flexible, endless tracks which were supported upon road wheels and which extended the full length of the chassis available behind the front wheels. The frame of the vehicle was a rigid, welded assembly consisting of two deep-webbed side members and thirteen closely-spaced cross-members. Armour plates were bolted beneath the frame, while smaller vertical plates protected the webs of the side members. The rigid construction of the frame itself, aided by the reinforcement of the "underbelly" armour plating and the armoured body, resulted in an extremely rigid body frame unit. The hull, open at the top, was welded and ballistically well shaped. It was made in two sections, secured together by bolted flanges behind the driving compartment. While *Ausf.* A, B and C had both bolted and welded armour plates, later versions starting with *Ausf.* D, had all welded construction.

Armour thickness of the frontal plate was 14·5 mm., while side plates were 8 mm. thick. The superstructure normally housed two seats for the driver and commander and two longitudinal benches to accommodate the rest of the crew. A centre aisle was provided, ending in a large double door in the rear of the vehicle for easy accessibility. Two visors were provided in the front vertical plate and one on each side of the driving compartment. Two large hatches on top of the engine compartment gave access to the power plant. The roof was open and covered only by a canvas tilt to protect the interior against the weather.

The engine was the standard six-cylinder water-cooled Maybach HL 42 TUKRRM petrol unit. Also built by Nordbau and Auto-Union, it had a bore of 90 mm. and a stroke of 110 mm. giving a displacement of 4,171 cc. Output was 100 b.h.p. at 2,800 r.p.m. It had an overhead camshaft.

The front axle beam was forged and was suspended on a single transverse leaf spring. Tubular wishbones braced the axle. Front wheels were of pressed steel with tyres of size 7,25–20 extra, or 190–18. Two shock absorbers completed the front axle assembly. No front wheel brakes were fitted. Each track of the rear suspension was carried by a driving spocket at the front and an idler wheel at the rear. Between these two were six pairs of staggered, rubber-tyred, pressed steel road wheels which carried the weight of the vehicle. The road wheels were suspended by transverse torsion bars, one to each wheel. They were housed in cross tubes of elliptical section, each carrying two torsion bars. The idler wheels also acted as track tensioners.

UNIQUE TRACKS

The light, flexible, lubricated track links were of unique and highly sophisticated construction—a special feature of the German half-track vehicles. The main body of each track shoe was cast and ribbed for strength, drilled and cored for lightness. Linked together by track pins, each was rigidly fixed to the forked end of one casting, while it was carried in needle

roller bearings in the opposite end of the adjacent shoe. A large tooth projected inwards from each shoe, while a rubber pad was fastened to the outside. The needle bearings were lubricated and thus required constant maintenance.

Torque from the engine was transmitted to the driving sprockets through a dry, twin-plate clutch (Fichtel & Sachs PF 220 K), a gearbox, a differential and two final drive units respectively. The gearbox was a Hanomag design, mounted in line with the power plant, but sufficiently set back to enable the differential unit to be situated transversely between the two. Short propeller shafts connected the clutch to the gearbox and the gearbox to the differential. The output shafts were connected to the final drive assemblies, which were part of the drive sprocket unit.

This SdKfz 251/1 shown here in Russia carried three frames on each side to mount either the 28 cm. high explosive or 32 cm. napalm rockets.
(Spielberger Collection)

Interior of the basic m.SPW as encountered in 1942 and 1943. This is normal squad vehicle, SdKfz 251/1. (Col. Robert Icks)

SdKfz 251/3/II, with antenna. This was the radio vehicle for tank co-operation. (Col. Robert Icks)

Engineer m.SPW Ausf. D, mounting bridging equipment and spare gasoline containers. They were used in numbers to assure mobility for tank formations. Mounting of both machine-gun 42s is clearly visible.　　(Col. Robert Icks)

SdKfz 251/11 shows the equipment as a telephone unit for the laying of field cables.　　(Col. Robert Icks)

m.SPW Ausf. C, in Russia. Spare tracks were carried on the front armour plate to provide additional protection.　　(Spielberger Collection)

The gearbox provided for a total of eight forward ratios and two reverse, since it was possible to select two alternative gear trains. A spur wheel differential was employed.

Steering was effected by a steering wheel, which had to be mounted at an inverted angle and connected to the steering column by angular gearing. The steering column itself incorporated disc type universal joints. The steering box was mounted on the left side and had two drop arms. The outer drop arm operated the front wheel steering in an orthodox manner, while the inner drop arm operated a spring connection to a cross-shaft and, via levers and cables, to internal expanding track brakes mounted on each side of the differential. Thus, normal steering through the front wheels was obtained by first movement of the steering wheel in either direction, while further movement brought the track brakes into operation. A front wheel position indicator was provided.

The hand brake operated through compensating cables to the track brakes on each side of the differential. The foot brake was air-servo assisted and operated on to internal expanding brake units, located inside the drive sprockets.

One fuel tank with a capacity of 35 gallons was mounted in the centre section of the frame. One Bosch, 300 watt, 12 volt generator supplied all electrical outlets and charged a battery on early models. Newer issues came equipped with two batteries. A 1·8 h.p. 12 volt Bosch starter was installed.

VARIANTS

The *mittlerer gepanzerter Kraftwagen* SdKfz 251 or "medium armoured vehicle" served as a basis for all medium armoured personnel carriers of the German Wehrmacht. The Hanomag type designation was H kl 6 p. The standard vehicle for the armoured infantry units was designated **SdKfz 251/1** *mittlerer Schützenpanzerwagen*. It carried a 12-man crew, two machine-guns 34 or 42, and two sub-machine-guns. It was followed by the **SdKfz 251/2**, a medium mortar carrier with a crew of eight, one machine-gun, two sub-machine-guns, and one 81 mm. mortar. Five versions of a wireless vehicle, *mittlerer Funkpanzerwagen* SdKfz 251/3 were designated. Of these, SdKfz 251/3 V was the so-called *Kommando Panzerwagen,* a vehicle intended for higher general staff officers. It was easily recognisable by its obvious frame antenna suspended around its superstructure. All these versions had a crew of seven, one machine-gun and two sub-machine-guns, but varied considerably in their radio equipment. **SdKfz 251/4** towed the light 7·5 cm. infantry howitzer (le IG), it also carried the ammunition for this weapon. Again, it had a crew of seven with one machine-gun and one sub-machine-gun. **SdKfz 251/5** was issued as an engineer vehicle, with a crew of eight, two machine-guns 34 or 42, two sub-machine-guns and various engineer equipment.

In 1940, J. Gast KG. of Berlin-Lichtenberg was ordered to design modifications for SdKfz 251 or 251/1 to fire either 28 cm. H.E. or 32 cm. jellied gasoline rockets from frames attached to the sides of the vehicles. The device consisted of six individual frames, mounted on the armoured side plates of the vehicle. Three rockets were carried on each side.

Gaubschat of Berlin also modified the SPW for use as an artillery observation vehicle. The order was issued on September 1, 1940, and the first vehicles thus equipped were ready for troop trial in the spring of 1942.

Next on the official list was **SdKfz 251/6**, a *mittlerer Kommando Panzerwagen* again intended for general

The 3·7 cm Pak was soon replaced by the 7·5 cm L/24, the former main armament of the Panzer IV. A substantial number of these vehicles, SdKfz 251/9, were used during the last two years of the war. They acted as support vehicles and added the necessary fire power to Panzergrenadier units. This is a later version with an Ausf. D. chassis.
(Col. Robert Icks)

staff officers. It was followed by two versions of an engineer vehicle, SdKfz 251/7 I and II. They carried a crew of eight, two machine-guns, two sub-machine-guns and assorted engineer equipment. The two versions of the *Kranken Panzerwagen* SdKfz 251/8 I and II, served as an armoured ambulance. With a crew of two, they were equipped to handle either four stretcher cases or up to ten lightly injured cases.

Buessing-NAG received an order from the Ordnance Department on March 31, 1942 to equip a proportion of the medium SPWs with the 7·5 cm. KWK L/24. These units were intended to serve as support vehicles and had a crew of three. 150 units were ordered initially with delivery starting in mid-June 1942. They were designated SdKfz 251/9.

In 1940 the platoon leader vehicles were equipped with a 3·7 cm. PaK and a crew of six. Designated SdKfz 251/10, these appeared with or without gun shields for their main armament.

Next on the list was SdKfz 251/11, a telephone cable vehicle with a crew of five. It was followed by the SdKfz 251/12, a survey section instrument carrier for artillery units. The artillery was also supplied with SdKfz 251/13, a sound recording vehicle. The artillery SdKfz 251/14, and 15 were a sound ranging vehicle and a flash spotting vehicle respectively. A flame-thrower unit was next, the *mittlerer Flammpanzer-wagen* SdKfz 251/16. In addition to one machine-gun and two sub-machine-guns, it had two 14 mm. flame-throwers mounted on either side of the super-structure, plus one hand-operated 7 mm. thrower for close action. SdKfz 251/17 mounted a 2 cm. Flak 38 as a self-propelled mount. Only a few of these vehicles saw action, however. Their three-man crew had one additional machine-gun 42 for self-defence purposes. SdKfz 251/18 was an observation post vehicle, while 251/19 carried equipment for a telephone exchange unit.

The research with infra-red battlefield illumination in 1944 also utilized the basic medium SPW. The SdKfz 251/20 acted as a support vehicle mounting a relatively large searchlight for Panther tank units equipped with infra-red sighting devices. The vehicle 251/21 appeared as a replacement for 251/17 at the end of 1944. It carried a triple AA. mount displaying 15 mm. former aircraft weapons. The series was concluded by SdKfz 251/22 mounting the 7·5 cm. Pak 40 L/48. It was heavily overloaded, since the complete anti-tank gun was installed with its original armoured shield. Only limited traverse was provided.

By 1944, the SdKfz 251/4, 5 and 10 were no longer in production. Some of the 3·7 cm. anti-tank guns had been replaced by the tapered bore, 2·8 cm. anti-tank rifle as early as 1942.

The version of the medium SPW SdKfz 251/22 mounted the 7·5 cm. Pak 40. This vehicle protected infantry against enemy tanks and appeared in ever-increasing numbers on the battlefield in 1944.
(Col. Robert Icks)

The HKp 603, developed by Hanomag, was an improved version of the medium SPW. It never went beyond the prototype stage.
(Imperial War Museum)

167

TACTICAL EMPLOYMENT

The beginnings of the *Panzergrenadier* development can be traced as early as 1931, when Colonel Guderian became Chief of Staff to the Inspector of Mechanized Troops. There the foundation was laid, especially in the area of organization, for the use of armoured infantry units within the first three Panzer divisions. Proper equipment was one of the major concerns. With light tanks available only for the tank regiments, all other vehicles possessed neither cross-country ability, nor was armour protection provided.

At this time, the infantry section of a Panzer division consisted of an infantry brigade, including one rifle regiment with two battalions and one independent *Kradschützen* battalion of infantry equipped with sidecar motorcycles. The rifle regiment in turn was equipped with four or six-wheeled troop transport vehicles. Four Light divisions were also established, each having one tank battalion only. Their infantry elements, again, were equipped with soft-skinned wheeled vehicles. Thus, the basic requirement for the armoured forces to have infantry support available at all times could not yet be met. Only a token number of armoured troop carriers were ready when the war started in 1939.

The first battle experience was translated into explicit training instructions during the winter of 1939–40. This, coupled with the availability of additional armoured vehicles, resulted in rapid combined movements during the campaign against France in 1940. One of the anticipated improvements was an increase in fire power. During this campaign, 1st Panzer Division already had a rifle regiment with three battalions, of whose 15 companies seven were equipped with SPWs. Most of their fighting was done from the moving vehicle. Dismounted infantry squads were only necessary to overcome stubborn pockets of resistance. It soon became obvious that this close co-operation between tanks and SPWs resulted in fewer losses for the infantry.

Invaluable experience was gained during the initial phase of the war against Russia. Tremendous distances had to be covered in close-co-operation between the various branches of many Panzer divisions, many of them already equipped with an SPW battalion. Here the experience of stretched supply lines and overwhelming maintenance problems brought about considerable improvements which had lasting results during the War.

PANZERGRENADIERS

By the spring of 1942, all Panzer divisions were equipped with SPW battalions. And, from July 5, 1942, all rifle regiments within Panzer divisions were renamed *Panzergrenadiers*.

Well suited for attack and defence alike, the armoured infantry vehicle established itself as an invaluable tool of war. It developed into the "eye" of the tank, whose limited vision proved to be a considerable handicap if a determined enemy resorted to close-battle tactics. Radio communication between vehicles also played an important rôle. Thus, *Panzergrenadier* units were exceptionally well suited for quick reconnaissance, protection of open flanks and carrying out raids against enemy flanks and rear.

During the winter of 1942–43, it was proven over and over again that *Panzergrenadier* units were also quite capable of fighting dismounted. The few remaining SPWs were used to provide back-up fire protection.

A tremendous increase in fire power was provided for the *Panzergrenadier* regiments in 1943. Guderian also improved considerably the training of armoured infantry units, with particular emphasis on the following: support of tank attacks in obstructed terrain, in forests, across rivers and in villages; attack against fortified mine fields or against anti-tank gun barriers; attack at night. During defensive actions the main tasks of *Panzergrenadier* units were: support of tank units during counter-attacks; attack against

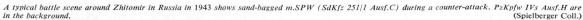
A typical battle scene around Zhitomir in Russia in 1943 shows sand-bagged m.SPW (SdKfz 251/1 Ausf.C) during a counter-attack. PzKpfw IVs Ausf.H are in the background. (Spielberger Coll.)

As a final version, the HKp 606 was intended to replace all previous series of armoured half-tracks and to act as the standard vehicle for both the light and medium SPW. Economic conditions during the war made it impossible for these improved vehicles to reach production stage.

exposed enemy flanks; quick securing of important objectives and their incorporation into the defence perimeter. All the battle experience gained was transferred as quickly as possible into instruction manuals and the training centres were advised to change training methods as new experience became available.

The Battle of Kursk in 1943 indicated clearly that the number of SPWs in service was still insufficient to assure exploitation of breakthroughs achieved by tanks. At this time, more and more Panzer and *Panzergrenadier* units found themselves acting as "Fire Brigades" to stop enemy attacks with resulting enormous losses which could not always be recovered.

The summer of 1944 saw *Panzergrenadier* units and their SPWs fighting against the Allied forces in France. Experience there quickly indicated that no armoured force could sustain itself without adequate anti-aircraft protection. Movements of any sort, including the supplying of units, had to be done during the brief night time. Only a few days of bad flying weather allowed for the traditional counter-attack pattern.

Against the assault from both East and West, only sporadic counter-measures could be launched, resulting normally in heavy casualties on both sides and losses of irreplaceable material to the German Armies. The Battle of the Bulge in 1944 saw for the last time combined German tank and armoured infantry assaults. The mountainous terrain of the Ardennes favoured the SPW, since its smaller dimensions and better fuel economy made it better suited for this kind of warfare.

Finally, a combined force of tanks and SPWs was established which, together with armoured engineers and self-propelled artillery units, fought delaying actions until the very end without being able to stem the tide.

It has to be repeated here that, in the German Armies of World War II, the tank found its classical partner in the SPW. Together, they fought the greatest armoured battles in history. The *Sonderkraft-fahrzeug* 251, despite its many shortcomings, served as an example for similar vehicles built by many other nations and established itself as one of the most important armoured fighting vehicles of its time.

SPECIFICATION

General
Designation: Mittlerer gepanzerter Mannschaftkraftwagen. Designation from 1942: mittlerer Schuetzenpanzerwagen. Ordnance No. SdKfz 251. Manufacturer's Type: Hanomag HL kl 6p.
Crew: 12—commander, driver, 10 men infantry squad in basic SdKfz 251/1.
Battle weight: 8·9 long tons.
Dry weight: 7·4 tons.

Dimensions
Length overall: 19 ft. (Ausf. A, B and C). 19 ft. 7½ in. Ausf. D.
Height: 5 ft. 9 in.
Width: 6 ft. 11 in.
Width over tracks/overall: 6 ft. 11 in.
Track centres/wheel base: 5 ft. 5 in./5 ft. 3 in.
Track width: 9¼ in.

Armament
Main: See description of Variants.

Ammunition
Rounds stowed: 2,010 7·92 mm. machine-gun for basic SdKfz 251/1 with two MG 34 or 42.

Communications
Varies between models.

Armour
Homogeneous welded and riveted armour plate.
Hull: 14·5 mm. at 14°.
Glacis: 10 mm. at 80°.
Sides: 8 mm. at 35°.
Rear: 8 mm. at 35°.
Floor: 6 mm. horizontal.

Engine
Maybach "HL 42 TUKRM" or TUKRRM. Petrol. 6 cyl. in-line. 4,171 c.c. 100 b.h.p. at 2,800 r.p.m. Fuel: 35 gallons in one tank between frame.

Transmission
Hanomag "021-32785U50". 4 forward, 1 reverse speeds with reduction. Crash gearbox.

Suspension
Front transverse leafspring, two tyres, 7.25–20, starting Serial No. 795091.—190-18.
Rear transverse torsion bars, steel tracks, rubber cushioned, lubricated 55–56 links per track. Type: Zgw 50/280/140 cast links. Type Zpw 50/280/140 pressed links.

Electrical System
Power supply and generators: Starter, Bosch EJD 1,8/12. Generator Bosch RKCN 300/12-1300. One or two batteries 12 volt 75 amps.

Performance
Max. road speed: 33 m.p.h.
Max. gradient: 24°.
Trench: 6 ft. 6 in.
Wading depth: 2 ft.
Fuel consumption 3·5 m.p.g.

Special Features
See SdKfz 251/1 to 251/22 listed in text under Variants.

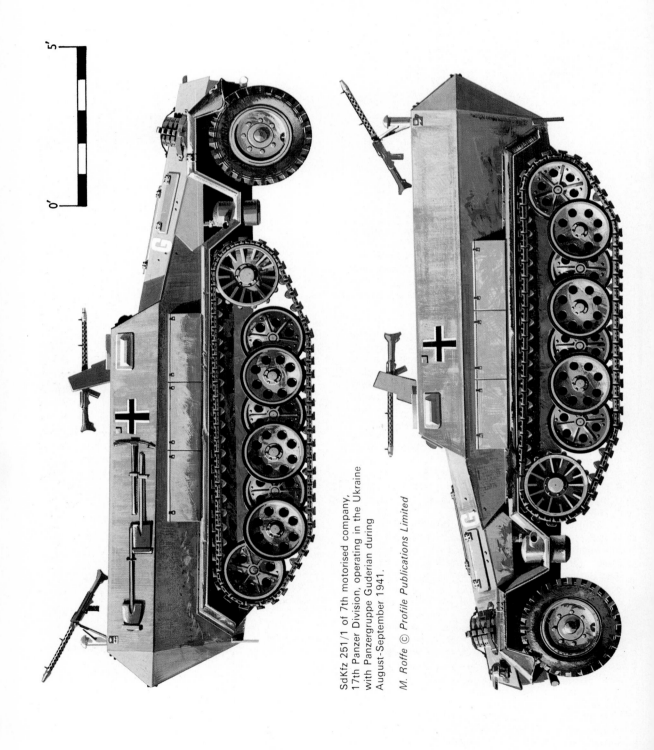

SdKfz 251/1 of 7th motorised company,
17th Panzer Division, operating in the Ukraine
with Panzergruppe Guderian during
August-September 1941.

M. Roffe © Profile Publications Limited

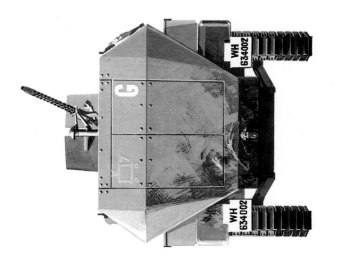

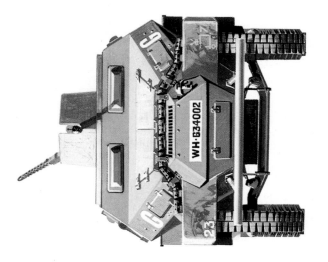

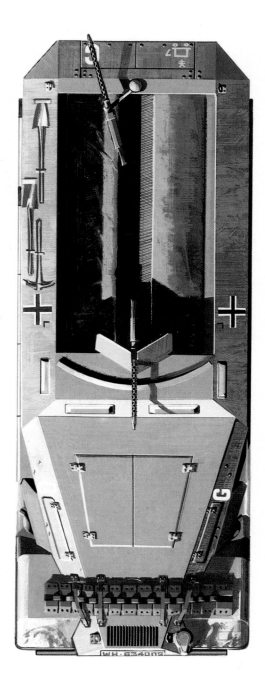

Leichter Funkpanzer SdKfz 250/3.III. This was one of the four radio vehicles that were among the variants of the Leichter Schuetzenpanzerwagen SdKfz 250 It carried a Fu 7 and a Fu 8, which was characterised by the frame antenna. It was used for ground-to-air communication.

Leichter Schützenpanzerwagen SdKfz 250

by Peter Chamberlain and Hilary L. Doyle

DEVELOPMENT

ALTHOUGH the Ordnance number *Sonderkraftfahrzeug 250* suggests otherwise, chronologically the SdKfz 250 followed the SdKfz 251. In importance also the SdKfz 250 was overshadowed by the SdKfz 251 which was the main troop carrier of the German Wehrmacht.

The development of the SdKfz 250 had its origin in an order received by Demag AG., of Wetter/Ruhr, in 1932. This order from the Army asked Demag to develop an all terrain tractor capable of towing a 1 ton load. The half-track solution was once again adopted and by 1934 Demag had their model D II. 1 under test. Numerous prototypes and development models followed in the next few years and resulted in series production of the Demag D 6 during 1937 and 1938. Numerous special tasks were envisaged for these 1 ton vehicles in addition to the primary requirement of towing anti-tank and light artillery pieces for the motorised infantry units. The most important variation was the use of this chassis as the self-propelled carriage for the 2 cm. Flak cannon. The success of the pre-production D 6 series led to the order for mass production of the Demag D 7 in 1939. This vehicle was officially called the *Leichter Zugkraftwagen 1t* and received the Ordnance number SdKfz 10.

In 1939, following the introduction of prototypes of the SdKfz 251, investigations revealed that an

armoured superstructure could be mounted on the Zgkw 1t chassis. At this time the Army had outlined requirements for three special vehicles, smaller than the SdKfz 251, which would provide support for motorised forces. The first requirement was for an armoured personnel carrier to transport a half group (section) of infantry during reconnaissance in depth. The smaller numbers in each vehicle and therefore the greater number of vehicles per reconnaissance battalion would give the flexibility required. Buessing-NAG of Berlin-Oberschoeneweide were entrusted with the design of the armoured body because of their recent experience in the development of the SdKfz 251. Armour protection was to be 14·5 mm. at the front and 8 mm. on the sides while accommodation was to be provided for the driver, commander and four troopers. The armoured body was to be as compact as possible so as to keep the weight low and maintain performance. In view of the superstructure designed by Buessing-NAG the length of the chassis was reduced by Demag who were still responsible for the chassis development. This was achieved by reducing the track on the ground, by removing the first axle following the drive sprocket, and by moving the complete trackwork forward. The elimination of one set of road wheels on each side with associated torsion bars and suspension further reduced the weight. Trials were held at Kummersdorf and an order was placed for production almost immediately.

The Ordnance number Sonderkraftfahrzeug 250 was allotted and the official designation was *Leichter Gepanzerter Mannschaftskraftwagen*. The Demag name for this armoured carrier and its chassis was Demag D 7p. The p stood for panzer.

An external factor which had a great bearing upon the development of the Demag D 7p was the conclusion drawn from experiments with a battery of prototype Assault Guns which were held during the late 1930s. It was concluded that for really effective operation the infantry assault guns would depend upon special support vehicles, armoured and capable of cross country travel, to re-supply them with ammunition and to provide observation facilities. Thus an outline was formed for the additional two requirements for half-tracks using the chassis of the Demag D 7p. Demag continued to be responsible for the chassis and took these requirements into consideration during their design study. As both latter vehicles were to be fully enclosed and were to have heavier armour than the basic SdKfz 250 this was a major factor for Demag. The ammunition vehicle received the Ordnance number Sonderkraftfahrzeug 252 and the official designation *Leichter Gepanzerter Munitionstransportkraftwagen*. Due to the limited payload capacity of these armoured vehicles the superstructure was cut back sharply from the middle of the fighting compartment. In this steeply angled rear plate were large double doors permitting speedy loading and transfer of ammunition. A crew of two was carried, commander and driver. They gained access through individual hatches in the roof of the driver's compartment. A small armoured trailer containing further stocks of ammunition was normally towed. The firm of Waggonfabrik Wegmann AG in Kassel-Rothenditmold were responsible for the armoured superstructure. The frontal armour of these vehicles was 18 mm. as opposed to the 14·5 mm. of the basic SdKfz 250.

The third and final vehicle to be introduced on the Demag D 7p chassis was the observation vehicle for the Sturmgeschuetz battalions. This vehicle was also developed by Demag and Wegmann, but was simply a roofed-in version of the basic SdKfz 250 fitted with equipment which suited it for the task required. To the left middle of the fighting compartment roof was a large rotating circular hatch with two doors which incorporated further smaller opening covers which in turn permitted a scissors periscope to project while the main hatches were closed. To the rear left was a rectangular access hatch and on the right side was the antenna for the radio equipment, namely an Fu 16 ultra-shortwave transmitter h and an Fu 15 receiver h both operating on the 23000-24950 Kc/s. band for communication with assault gun units. The Ordnance number for these vehicles was Sonderkraftfahrzeug 253 and the official designation was *Leichter Gepanzerter Beobachtungskraftwagen*.

Early in 1940 the Sturmgeschuetz batteries were already being issued with the SdKfz 252 ammunition carriers, and a considerable number of the SdKfz 253 observation vehicles had been delivered by the time the Blitzkrieg on France began in May 1940. There is no indication of deliveries of the SdKfz 250 basic vehicle before the latter part of 1940. However, before long the special purpose versions SdKfz 252 and 253

were dropped in favour of less expensive adaptations of the basic SdKfz 250. By 1943 there were twelve official sub-classifications of this vehicle which was being produced in large numbers.

PRODUCTION

The basic SdKfz 250 *Leichter Gepanzerter Mannschaftskraftwagen* entered production in 1940 and was officially manufactured until the end of 1944, but due to disruption contracts were still uncompleted at the end of the war. Initially the chassis Demag D 7p

Leichter Zugkraftwagen 1t SdKfz 10. Manufacturer's type was Demag D 7. Mass production was ordered in 1939.

Leichter Schuetzenpanzerwagen SdKfz 250/1, the basic vehicle.

Leichter Gepanzerter Munitionstransportkraftwagen SdKfz 252, the ammunition vehicle of the series.

Leichter Gepanzerter Beobachtungskraftwagen SdKfz 253, the observation vehicle which was later replaced by the SdKfz 250/4.

was manufactured alongside the regular tractor chassis, Demag D 7, at the Wetter/Ruhr plant. However, as the importance of the SdKfz 250 and its derivations grew, Demag gradually substituted D 7p production lines for those of the D 7. The tractor production was taken up by the Saurer Werke in Vienna, while Buessing-NAG and Adler also participated. Mechanische Werke in Cottbus were responsible for production of both D 7 and D 7p chassis. DEW Hannover and Steinmueller of Gummersbach built the armoured bodies. Most of the armour plating used for the SdKfz 250 bodies was produced by the Bismarckhuette in Upper Silesia. The assembly of the SdKfz 250 took place at the works of Evens & Pistor in Helsa, Thuringia. In 1941 the two special variants SdKfz 252 and SdKfz 253 were removed from the production program in favour of increased production of the basic SdKfz 250 unit which could be readily adapted for the various roles. During 1942 a more suitable official designation was applied; *Leichter Schuetzenpanzerwagen* invariably abbreviated to *le. SPW*. Currently available official figures indicate that 5,930 *le.SPW* were manufactured in the years 1942 to 1944.

In 1943 the SdKfz 250 underwent a considerable redesign, simultaneously with the redesign of the SdKfz 251. The object of this exercise was to simplify production rather than to effect technical improvements, thus the chassis, running gear and automotive parts remained virtually unchanged. The new armoured body represented a considerable saving in fabrication time, having almost 50 per cent less separate armoured plates. The squared-off body was just as effective in providing protection against small arms fire and the internal capacity was considerably increased. The 3 ton SdKfz 251 Ausf. A, B and C had appeared by 1940 and the 1943 redesign of the SdKfz 251 became the Ausf. D. The smaller SdKfz 250 on the other hand arrived much later in the front line and no modifications were permitted lest they cause delays in production. Even when the vehicle was redesigned in 1943 no Ausf. code appears to have been allotted. During 1939 and 1940 Demag had projected an improved D 8 chassis but this was never advanced beyond the project stage. However, from 1940 to 1944 Demag cooperated with Hanomag to find a standard solution to replace both the 1 ton and 3 ton tractors and SdKfz 250 and SdKfz 251 carriers. This development was to be the HK 600 series described in the Profile of the SdKfz 251.

SdKfz 250 DESCRIBED

The layout and construction of the SdKfz 250 was very similar to that of the larger SdKfz 251. The front axle was suspended by a transverse leaf spring, and axle and suspension were anchored as on the SdKfz 251. The pressed steel disc wheels carried 600 x 20 tyres. Unlike contemporary US half-tracks the German vehicles did not have a powered front axle, which made the steering very heavy and driving tedious. For normal turns the front wheels steered the vehicle but when a hard turn had to be made the movement of the steering wheel automatically actuated a mechanical link to the steering brakes mounted in the differential unit. These steering brakes controlled the

drive to the tracks and allowed the tracks to assist steering. The steering wheel of these vehicles was inverted to accommodate the frontal sloped armour plate and this made the steering even more difficult. The only brakes provided on these vehicles controlled the tracks and these were operated hydraulically. The handbrake was a mechanical linkage to the same units. Lubricated needle roller bearing tracks similar to those of the SdKfz 251 were used, though the links were normally of forged steel on the SdKfz 250 and cast steel on the tractor version SdKfz 10. Track type was Zpw. 51/240/160, with a width of 240 mm. and a pitch of 160 mm.; 38 links completed each track. The running gear consisted of four transverse torsion bars each acting on a swing arm hinged in a forward direction. To accommodate the torsion bars the right side running gear was further forward than the left. The wheels were pressed steel discs fitted with solid rubber tyres. These wheels were of the interleaving and overlapping type common to most half-tracks. The drive sprocket at the front was connected to the differential by short propeller shafts while the sprockets themselves housed a final reduction gear. The idler sprocket at the rear could be adjusted for track tensioning and was fitted with a shear bolt safety device.

The SdKfz 250 and SdKfz 251 were powered by the same standard Maybach six-cylinder watercooled petrol engine: the 4171 cc. HL 42 TRKM which developed 100 b.h.p. at 2800 r.p.m. The transmission, however, was totally different. The SdKfz 10 and SdKfz 250 had a Maybach Variorex VG 1202128 H unit. This gearbox was a pre-selector type which provided seven forward and three reverse speeds, thus eliminating the normal requirement for a two speed transfer box. But the Variorex unit was complex and required good maintenance. The engine and gearbox were coupled through a Fichtel & Sachs PF 220 Komet clutch. A Cletrac differential completed the power train. The engine and power train of these vehicles was mounted offset to the right side so that the gearbox was alongside and to the right of the driver.

The armoured body was manufactured in two parts; the front section enclosed the engine while the back section included all the driver and crew compartments. The two halves were bolted together during final assembly. As mentioned already the driver sat alongside the gearbox on the left side of the vehicle. In front of him was a large vision port which could be opened and was fitted with splinter-proof glass blocks when closed. On the side wall was a single vision slit also with a glass block. Also in front of the driver was the inverted steering wheel, while slightly to the right was the main control panel, the most important instrument being a very large tachometer. The commander, on the right of the driver, had similar vision facilities and ahead of him was mounted the radio set which was the usual Fu Spr.Ger.f for inter-vehicle communication. Along the left wall of the vehicle was a bench seat for three soldiers and the remaining one was provided with an individual seat to the rear centre of the fighting compartment in front of the main petrol tank. The right wall of the vehicle was enclosed by a stowage box which was used to store the armament of the vehicle and troops along with other items, including ammunition.

SdKfz 250 with post-1943 body.

SdKfz 250/5.II. Originally classified as a Leichter Beobachtungspanzerwagen, together with the SdKfz 250/5.I, the vehicle was given the title of Leichter Aufklaerungspanzerwagen in 1944.

View of SdKfz 250/1 interior showing position of righthand side storage. A Radio B 1 x 9 mm. MP 38 with six ammunition magazines C 1 x 7·92 mm. MG 34 in storage D AA defence pivot for MG 34 E Verey pistol and 12 rounds of signal ammunition F Heavy field mounting for MG 34.

Late pattern SdKfz 250/9 with the new six-sided turret that was also being produced for the SdKfz 234/1 eight-wheeled armoured car. The vehicle also had the new pattern SdKfz 250 body.

Leichter Beobachtungspanzerwagen SdKfz 250/4 which replaced SdKfz 253.

(Courtesy A. L. Sohns)

SdKfz 250/8 was armed with the 7·5 cm. KwK 37 L/24.

The armament of a SdKfz 250 was one le.MG 34 which was mounted behind a pivoting shield on the roof of the driver's compartment. On the rear wall top there was a pedestal for an additional MG 34 which was carried either for AA defence or with a heavy field mounting for ground use. The crew were personally armed with four 7·92 mm. Kar. 98K rifles while the commander had a 9 mm. MP 38 machine pistol. A small saddle type seat was mounted on top of the gearbox for the front machine gunner to use when firing the gun.

The fuel tank at the rear right of the SdKfz 250 had capacity for 140 litres (31 gallons) which allowed a normal operating radius of between 300 and 175 kilometres (186/109 miles). The basic vehicle weighed 5.38 tonnes and had a maximum speed of 60 Km.p.h. (37 m.p.h.) on roads.

Normal exit and entry were effected through a single door in the tail plate. This door was also fitted with a vision port for rear observation. In action the troops frequently used the open roof as a quicker method of disembarkation. This open roof could be fitted with a tarpaulin, carried in the vehicle, during inclement weather.

VARIANTS (SdKfz 250/1–12)

The *Leichter Schuetzenpanzerwagen* was manufactured in twelve official variants each with a unique Ordnance number. However, there were often numerous different official models within each classification. Finally there were a number of other models for which no official records have been located.

The basic **SdKfz 250/1** has already been described in detail. This vehicle was intended to carry a half section (halbgruppe) into action. There was also another model of the SdKfz 250/1 which was very important. This was the vehicle carrying schwerer MG 34 halbgruppe. The MG shield was not fitted on the roof over the driver's compartment as these vehicles were to carry an MG 34 on the heavy mounting. This configuration permitted sustained heavy

automatic fire to be directed on distant targets at a moment's notice. These vehicles also carried a second MG 34 which could again be mounted in the rear AA pivot or taken out of the vehicle and fired from a heavy field mounting stowed on the rear armour plate. Both these versions existed in both the pre- and post-1943 body forms.

The next vehicle on the official list was the *Leichter Fernsprechwagen* **SdKfz 250/2**. This was a handy little vehicle used by the communications troops for laying field telephone cables. The cables were held on reels. Racks to hold these reels during laying operations were fitted to both the front mudguards and to the top of the petrol tank at the rear right-hand side of the vehicle. This meant that cable could be paid out on either side into a ditch for example, or simply reeled out to the rear as the driver moved forward across open country. Special equipment for these vehicles included long poles which were used to guide the cable clear from the side of a road during laying.

Four official versions of the **SdKfz 250/3** *Leichter Funkpanzer* were in existence. Each of these was a radio vehicle with equipment to suit the particular formation which it was to accompany and the command to which it was to report. Thus the model attached to motorised forces was equipped with the Fu 12 radio set, which was the normal ground forces link with such formations. The Fu 12 was a medium wave receiver operating on the 835-3000 Kc/s. band and an 80 watt transmitter which used the 1120-3000 Kc/s. band. A 2 metre rod with star antenna at the top was the aerial for these Fu 12. This aerial was carried on the rear left of the fighting compartment while the usual 2 metre rod aerial for the inter-vehicle Funksprechgeraet f was on the front right. The radio set itself was carried on top of the petrol tank which was reduced in height. A crew of four operated these radio vehicles. The main armament was one MG 34. Again both pre- and post-1943 bodies were to be seen.

The second type of radio vehicle had an Fu 7 radio set which consisted of an ultra-shortwave receiver d1 and a 20 watt transmitter d which operated on the 42100-47800 Kc/s. band. The Fu 7 was used to contact Luftwaffe support groups inside a range of 50 km. The aerial was again a 2 metre rod aerial.

The third model was another ground-to-air co-ordination vehicle and as such was usually operated by Luftwaffe personnel and therefore had the WL number plate of the Luftwaffe. Not only did these vehicles carry a Fu 7, the aerial for which was mounted on top of an armoured container at the rear, but also a Fu 8 which was characterised by the massive frame antenna. These Fu 8 sets were for contact with the main divisional command at ranges up to 40 Km. On later models the frame antenna was replaced by an 8 metre winched mast aerial with a star antenna on top which could be raised and lowered as required. The 8 metre mast increased the range to 50 Km. The Fu 8 was a medium wave receiver c for the 835-3000 Kc/s. band while the earlier model b was for the 580-3000 Kc/s. band. The transmitter was a 30 watt unit operating between 1130 and 3000 Kc/s.

The final model of the radio vehicles seems to have been a general type with no specific radio sets mentioned in official documents. However, reports indicate that they were fitted with Fu 15 or Fu 16 for contact with assault gun formations, and with the Fu 10 when attached, for example, to armoured car groups. The Ordnance numbers for these vehicles were: SdKfz 250/3.I, SdKfz 250/3.II, SdKfz 250/3.III and SdKfz 250/3.IV.

The official list indicated that the next variant was ordered as a *Leichter Truppenluftschuetzpanzerwagen* **SdKfz 250/4**. This was to have been an anti-aircraft vehicle, but it never materialised and had been removed from the Ordnance list dated 7th June 1943. After the redesigned body was introduced the designation SdKfz 250/4 reappeared, this time for a *Leichter Beobachtungspanzerwagen,* an armoured observation vehicle specially for the assault gun formations. This was therefore a replacement for the earlier discontinued SdKfz 253 *Leichter Gepanzerter Beobachtungskraftwagen.* The observation equipment primarily consisted of a pivoting mount for a scissors periscope type 14 Z Si, with an adjustable seat rotating with this equipment. As one would expect the radio sets were the Fu 15 and Fu 16 of the assault guns. The Fu 15 was an ultra-shortwave receiver h operating on the 23000-24950 Kc/s. band and the Fu 16 was a combination of an ultra-shortwave receiver h with a 10 watt transmitter h which also operated on the same wave-band. Two normal 2 metre rod aerials were used for these radios, and a third aerial for the Fu Spr.Ger. f intercom.

The **SdKfz 250/5.I** was also a *Leichter Beobachtungspanzerwagen* which was issued at a much earlier date to the artillery batteries. Since the radio equipment consisted of a Fu 8 and a Fu 4 the vehicle was difficult to distinguish from the radio vehicles SdKfz 250/3. Earlier models had a frame antenna for their Fu 8. The second version was in fact classed as a replacement for the first and was designated SdKfz 250/5.II. The main difference was the installation of the Fu 12 radio set. From 1944 these SdKfz 250/5.II were given a new official title *Leichter Aufklaerungs-panzerwagen* or light reconnaissance vehicles. By this time only the late type of body would have been issued.

As already mentioned the special SdKfz 253 ammunition carrier for assault guns was discontinued in 1941. The replacement from the basic SdKfz 250 series was given the Ordnance number **SdKfz 250/6.** There were two models. The first was designated *Leichter Munitionspanzerwagen Ausf. A. – fuer Sturmgeschuetz 7·5 cm. Kanone (Kurz) Ausf. A bis E.* As indicated by this official designation the carrier supported the assault gun batteries which were equipped with Sturmgeschuetz Ausf. A to E, that is those with the 7·5 cm. Stu.K L/24 cannon. These guns used a fairly small round of ammunition which was normally stored two to a small pressed steel box with a carrying handle. The SdKfz 250/6 Ausf. A had internal racks for 35 such boxes containing 70 rounds of ammunition. A trailer similar to that towed by the SdKfz 252 was used to transport a supplementary supply of ammunition. A crew of two had all the usual equipment provided in the SdKfz 250 series vehicles including one MG 34 as the main armament.

With the advent of the Sturmgeschuetz 40 Ausf. F and Ausf. G starting in 1942 a new model of the ammunition carrier had to be ordered. Externally similar to the Ausf. A the SdKfz 250/6 Ausf. B was internally modified to carry the long shells of the new more powerful 7·5 cm. Stu.K 40 cannons. The changes consisted of fitting a rack each side of the vehicle into which 30 canisters could be placed. These were tubular steel containers with a screw top; each carried one 7·5 cm. Stu.K. 40 round. A total of 60 rounds were carried internally; others might be towed in a trailer.

All the vehicles so far described were issued as transporters or carriers of equipment or men. The next five models were weapons carriers which were intended to act as fighting support vehicles. **SdKfz 250/7** *Leichter Schuetzenpanzerwagen (Schwerer Granatewerfer)* mounted an 8 cm. Gr.W 34 mortar. In the centre of the fighting compartment was a fixed base which permitted a limited arc of traverse for the mortar. A mortar crew of three was accompanied by the usual vehicle commander and driver. Internal stowage was only for 21 boxes of mortar rounds due to the very crowded interior. However, it was essential to have a method of bringing the mortars into action quickly in support of the grenadiers who travelled in similar fast crosscountry vehicles. A normal ground base plate for the mortar was stowed on the rear of the carrier so that the mortar could be dismounted for firing and thus leave the carrier mobile. In order to provide a clear field of fire from within, these vehicles were never fitted with a forward machine gun position and its associated shield. However, there was a pivot mounting at the rear for the AA. MG 34 which was carried along with a field mounting inside the mortar carrier. To overcome the chronic shortage of mortar bomb space in the mortar carriers there was another version of the SdKfz 250/7 which was designated the *Leichter Schuetzenpanzerwagen (Munitionsfahrzeug).* These Munitionsfahrzeug were identical to the mortar carrier, even having the fixed base plate to take a mortar, but by not installing a number of items, including the mortar itself, a total of 66 rounds could be carried. A crew of only four also allowed the extra space for radio equipment in some of these vehicles. The normal MG 34 mounting at the front was provided. One Munitionsfahrzeug was issued for every two mortars and was commanded by the section leader. Where possible platoon commanders used the very same vehicle with the extra radio equipment, thus further increasing the ammunition supplies of the platoon.

The designation **SdKfz 250/8** was reserved for a vehicle armed with the 7·5 cm. KwK 37 L/24 which was similar to the larger SdKfz 251/9. However, it was not until late 1943 that these *Leichter Schuetzenpanzerwagen mit 7·5 cm. KwK 37* actually entered production. The chassis was that of the late model SdKfz 250 and the mounting itself represented an improvement over earlier fittings in the SdKfz 251/9 and the SdKfz 233 armoured car. This mounting was fixed on top of the standard chassis and required no special structural modification unlike the earlier types. The silhouette was very high but speedy construction made this solution preferable. The 7·5 cm. KwK 37 L/24 became available in 1943 in large numbers when it was removed from the Panzerkampfwagen IV and Sturmgeschuetz for replacement by the long barrelled 7·5 cm. KwK 40 or Stu.K 40. Later models of the SdKfz 250/8 were also called *Leichter Schuetzenpanzerwagen fuer 7·5 cm. K.51 Sf.* A feature of these vehicles was the co-axial mounting for the MG 34 or MG 42 which permitted machine

gun fire to be laid on the target of the main armament. These vehicles were primarily seen as a replacement for the SdKfz 250/10 which was armed with the obsolete 3·7 cm. Pak anti tank gun.

The **SdKfz 250/9** *Leichter Schuetzenpanzerwagen (2 cm.)* was a far more interesting vehicle than its official designation suggests. It was, in fact, a half-track armoured car introduced to make the operations of the reconnaissance patrols more effective. In Western Europe and North Africa the SdKfz 222 Horch 4 x 4 wheeled scout cars proved quite effective, but in Russia this was not the case and missions frequently failed due to the inability of these wheeled vehicles to negotiate the difficult roadless terrain especially during the winter. The urgency of this problem made it impossible to consider the design of new scout vehicles and the Ordnance department therefore ordered a compromise in the form of the SdKfz 250/9. The complete turret assembly of an SdKfz 222 armoured car was mounted on the SdKfz 250 body thus providing the troops with what was often unofficially known as the *Leichter Spaehpanzerwagen (2 cm.)* SdKfz 250/9. A crew of three operated these reconnaisance half-tracks. The basic vehicle was much the same as those of the SdKfz 250 series, but the rotating turret of the SdKfz 222 added a new dimension to its capabilities. The ten-sided turret was open topped so as to permit clear all-round vision. Wire mesh covers protected the crew from grenades and other such missiles. The armament was a 2 cm. KwK 38 L/55 autocannon with a coaxial MG 34. In addition to the 360 degree traverse provided by the turret mounting, the armament had an unusually high elevation of 80 degrees. This elevation made it possible to successfully engage air targets. 2 cm. ammunition was fed from ten-round boxes, so only limited automatic fire could be maintained. The radio equipment of these units was the Fu 12 already described. After 1943 the new pattern body was introduced and along with it came the new shaped

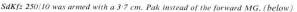
SdKfz 250/9 was a half-track armoured car which had the complete turret assembly of an SdKfz 222 armoured car on a SdKfz 250 body. The armament was a 2 cm. KwK 38 L/55 autocannon with a coaxial MG 34.

SdKfz 250/10 was armed with a 3·7 cm. Pak instead of the forward MG. (below)

A B C D

SdKfz 250/11 was similar to the SdKfz 250/10 but was armed with the 2·8 cm. schwere Panzerbuechse 41 which had a cone bore. A 2·8 cm. s.Pz.B. 41 field carriage wheel section B Tarpaulin cover C 2·8 cm. schwere Panzerbuechse 41 D Trail section of field carriage.

SdKfz 250/12 was an artillery survey vehicle. This view of the interior shows A Respirator B Scissors periscope and direction finder C 1 x MP 38 and ammunition D Tripod field mounting for dismounted use of periscope and direction finder E Stowed MG 34 F 4 x Kar 98K rifles G Baggage container H Cover hoops I Tarpaulin opening section J Pivot for AA MG 34 mount and armoured shield, or for survey equipment.

A B B C D E F

G H I J

turret which was now in production for the SdKfz 234/1 eight-wheeled armoured car. By this time the four-wheeled cars were no longer manufactured. The turret was six-sided but other than that was similar to the earlier ten-sided type.

As early as 1940 the platoon leader of a grenadier unit was equipped with an SdKfz 251 in which a 3·7 cm. Pak anti-tank gun replaced the forward MG. A corresponding vehicle on the light half-track chassis was given the designation **SdKfz 250/10** and was introduced at an early stage. As on the SdKfz 251 there were several variations of gun shield protecting the gunners operating the 3·7 cm. Some vehicles had only the bare gun itself, others had a shield only for the gun layer, and finally there were those with the complete gun shield as found on the field mounting of the anti-tank gun.

Even by the time it was introduced on the SdKfz 250/10 the 3·7 cm. Pak was an ineffective and obsolete weapon and it was envisaged that all such units be replaced by the SdKfz 250/8 armed with the 7·5 cm. Due to production delays, however, the latter vehicle did not appear at the time expected and a replacement for the SdKfz 250/10 was found in the **SdKfz 250/11**, a similar vehicle armed with the 2·8 cm. s.Pz.B. 41. This light anti-tank gun was introduced for infantry use in late 1941. The main feature was the use of a cone bore. A 2·8 cm. round was squeezed down a cone-shaped barrel with the driving rings being forced into an annular recess in the shell. The effect was a greatly increased muzzle velocity as the round left

the 2 cm. muzzle, in this case over 4,600 feet per second. The performance at shorter ranges was far better than the 3·7 cm. Pak and the versatility of the SdKfz 250/11 was greatly increased since the s.Pz.B. 41 could be dismounted for field use. The gun wheels and carriage section were carried on the rear plate and the trail section on a rack along the right-hand front mudguard. The field carriage was of the "Airborne" variety, a very lightweight tubular unit normally issued to paratroops and airborne forces. Unlike the airborne gun a shield was provided for the crew. The official designation was *Leichter Schuetzenpanzerwagen (Schwere Panzerbuesche 41)*.

The final model of the SdKfz 250 which was shown on official Ordnance lists was the *Leichter Messtruppanzerwagen* **SdKfz 250/12**. This was an artillery survey vehicle equipped with an Fu 8 initially and with an Fu 12 in later models. A scissors periscope with a special direction finder attachment could be mounted on either the front or rear MG pivots. A survey section of four men used these vehicles.

Obviously, with such a widely issued and much used vehicle as the SdKfz 250 there were many improvised modifications effected by field workshop units. These are of little importance to the overall story. However, pictorial evidence suggests that two further models were manufactured by factories rather than field units. It will be remembered that the *Leichter Truppenluftschuetzpanzerwagen* SdKfz 250/4 did not materialize and the designation was used for another vehicle. Photographs dating from late 1944 onwards indicate SdKfz 250 vehicles mounting 2 cm. Flak guns or 2 cm. KwK 38 in mountings suitable for anti-aircraft use. The second, apparently purpose-built version, is on display at the Yugoslav Military Museum in Belgrade. This version has a 5 cm. Pak 38 anti-tank gun. The interior of the vehicle is very carefully laid out and modified to suit the mounting of such a heavy weapon. The most notable change is the extension of the rear of the vehicle so that the back plate is at a negative angle unlike all others in the SdKfz 250 series. This vehicle used a post-1943 type body.

TACTICAL EMPLOYMENT

The tactical employment of the specialised types of SdKfz 250 is self-explanatory. The ammunition carriers and observation vehicles improved the performance of the assault gun batteries. The radio and telephone cable layers contributed to the communications of all branches of the Wehrmacht, while the survey vehicles supported the artillery batteries. The essential purpose of the SdKfz 250 *Leichter Schuetzenpanzerwagen* was to transport and provide support for the half groups of the armoured reconnaissance battalion or *Panzer Aufklaerungs Abteilung*. Obviously, the internal organisation of each Panzer Aufklaerungs Abteilung differed, depending upon the strength and location of the division to which it belonged; but the recommended requirements for these units indicated the importance of the SdKfz 250. The Leichter Panzer Aufklaerungs Kompanie was to incorporate four platoons each with seven SdKfz 250 vehicles, those of the first three platoons being the basic SdKfz 250/1 and, if available, the platoon leaders in the SdKfz 250/10 or SdKfz 250/11. The fourth platoon was the heavy support platoon and was normally to be equipped with four SdKfz 250/7 mortar carriers, two actually carrying the mortars while the section leader and platoon leader used the ammunition vehicles. Two SdKfz 250/8 armed with the 7·5 cm. KwK 37, and a section leader in an ammunition carrier completed the equipment. The headquarters section of the company used two SdKfz 250/3 radio vehicles.

Also in the battalion establishment for the 1944 type Panzer Divisions was the Panzer Spaehwagen Kompanie which had amongst its equipment twenty-five SdKfz 250 vehicles – sixteen being SdKfz 250/9 scout cars and the remaining nine being either SdKfz 250/8 (7·5 cm. KwK 37 guns) or basic vehicles. In the 1943 establishment there were sixteen SdKfz 250/9 and nine SdKfz 250/1 only. The total suggested establishment for the 1944 type Panzer Division was

fifty-five le. SPW. The le. Panzer Spaehwagen Kompanie of the Panzergrenadier Division for 1943 and 1944 was also to have up to eighteen SdKfz 250 of various types.

The "Provisional Directive Program IV" which provided the guidelines for industry for 1945 was issued in mid-July 1944. This document shows that the SdKfz 250 was to be eliminated from production in favour of standardisation on the SdKfz 251 type, and with that in mind the establishment tables for Panzer and Panzergrenadier Divisions for 1945 were adjusted to show only the SdKfz 251 in the Panzer Aufklaerungs Abteilung. This was logical since the material requirements for construction of the larger vehicle were not much greater while the simplification of manufacture would certainly have increased output. Versatility in the field would have been increased and above all spare parts duplication would have been eliminated. Finally, training would have been simplified. However, such measures were of little importance at such a late stage in the war with the Allied and Soviet Forces closing in on Germany.

SPECIFICATION

Designation: Leichter Gepanzerter Mannschaftskraftwagen (le. MTW).
Designation from 1942: Leichter Schuetzenpanzerwagen (le. SPW).
Ordnance No.: SdKfz 250.
Crew: 6 – commander and driver, 4 men of Infantry section in basic SdKfz 250/1.
Battle weight: 5·7 tons.
Dry weight: 5·4 tons.

Dimensions
Length overall: 15 ft.
Height: 5 ft.
Width: 6 ft. 4½ in.
Track centres/wheel base: 5 ft. 3½ in./5 ft. 2 in.
Track width: 8 in.

Main armament
See description of variants.

Communication
Varies between models, but all have Fu.Sp.Gr.f inter-vehicle radio telephone.

Armour
Homogeneous welded and riveted armour plate.
Hull: 14·5 mm. at 12°.
Glacis: 10 mm. at 83°.
Sides: 8mm. at 40° upper, and 28° lower.
Rear: 8 mm. at 23°.
Floor: 6 mm. horizontal.

Engine
Maybach HL 42 TUKRM or TUKRRM petrol, 6 cyl. in line. 4171 cc. 100 b.h.p. at 2,800 r.p.m. Fuel: 31 gallons in tank on rear right hand side of fighting compartment.

Transmission
Maybach Variorex VG 120128 H. 7 forward and 3 reverse speeds. Preselector gearbox.

Suspension
Front: transverse leaf spring, two tyres 600 x 20.
Rear: transverse torsion bars, forged steel tracks, rubber cushioned, lubricated, 38 links per track. Type Zpw 51/240/160 or cast links type Zgw 51/240/160.

Electrical system
Power supply and Generators: Starter Bosch EJD 1, 8/12. Generator Bosch RKCN 300/12-1300. 12 volt battery 75 amps.

Performance
Max. road speed: 37 m.p.h.
Max. gradient: 24°.
Wading depth: 2 ft. 4 in.
Range: 186 miles on roads/109 miles cross country.

Special features
See SdKfz 250/1 to SdKfz 250/12 described in text.

Schwerer Panzerspähwagen (8 Rad) Sd Kfz 233 had an open superstructure in which was mounted a 7·5 cm StuK (SturmKanone) L/24. The 233's assault gun was intended to provide supporting fire for the more lightly-armed 8 Rad 231 and 232 cars. (RAC Tank Museum)

German Armoured Cars

by Major-General N. W. Duncan

Although the Germans played a prominent part in the development of the internal combustion engine they were slow in the application of this invention to military use. In 1904 the firm of Austro-Daimler in Austria built an armoured car with four-wheel drive and a revolving turret in which was mounted a water-cooled machine-gun. Nothing came of this but in 1906 the German firm of Ehrhardt who had close technical connections with Austria and who had been concerned with the early petrol engines, built an armoured car as a private venture. This extremely interesting vehicle was intended to provide high angle fire against balloons: it mounted a 50 mm gun in a turret with a traverse of 90 degrees either side of the centre line of the car which could fire at all elevations from 0 to 90 degrees. This is the first recorded instance of an AA armoured car and foreshadows those built during World War II. It indicates the attention paid in Germany, even at that early date, to the possible dangers of aerial reconnaissance. Although the aeroplane was not at that time a practical military proposition, both balloons and man-lifting kites were in use and had achieved results which made the provision of fire against them a valuable selling point for a private venture such as Ehrhardt's. However novel the point of view it failed to impress the German General Staff and nothing more was heard of this design, although Krupp's produced several experimental models of 57 mm AA guns on both armoured and unarmoured Daimler chassis between 1909 and 1911.

The potential of the armoured car continued to attract

inventors and up to 1914 various prototype vehicles were constructed—although none of them were officially adopted for use in the German Army, which at that time was organised on a horse-drawn basis: motor cars were rare and motor lorries virtually non-existent. German military thought relied chiefly on man-power for victory and discounted the possibility of using machines on a large scale, either to reduce casualties or to achieve victory at a greater pace than that at which a horse could move.

Austro-Daimler 1904 armoured car after modification with two machine-gun ports in the revolving turret. (via Col. R. J. Icks)

The first AA armoured car: Ehrhardt 1906 with 5 cm BAK (Ballon Abwehr Kanone). Chain drive to near side rear wheel visible.

5·7 cm FlAK (Fleiger Abwehr Kanone) on Daimler Panzerkraftwagen 1909. 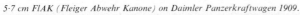 ('The Times' History of the War)

During the advance into Belgium in 1914, the leading Germans were frequently engaged by improvised armoured cars manned by British or Belgian troops. These civilian pattern vehicles, clad with sheets of boiler plate to provide some protection for the driver and the machine-gun which they carried, were quickly replaced by cars with bodies designed for their task, protected by proper armoured plate and eventually equipped with revolving turrets mounting machine-guns.

In response the Germans built a range of armoured cars of the same general pattern as those produced by the Allies, but which, instead of using touring car chassis, were derived from 4-wheel drive commercial chassis. Prototypes were produced in 1915 by the Büssing, Daimler and Ehrhardt firms. They were considerably heavier than contemporary Allied armoured cars, weighing between 8 and 10 tons (and the Büssing was over 30 feet long) and all had duplicate driving positions at the rear. The Büssing in addition steered on all four wheels. The three cars were sent to the Western Front early in 1916 but do not appear to have taken part in any operations there. By the time they appeared the line had stabilized, trench warfare was in full swing and the chances of armoured car operations were reduced. They were, however, later used on the Russian front where they encountered Russian armoured cars. Subsequently, more, improved cars of the Ehrhardt type were built and used chiefly on the Russian front, but German armoured vehicles made no significant contributions to the campaigns in that part of the world.

Under the Treaty of Versailles Germany was forbidden to build tanks and was allowed only a limited number of armoured cars, primarily for internal security use.

Those built for the Army were prohibited under the Treaty from having revolving turrets and the design was also limited in other ways to prevent them being used as fighting vehicles. The standard Army vehicle, designated

Ehrhardt Panzerkraftwagen 1915. (O. Munzel)

Sdkfz 3, was produced as an armoured personnel carrier although some were subsequently converted to wireless command vehicles. The 4-wheel drive chassis was a modified version of the Daimler DZVR used during the war. The Police armoured cars (Polizeisonderschutz-wagen), which were used for internal security duties, were much more formidable vehicles. There were three models —Daimler, Ehrhardt and Benz. The first Daimlers were built in 1919, but improved Daimlers were built in 1921–1922, together with the Benz and Ehrhardt types. Four-wheel drive chassis of similar type to that of the Sdkfz 3 were used for the Police vehicles but with the addition of rear steering wheels; and the armoured hulls had twin machine-gun turrets, command cupolas and searchlights. All these vehicles were heavy and cumbersome and, despite their four-wheel drive, virtually road-bound.

Büssing Panzerkraftwagen 1915. The vehicle was over 30ft long and steered on all four wheels. (via B. T. White)

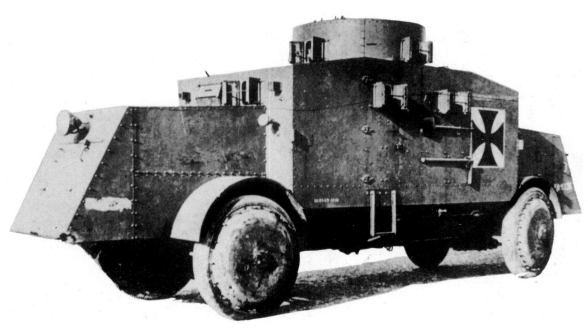

Ehrhardt Panzerkraftwagen 1917: snow chains on wheels for operations on Eastern Front. Identification painted on bonnet is 'Zug 6'.
(Imperial War Museum)

Despite the absence of suitable vehicles for training, interest in the postwar German Army centred on the possibilities of the armoured car for medium and distant reconnaissance for which it was specially suited: it fitted the concept of the reborn German Army, envisaged by its creator General von Seekt, as a compact mobile hard-hitting, fast-moving force. The armoured car was used by the Germans to back up the motor-cyclists, both solo and side-car borne, who were the spearhead of the reconnoitring thrust. As thought and experience crystallised, both armoured cars and motor-cyclists were to be found in the reconnaissance battalions of Panzer divisions, but it took the Germans a long time to mount anything heavier than a 20 mm gun in their armoured cars despite the important role assigned to them in the search for information.

The development of armoured cars in all countries has nearly always followed the same pattern: early models are usually civilian pattern vehicles with an armoured body (amounting almost to a standard pattern everywhere) clapped on to a chassis which may or may not be reinforced to carry the extra load. In due time the limitations of 4 × 2 drive (or even 4-wheel drive not designed for the job) become so obvious that recourse is had to the specialised lorry with multiple axles or four-wheel drive. The advantages of using a standard chassis in reducing cost and production time are so obvious that the next step is always delayed as long as possible. However, eventually it is always impossible to avoid recognition of the fact that the armoured car is a specialised weapon and it can only achieve its ultimate possibilities if it is built for its particular task.

The German Army reached this last stage in 1927 when a specification for a future armoured car was issued:
1. On good level roads the car must have a maximum

speed of 41 m.p.h. and a circuit of action of 125 miles at an average speed of 20 m.p.h.
2. The armoured car must climb a slope of 1 in 3.
3. The armoured car must cross a ditch $1\frac{1}{2}$ metres wide without bellying and without any external assistance.
4. The armoured car must wade in water 1 metre deep.
5. Provision must be made for movement in either direction. The change over from forward to reverse driving position must not take more than 10 seconds.
6. The weight of the chassis must not exceed 4 tons and the complete car $7\frac{1}{2}$ tons.
7. Ground clearance must be ·3 metre.
8. The track of the car must be of such a width that it could be adapted to run on rails if required.
9. The crew was to consist of five men: commander, driver, two gunners and a wireless operator.

It was obvious that no standard chassis could possibly meet these requirements: the stage was thus set for the appearance of a purpose built vehicle, a point that Great Britain, which had been the leading protagonist for the armoured car, only reached years later.

Development contracts for multi-wheeled armoured cars were accepted in 1929 by three firms, Daimler-Benz, Magirus and Büssing-NAG. The first two produced 8-wheeled versions while Büssing-NAG built a 10-wheeled prototype. The Daimler-Benz vehicle, known as ARW/MTW1, had several advanced design features including chassis-less construction, with the automotive components being attached direct to the hull, and was amphibious. The 10 wheeled Büssing-NAG model was also amphibious, as was the Magirus. All three models were tested extensively in secret in Germany and, by special arrangement, in Russia. Development would probably have resulted in a very effective design for production but this was ruled out in 1930 because these specialised multi-wheeled armoured cars were too expensive.

The same three firms—Daimler, Magirus and Büssing-NAG—had in the meantime been engaged in the development of a 6-wheeled armoured car on the commercial chassis which were on offer for the public. The Daimler-Benz models were first on the scene and appear to have played the greater part in the evolution of the production model, but nevertheless all three firms eventually built cars of this type for the Army on their own chassis up to 1935–1936. There were three versions in service, with different functions as follows:

Schwerer Panzerspähwagen Sd Kfz 231 —6-wheeled armoured car with 2 cm gun and one MG.

Schwerer Panzerspähwagen Sd Kfz 232 —6-wheeled armoured car with same armament and a medium range wireless set.

Panzerfunkwagen Sd Kfz 263 —6-wheeled armoured car with non-revolving turret and long range wireless set.

Side by side with the development of the heavy 6-wheeled armoured cars the German Army also put out a requirement for a light 4-wheeled armoured car. By 1933 this had been produced in two versions, the first, Kfz 13, carrying an MG, protected by a small shield and carried on a pivot mounting in an open body. The second version, Kfz 14, carried a wireless set but had no armament: the crew of this car was increased to three men in place of the two in the gun car version. Both types had their engine in front, and had armour 8 mm thick.

These small lightly armoured four-wheeled vehicles were the forerunners of Germany's light armoured cars. They were issued to cavalry regiments which had been converted to the armoured role. Easy to produce and

Ehrhardt Panzerkraftwagen 1919 was externally similar to the 1917 model. (via B. T. White)

Standard German Army vehicle in post-Versailles period was the MTW (Mannschaftstransportwagen) Sd Kfz 3 produced as an armoured personnel carrier. Some were converted to wireless command vehicles. On the left is a Pz SpWg (Panzerspähwagen) Sd Kfz 221. (Col. R. J. Icks)

Three-quarter front view of MTW Sd Kfz 3 converted to a wireless command vehicle (left) with Pz SpWg Sd Kfz 221. (O. Munzel)

Side view of MTW Sd Kfz 3, Daimler 1921. ('Taschenbuch der Tanks')

There were three models of the formidable armoured cars built for the German Police in the post-Versailles period. These Polizeisonderwagen were—

the Ehrhardt 1921—

the Daimler 1921, and—

the Benz 1921.

relatively inexpensive they met the immediate requirements of the newly elected Nazi government for something in the shop window to stimulate Germany's rising pride in her armed forces.

By 1935 the Kfz 13s had proved their value and a fresh requirement for a more sophisticated car was issued. In 1937 the 4-wheel drive SdKfz 221 series was in production, with a rear-mounted engine of 3·5 litres, armour varying between 14 and 8 mm, and a top speed of 50 m.p.h. The chassis in its normal front engine version was also used for other purposes, as an artillery tractor and as an APC: it was designed by Horch and the armoured car version had an open-topped turret with 360 degree traverse mounting a 7·92 mm MG.

There were six versions in the 221 series:

Leichter Panzerspähwagen Sd Kfz 221 (MG)—	mounting MG only.
Leichter Panzerspähwagen Sd Kfz 221 (2·8 cm. PzB41)—	mounting an anti-tank rifle in an open-topped turret.
Leichter Panzerspähwagen Sd Kfz 222 (2 cm)—	mounting 2 cm gun and machine-gun in turret with a hinged wire grille head cover.
Leichter Panzerspähwagen Sd Kfz 223 (Fu)—	MG version but with a medium range wireless set.
Kleiner Panzerfunkwagen Sd Kfz 260—	Both these vehicles were special wireless cars with long range sets.
Kleiner Panzerfunkwagen Sd Kfz 261—	

In 1935, with the Rhineland re-occupied and Germany re-established in her own eyes, the provisions of the Versailles Treaty were openly defied and there was much activity in the German armoured world. As far as armoured cars were concerned the 8- and 10-wheeled designs which had been rejected in 1933 were again examined and were developed into an 8-wheeled armoured car which appeared in the following versions in 1938:

Schwerer Panzerspähwagen (8 Rad) Sd Kfz 231—	armed with 2 cm gun and machine-gun.
Schwerer Panzerspähwagen (8 Rad) Sd Kfz 232 (Fu)—	as above, but with a wireless set.
Schwerer Panzerspähwagen (8 Rad)—Sd Kfz 233—	armed with 7·5 cm gun Stuk L/24.
Panzerfunkwagen (8 Rad) Sd Kfz 263—	no turret, heightened hull with MG in front plate. Long range wireless vehicle.

For some reason the Germans gave these 8-wheeled vehicles the same vocabulary number as those of the earlier 6-wheeled cars. To distinguish between the two the description (6 Rad) or (8 Rad) was added to the vocabulary number. The 231 series (6 Rad) were used by the armoured car companies of the Panzer divisions from 1935 onwards until the 8-wheelers took their place. Some of them were in action in Poland and in the early stages of the campaign in France in 1940.

Two years after the appearance of the Sd Kfz (8 Rad) 231 series there was a further demand from the German Army in August 1940 for armoured cars specially adapted for work in tropical conditions; the North African campaign was then the only active war theatre. They were to be powered by an air-cooled CI engine, to have a more powerful armament than the earlier 8-wheelers and were to carry more armour. This new 234

Three-quarter rear view of the 10-wheeled ZRW (Zehnradwagen) Büssing-NAG prototype, 1929–30. The vehicle was amphibious. (B. H. Vanderveen)

range proved very successful: they were formidable cars and proved very good performers across country, a characteristic also of the earlier 8-wheelers. Their secret lay in the fact that all eight wheels were both driven and steered.

Hitler himself ordered the installation of the long 7·5 cm gun on the 234 chassis. It would have been ideally suited to the anti-tank role and the possibilities inherent in these cars in combination with tanks or static anti-tank guns are enough to make any tactician's mouth water.

The list of variants of the SdKfz 234 is as follows:

Schwerer Panzerspähwagen Sd Kfz 234/1— armoured car with 2 cm Kwk and machine-gun in open turret with hinged wire grille top.

Schwerer Panzerspähwagen Sd Kfz 234/2 (Puma)— 5 cm Kwk L/60 and co-axial machine-gun in enclosed turret.

Schwerer Panzerspähwagen Sd Kfz 234/3— turretless: 7·5 cm Stuk L/24 in open mounting.

Three-quarter front view of the Daimler-Benz 8-wheeled ARW/MTW 1 (Achtradwagen/Mannschaftstransportwagen) during development. The vehicle, which was amphibious, had a chassis-less construction. (via RAC Tank Museum)

Schwerer Panzerspähwagen (6 Rad) Sd Kfz 231 with 2 cm gun and rail round commander's hatch for AA machine-gun. The long gap between the front and rear wheels was a noticeable characteristic of the six-wheelers. (via RAC Tank Museum)

Light 4-wheeled scout car with machine-gun, Maschinengewehr-Kraftwagen Kfz 13, in Russia, summer 1941. (via RAC Tank Museum)

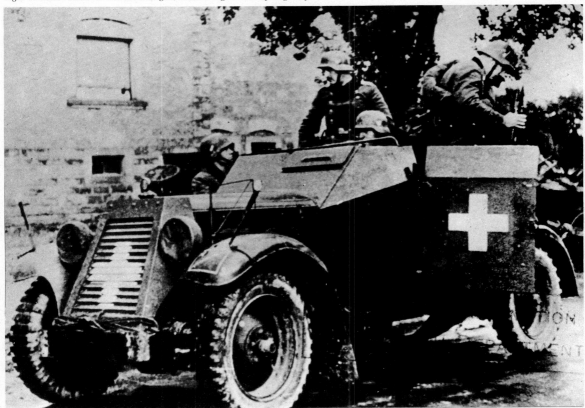

Schwerer Panzerspähwagen (6 Rad) Sd Kfz 232: the wireless-equipped version of the Sd Kfz 231, showing the turret swung beneath the frame aerial.
(via RAC Tank Museum)

Leichter Panzerspähwagen Sd Kfz 221 (MG) at English Channel coast, 1940.
(B. H. Vanderveen)

Schwerer Panzerspähwagen   turretless: 7·5 cm Pak
Sd Kfz 234/4—   L/48 in open mounting.

AMPHIBIOUS ARMOURED CARS

Prototype amphibious armoured cars were designed by Hans Trippel and built by the Trippelwerke in 1941 and 1942. Three versions, Schildkröte (Turtle) I, II and III, were produced armed respectively with a single MG, with two MGs, and finally with a 2 cm gun. Armour was originally on a 7 or 7·5 mm basis but this was later increased to a maximum of 10 mm. An air-cooled V8 Tatra was installed and performance on the road was quite satisfactory; the cars behaved quite well in the water but the three prototypes came up against the usual difficulty experienced by all designers trying to provide inherent buoyancy within the confines of the vehicle: to obtain anything like sufficient flotation the vehicle has to be very lightly constructed, which rules out the possibility of carrying either a weapon large enough to be of any value against hostile AFVs or sufficient armour to confer

Leichter Panzerspähwagen Sd Kfz 221 (2·8 cm PzB41) with a 2·8 cm Panzerbusche anti-tank weapon in place of the machine-gun. The turret was cut away in front and back to accommodate it. Note wire grille for protection on side wing of original turret.
(RAC Tank Museum)

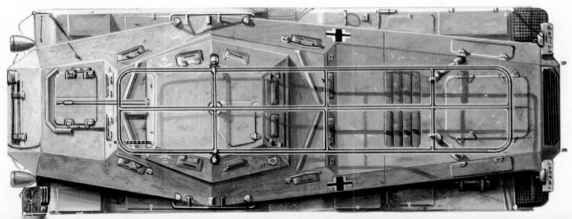

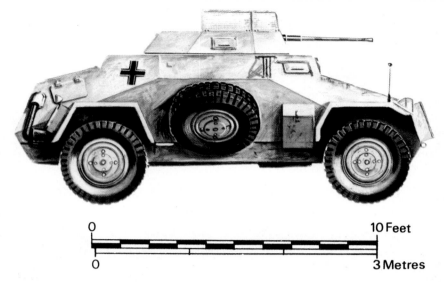

0   10 Feet

0   3 Metres

Above: Leichter Panzerspähwagen Sd Kfz 222 in winter camouflage.

Left: Four views of Schwerer Panzerspähwagen (8 Rad) Sd Kfz 232 (Fu) of the Afrika Korps.

Below: Schwerer Panzerspähwagen (6 Rad) Sd Kfz 231 at the time of the Polish campaign, September 1939.

Bottom: Schwerer Panzerspähwagen Sd Kfz 234/2 (Puma).

T. Hadler © *Profile Publications Ltd.*

Leichter Panzerspähwagen Sd Kfz 222 in North Africa. The 222 had a 2 cm KwK (KraftwagenKanone) L/55 as its main armament, with a 7·92 mm coaxial machine-gun. Overhead protection in the turret was given by a hinged wire grille.   (RAC Tank Museum)

Captured Sd Kfz 222 in North Africa. The two-part wire grille that gave side, front, and overhead protection has been opened to allow room for the special armament installation. (South African National War Museum)

any appreciable measure of immunity against hostile fire.

Great trouble was experienced by Trippelwerke in obtaining the materials needed for the construction of their vehicles and the project was abandoned in 1942.

ARMOURED CARS OF OTHER COUNTRIES USED BY GERMANY

Germany was not a great user of armoured cars and produced most of what she required for her own use. However there were a few types built by other countries which she did incorporate in her own forces. In 1930 Austria built a wheel-cum-track machine which eventually developed into Type RR 7. Fifteen of them had been built by January 1937 and these were afterwards taken into German service as Sd Kfz 254: production was continued until a total of 128 was built. By 1940 RR 9 had appeared, still with wheel and track capacity, but fitted with a revolving turret mounting a machine-gun. This machine and its proposed later developments interested not only the German Army but also the Waffen SS. Despite such powerful backing nothing further was heard of the project which was abandoned in 1942. About

50 Austrian 8-wheeled armoured cars were also taken into German service—these were the Austro-Daimler type ADGZ.

After the fall of France in 1940 the Germans requisitioned about 200 French Panhard armoured cars, Type 178, and gave them the vocabulary number Pz Spw.P 204(f). They were four-wheel drive cars, with a four man crew and were armed with a 25 mm gun and a machine-gun. They were powered by a 4-cylinder Panhard engine of 100 h.p. and, with up to 20 mm of armour, weighed 8·2 tons.

CONSTRUCTIONAL FEATURES

Maschinenegewehr—Kraftwagen mit MG: Kfz 13

This car was of conventional construction with 4×2 drive; it had a front-mounted Adler 6-cylinder engine of 60 h.p. coupled to a sliding pinion 4-speed gearbox and a back axle of normal pattern. The car had a crew of two men, carried in an open-topped body which had one MG mounted on a pivot with a small shield for the commander/gunner. It weighed $2\frac{1}{2}$ tons and the armour was 8 mm thick.

Kfz 14

This wireless car used the same chassis as the Kfz 13 but it had no armament. This was the inevitable disadvantage of a bulky wireless set and had to be accepted until a small and compact set had been developed. Kfz 14 had the same open body as the fighting version and carried a frame aerial almost as big as the ground plan of the car: this could be lowered in the interests of concealment. The reputed range of the set was 20 miles. In Great Britain, the No 1 set was produced in 1931 and fitted into a light tank with a speech range of between 3 and 5 miles albeit with a performance that was both chancy and temperamental. Nonetheless special wireless tanks were not needed.

Pz Spw (6 Rad) Sd Kfz 231

These 6-wheeled armoured cars were the production versions of prototypes submitted by Daimler-Benz, Büssing-NAG and Magirus from 1929 onwards. The first prototype, Daimler-Benz Type G3(p), weighed 4·9 tons, the chassis having a notably long gap between the front wheels and the rear pair of axles: this remained a characteristic of the six-wheelers. A revolving turret mounted one 7·92 MG and a 6-cylinder 70 h.p. Daimler engine drove a standard sliding pinion gearbox, the drive being taken thence by a normal propellor shaft to the three axles, each of which had its own differential. Adjustable tracks could be fitted round the rear wheels to increase cross-country performance in bad going.

After experience with this model Daimler-Benz produced another version, Type G3a(p), which was successfully tried out on manoeuvres in company with a Büssing-NAG version of the car, Type G31(p), which had a 4-cylinder engine. The Magirus model was Type M206(p) and, like the Daimler-Benz, had a 6-cylinder

engine. Out of these cars came the production versions which first appeared in 1933 as Sd Kfz 231. Weight had increased to approximately 6 tons and the crew had become four. A 2 cm gun was mounted in the revolving turret: duplicate steering positions with alternative controls were fitted, the second steering wheel and the controls coming into action when reverse gear in the direction gearbox was engaged. A coaxial MG was added together with a ring round the commander's hatch to allow a light MG to be used for AA defence. The long gap between the wheels was still evident and to reduce the chance of the car "bellying" a roller the complete width of the car was fitted across the middle of the chassis.

Pz Spw (6 Rad) Sd Kfz 232

This was the same car as 231 but was fitted with a wireless set and also mounted a coaxial MG. A horizontal frame aerial consisting of parallel tubes was carried on two outriggers at the back of the car. The frame had a central bearing which rested on a turret support shaped like an inverted "U". This allowed the turret to turn beneath the aerial without transmitting any movement to it. No provision was apparently made to avoid the danger of shooting away the rear aerial supports when the turret was turned to 160 and 200 degrees.

Panzerfunkwagen (6 Rad) Sd Kfz 263

This was an ordinary 231 chassis fitted with a non-rotating turret carrying in its front plate only one MG for defensive purposes. The extra space within the hull was used to house a long range wireless set. A frame aerial of similar design to that on Sd Kfz 232 (Fu) but of slightly different shape was supported at four points and could be lowered if necessary. Provision was made for trans-

Schwerer Panzerspähwagen (8 Rad) Sd Kfz 231 was armed with a 2 cm KwK and a coaxial 7·92 mm MG. (R. Surlémont)

Schwerer Panzerspähwagen (8 Rad) Sd Kfz 232 was the same car as the 231 and mounted the same armament, but it had a medium range wireless set with a frame aerial.
(RAC Tank Museum)

mission through a mast aerial if greater range was needed.

The 6 Rad range of cars were robust and well-built with a good cross-country performance, though hampered by their tendency to belly in bad going even when fitted with the cross-car roller. It is possible that this weakness may have revived interest in the 8- and 10-wheeled designs which were submitted for consideration in 1929 when the question of multi-wheeled cars first came up. However, before going on to describe the range of 8-wheeled cars that came into service, there was the range of 4-wheeled armoured cars that came into service with the German Army from 1938 onwards.

Pz Spw Sd Kfz 221—Light four-wheeled armoured cars

These cars were built to meet a requirement for a range of light armoured cars and came into production in 1937. A 75 h.p. water-cooled V8 Horch petrol engine was mounted at the rear and the drive was taken to a sliding pinion gearbox of conventional design giving five forward speeds and one reverse gear. From this box the drive was taken to front and rear differentials and thence to the wheels. These were independently sprung, each having two radius arms controlled by parallel coil springs. Bullet-proof tyres were fitted and the car weighed 4 tons.

Pz Spw Sd Kfz 222

This was a later development of Sd Kfz 221 and appeared a year later in 1938. The same chassis was used but the front armour plate was increased in thickness to 14·5 mm which raised the weight to 4·8 tons. The engine power was increased to 81 and later 90 hp. The turret was

higher and was provided with overhead cover in the form of a hinged wire grille. A 2cm KwK L/55 gun was mounted with a coaxial 7·92 mm MG and the crew was increased to 3 men.

Pz Spw (Fu) Sd Kfz 223

These cars were similar to the 222s but carried a medium range wireless set and were armed only with a 7·92 mm MG mounted in a small turret set on the top of the superstructure. A rectangular frame aerial was mounted on four supports hinged to the body and could be lowered when necessary to reduce the silhouette. This aerial, which was of a different pattern to that fitted to the multi-wheeled wireless cars, did not prove satisfactory and was replaced by a vertical rod.

One other version of these cars must be mentioned. In some cases the turret of the 221 pattern was cut back and a 2·8 cm Panzerbusche was mounted in it. This weapon was really an anti-tank rifle firing solid shot and using a "squeeze" device to obtain higher MV. It was a large gun and had to be mounted above the turret ring. A shield was provided for the gunner's protection and the side wings of the original turret were retained, but the protection could only be described as scanty at best.

Pz Spw (8 Rad) Sd Kfz 231

While the 6-wheeler armoured cars grew up from existing commercial chassis, however much these were altered in the process, the 8-wheelers were a new design from the beginning. The engine and gearbox were situated at the rear of the hull in a chassis of light construction which served to locate the various components, rigidity of the car as a whole being assured by the

194

armoured hull. This seems a clumsy form of construction and the British system of dispensing with the chassis and using the hull to locate components and give rigidity seems preferable, at least on grounds of weight saving.

The eight wheels were mounted as two bogies of four, each wheel being linked to the hull by two parallel swinging arms. Each pair of wheels shared an inverted semi-elliptic spring, which pivoted at its centre about the extensions of two tubular cross members which ran across the chassis. Alternative steering positions were provided, with controls that could be engaged by a lever on the steering column.

A 155 h.p. Büssing V8 petrol engine drove a three-speed constant mesh gearbox which had an auxiliary two-speed box incorporated with it, giving a total range of six speeds. A separate direction box was provided which gave a full range of gears for forward and reverse movement. The drive was taken from these boxes to two auxiliary transfer boxes in the middle of the two bogies. From these transfer boxes limited slip differentials took the drive to the four wheels of the bogie concerned. All eight wheels were both steered and driven which involved some complicated design work especially over the geometry of the steering layout. The middle wheels have to turn less than those at either end of the car, and to compensate for the difference in the various radii a De Lavaud type of differential was incorporated in each of the transfer boxes. The layout sounds very complicated but it contributed in no small measure to the very good cross-country performance of these cars. On a curve

Pz SpWg (8 Rad) Sd Kfz 232 after capture in the Middle East. (Imperial War Museum)

Above the Australian officer's head as he lectures on the characteristics of a captured Sd Kfz 232 (8 Rad) in the Middle East can be seen one of the legs on the turret with which the arms from a central pivot engaged to support the front end of the frame aerial. (Imperial War Museum)

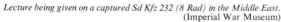

Lecture being given on a captured Sd Kfz 232 (8 Rad) in the Middle East. (Imperial War Museum)

Panzerfunkwagen (8 Rad) Sd Kfz 263 was a specialised wireless armoured car with a crew of five, as against four in the 8 Rad 231 and 232. Its only armament was a 7·92 mm MG 34 in the front plate of the heightened superstructure which formed a rigid turret. Frame aerial had an extra pair of supports compared with the 232's and no arrangement for pivoting in front. Rod aerials replaced frame aerials in 1942. (RAC Tank Museum)

Schildkröte (probably III) in water—front view. The Schildkröte project, begun in 1941, was abandoned in 1942. (Imperial War Museum)

Schildkröte (Turtle) prototype during swimming trials.
(RAC Tank Museum)

Schwerer Panzerspähwagen Sd Kfz 234/2 (Puma) was armed with a 5 cm KwK L/60 and a co-axial 7·92 mm MG in a totally enclosed turret. The 234 series came into service in 1943. It can readily be distinguished from the earlier eight-wheeled armoured cars by the different mudguard arrangement, the earlier cars having a break between the front pair and rear pair of mudguards on each side. (RAC Tank Museum)

Schwerer Panzerspähwagen Sd Kfz 234/3 was a close support armoured car mounting a 7·5 cm StuK L/24 in an open body. (RAC Tank Museum)

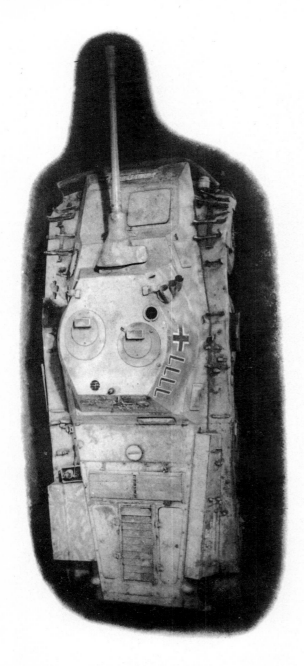

Top view of Pz SpWg Sd Kfz 234/2 (Puma). (RAC Tank Museum)

every wheel exactly tracked the one in front of it, in contrast to the conditions obtaining in the usual 6-wheeled model where the middle wheel has literally to be dragged sideways on a curve to follow the track of the steered wheel in front of it.

Sd Kfz 231 (8 Rad) appeared with a 2cm KwK gun and a 7·92 mm MG in the turret which, although larger, resembled that of the 6-wheeled 231 but had a front plate coming down to the hull, thereby eliminating the dangerous re-entrant angle below the gun which was a characteristic feature of the earlier car. Later cars of the 231 (8 Rad) series, built from 1939 onwards, had the engine h.p. increased to 180.

Pz Spw (8 Rad) Sd Kfz 232

This was the same car as the 231 and mounted the same armament but it was fitted with a medium range wireless set. It had a frame aerial with fixed supports at the back of the car: the front end was supported on a central pivot which engaged with bipod legs erected on the turret and allowed this to turn without disturbing the aerial.

Pz Spw (8 Rad) Sd Kfz 233

This car was intended to provide covering fire for the 231-232 cars which only mounted a 2 cm gun. 233 had an open turret in which was mounted a 7·5 cm StuK L/24 gun with limited traverse. The car was open from the top of the superstructure and the low velocity 7·5 cm gun was enclosed in a curious box-shaped mantlet.

Panzerfunkwagen (8 Rad) Sd Kfz 263

The range of 8-wheeled armoured cars was completed by a specialised wireless car, the sides of the crew compartment being built up to provide accommodation for the wireless gear. The superstructure was higher than in the gun cars but the general outline resembled them so that at a distance it was difficult to differentiate between 263 and 232, except for the fact that the frame aerial for 263 was slightly larger. In 1942 the frame aerials on both type of car were abolished and were replaced by a rod pattern. 263 carried one 7·92 mm MG in a ball-mounting in the front plate, but was otherwise unarmed.

Pz Spw Sd Kfz 234 series

The general layout of the (8 Rad) 231 cars was retained in these "Tropical" armoured cars, except for minor alterations and modifications. The thickness of the front armour was increased to 30 mm and a 220 h.p. Tatra V12 air-cooled CI engine replaced the water-cooled Büssing used in the (8 Rad) 231 series. This Tatra engine gave considerable trouble when first installed but this trouble was eventually cured, the 234 series coming into service in 1943. Production models weighed between 10½ and 11½ tons with a consequent reduction of top speed to 53 m.p.h. in place of the 62 m.p.h. of the earlier cars. The general layout of gearboxes, transferboxes and differentials remained the same. The first car to appear, Sd Kfz 234/1, mounted a 2 cm gun and a coaxial MG in an open-topped turret which resembled that of Sd Kfz 222, the earlier 4 × 4 car. For the size of the car the armament appears very inadequate but this was to be rectified with the next model.

Type	Weight	Length	Width	Height	Engine bhp/rpm	hp/ton	Transmission	Speed mph	Radius of Action miles	Armament/Amn. Main	Armament/Amn. MGs	Armour Max/Min mm	Crew	Remarks
Ehrhardt BAK 1906	3·2				Ehrhardt 4 cyl. 60 hp.	18·8		28°	100	50mm/100		3/	5	Solid tyres. Twin turrets. Similar type of machine was also produced by Ehrhardt and Daimler. Dimensions and performance virtually as for the Benz version. Daimler Benz prototype 8-Wheeler—basis for 231–234 8-Wheelers
Pz Kw Daimler M 1915	9	19' 9½"	8' 8"	11' 2½"	Daimler M 1464 4 cyl. 80/1200	8·9		23·5	150	—	3 × 7·92mm	7/5	8-9	
M21 Sonderschutz-wagen Benz. 1920	7	18' 2"	7' 7"	7' 1"	Daimler UT 1574 4 cyl. 100/1200.	14·3		31		—	2 × 7·92mm/ 6000	9/7	7-9	
ARW/MTWl. 1929	7·8				Daimler Benz M36 6 cyl. 105/2350	13·5		40	150	1 × 3·7cm	1 × 7·92mm	13·5	5	
6—Wheeled Cars														
Daimler Benz G3a 1929	4·9	18' 8"	6' 2"	7' 10"	Daimler Benz MO9 6 cyl. 68/2900	14	3-speed sliding pinion with addtl. 2-speed box. Separate change direction box. All axles were driven	38	150		1 × 7·92mm	14·5/8	4	DB. G3(p)—60hp. DB. engine at 2800 rpm. Wt. 5·5 tons: hp/ton 10·9 Bussing NAG. G31 (p)—4 cyl Bussing-NAG 65 hp at 2000 rpm. Wt. 5 tons: hp/ton 13. These machines and Magirus M206—Magirus 70 hp—were pre-production armd. cars before the issue of Sd Kfz 231 (6 Rad) Bussing-NAG and Klockner-Humbolt also built this car to the same design but using a 4 cyl 60hp Bussing-NAG and a 6 cyl 70hp Magirus engine respectively.
PzSpw (6 Rad) Sd Kfz 231 1933	5	18' 8"	6' 2"	7' 6"	Daimler Benz MO9 6 cyl. 68/2900	13·6	"	38	150	1 × 2cm/ 200	1 × 7·92mm/ 2000	14/8	4	
Pz Spw (6-Rad) Sd Kfz 232 (Fu)														Mechanically these vehicles were the same as Sd Kfz 231. 263 did not have a revolving turret and was purely a wireless vehicle with one mg. for defensive purposes. 232 had a frame aerial and a medium range wireless set. The turret could revolve below the aerial. Some of the 231 range were fitted with belly rollers running across the cars, between the front and back wheels. Dimensions for 232 and 263—as for 231
Panzerfunkwagen (6 Rad) Sd K/3 263														
4—Wheeled Cars														
Mg-Kw. Kfz 13	2·3	14' 0"	6' 8"	5' 0"	Adler 65—6cyl: 60/2406	26·7	4 × 2	31	150	—	1 × 7·92mm/ 2000	8	3	Sd Kfz 14 was the same car unarmed but carrying a medium range wireless set.
Pz Spw Sd Kfz. 221 1937	4	16' 0"	6' 6"	6' 0"	Horch 108 V8. 81/3600	20·3	Sliding pinion gearbox. 5FlR Front and rear differential giving 4-wheel drive.	50	200	1 × 2·8cm or	1 × 7·92mm/ 2000	8/6	2	This car had a long cut away turret when the 2·8 cm was mounted
Pz Spw. (Fu) Sd Kfz 223	4·4	"	"	"	"	18·4	"	"	"	—	1 × 7·92mm	8/6	3	This was a 221 adapted to take a medium range wireless set.
Kl. Pz. Funkwagen (Sd Kfz 260 and 261)	"					"		"	"	—	—	8/6	3	Both these machines were unarmed versions of 221 adapted to take a long range wireless set.
Pz Spw Sd Kfz 222 1938	4·8	16' 0"	6' 6"	6' 10"	Horch 108 V8. 81/3600	17	As for 221.	50	175	1 × 2cm/ 220	1 × 7·92mm/ 2000	14·5/10/5	3	Redesigned version of 221 with wire enclosed turret and slightly higher superstructure.
8—Wheeled Cars														
Pz Spw (8 Rad) Sd Kfz 231 1938	8·3	19' 6"	7' 4"	7' 9"	Bussing-NAG. L8V–GS 150/3000	18	3 speed Constant mesh gearbox with 2 speed auxiliary box. Separate direction change box. Two transfer boxes each with limited slip differential to four wheels. De Lavaud type differential in each transfer box	62	185	1 × 20mm/ 180	1 × 7·92mm/ 1000	14/10/8	4	WT with rod aerial sometimes fitted Sd Kfz 232 was the same car as 231 but had a medium range wireless and a frame aerial fitted. All the (8 Rad) 231 series had two mudguards each side, each one covering two wheels.

Table continued overleaf

8—Wheeled Cars (Continued)

Type	Weight	Length	Width	Height	Engine bhp/rpm	hp/ton	Transmission	Speed mph	Radius of Action miles	Armament/Amn. Main	Armament/Amn. MGs	Armour Max/Min mm	Crew	Remarks
Sd Kfz 233 (8 Rad)	8·3	19'6"	7'4"	7'9"	Bussing-NAG L8V–GS 150/3000	18	3 speed Constant mesh gearbox with 2 speed auxiliary box. Separate direction change box. Two transfer boxes each with limited slip differential to four wheels. De Lavaud type differential in each transfer box	62	185	1 × 7·5cm/85	1 × 7·92mm/1000	14/10/8	5	No turret, and no head cover for crew. Limited traverse for gun.
Pz Fu Wg Sd Kfz 263 (8 Rad)	8·1	"	"	"	"	18·4	"	"	"	—	1 × 7·92mm/1000	"	5	Fitted with long range wireless set. Frame aerial.
Pz Spw (8 Rad) Sd Kfz 234/1	10·5	20'1"	7'10"	7'0"	Tatra 103 12 cyl air cooled V12 C.I. engine 220/2250	21	"	53	375	1 × 2cm/280	1 × 7·92mm/1000	30/15/8	4	6 sided open topped turret. Wire mesh anti-grenade screen. The 234 series have one long mudguard each side covering all four wheels
Sd Kfz 234/2 (Puma)	11	20'1"	7'10"	7'7½"	"	"	"	"	"	1 × 5cm/55	1 × 7·92mm/1000	100/10	4	Totally enclosed turret—5cm KwK L/60 gun.
Sd Kfz 234/3	10·5	"	"	7'0"	"	"	"	"	"	1 × 7·5cm/60	1 × 7·92mm/1000	30/15/8	5	No turret and no head cover for crew. Limited traverse for gun. 7·5cm StuK L/24 gun.
Sd Kfz 234/4	10·5	"	"	"	"	"	"	"	"	1 × 7·5cm/60	1 × 7·92mm/1000	"	5	No turret and no head cover for crew. Limited traverse for gun 7·5cm Pak L/48 gun.

Pz Spw Sd Kfz 234/2 (Puma)

234/2 was armed with a 5 cm KwK L/60 gun and a coaxial 7·92 mm MG. These were mounted in a totally enclosed oval-shaped turret with steeply sloping sides, giving a very good ballistic shape. Puma was the most powerfully armed armoured car that the Germans had and was a very formidable weapon. In common with all the 234 range it was fitted with wireless and carried a rod aerial which terminated in three points on the near side mudguard at the back of the car.

Pz Spw Sd Kfz 234/3

This car mounted the 7·5 cm StuK L/24 in an open body of the same pattern as that used in Sd Kfz (8 Rad) 233.

Pz Spw Sd Kfz 234/4

This car owes its existence to a personal order of Hitler's. The 234 body was modified to mount the 7·5 Pak L/48 and in this guise it was really more of an S.P. anti-tank weapon than an armoured car. The HV gun made this car a most formidable weapon.

GUN POWER AND THE GERMAN ARMOURED CAR.

Armoured car production for the German Army was on a relatively small scale: it was not a weapon on which the Army put great reliance, except to back up reconnaissance troops, and consequently it never received anything like the attention that was lavished on the development of German tanks. The cars were soundly constructed, capable of carrying out their appointed tasks, but they relied on speed, manoeuvrability and lightness to achieve their ends: to this end they sacrificed armour protection and, very curiously for the Germans, gun-power. It was not until 1944 that they introduced a 5 cm gun and mounted it in an enclosed revolving turret.

Up till then the heaviest gun mounted in a fully traversing turret—the criterion of the true armoured car—had been the 2 cm. The Puma with its 5 cm gun put the German armoured car on an equality with the British Daimler for the first time. However, in drawing this comparison it must be remembered that both 8-wheeled chassis, the 231 and 234, had been adapted to mount the short 7·5 cm gun StuK L/24, primarily to support the operations of the machine-gun armed cars.

Other variations in armament comprised the 2·8 cm anti-tank rifle which was fitted with a "squeeze" device to obtain higher muzzle velocity against hostile AFVs, and the high velocity 7·5 cm gun Pak L/40 which was mounted on the 234 8-wheeled chassis.

Post-war thinking in the British Army has recognised the need for a good HE and shot firing weapon in armoured cars and this is typified in the 76 mm gun found in the Saladin armoured car. This need was appreciated by the Germans for tanks quite early in World War II: by this standard German wartime armoured car armament falls short.

10.5cm (f) auf PzKpfw Mk VI (e)
A small number of captured British light tanks of the Mk VI series were converted as mobile mounts for the French 105mm gun.
(Bundesarchiv Koblenz)

Illustrated Summary of German Self-Propelled Weapons 1939–1945

by Peter Chamberlain and Hilary L. Doyle

INTRODUCTION

EVEN before the outbreak of the Second World War, German Panzer experts had called for the introduction of self-propelled guns to accompany the Panzer Divisions then in the process of being formed. These demands, of course, referred primarily to self-propelled carriages for the field guns of the artillery regiments which would support the main fighting units, the tanks, in both attack and defence. However, due to the heavy production requirements for tanks and the limited war effort during the period from 1939 to 1941, plans to produce self-propelled artillery were neglected to a great extent and only a few attempts were made to introduce mobile guns.

Events in Russia during the latter part of 1941 forced an unforeseen development—the hurried introduction of large numbers of improvised self-propelled anti-tank guns. The carriages used were converted from the now obsolete light tanks which constituted so much of the strength of the Panzer Divisions and occupied so much space on the production lines of numerous German tank factories. These self-propelled guns were not the carefully designed weapons which had been urged before the war, but were instead a panic attempt to make up for the very low number of medium tanks available and even the inferiority of these same medium tanks. Such make-shift equipments were not the answer to the problems, and field units soon complained and demanded better tanks and tank destroyers. However, production was continued until the end of the war by the utilisation of otherwise useless stocks of captured foreign tank chassis and guns; such production being justified on the grounds that

the mobility of these anti-tank guns was worthwhile during the many defensive battles that were the order of the day. Fortunately, a true anti-tank weapon became available through the up-gunning of the infantry assault gun or Sturmgeschuetz, and by its more developed successor the Jagdpanzer. Heavily armed and armoured these low vehicles were ideal for defensive warfare and proved very successful, so much so that in the final years of the war far more of this type of vehicle were produced than tanks.

Meanwhile, the much neglected mobile artillery was provided by using a proportion of the already mentioned obsolete light tank chassis. Again the improvised nature of these self-propelled guns caused difficulties, and improvements were requested by artillery units in the front line. This led to the interesting development of the Waffenträger. Basically it was hoped to produce a gun with all-round traverse which could be dismounted from its self-propelled carriage when required. Several advanced projects were not finalised due to the pressure on German industry as the war situation deteriorated.

A notable exception in this story were the anti-aircraft guns which were given self-propelled carriages of a semi-tracked type from the start of the war. However, the development of a fully tracked and armoured anti-aircraft mounting was continually left over and this problem was only tackled in the last years of the war when Allied air power began to cripple the mobile formations of the German Army.

There were a vast number of different types of self-propelled gun and these can be classified either by the carriage or by the type of weapon. As the prime purpose for building all these self-propelled guns was to mobilise a specific weapon, any and every type of chassis could be and was used.

For this reason the authors have divided this Summary into sections according to the type of weapon used, ie. Anti-Tank (Pak), Assault Gun (StuG), and so forth, and then they have catalogued the equipments within these sections in chronological order by the calibre of the gun.

Reference to the glossary of German terms will explain the full meaning of any of the vehicle designations given in the picture captions.

This Summary is the first fully comprehensive coverage of all known German operational, improvised and experimental self-propelled weapons to be mounted on wheeled, tracked or semi-tracked vehicles during the period from 1939 to 1945 and the authors would like to thank the following individuals for the assistance they have given ie: Col. R. J. Icks, J. de Voss, Masami Tokoi, J. Milsom, R. Hunnicutt, W. Spielberger. Grateful acknowledgements also to Derek Mayne of the Imperial War Museum and to Dr Haupt of the Bundesarchiv Koblenz.

GLOSSARY OF GERMAN TERMS USED IN THIS SUMMARY

Abbreviation	Full Term	English Translation
	Auf	Upon, on
Ausf.	Ausfuehrung	Model, Mark
	Bis	To
(f)	Franzoesisch	French
Fgst	Fahrgestell	Chassis
FH	Feldhaubitze	Field Howitzer
FK	Feldkanone	Field Gun
Flak	Fliegerabwehrkanone	Anti-Aircraft Gun
	Flakpanzer	Anti-Aircraft tank
	Frueher	Formerly
	Fuer	For
	Geraet	Weapon
gep	Gepanzert	Armoured
gl	Gleiskette	Track(ed)
GrW	Granatewerfer	Mortar
GW	Geschuetzwagen	Gun Motor Carriage
Haub	Haubitze	Howitzer
I	Infanterie	Infantry
IG	Infanteriegescheutz	Infantry Gun
JgdPz	Jagdpanzer	Tank Hunter
Kwk	Kampfwagenkanone	Tank Gun
le	Leicht	Light
leFH	leichte Feldhaubitze	Light Field Howitzer
Lkw	Lastkraftwagen	Lorry, Truck
m	Mittler	Medium
MG	Maschinengewehr	Machine Gun
	Mit	With
Mrs	Moerser	Heavy Mortar/Howitzer
NbW	Nebelwerfer	Chemical/Smoke Projector
(O)	Oesterreichisch	Austrian
	Oder	Or/Alternatively
Pak	Panzerabwehrkanone	Anti-Tank Gun
Pjk	Panzerjaegerkanone	Anti-Tank gun adapted for use in Tank Hunter vehicles
Pz	Panzer	Tank
PzB	Panzerbüchse	Small Anti-Tank Gun with tapered bore
PzH	Panzerhaubitze	Howitzer adapted for fitting in armoured vehicles
PzJaeg	Panzerjaeger	Tank Destroyer/Fighter
PzKpfw	Panzerkampfwagen	Battle Tank
PzSpWg	Panzerspähwagen	Armoured Reconnaissance Car
(r)	Russisch	Russian
Raup	Raupe	Caterpillar Track
RaupFzg	Raupenfahrzeug	Self-Propelled full tracked vehicle
RSO	Raupen Schlepper Ost	Tracked Carrier East
RW	Raketenwerfer	Rocket Projector
s	Schwer	Heavy
Saukopf	Saukopfblende	Boars Head/Cast gun mantlet
SdKfz	Sonderkraftfahrzeug	Special Purpose Motor Vehicle
SdFgst	Sonderfahrgestell	Purpose built chassis
sFH	Schwere Feldhaubitze	Heavy Field howitzer
Sf(Sfl)	Selbstfahrlafette	Self-Propelled Carriage
sIG	Schwere Infanteriegeschütz	Heavy Infantry Gun
sPzSpWg	Schwere Panzerspähwagen	Heavy Armoured Reconnaissance Car
SPW	Schützenpanzerwagen	Armoured Infantry Vehicle
StuG	Sturmgescheutz	Assault Gun
StuH	Sturmhaubitze	Assault Howitzer
StuK	Sturmkanone	Assault cannon
StuMrs	Sturmmoerser	Assault Mortar
(t)	Tchechoslowakisch	Czechoslovakian
	Und	And
	Vierling	Quadruple
VK	Voll Ketten/ Versuchkonsruktion	Fully tracked/Experimental prototype vehicle
	Waffentraeger	Weapons Carrier/Transporter
Werf	Werfer	Projector
Zgkw	Zugkraftwagen	Prime Mover/Semi-Tracked Vehicle
	Zwilling	Twin/Dual

Assault Guns (Sturmgeschuetz)

From experience gained during World War I, the German Army requested an armoured mobile gun able to advance with the infantry and destroy local strong points where supporting artillery was not available or capable of doing this task. The design eventually adopted was that of a turretless tank mounting a low velocity gun in the front hull.

The turret was replaced by a squat superstructure, and a short barrelled 7,5cm KwK L/24 gun was mounted low in the hull front, the gun having a limited traverse.

Gepanzerte Selbstfahrlafette fuer Sturmgeschuetz 7,5cm Kanone Ausf. A SdKfz 142 or Sturmgeschultz III Ausf. A
Based on the Panzerkampfwagen III Ausf. E, this was the first of the series to go into production, during 1940. Crew 4. Weight 19.5 tons.

Gepanzerte Selbstfahrlafette fuer Sturmgeschuetz 7,5cm Kanone Ausf. B, C and D SdKfz 142 or Sturmgeschultz III, Ausf. B bis D
Produced from 1941 these three models were basically similar to StuG Ausf. A. There was little external difference between these models except for variations in the chassis, Ausf. F, G and H respectively. Crew 4. Weight 22 tons.

Sturmgeschuetz III, Ausf. E SdKfz 142
Produced in 1942, this was the last model to be armed with the short barrelled 7,5cm KwK L/24. Though similar to the previous models, this vehicle was fitted with an additional armoured pannier on the right side to carry extra radio equipment when in use as a Zugführerwagen (Unit Commander's vehicle).

7,5cm Sturmgeschuetz 40, Ausf. F SdKfz 142/1 or Sturmgeschuetz III Ausf.F
Early in 1942 the first StuG models with a long barrel 7,5cm StuK 40 L/43 were introduced. This was a development of the KwK 40 tank gun adapted for use in the assault type of vehicle. Based on a chassis similar to that of the StuG III Ausf. E, this vehicle had a modified superstructure fitted with an electric fan on top to ventilate the fighting compartment. Crew 4. Weight 21.6 tons.

7,5cm Sturmgeschuetz 40 Ausf. F/8
Only a small series of the StuG III Ausf. F were armed with the L/43 gun. The Ausf. F/8 was then fitted with a longer gun, the 7,5cm Sturmkanone (StuK) 40 L/48.

7,5cm Sturmgeschuetz 40 Ausf. G SdKfz 142/1 or StuG III Ausf. G fuer StuK 40 L/48
This model appeared at the end of 1942 and was based on the Panzerkampfwagen III Ausf. J. Again various changes had taken place. The longer gun, the Sturmkanone 40, was fitted and the nose frontal armour increased. The roof of the superstructure was equipped with a circular commander's cupola, with seven episcopes—previously the commander had had a fixed hatch through which the artillery scissors periscope projected. Also on the roof was a small armour shield for use with the machine gun. Later vehicles were fitted with armoured skirting and treated with Zimmerit (Anti-magnetic grenade plaster). Crew 4. Weight 23.9 tons.

7,5cm Sturmgeschuetz 40 Ausf. G (Saukopf) SdKfz 142/1
This was the final production version of the Sturmgeschuetz III and was similar to the Ausf. G, but it had heavier armour and a cast gun mantlet called a Saukopfblende or Saukopf (Pig's Head). Final production vehicles were equipped with a remote controlled machine gun on the turret roof. Crew 4. Weight 24.5 tons. (Bundesarchiv, Koblenz)

**Sturmgeschuetz IV L/48 (7,5cm StuK 40) SdKfz 163
or StuG IV fuer 7,5cm StuK 40**
Produced from 1943, this equipment consisted of the 7,5cm StuK 40 mounted on the chassis of the Panzerkampfwagen IV Ausf. H or J. The superstructure was modified from that of the StuG III Ausf. G, late model with Saukopf mantlet. Armour protecting was increased by the addition of slabs of concrete six inches thick attached to the front plate and roof over the driver's compartment.

Late models were equipped with a remote-controlled machine gun on the roof. Crew 4. Weight 23 tons.

10,5cm Feldhaubitze 42 SdKfz 142/2   or Sturmhaubitze 42 Ausf. F
With the adoption of the long L/43 7,5cm gun in place of the short 7,5cm low velocity gun on the StuG III models there remained a limited requirement for howitzer-armed vehicles for the close support role. As developed, this close support weapon had the usual characteristics of the StuG but was confined to a purely anti-personnel role, firing high explosive and not armour-piercing ammunition as did the up-gunned StuG models. Produced in 1942, the first of the assault howitzer vehicles were armed with the 10,5cm le FH 18, a light field howitzer adapted for use in the StuG. Identical to Sturmgeschuetz 40 Ausf. F, only a few of these vehicles were built. Crew 4. Weight 23 tons.

Late production model above showing remote-controlled machine gun on roof.

10,5cm Sturmhaubitze 42 Ausf. G, SdKfz 142/2   or Sturmgeschuetz III mit 10,5cm StuH 42 L/28 3   or StuG III fuer 10,5cm StuH 42
This equipment with respect to the chassis and superstructure was identical to the Sturmgeschuetz 40, but it was armed with the 10,5cm Sturmhaubitz 42 L/28 (Assault Howitzer) that had been adapted to this role. Late production models had no muzzle brakes and were fitted with remote-controlled machine guns on the roof. Some vehicles in this series were fitted with a modified version of the cast gun mantlet Saukopf. Crew 4. Weight 24 tons.

10,5cm Sturmhaubitze 42 Ausf. G without muzzle brake. Equipped with armour skirting.

10,5cm Sturmhaubitze 42 Ausf. G with Saukopf.

Mid-production Brummbaer showing driver's housing with periscope.

Late production Brummbaer with front ball-mounted machine gun, and new type of commander's cupola equipped with anti-aircraft machine gun.

StuPz 43 or Sturmpanzer IV Brummbaer
or Sturmhaubitze 43 L/12 auf Fgst PzKpfw IV (Sf) SdKfz 166

Designed as a heavy armoured assault vehicle this equipment was the final development of the 15cm sIG 33 assault gun carriages. Based on the Panzerkampfwagen IV chassis models F, G, H and J this version was equipped with the 15cm Sturmhaubitze L/12 that had been developed from the sIG 33. This short 15cm howitzer was ball-mounted in a heavily armoured box-type superstructure with a frontal thickness of 100mm.

Variations of this equipment existed. In early vehicles the driver had direct vision through a visor of the vertical sliding shutter type arranged in the front plate of the superstructure, this was as used on the Pz VI Tiger tank. Mid-production machines were fitted with a built-up cab with no visor, the driver using a fixed periscope in the cab roof. The late production version carried a ball-mounted machine gun high up on the left side of the front superstructure plate. The armour arrangement of the front and rear of the superstructure was also changed, the front now consisting of two plates instead of one. 313 machines were built. Crew 5. Weight 28.2 tons.

38cm RW 61 auf StuMrs Tiger
or Sturmmoerser 38cm, RW 61, Sturmtiger

This equipment was designed at the request of the army for a self-propelled 21cm howitzer, capable of following the advancing troops and able to engage difficult targets with high angle fire.

As no suitable howitzer of 21cm calibre was available however, it was decided to use the 38cm Raketenwerfer 61 L/54, a weapon that had originally been developed as a naval anti-submarine projector.

The mobile mount for this breech loading rocket projector was the chassis of the PzKpfw VI Tiger E with the normal superstructure and turret replaced by a heavy rectangular superstructure of the type used on the Panzerjaeger SP equipments, the projector being mounted offset to the right of centre in the front plate. A small crane for loading the rocket projectiles through a hatch in the rear roof plate into the interior of the vehicle was mounted on the right rear corner of the superstructure. Racks were provided on either side of the fighting compartment to accommodate 12 rounds, while an additional round could be carried in the projector tube.

This vehicle entered limited production during 1944, a total of 10 Tigers being converted. Crew 5. Weight 68 tons.

Close Support 7,5cm Kwk L/24

As the short barrelled 7,5cm gun became available, being no longer required for use with the Panzerkampfwagen IV and Sturmgeschuetz vehicles, it was used for mounting in armoured cars and armoured personnel carriers, adapting these vehicles to the close support role. It was first used on the SdKfz 251/9 armoured personnel carrier and the SdKfz 233 eight-wheeled armoured car, both mountings requiring structural modifications of the basic vehicle.

The gun was mounted on a low pedestal, and the right half of the driver's visor plate was cut away to make room for the barrel. A small sloping armour plate was arranged over the gun to provide protection for the gun crew. Traverse of the gun was limited, being 12 degrees each way, with a maximum elevation of 20 degrees. During mid-1943 a new mounting was developed that enabled the gun to be fixed on top of any suitable structure with only minor alterations. This new gun mounting was used for the armoured personnel carrier, SdKfz 250, similar equipment being used with the SdKfz 234 eight-wheeled armoured car.

Mittlerer Schuetzenpanzerwagen (7,5cm KwK L/24) SdKfz 251/9
Armoured Personnel Carrier SdKfz 251 with 7,5cm KwK L/24 in the early recessed gun mounting. Crew 3. Weight 8.53 tons.

Front view of the SdKfz 251/9. Dial sight and commander's periscope are shown behind the gun.

SdKfz 251/9 with 7,5cm gun in new mounting.

Leichter Schuetzenpanzerwagen mit 7,5cm KwK L/24 SdKfz 250/8
Light Personnel Carrier SdKfz 250 equipped with the short 7,5cm gun in new mounting. An MG 42 machine gun was mounted on the gun to give co-axial fire and also to act as a ranging gun for the latter. Crew 3. Weight 6 tons.

Panzerspähwagen (SdKfz 233) mit 7,5cm StuK L/24
or Schwerer Panzerspähwagen (sPzSpWg) (7,5cm L/24)
SdKfz 233, 8-Rad
Heavy eight-wheeled armoured car SdKfz 233 with early cut-away gun mounting. Crew 3. Weight 7.55 tons.

SdKfz 233 with modified recessed gun mounting.

Schwerer Panzerspähwagen (sPzSpWg) (7,5cm L/24)
SdKfz 234/3, 8-Rad
or Panzerspähwagen (SdKfz 234/3) mit 7,5cm StuK L/24
Improved model of the eight-wheeled armoured car series, SdKfz 234
equipped with the 7,5cm L/24 gun in new mounting. Crew 4. Weight
9.7 tons.

SdKfz 234/3. View of the gun compartment.

Heavy Infantry Artillery (Schweres Infanteriegeschuetz 33)

Prior to the appearance of the heavy armoured assault howitzers, a self-propelled lightly armoured howitzer was improvised and used in the Polish and Flanders campaigns to give high angle support fire to the attacking German infantry units.

The weapon used, based on the chassis of the obsolete Panzerkampfwagen I, was the 15cm sIG 33 (Schweres Infanterie Geschuetz 33) a standard German infantry support howitzer that could be used for either high or low trajectory shooting.

As this weapon proved successful, able to open fire instantly and to come into position with comparative rapidity as compared to the horse or tractor drawn standard 15cm Infantry Howitzer, similar equipments based on the Panzer II, III and 38(t) chassis were built.

All these SP equipments, with the exception of the Panzer III version, were only armoured against shell fragments or small arms fire, and suffered from the disadvantage of being open at the top and rear. By the end of 1943 this type of equipment had become obsolete and was gradually replaced by the 10,5cm Sturmhaubitze or 15cm Sturmpanzer IV (Brummbaer).

**15cm sIG 33 L/12 auf PzKpfw I Ausf. B
or GW I fuer 15cm sIG 33
of 15cm sIG 33 auf Geschuetzwagen I Ausf. B**
Produced in 1939, this equipment consisted of the 15cm sIG 33 infantry howitzer complete with shield, wheels and trails mounted on the chassis of the Panzerkampfwagen I Ausf. B. The howitzer and crew were protected by a large armoured box-shaped superstructure, open at the top and rear. 38 were built. Crew 4. Weight 8.5 tons.

**15cm sIG 33 auf Fgst PzKpfw II (Sf) Verlaengert
or GW II fuer 15cm sIG 33**
This modified version appeared in 1943, equipped with a lengthened chassis and an additional road wheel to replace the five-wheel version that was over-loaded.

15cm sIG 33 auf Fgst PzKpfw II (Sf) SdKfz 121 or GW II fuer 15cm sIG 33 or 15cm sIG 33 L/12 auf Pz II
This self-propelled equipment entered service in 1942 and was a conversion of the Panzerkampfwagen II Ausf. C modified to mount the sIG 33 howitzer. The gun was mounted in a low superstructure welded to the front glacis plate, and this superstructure was extended to the sides to close in the whole length of the chassis. Crew 5. Weight 12 tons.

**15cm sIG 33 (Sf) auf Panzerkampfwagen 38(t) Ausf. H, Bison
SdKfz 138/1 or 15cm sIG 33 L/12 auf (Sfl) 38(t)
or 15cm sIG 33 auf Geschuetzwagen 38(t)**
*Produced in 1942 this equipment consisted of the 15cm sIG 33 howitzer
carried on the chassis of the Panzerkampfwagen 38(t). The gun was
positioned at the front of the vehicle within an armoured open top superstructure that sloped towards the rear of the chassis. The front plate overlapped the gun shield that had been retained; a further plate which moved
with the gun was fitted over the barrel and recuperator. Crew 4. Weight
12.7 tons.*

**15cm sIG 33 L/12 auf (Sf) 38(t) Ausf. M
SdKfz 138/1 or GW38 fuer sIG 33/1
or 15cm Schweres Infanteriegeschutz 33/1 auf
GW 38(t)**
*Produced in 1943, this was an improved version of the above model. The
engine was re-positioned centrally in the chassis and the fighting compartment moved to the rear. This was a similar arrangement to that
adopted for the Panzerjäger 38(t) Ausf. M. A total of 370 vehicles of
both versions of the 15cm sIG 33 auf Pz 38(t) were built. Crew 4. Weight
12 tons.*

**Sturm-Infantriegeschuetz 33 B Sfl or 15cm sIG 33 auf Pz III
or StuIG 33 auf Fgst PzKpfw III**
*Produced in 1941 and based on the chassis of the Panzerkampfwagen III Ausf. H, twelve pre-production vehicles were built and then production was
cancelled. For this conversion the 15cm sIG 33 howitzer was completely enclosed within an armoured superstructure. Crew 5. Weight 22 tons.*

(Bundesarchiv, Koblenz)

Self-Propelled Anti-Tank Guns (Panzerjaegers)

The largest proportion of the German self-propelled artillery consisted of the type known as the 'Panzerjäger' or Tank Hunter. These vehicles were characterised by their slightly modified, or unmodified tank chassis, their light, bullet-proof open topped superstructure and their armament which was practically unmodified from the field mounted version. Most of these equipments were improvised to make available the self-propelled mounting of as many guns as possible in the shortest possible time, some of these guns being of French, Russian or Czech origin.

Although the bulk of this class of equipment was mounted on standard German tank chassis and semi-tracked vehicles, a number of them were based on captured French or Czech tank chassis converted to this role. Various types of wheeled vehicles were also adapted to carry certain anti-tank guns.

LIGHT INFANTRY ANTI-TANK GUNS

Leichter Panzerspähwagen SdKfz 221 mit 2,8cm Panzerbuechse 41 or 2,8cm sPzB 41 auf SdKfz 221
Produced in late 1941, this equipment consisted of the tapered bore light anti-tank gun mounted on the SdKfz 221 four-wheeled light armoured car. The normal 7,92mm MG 34 was removed and the front of the open top turret was cut away to mount the gun which retained its normal gun shield. Crew 2. Weight 4.5 tons. (Bundesarchiv, Koblenz)

3,7cm Pak auf I ge Lkw(o)
3,7cm Pak and field carriage mounted on a 6 × 4 Krupp light truck type L2H43. This was a field improvisation. The gun had a restricted traverse.

Leichter Schuetzenpanzerwagen (Schwere Panzerbuechse 41) SdKfz 250/11 or leSchtzPzWg (sPzB 41)
The light personnel carrier SdKfz 250 adapted to mount the anti-tank gun 2,8cm sPzB 41. The weapon was dismountable and for this purpose a field carriage (airborne type) was carried, the wheel section at A the trail portion at B. Crew 4. Weight 5.53 tons.

Medium personnel carrier SdKfz 251 equipped with the 2,8cm anti-tank gun. This was not a standard fitting on this class of vehicle.

3,7cm Pak auf Fahrgestell Bren(e)
Conversion of the British Bren carrier to a self-propelled mount for the 3,7cm Pak. Only a few were so converted, the gun and shield being mounted on the engine behind the driver's compartment.

3,7cm Pak (Sf) auf Infantrie Schlepper UE (f)
The French Chenillette infantry carrier adapted, with minor modifications, as a mobile mount for the 3,7cm Pak. Crew 3. Weight 2 tons.

3,7cm Pak auf gep Artillerieschlepper(r)
This was a typical field improvisation and consisted of the 3,7cm Pak mounted on the Russian artillery tractor STZ Komsomolets.

3,7cm Pak auf le Zgkw
This was a field conversion and consisted of the 3,7cm Pak with field carriage mounted on the SdKfz 10. A number of variants of this improvised mounting existed, some of the vehicles being fitted with make-shift armour plate. Crew 5. Weight 5.5 tons approx.

3,7cm Pak (Sf) auf Zgkw1t
To provide additional mobility for the 3,7cm Pak used by the motorised infantry units, a number of these guns were removed from their field carriages and mounted on the SdKfz 10, a pedestal mount being provided. Crew 5. Weight 4.9 tons.

Leichter Schuetzenpanzerwagen (3,7cm Pak) SdKfz 250/10
Produced during 1942, this equipment consisted of the 3,7cm Pak mounted on the light personnel carrier SdKfz 250. Several variations existed as regards the gun shield. One version was fitted with the normal gun shield, another was equipped only with a small armour shield on the gunner's side, while on a third version the gun shield was dispensed with altogether. Crew 4. Weight 5.67 tons.

Mittlerer Schuetzenpanzerwagen (3,7cm Pak) SdKfz 251/10
This was the first adaptation of the 3,7cm Pak to be mounted on a semi-tracked personnel carrier. Produced in 1940 this equipment was similar to the SdKfz 250/10 with variations to the gun shield. Later models were equipped with a new pattern gun shield to decrease the silhouette of the vehicle. Crew 6. Weight 8.15 tons.

Late model of SdKfz 251/10 with lower gun shield.

4,7cm Pak (t) Sfl auf PzKpfw I Ausf. B   or Panzerjaeger I fuer 4,7cm Pak (t)
Introduced into service in 1940, this was the first self-propelled anti-tank gun to enter German service. Based on the chassis of the Panzerkampfwagen I Ausf. B, this equipment was fitted with a Czech 4,7cm anti-tank gun L/43 mounted within a three-sided gun shield. Crew 3. Weight 6 tons.

Top left
4,7cm Pak 181 oder 183(f) auf PzJaeg Lorraine Schlepper (f)
Produced in limited numbers during 1941, this equipment consisted of the unmodified French Lorraine Tracteur Blindé 38L with either the French 47mm M/E 1937 or M/E 1939 anti-tank gun mounted on a pedestal at the rear of the vehicle. Crew 3. Weight 6 tons.

Top right
4,7cm Pak (t) auf PzKpfw 35R (f)
or 4,7cm Pak (t) auf Panzerjaeger Renault R35 (f)
Based on the French Renault R35 tank, this conversion appeared in early 1943. The turret was replaced by a large open top superstructure mounting a 4,7cm Czech anti-tank gun. Crew 3/4. Weight 10.5 tons.

4,7cm Pak(f) auf Panzerspähwagen P 204(f)
A small number of captured French Panhard 178 armoured cars were converted to anti-tank vehicles. The vehicle's turret was removed and replaced by an open top three-sided superstructure, in the front of which was installed a 47mm gun retaining its original shield.

(Bundesarchiv, Koblenz)

47cm Pak(f) auf Infanterie Panzerkampfwagen Mk II(e)
Improvisation of the British Infantry Tank Mk II (Matilda) to mount the French 4,7mm anti-tank gun. Only one converted.
(Bundesarchiv, Koblenz)

5cm Pak 38 (Sf) auf leichter Selbstfahrlafette
To increase the mobility of the 5cm Pak, some of them were carried on the SdKfz 10 semi-tractor on a pedestal mounting.
(Bundesarchiv, Koblenz)

Borgward PzSfl Ia fuer 5cm Pak 38 L/60
Based on the Borgward ammunition carrier VK 301, two prototypes were converted to mount the 5cm Pak 38 during 1940. Project dropped.

5cm Pak 38 auf leichter Schuetzenpanzerwagen SdKfz 250
5cm Pak mounted on the light semi-tracked personnel carrier SdKfz 250. Nothing known, believed to be a trials vehicle.

◄ **5cm Pak 38 auf Fgst PzKpfw II**
Developed during 1942, this equipment consisted of the 5cm Pak 38 mounted on the chassis of the PzKpfw II. As this weapon proved unsuitable it was replaced by the 7,5cm Pak 40/2 auf Sfl II. Marder II.
(Bundesarchiv, Koblenz)

5cm Pak 38 L/60 auf PzKpfw II n.A (Sd 7gst VK901) or Pz Sfl Ic fuer 5cm Pak 38
(No picture available)
Two test vehicles were built from the chassis of the VK901 which was the prototype for advanced models of the PzKpfw II. These vehicles were used in Russia early in 1942 as light anti-tank units. Crew 4. Weight 10.5 tons.

7,5cm Sfl L/40.8   or 7,5cm Selbstfahrlafette L/40.8
Based on an early model of the Buessing-NAG 5-ton semi-tractor series, this vehicle and two other prototypes were developed during 1934–1935 as anti-tank vehicles designed to co-operate with cavalry units. The engine was moved to the rear and the vehicle was fitted with an armoured body mounting a 7,5cm L/40 Pak gun in a rotating turret. One prototype was used in North Africa. Crew 4. Weight 6 tons approx.

Schwerer Panzerspähwagen (7,5cm lang) SdKfz 234/4
This conversion was produced on Hitler's personal orders. It was practically identical to the SdKfz 234/3 except for the longer gun. The complete gun (7,5cm Pak 40 L/48), less wheels and trails, was mounted on a pivot in the centre of the SdKfz 234 fighting compartment. This vehicle was often referred to as the 'Pakwagen'.

**7,5cm Pak 40 (Sf) auf PzJaeg RSO
or 7,5cm Pak 40/1 auf RSO (Sf)**
This conversion appeared in 1944 and consisted of the fully tracked cargo tractor Steyr Raupenschlepper Ost (Tracked Tractor East) or RSO modified to carry the 7,5cm Pak 40 gun. It carried no protective armour other than the gun shield and was constructed without a cab to the driver's compartment. The two sides and tail gate were made of wood and could be lowered to the horizontal position to make additional space for a gun platform. Crew 4. Weight 4.5 tons.

**7,5cm Pak 40/1 auf Lorraine Schlepper(f) (Marder I) SdKfz 135
or Panzerjaeger fuer 7,5cm Pak 40 (Sf) Lorraine Schlepper
or PzJaeg LrS fuer 7,5cm Pak 40/1**
Produced in 1942, 184 Lorraine tractors were converted as self-propelled mounts for the 7,5cm Pak 40/1. The gun was mounted within a high open top armoured box with the original gun shield overlapping the front superstructure. Crew 5. Weight 8 tons.   (Bundesarchiv, Koblenz)

7,5cm Pak 40 L/46 auf mittlerer Schuetzenpanzerwagen, SdKfz 251/22
This was the last official variant of the SdKfz 251 series. It stemmed from a personal order from Hitler that as many anti-tank guns as possible be self-propelled to combat the increasing numbers of enemy tanks. This equipment entered service during November 1944 and consisted of the 7,5cm Pak 40, without its wheels and gun trails, mounted on a sub-frame within a SdKfz 251 armoured carrier. Part of the driver's compartment roof was removed to permit limited traverse of the gun. Crew 4.

**7,5cm Pak 40 L/46 auf mittlerer Schuetzenpanzerwagen, S 307(f)
or 7,5cm Pak 40 L/46 auf ZgkwSomua(f)**
Produced in mid 1944, 16 French Somua semi-tracked vehicles were converted as self-propelled mounts for the 7,5cm Pak 40. Crew 3/4. Weight 9 tons approx.

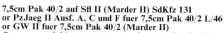

7,5cm Pak 40/2 auf Sfl II (Marder II) SdKfz 131
or PzJaeg II Ausf. A, C und F fuer 7,5cm Pak 40/2 L/46
or GW II fuer 7,5cm Pak 40/2 (Marder II)
Prototypes of this equipment were first tested with the 5cm Pak 38 (5cm Pak 38 auf Fgst PzKpfw II) but the production version was fitted with the more powerful 7,5cm Pak 40/2. These equipments entered production during 1942. The basic chassis used for this conversion was the PzKpfw II Ausf. A, C and F. The engine was removed to the rear and the 7,5cm gun with its original shield was mounted on a platform on the front of the vehicle, being protected by a 10mm armour shield that sloped to the rear. 1217 of this equipment were built. Crew 4. Weight 10.8 tons.

Panzerjaeger 38(t) Ausf. M SdKfz 138
or 7,5cm Pak 40/3 (L/46) Marder III auf GW 38
This self-propelled mount consisted of the 7,5cm Pak 40 mounted on a considerably modified PzKpfw 38(t) chassis. As the previous Marder III had suffered difficulties because it was nose heavy, the engine was re-positioned centrally in the chassis and the gun moved to the rear. The superstructure of 10mm plates was extended over the tracks to the extreme rear of the vehicle, this arrangement bringing the fighting compartment more conveniently to the back of the hull. A total of 799 vehicles were converted, production beginning in mid-1943. Crew 4. Weight 10.5 tons.

7,5cm Pak 40/3 (L/46) auf PzJaeg 38(t) SdKfz 138
or 7,5cm Pak 40/3 auf Sfl 38(t) Ausf. H
or Panzerjaeger 38(t) Marder III
Produced in late 1942 as an interim tank destroyer, this equipment consisted of the 7,5cm Pak 40 mounted on the chassis of the ex-Czech Praga TNH/LT38 tank chassis, designated by the German Army as Panzerkampfwagen 38(t). The gun was positioned at the front of the vehicle protected by a three-sided open top gun shield constructed of 10mm-15mm armour plate. Total number converted was 418. Crew 4. Weight 10.8 tons.

7,5cm Pak 40 auf GW 39H(f)
Produced during 1942, the basic chassis used as a self-propelled mount for this equipment was the French Hotchkiss H39 tank, a total of 24 being converted. This conversion was similar to that of the Marder 1, the gun being mounted forward within a high open top armoured superstructure with the gun shield overlapping the front plate. Crew 5. Weight 12.5 tons.

7,5cm Pak 40 auf GW FCM(f)
Entering service during 1943, this conversion was based on the French FCM tank chassis. Only 10 of these vehicles were converted. The design of the superstructure was similar to that of the previously converted French tanks. Crew 3/4. Weight 13.5 tons.

FOREIGN ANTI-TANK GUNS

7,5cm Pak 97/38 auf m Beute Panzer T 26
This was an experimental equipment built in 1943, and consisted of the French 75mm gun Model 1897 mounted on the chassis of the Russian light tank T 26. The gun, of which large stocks had been captured in France, had originally been adopted into the German Army in 1942, where it had been remounted on the field carriage of the German 5cm Pak gun and fitted with a long perforated muzzle brake. The modified gun was designated 7,5cm Pak 97/38. (Bundesarchiv, Koblenz)

7,62cm Pak 36(r) auf Panzerjaeger Selbstfahrlafette Zugkraftwagen 5t, Diana
Nine of these equipments were built during 1941–42. They consisted of the Russian 7,62cm FK 296 gun on its wheeled carriage, with the split gun trails shortened, mounted on the chassis of the 5 ton Buessing-NAG semi-tracked tractor SdKfz 6. For this conversion a high box type armoured superstructure was built behind the driver's compartment, consisting of two sides and a back plate, all of which were fitted with hinged doors. Frontal protection was provided by the gun shield set behind partly built-up front plates. Crew 5. Weight 10.5 tons. (Bundesarchiv, Koblenz)

Panzerselbstfahrlafette II fuer 7,62cm Pak 36(r) SdKfz 139, Marder III or Panzerjaeger 38(t) fuer 7,62cm Pak 36(r)
This vehicle appeared early in 1942 and was an expedient for a tank destroyer to counter the large numbers of new enemy tanks (T 34 and KVs) appearing on the Russian front. As the only effective anti-tank gun available was the Russian 7,62cm FK 296, of which large numbers had been captured during the early fighting in Russia, it was decided as an interim measure to mount these guns on the chassis of the Czech 38(t) tank. To speed production the conversion was made as simple as possible. The turret and forward deck plates were removed and replaced by a cruciform on which the gun less its undercarriage was mounted. A low armoured superstructure was fitted around the vehicle to protect the gun mounting and crew. A total of 344 were built. Crew 4. Weight 10.8 tons.

PzSfl fuer 7,62cm Pak 36(r), Sd Kfz 132 (Marder II) or 7,62cm Pak 36(r) L/54.8 auf Fgst, PzKpfw II (Sfl) or PzJaeg II Ausf. D, E fuer 7,62cm Pak 36(r) or 7,62cm Pak 36(r) (Sfl im PzKpfw II)
This vehicle also appeared early in 1942, and like the early Marder III was an interim design for a mobile tank destroyer. Based on the chassis of the Panzerkampfwagen II Models D and E, this version was also armed with the Russian 7,62cm FK 296 anti-tank gun. Like the Marder III (SdKfz 139) the gun and shield were mounted above the superstructure, whereas the normal practice was to enclose the gun within the armoured superstructure. Later in the war some vehicles of this conversion were equipped with the German 7,5cm Pak 40/2. Crew 4. Weight 11.5 tons.

SUPER-HEAVY ANTI-TANK GUNS

8,8cm Kw K 43 L/71 auf mittlerer Schuetzenpanzerwagen
Developed during 1943, this was an experimental mounting of the 8,8cm Kw K (tank gun) carried on a modified chassis of the SdKfz 251.

8,8cm Flak 18 auf Selbstfahrlafette Zugkraftwagen 12t
Produced in limited numbers during 1940, this was an early attempt to employ the 8,8cm Flak gun in the role of a self-propelled anti-tank gun. The mobile carriage used for this conversion was the 12 ton semi-tracked tractor, SdKfz 8 which had been armoured in front. At the back of the chassis was a platform on to which the gun mounting was fixed.
(Bundesarchiv, Koblenz)

8,8cm Pak 43/3 auf Panzerjaeger 38(t)
Developed late in 1944, this was a prototype machine for a proposed new series of Panzerjaegers. This version was based on a modified 38(t) chassis with the engine moved to the front. It was armed with the 8,8cm Pak 43/3. Crew 4. Weight 11 tons.

8,8cm Panzerjaeger 43 auf Sfl 38(d)
This pilot model built by Rheinmetall-Borsig and Ardelt appeared in 1945. The carriage used for this conversion was a purely German re-designed and enlarged version of the Panzerjaeger 38(t), powered by a new Tatra diesel engine that had now been moved to the front of the vehicle. The 8,8cm Pak 43 was mounted at the rear of the chassis in an open top armoured turret that had all-round traverse. Designated 38(d) this modified chassis had been developed as a self-propelled mount for the Waffentraeger series on which it was planned to carry anti-tank, field or medium guns mounted on their field carriages and which should, when required, be dismountable to permit firing from the field carriage on the ground. Crew 4. Weight 15.5 tons.

8,8cm Pak 43/1 (L/71) auf Fgst PzKpfw III/IV (Sf), SdKfz 164 or Panzerjaeger III/IV Nashorn frueher Hornisse or 8,8cm Pak 43/1 L/71 auf GW III/IV
Introduced into service in November 1942, this equipment consisted of a modified Pz IV chassis with the engine moved forward and installed directly behind the transmission to provide a clear space for the fighting compartment at the rear. The gun was mounted over the engine, and both gun and crew were protected against small arms fire by a high open-topped superstructure of thin armour plate, 30mm at the front and 20mm at the sides. The transmission and drive were the same as those used on the Pz III. Two types of driver's hatches were used on these vehicles, of which 473 were built. Crew 5. Weight 26.5 tons.

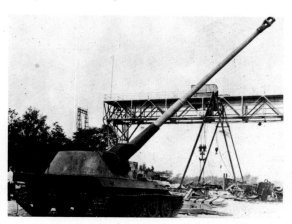

8,8cm Pjk43/3 auf Krupp/Steyr Sfl 38(d)
Also produced in 1945, this was a similar type of vehicle to the Rheinmetall-Borsig and Ardelt vehicle, except that the chassis incorporated the suspension units of the Steyr Raupenschlepper Ost (East Front tractor). Crew 4. Weight 15.5 tons.

12,8cm K 40 auf Versuchsfahrgestell (VK 3001) H or 12,8cm Kanone 40 auf Sfl VK 3001 (H) or 12,8cm Selbstfahrlafette L/61 (Panzer-Selbstfahrlafette V)
Produced in 1942, the chassis used for this equipment was that of a Henschel prototype for a tank in the 30 ton class, four of which were built in late 1941, but were made obsolete by the appearance of the Russian T 34 tank. Two of the four VK 3001 chassis were converted as self-propelled mounts for the 12,8cm Kanone to test its feasibility against fortifications and as an anti-tank gun. The 12,8cm Kanone had originally been developed as a Flak gun. The converted vehicles were lengthened, the rear idler wheels being moved back a considerable distance to accommodate the large fighting compartment that consisted of an open top lightly armoured superstructure. The two vehicles were sent to Russia for trials during 1942. Crew 5. Weight 35 tons.

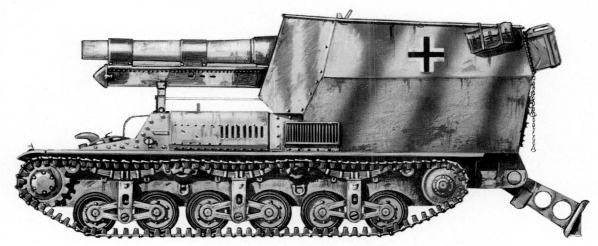

15cm sFH 13 Sfl Lorraine (SdKfz 135/1)

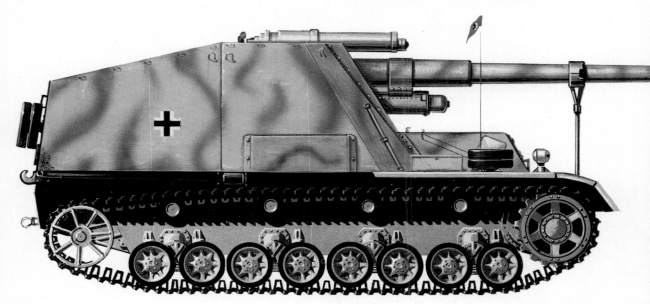

Geschuetzwagen III/IV 'Hummel' (SdKfz 165)

Sturmgeschuetz III Ausf.D (SdKfz 142)

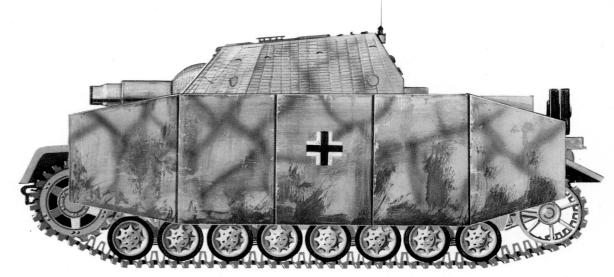

Sturmpanzer IV 'Brummbaer' (SdKfz 166)

7.5cm PaK 40/2 auf Sfl II 'Marder II' (SdKfz 131)

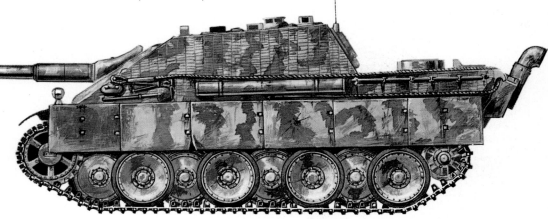

Jagdpanzer V Jagdpanther (SdKfz 173s)

Tank Hunters (Jagdpanzers)

The increased casualties and lack of effectiveness of the traditional towed anti-tank guns led at first to the simple self-propelled mounts described in the section on anti-tank guns. These self-propelled guns had mobility and could be brought into action without loss of time. However, they lacked protection for the crews, as did the wheeled anti-tank guns, but they were without the latter's facility for concealment. In 1942 the long 7,5cm cannons were first mounted in the assault vehicles (Sturmgeschuetz) and this development introduced a highly successful anti-tank weapon which had not only mobility but also the protection of armour and a low silhouette. This basic concept was now developed and improved so that a new class of vehicle was introduced, able to carry out the dual role of both tank destroyer and assault gun. These vehicles were known as Jagdpanzers. The powerful anti-tank gun was butted in the lowest possible vehicle with the heaviest armour it was capable of carrying. Special care was taken to increase protection with sloped armour.

Jagdpanzer IV Ausf. F (7,5cm Pak 39 L/48) SdKfz 162 or Panzerjaeger 39
In an effort to improve the StuG III concept this vehicle was designed upon the chassis of the PzKpfw IV which could be manufactured in large numbers. Sloped armour and substantially improved gun mounting and mantlet characterised the design. From an early stage it was intended to use the 7,5cm StuK 42 L/70 cannon based upon the high velocity weapon of the Panther tank, but delays and shortages in 1943 led to the introduction of this vehicle late in that year, armed with the 7,5cm Pak 39 L/48 which was based upon the 7,5cm StuK L/48. Late production models dispensed with the muzzle brake and the machine gun port on the left hand side of the front plate. Crew 4. Weight 23.6 tons.

7,5cm Pak 39 L/48 auf PzJäg 38(t) Hetzer (SdKfz 138/2) or Jagdpanzer 38(t)   or JagdPz 38 fuer 7,5cm Pak 39 L/48
The large production facilities of the Czechoslovak Praga and Skoda works were used to mass produce the Hetzer from 1943. The anti-tank gun was the same 7,5cm Pak 39 L/48 mentioned above. This lighter chassis had less armour and a very cramped interior but proved to be effective support for the infantry units to which it was attached. Some 1577 were manufactured before the end of the war, including about 100 guns with rigid mountings. These latter guns were fitted in a simple ball mount and possessed none of the usual recoil gear as the recoil forces were absorbed by the vehicle itself. While the guns performed successfully, difficulty was encountered with the sighting devices; the solution had not been introduced by 1945. Crew 4. Weight 15.8 tons.

Late production model of the Jagdpanzer IV, equipped with mild steel skirting plates (Schürzen) and coated with Zimmerit, an anti-magnetic compound to stop the attachment of magnetic demolition charges.

Left **Panzer IV/70 SdKfz 162/1   or Jagdpanzer IV mit 7,5cm StuK 42 L/70**
This was the 7,5cm StuK 42 using the Jagdpanzer IV chassis as originally intended. Muzzle brakes were not fitted on these equipments due to the proximity of the gun to the ground and consequent problems of dust created by the back blast. Later models had only three return rollers and steel-tyred resilient wheels in place of the rubber-tyred ones on the front road wheels. The reason for the change was the damage caused to the tyres by the heavy front of the vehicle (80mm) and the long overhang of the gun.
  Produced in late 1944 this vehicle was intended to replace the Panzerkampfwagen IV, hence the designation. 1531 Jagdpanzer IV chassis were produced and were equipped with both types of guns. Crew 4. Weight 24.5 tons.

Right **Panzer IV/70**
Late production model with minor modifications and three return rollers.

Panzerjaeger Tiger (P) Ferdinand
fuer 8,8cm Pak 43/2 oder StuK 43/1 (SdKfz 184s)
or 8,8cm Pak 43/2 L/71
auf PzJaeg Tiger (P) Elefant früher Ferdinand
or Jagdpanzer Tiger (P) Elefant mit 8,8cm Pak 43/2 L/71
This equipment was a conversion of the VK 4501 (P) the Porsche Tiger that had been built to compete with the VK 4501 (H) Henschel Tiger. As the production of the Porsche Tiger had begun and 90 had been authorised before the result of the trials in which the Henschel Tiger was chosen, it was decided to convert the Porsche Tiger chassis as self-propelled mounts for the 8,8cm Pak 43. Introduced into service during 1943.
Later re-worked Elefants were armed with a hull machine gun and a new commander's cupola. 90 built. Crew 6. Weight 71.7 tons.

Panzer IV/70 Zwischenloesung
The urgency to mount the 7,5cm StuK 42 in as many vehicles as possible led to Hitler's order in August 1944 that all PzKfw IV production be immediately switched to building the Panzer IV/70. Obviously, instant change could not be undertaken by industry and so an interim vehicle was improvised with the modified superstructure of the Panzer IV/70 on top of the standard Panzerkampfwagen IV chassis.
Only a small number of these vehicles were built during 1944–1945. Crew 4/5. Weight 28 tons.

8,8cm Pak 43/3 auf Panzerjaeger Panther SdKfz 173s
or Jagdpanther
The lack of success of the self-propelled 8,8cm Pak 43 Nashorn using a lightly armoured Pz III/IV chassis and the limited number of technically unsuccessful Elefant vehicles led to the development of a Panther chassis to carry the 8,8cm Pak 43. Minor differences appeared between the vehicles from different manufacturers, one type having a welded gun mounting and the other a heavy bolted-on type. Only 382 Jagdpanthers were built, mainly during 1944. Crew 5. Weight 46 tons.

Jagdpanther with heavy bolted gun mantlet.

Jagdtiger fuer 12,8cm Pak 44 L/55 SdKfz 186s   or PzJaeg Tiger Ausf. B fuer 12,8cm Pak 44
The race between armour and anti-tank guns reached its wartime limit with the use of the 12,8cm gun as an anti-tank gun. Obviously performance was good but such guns were too heavy for normal field use. For such a large gun a Jagdpanzer based upon the chassis of the Koeningstiger (PzKpfw Tiger Ausf. B) was developed. This massive vehicle had armour to match with 250mm frontal plates. An order for 150 was placed, though records indicate that only 48 were completed by the end of the war. Porsche developed a new form of longitudinal torsion bar suspension for these vehicles to replace the Henschel transverse torsion bar suspension, but only a few vehicles were equipped with this Porsche suspension. At one period several of these vehicles were armed with the 8,8cm Pak 43/3; this was due to the delay, caused by Allied bombing, of the production of the 12,8cm Pak 44. Crew 6. Weight 76 tons.

Mobile Flak Guns

Early versions of self-propelled anti-aircraft guns were made by the mounting of small calibre 2cm and 3,7cm Flak guns on wheeled and semi-tracked vehicles to give mobile anti-aircraft protection to transport and armoured convoys against Allied air attacks. These light weapons could also be used against ground targets, being provided with armour-piercing ammunition in addition to high explosive rounds.

The first full-tracked vehicle to be used as a self-propelled mount for the anti-aircraft role appeared in 1943. This was the Flakpanzer 38(t) based on the chassis of the Czech 38(t) tank. It was followed by other models of Panzerflak with increased firepower, the Flakpanzer IV series that utilised the chassis of the Panzerkampfwagen IV. The final stage of development in this series

was the leichte Flakpanzer IV Kugelblitz armed with two 3cm automatic cannon in an enclosed armoured power-operated turret. Only five of these vehicles had been built by the time the war ended.

During the war, various attempts were made to make the 8,8cm Flak gun mobile by employing the 12- and 18-ton semi-tracked vehicles as self-propelled mounts for this equipment. Fourteen of the 18-ton vehicles were converted to carry the 8,8cm Flak 37. Designs were also projected to mount the 8,8cm gun on a full-tracked chassis. Only one of these vehicles was developed. Designated Flakpanzer fuer schwere Flak, this equipment was mounted on a composite chassis consisting of Panzerkampfwagen IV and semi-track suspension components.

FLAK MACHINE-GUNS

Leichter Truppenluftschutz-Kraftwagen, Kfz 4
Used in motorised convoys for air defence, this was a light 4 × 4 Stoewer personnel car with the Zwillingslafette 36 installed in the rear compartment.

MG Doppelwagen 36
Used for anti-aircraft protection of infantry on the march. The 7,92mm MG 34 machine guns of some units were carried in a single axle horse drawn limber known as the MG Doppelwagen. The MGs were mounted in pairs on a combined seat and pedestal mount known as the Zwillingslafette 36 (Twin machine gun mount, Model 36). When used in this defence role, the MGs were equipped with a special anti-aircraft sight. The normal ground tripods were carried strapped at the rear of the limber.

The Zwillingslafette 36 was a universal MG mount that could be adapted to fit most vehicles, including rail-wagons. The picture shows the mount on a medium type truck.

Zwillingslafette 36 close up.

MG 151/15 oder 151/20 Drilling auf mSchtzPzWg SdKfz 251/21
Introduced in late 1944, this equipment consisted of 1,5cm MG 151/15 or 2cm MG 151/20 aircraft guns on a pedestal triple mounting. This weapons system was installed on a 3-ton armoured semi-tracked personnel carrier SdKfz 251. Though designed for light anti-aircraft defence in armoured convoys the guns could also be used in an anti-tank role. Crew 4/6.

LIGHT FLAK GUNS

Leichte Selbstfahrlafette (DemagDII, 3) 2cm Flak 30
Experimental mounting of the 2cm Flak gun on the third prototype vehicle of the SdKfz 10 series to test the feasibility of adopting this vehicle as a standard self-propelled carriage for the 2cm Flak. Crew 7. Weight 5 tons.

2cm Flak 30 als Selbstfahrlafette auf E-Fahrgestell sPkw
2cm anti-aircraft gun model 30 mounted on the heavy 4 × 4 Auto-Union personnel car fitted with a special body with drop sides to form extension of rear body. Used mainly by Luftwaffe units for convoy defence.

Leichte Selbstfahrlafette (2cm Flak 30) SdKfz 10/4
2cm Flak gun mounted on 1-ton semi-tracked vehicle SdKfz 10. The sides of the vehicle were dropped when in action to facilitate all round traverse. Spare ammunition was carried in a towed two-wheeled limber. Crew 7. Weight 5.5 tons. (Bundesarchiv, Koblenz)

Mittlerer Schuetzenpanzerwagen (2cm)
This equipment consisted of the 2cm Flak 30 mounted on an unmodified SdKfz 251. Only a limited number of these vehicles were converted.

Leichte Selbstfahrlafette (2cm Flak 38) SdKfz 10/5
This was a modified version of the SdKfz 10/4 with an armoured cab and armed with the 2cm Flak model 38, a weapon with an increased rate of fire. Crew 7. Weight 5.5 tons.

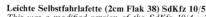

2cm Flak 38 auf Mannschaftskraftwagen
2cm anti-aircraft gun model 38 in the rear compartment of an Auto-Union 4 × 4 personnel car. The weapon was mounted on a raised platform.

2cm Flak 38 auf le gl Lkw Kfz 70
This was a standard conversion, and consisted of the 2cm Flak gun carried in the rear compartment of a 6 × 4 light truck, (Type Krupp L2H143) used by the Luftwaffe.

Luftwaffe, mSchtzPzWg (2cm Flak 38)
Developed for the Luftwaffe Flak troops, several were built and tested in troop trials. This equipment consisted of the 2cm Flak 38 on a modified SdKfz 251. To allow the gun to be installed in the fighting compartment, the body was redesigned so that the sides of the vehicle could be folded down to allow full traverse of the gun. (Bundesarchiv, Koblenz)

mSchtzPzWg mit 2cm Flak 38 SdKfz 251/17
Developed as a flak vehicle in 1944, and built in limited numbers this series became standard equipment. The gun, in a small armoured turret, was positioned behind the driver's compartment with the gun barrel projecting over the armoured cab of an SdKfz 251. Crew 4/6.

Leichte Flakpanzer 38(t) SdKfz 140
Built during 1943, this was the first full-tracked vehicle to be used as a self-propelled mount for an anti-aircraft weapon. A 2cm Flak 38 was mounted at the rear of a modified PzKpfw 38(t) tank chassis and enclosed by an octagonal shield 10mm thick. The upper part of each of the eight sides of the shield was hinged at the bottom; these could be folded outwards when going into action. Crew 4. Weight 9.8 tons.

2cm Flakvierling 38 auf m Lkw
These vehicles appeared in 1943 and consisted of the 2cm quadruple anti-aircraft guns mounted on 4 × 4 or 4 × 2 3-ton medium trucks. The driver's compartment and the engine were armoured and the vehicle's sides could be lowered to allow full movement for the gun and crew.
A two-wheeled trailer was towed carrying extra ammunition.
(B. L. Davis)

Mittlerer Zugkraftwagen 8(t) mit 2cm Flakvierling 38 SdKfz 7/1 or Selbstfahrlafette 2cm Flakvierling 38
This equipment consisted of the 2cm Flakvierling 38, a quadruple version of the 2cm Flak 38, mounted on the rear of the 8-ton semi-tracked vehicle SdKfz 7. Developed in 1941, the combination of the four guns under one fire control increased the rate of fire to 800 rpm. Crew 10. Weight 11.5 tons.

Late production mZgkw 8(t) mit 2cm Flakvierling 38 with gun shield and the front of the vehicle armoured. (Bundesarchiv, Koblenz)

Flakpanzer IV, (2cm Flakvierling 38) auf Fgst PzKpfw IV Möbelwagen
For the defence of German armour against the increasing Allied fighter-bomber attacks attempts were made to develop a more satisfactory anti-aircraft vehicle than that of the leichte Flakpanzer 38(t). Entering service during 1943, this equipment consisted of the 2cm quadruple anti-aircraft guns mounted on the chassis of the PzKpfw IV Ausf. H and J. The guns and crew were protected by four hinged 10mm armoured plates, which were lowered in action to allow full traverse. A counter-part of this vehicle mounted the 3,7cm Flak 43. Crew 5. Weight 25 tons.

leichte Flakpanzer IV (3cm) Kugelblitz
This vehicle was the last in the series of the Flakpanzers, and was designed to give complete protection to the gun crew and to mount an armament with greater penetration power against the armoured fighter-bombers. The PzKpfw IV chassis was also used for this development, which carried an armoured power-operated turret. Mounted within the ball turret were two Mk 103/38 aircraft guns; these were quickfiring cannon with automatic belt feed. Only five of these vehicles were built by the end of the war. Crew 5. Weight 24 tons.

Flakpanzer IV (2cm) auf Fgst Pz IV/3 Wirbelwind
This vehicle was designed to give the crew better armoured protection and entered service at the end of 1943. Based on the chassis of the PzKpfw IV Ausf. J, the 2cm quadruple guns were now mounted within a 16mm armoured revolving open turret. A counter-part of this vehicle, the Ostwind, mounted the 3,7cm Flak 43. Crew 5. Weight 22 tons.

MEDIUM FLAK GUNS

3,7cm Flak 36 auf Lkw Mercedes-Benz, 4500A
3,7cm Flak mounted on the chassis of the 4 × 4 Mercedes-Benz 4.5-ton cargo truck, Type 4500A. The vehicle was considerably modified for this adaptation.

3,7cm Flak 43 auf Schwerer Wehrmachtsschlepper
3,7cm Flak 43 mounted on the chassis of the SWS half-track, a vehicle that had been designed to replace the 5-ton semi-tracked vehicle, SdKfz 6.

mZgkw 8t mit 3,7cm Flak 36 SdKfz 7/2
3,7cm Flak mounted on the chassis of the 8-ton semi-tracked vehicle, SdKfz 7.

Reworked version of the SdKfz 7/2 with armoured cab.

3,7cm Flak 36 (Sf) auf Zugkraftwagen 5t SdKfz 6/2
3,7cm Flak 36 mounted on the 5-ton semi-tracked vehicle SdKfz 6.

3,7cm Flak 36 auf Maultier
This equipment consisted of the 3,7cm Flak gun mounted on a Ford 2-ton semi-tracked cargo vehicle. (Gleisketten-Lkw, 2t (Maultier))
(Bundesarchiv, Koblenz)

3,7cm Flak 43 auf Sf IV Möbelwagen
This was a similar carriage to that of the Flakpanzer IV, but armed with the 3,7cm Flak 43 in place of the 2cm Flakvierling 38. Both vehicles appeared at the same time.

3,7cm Flak 43 auf Sf Ostwind
A similar vehicle to the Wirbelwind, but mounting the 3,7cm Flak 43 in the armoured turret.

HEAVY FLAK GUNS

Flakpanzer fur schwere Flak (8,8cm Flak 37) or 8,8cm Flak 37 auf Sonderfahrgestell
Developed in 1943, this experimental equipment was the 8,8cm Flak 37 mounted on a full-track chassis, consisting of Panzer IV and semi-track suspension components. The gun, which retained its normal gun shield, was protected at the sides and rear by armour shields, which could be lowered to allow full traverse of the gun. Crew 8. Weight 20 tons.

8,8cm Flak 37 (Sf) auf Zugkraftwagen 18t
Though the 8,8cm Flak gun had in 1940 been mounted on a semi-tracked vehicle to create a mobile mount for this gun, this conversion had been developed purely as an anti-tank weapon. In 1943 a series of 14 of the 18-ton semi-tracked vehicles SdKfz 9, were converted to mount the 8,8cm Flak 37 for the dual role of Pak and Flak. The cab and engine were armoured and outriggers or jacks were attached to the vehicle's sides; these could be lowered to increase the stability of the gun when in action. Crew 9/10. Weight 25 tons.

Below left
8,8cm Flakpanzer with the three protecting armoured shields lowered.

8,8cm Flak 41 auf Sonderfahrgestell
This was the special chassis mounting the 8,8cm Flak 41 model replacing the Flak 37. Experimental only.

Mobile Field Artillery

Medium and Field self-propelled artillery was introduced about the middle of 1942. Employed with the armoured and motorised divisions, various models of the 10,5cm and 15cm guns mounted on German and captured French tank chassis were used.

During 1942/43 plans were made for the development of a new range of weapons called Waffenträgers (Weapon Carriers). These equipments were to consist of Anti-tank, Field and Medium guns mounted on their original field carriages, the complete units to be carried on a lightly armoured tracked chassis and, where possible, to be dismountable as field pieces, power-driven mechanism being carried for this purpose. To be constructed with standard tank components, the Weapon Carriers consisted of three groups: Heuschrecke (Grasshopper), Grille (Cricket), and a third series based on the chassis of the modified 38(t) Czech tank. Though many of these projects existed as wooden models or as designs on the drawing board, only a few prototype machines were built.

LIGHT FIELD HOWITZERS

**le FH 18/2 auf FgstPzKpfw II (Sf) SdKfz 124 Wespe
or GW II fuer 10,5cm le FH 18/1 Wespe**
Introduced in 1942 for employment with the armoured regiments, this equipment consisted of the 10,5cm gun howitzer mounted at the rear of a Panzer II Ausf. F chassis. The fighting compartment was open at the top and rear. Crew 5. Weight 11.5 tons.

10,5cm le FH 16 auf GW FCM (f)
This conversion consisted of the 10,5cm gun howitzer model 16 mounted on the chassis of the French FCM tank. Ten of this model were produced and taken into service during 1942. Crew 4/5. Weight 13.5 tons.

10,5cm le FH 18 auf GW Lorraine Schlepper (f)
This lightly armoured mobile gun howitzer appeared in mid 1942. Based on the French Lorraine carrier chassis 24 were produced. Crew 4. Weight 8.5 tons.

**10,5cm le FH 18 auf GW 39H (f)
or 10,5cm Panzerhaubitze 18 auf Sfl39H (f)**
Based on the chassis of the French Hotchkiss tank type H39, forty-eight conversions of this type appeared during 1942. Crew 4/5. Weight 13 tons.

**leFH 18/1 (Sf) auf GW IVb
or 10,5cm leFH 18/1 auf GW IVb SdKfz 165/1**
This was an experimental Panzerartillerie type using a shortened PzKpfw IV chassis as the self-propelled mount. A total of eight vehicles was built during 1942 and these later saw service in Russia. Crew 5. Weight 17 tons.

10,5cm le FH 18/3 (Sf) auf GWB2 (f)
A limited number of this equipment was introduced into service in 1942. The 10,5cm gun was mounted in the front of an open topped compartment placed well forward on a French Char B1bis hull. Crew 5. Weight 32 tons.

GW IVb fuer 10,5cm leFH 18/1 (Heuschrecke IVb)
or 10,5cm leFH 18/1 L/28 auf Waffentrager, GW IVb
Based on a modified chassis of the PzKpfw IV, eight of these experimental Weapon Carriers were built during 1942. The turret which was fully rotating could be removed by a block and tackle assembly that was attached to a girder frame, and placed on the ground in the ground defence role of an armoured pillbox. This lifting gantry was arranged on both sides of the vehicle. The turret could, when required, be towed behind the vehicle. This was accomplished by placing the turret on a small girder frame with two wheels; these components were also carried on the vehicle. When towing the turret the vehicle was used as an ammunition carrier. Crew 5. Weight 17.3 tons.

This picture shows the Heuschrecke IVb towing the turret on wheels. The gantry is still in the lifting position.

leFH 18/40 (Sf)   or 10,5cm leFH 18/40 auf Fgst GW III/IV
This vehicle was also developed as a Weapon Carrier and carried the gun, gun carriage, and gun shield within an armoured superstructure, with the gun mounted to fire forward within a limited traverse. The gun wheels and trails were carried at the rear of the vehicle. When required for ground action, the weapon was removed by a block and tackle and with the wheels and trails was assembled on the ground as a normal field piece.

Rear view of leFH 18/40 (Sf) showing the two gun wheels and trails.

10,5cm K 18 auf Panzer-Selbstfahrlafette IVa
or 10,5cm leFH 18 L/52 auf PzSfl IVa
Based on the chassis of the PzKpfw IV Ausf. D, only two of this experimental vehicle were produced, in 1942. The gun howitzer that was developed from the 10cm sFK 18 field gun was installed in an open top fighting compartment. Tested in Russia this equipment proved unsatisfactory. Crew 5. Weight 25 tons.

15cm Panzerfeldhaubitze 18M auf GW III/IV SdKfz 165 (Hummel) or 15cm schwere Panzerhaubitze 18/1 (Sf) auf Fgst PzKpfw III/IV or Geschützwagen III/IV Hummel

Produced in 1942, this lightly armoured mobile heavy howitzer was carried on a self-propelled mount made of components from the PzKpfw III and IV series. Early versions were equipped with muzzle brakes but these were later eliminated. From mid 1944 the Hummel's driver's compartment was redesigned to a straight front. Crew 5. Weight 23.5 tons.

A late production Hummel with the redesigned front superstructure.

(Warpics)

15cm sFH 13 Selbstfahrlafette Lorraine SdKfz 135/1 or 15cm sFH 13 auf GWLrS (f)

This mobile artillery equipment consisted of a French Lorraine chassis (Tracteur Blindé 38L) on which was mounted the 15cm sFH 13, a medium howitzer of World War I. The howitzer was mounted at the rear of the vehicle within an open top fighting compartment. A hinged spade at the rear of the vehicle was lowered when the gun was in action. A total of 102 conversions were made from 1942 on. Crew 4. Weight 8.36 tons.

Hummel fitted with the Ostkette (East track). This was a lateral extension to the normal tracks for improved ground pressure and better traction over soft ground.

SUPER-HEAVY ARTILLERY

Grille 17/21 fuer 17cm K 18 oder 21cm Mrs 21

Designed as a mobile mount for the 17cm K 18 gun or 21cm Mrs 21 heavy howitzer, this consisted of a lengthened PzKpfw Tiger Ausf. B chassis with a built-up superstructure. One pilot model was nearly completed by the end of the war. Crew 8. Weight 58 tons.

Wooden model of the Grille 17/21.

60cm Moerser (Geraet 040) and 54cm Moerser (Geraet 041) Karl

This was the biggest weapon to be mounted on a self-propelled carriage. Projected in 1937 the first of the 60cm series appeared in 1939. This equipment was designed as a super-heavy self-propelled howitzer capable of firing a very large explosive projectile with a high trajectory to penetrate the deepest fortifications. Though initially developed for use against the French Maginot Line, with the fall of France the Karl was later used on the Russian Front, participating in the siege of Sevastopol, at Brest-Litovsk and later in the Warsaw rising.

Six of the 040 equipment were built, having two different tracked systems, either eleven twin road wheels and six twin return rollers or eight twin road wheels and eight twin return rollers. To increase the range of these weapons, some of the 040 equipments in 1942 were re-equipped with new 54cm howitzers, these being interchangeable with the 60cm barrel, and were re-designated Geraet 041.

Because of the size of these guns special means were provided for transporting them over distances too great to be negotiated as a self-propelled unit. For transporting by rail, the unit was suspended between two special railway trucks by means of a special steel truss. For movement by road, the equipment was partially disassembled and carried on special trailers.

To supply ammunition to these guns a special armoured carrier was developed, based on the PzKpfw IV Ausf. F chassis. This was equipped with a 2.5-ton crane to lift the three rounds of 60cm or 54cm ammunition that it carried and place them on the loading tray of the howitzer.

Weight 60cm Moerser/125 tons. Weight 54cm Moerser/132 tons.

54cm Moerser (Geraet 041).

Munitionpanzer IV loading 54cm shell on to Geraet 041 loading tray.

Mobile Mortars

SdKfz 250/7 8cm GrWWagen (Granatewerferwagen)
In service by 1943 this was a later version of the semi-tracked personnel carrier as a mobile mount for the standard mortar. In this case the mount used was the one-ton SdKfz 250 adapted to carry the 8cm mortar (sGrW 34).
    The mortar could be fired forward from the vehicle or from a ground position, a baseplate for the ground role being carried at the rear of the vehicle. A similar vehicle was converted to carry spare mortar ammunition. Crew 5. Weight 5.61 tons.

SdKfz 251/2 mSchtz PzWgGrW
or Mittlerer Schuetzenpanzerwagen (Granatewerfer)
Produced in 1942 the three-ton semi-tracked personnel carrier SdKfz 251 was modified to carry the 8cm mortar model 34. The mortar was sighted to fire forward over the driver's cab. A base plate was carried for use with the mortar when firing from the ground position. Crew 8. Weight 7.84 tons.

1/2   8cm Schwerer Granatewerfer 34 auf PzSpWg AMR (f)
or Moersertraeger AMR (f)
This was a conversion of the French light tank AMR (Renault Type ZT) as a mobile mount for the 8cm mortar. Two types of this conversion were constructed: One (above right) with a high superstructure open at the rear with the mortar sighted to fire forward; the other (right) similar, but equipped with a small armoured cab at the rear of the vehicle and a pulpit type of cupola on the front.

Mittlerer Schuetzenpanzerwagen S 307(f) mit Reihenwerfer
Produced in 1944, this equipment consisted of the French Somua semi-tracked vehicle adapted to carry 16 French 81mm mortars. These were arranged in two rows on a frame mounted at the rear of the vehicle. The bombs were discharged simultaneously. A similar device using German 8cm mortars was mounted on a truck.

Rocket Projectors

8cm R-Vielfachwerfer auf gep Mannschaft Wg Somua (f)
This experimental equipment was developed late in 1944 and consisted of 24 fin-stabilised 8cm nose-fused rockets (Raketen Sprenggranate) *fired from a multiple projector known as the 8cm R-Vielfachwerfer. The projector assembly consisted of 24 launcher rails arranged in two rows of 12 on a rotating base mounted at the rear of a modified armoured French Somua semi-tracked vehicle.*
(Bundesarchiv Koblenz)

Kleinpanzer Wanze
Produced towards the end of the war, this equipment consisted of four 8,8cm Raketen Panzerbüchse 54 (Rocket Launchers Model 54) mounted together within a metal frame on the chassis of the Borgward B IV, converting the vehicle into a one-man tank.
The 8.8cm RP 54 was the German equivalent of the American Bazooka. It fired a large hollow-charged rocket electrically, the current being obtained from a small generator located underneath the tube.
The Borgward B IV (Schwerer Ladungstraeger, SdKfz 301) was a radio-controlled tracked demolition vehicle that had been designed to carry and drop an explosive charge by remote control. Crew 1.

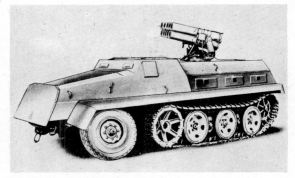

15cm Panzerwerfer 42 auf 'Maultier' (Opel) SdKfz 4/1

Rocket projectors were introduced in 1940 for laying heavy concentrations of smoke and high explosive on target areas, the original 15cm 6-barrel projector equipment being mounted on a two-wheeled towed carriage. To increase the mobility and rate of fire of this weapon, ten projector tubes were mounted on a converted semi-tracked cargo vehicle.

The mobile mount used for this conversion was the 2-ton Opel 3.6.36 Type S/SSM that had been fitted with a light armoured body. The projectors in two horizontal rows of five were mounted at the rear of the vehicle on a turntable with a 360 degree traverse. An additional ten 15cm rocket rounds were carried inside the vehicle. Crew 3. Weight 7.1 tons.

15cm Panzerwerfer 42 (Zehnling) auf Schwerer Wehrmacht-Schlepper

Projected in 1942, the construction of this simplified design for a heavy military semi-tracked tractor (SWS) was personally sanctioned by Hitler for the Infantry Programme to replace the 5-ton semi-tracked vehicle SdKfz 6 which was to be discontinued. The SWS entered into service late in 1944 and a number of them were converted to self-propelled carriages for the 15cm Nebelwerfer projectors to replace the Maultier.

An additional 26 rocket rounds were carried stowed inside the vehicle. Crew 5. Weight 14 tons.

Mittlerer Schuetzenpanzerwagen mit Wurfrahmen, SdKfz 251/1

Introduced into service during 1940, this equipment consisted of the standard 3-ton semi-tracked personnel carrier SdKfz 251 equipped with externally mounted pivoting racks for launching the heavy 28 or 32cm rockets. The racks known as the Schweres Wurfrahmen 40 (SWR 40) were attached, three on each side of the vehicle, and were designed to fire the rocket from the crate that it was packed in, thereby utilising the crate as the projector. The pivoting plates within the SWR 40 frames or racks were adjustable for elevations from 5 to 45 degrees and the rockets were aimed by manoeuvre of the vehicle. These vehicles were also known as Stuka zu Fuss (Infantry Stuka). Crew 7.

(Bundesarchiv, Koblenz)

Gepanzerter Munitionsschlepper UE(f) mit Wurfrahmen or RW auf UE(f)

This was the French Chenillette infantry tractor with four Wurfrahmen 40 mounted, two each side of the vehicle, for launching four 28 or 32cm rockets. The method of aiming and firing was the same as for the Stuka zu Fuss. Crew 2.

Infanterie Schlepper UE(f) für 28/32cm Wurfrahmen

This version of the rocket launching Chenillette carried the crated 28/32cm rockets on a raised metal platform that had been constructed over the stowage bin at the rear of the vehicle. The platform was hinged to obtain elevation and the method of aiming was the same as its counter-part.

A close-up of the sighting vane is shown in the picture of this vehicle, which is being inspected by Field-Marshal Rommel (centre of the group). (Bundesarchiv Koblenz)

28cm rocket launched from Hotchkiss H35. UE Chenillette with 28/32cm crated rockets is on the left. *(Bundesarchiv Koblenz)*

28/32cm Wurfrahmen auf PzKpfw 35H(f)
The rocket launching equipment on this vehicle, a French Hotchkiss H35 tank, was a modified device and consisted of a frame with two metal projectors bolted to movable plates, one frame being attached to each side of the vehicle. The projectors were shaped to the contours of the 28/32cm rockets and were designed as permanent launchers, additional rocket rounds being carried by a munitions vehicle.
Elevation of the launchers was achieved with the movable plates, the rockets being aimed by manoeuvre of the vehicle. *(Bundesarchiv Koblenz)*

Flame Throwers

Mittlerer Flammpanzerwagen, SdKfz 251/16   or m Flamm PzWg
Introduced in 1942, this was the 3-ton semi-tracked armoured personnel carrier SdKfz 251 equipped with flame-throwing weapons. Two 1,4cm flame-projectors protected by armoured V-shaped shields were mounted at the rear, on either side of the vehicle, and could be traversed 160 degrees.
A 154 gallon flame-fuel tank was fitted against the rear inner side of the vehicle and was sufficient for 80 bursts of 1 to 2 seconds at a range of 40 to 50 yards.
A portable 7mm flame-projector for use with a dismounted crewman against difficult targets was also carried. When in use the portable equipment was connected to the vehicle's flame-fuel tank by a 33 ft hose pipe. This equipment was dispensed with on later production models of the SdKfz 251/16. Crew 4. Weight 8 tons.

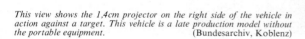

This view shows the 1,4cm projector on the right side of the vehicle in action against a target. This vehicle is a late production model without the portable equipment. *(Bundesarchiv, Koblenz)*

Flammpanzer I
A number of Panzerkampfwagen I Ausf. A were converted in the field by the Afrika Korps to the role of flame-throwers. The machine gun in the right of the turret was removed and replaced by a projector of a light infantry flame-thrower Model 40. The cylinders containing the flame-fuel and compressed air were installed inside the turret.

PzKpfw II (F) SdKfz 122

This equipment was a conversion of the Panzerkampfwagen II Ausf. D and E to the role of a flame-throwing tank, production of which began in 1940. Two remote controlled armoured turrets containing the flame projectors were mounted on the front of each track guard. These projectors with a range of 35 yards and a traverse of 180 degrees were controlled by the tank commander.

Each projector was supplied separately with flame fuel from a 35 gallon armoured tank carried externally on the track guards. At the rear of each fuel container was mounted a triple smoke generator discharger. Crew 3. Weight 11 tons.

Panzerkampfwagen III (F) SdKfz 141/3   or Flammpanzer III

Produced from 1942, this vehicle was the basic Ausf. L or M of the the Panzer III series converted to a flame-throwing tank. The flame-projector was contained inside a steel tube about 5 ft long and was mounted co-axially in the turret with a machine gun replacing the normal 5cm gun. A total of 225 gallons of flame-fuel was carried internally, being contained in two tanks within the hull. This enabled the projector to give 70 to 80 flame jets of 2–3 seconds at ranges of up to 65 yards maximum. Crew 3. Weight 23 tons.

Flammpanzer 38(t)

Produced in late 1944, the flame-projector was mounted on the offside front of a Panzerjäger 38(t) replacing the 7,5cm Pak 39. Two tanks containing 154 gallons of flame-fuel were carried internally. The range of the projector was 55 to 66 yards.

PzKpfw B1 Bis(f) Flamm

Twenty-four French Char B1 Bis heavy tanks were converted during 1943 to flame-throwing tanks. A flame-projector was installed in the front of the hull replacing the 75mm gun and the tank for the flame-fuel was placed at the rear of the vehicle within an armoured housing. Crew 4. Weight 34 tons.

Index

Panzer Division in action.

"Only Movement Brings Victory"

The Achievements of German Armour

by Brigadier H. B. C. Watkins

"ONLY movement brings victory": the title epitomises the spirit and tactical philosophy of the German armoured troops between 1919 and 1945, coming as it does from an article on the use of armour published in October 1937 in the journal of the National Union of German Officers.

The end of the first World War found the Germans in the embarrassing position of having had their Army reduced to a mere hundred thousand men and so stripped of offensive power as to be little more than a gendarmerie. Paradoxically, it was the very harshness of the terms of the Versailles Treaty that created a situation in which German military thinkers, no longer inhibited by the trappings of large conscript forces, were able to concentrate on two things. They began to rethink the whole concept of warfare on land and to set about training their small regular force as a cadre of high-class professionals round which an expanded Army could be built quickly when the need and opportunity arose.

When considering the origins of German thought on the subject of increased tactical mobility, the starting point is often seen to lie in the recognition of the work of Fuller and Liddell Hart by a handful of forward-looking soldiers. In fact the real seeds are to be found in the writings and stewardship of the new Reichswehr's first Commander-in-Chief—General Hans von Seeckt, who took up his appointment in March 1920.

This dynamic man had recognised the possibilities of infiltration tactics whilst Chief of Staff to von Mackensen in 1915. It was who now appreciated the golden opportunities for the future which the barren state of the Reichswehr was offering, believing, as he did, in the superiority of small, highly-trained armies over huge conscript forces. He therefore concentrated upon training all his four thousand officers and ninety-six thousand men to be leaders and instructors, in readiness for the great day when Germany would come into her own again.

Recognising the need to keep abreast of technical developments elsewhere, von Seeckt sent his officers to serve with and study other armies and to learn what they could about the use of tanks and aircraft in mobile warfare. Though not a tank man himself, but one who based most of his theories upon the advantageous use of cavalry, it was his broad tactical philosphy that gave the initial impetus to the work of the new generation of armoured disciples.

This philosophy is best expressed in von Seeckt's own words—"In brief, the whole future of warfare appears to me to lie in the employment of mobile armies, relatively small but of high quality and rendered distinctly more effective by the addition of aircraft . . ."[1] Convinced of the importance of surprise and of flexibility in the

---

[1] Hans von Seeckt "Thoughts of a Soldier", 1928.

1

General Heinz Guderian. His appointment to the Motorized Troops Department as a captain in 1922 marks the first milestone in the history of German armour.

handling of reserves to exploit a weakness or break-through, he saw what a vital part good communications and resolute leadership from the forward edge of the battle would have to play in mobile operations.

Though his teaching was more a masterly analysis of the true potential of modern arms as he knew them, rather than any form of military clairvoyance, the fact remains that as we follow the story of German armour over the years, that teaching will be repeatedly vindicated and reflected in all the Army's most striking successes. In passing, it is interesting to find that, as a young officer, Marshal Zhukov sat at the feet of von Seeckt in Germany between 1921 and 1923.

THE DEVELOPMENT OF THE PANZER DIVISION

One of the most fascinating aspects of military history is the influence that personalities have upon an army. The story of German armour is no exception. Indeed it centres very largely round the extraordinary fluctuations, between enthusiastic co-operation and open clash, that characterized the relationship of Adolf Hitler and General Heinz Guderian and, to a lesser extent, of Hitler and his other senior Generals. Not since the days of Frederick the Great had a German head of state so influenced the development of the Army or presumed to exercise such personal control of its operations. Never before in history has a megalomaniac contributed so decisively to the destruction of a magnificent machine for which, in his saner moments, he had provided the main impetus of its creation.

On April 1, 1922, Captain Heinz Guderian, a Jaeger officer and a member of the German General Staff, was appointed to the Motorized Troops Department of the Ministry of Defence in Berlin. This appointment marks the first milestone in our story. Entering into a semi-

technical field of employment for the first time, Guderian began to study the work of Fuller, Liddell Hart and Martel. These studies fired his interest in the use of mobile troops for long range strokes against enemy communications and in the concept of grouping mechanized infantry and tanks in armoured divisions. In 1923–4 he worked with Lieutenant Colonel von Brauchitsch (later to become a Field Marshal and C-in-C of the Army) on a series of exercises designed to study the co-operation of motorized troops and aircraft. Clearly, the influence of von Seeckt was at work and the shadow of the Stuka on the wall!

It would be quite wrong to think of Guderian as a lone wolf in his enthusiasm for armour and mobility. A number of others, more senior than he, were also at work. As a result, we find that by 1926 the Ordnance Board had put orders in hand for pilot models of turreted medium and light tanks and that a Captain Pirner had been sent to Kazan in Russia to carry out development work there (the Versailles Treaty forbade tanks for the German Army).

Guderian visited Kazan and got a good deal out of his discussions with Pirner on the subject of tank design. However, despite the progress being made, he and his fellows found themselves in conflict with the more reactionary generals at the top of the Army and it was really not until Hitler came into power that they began to get their own way—though, as we shall see, the battle was by no means won. Indeed Guderian was to encounter continuous opposition and prejudice as late as 1943, when he became Inspector General of Armoured Troops.

In 1928 he was established as an instructor in armoured warfare and began to hold small exercises with all sorts of canvas and metal mock-ups to evolve new tactics with tanks. He has acknowledged the debt he owed to the British at that time and the value to the German Army of the standard British handbook, newly written by Brigadier Charles Broad. This was the famous "Purple Primer", properly known as "Mechanized and Armoured Formations". It was translated into German and issued as a basic training manual. In his memoirs, Liddell Hart remarks how bitter the pill was to swallow, both for him and for his British colleagues, when the Panzer Divisions swept to victory in France in 1940. They employed a tactical policy which these Britons had for long ex-pounded but had seen repeatedly rejected by the higher echelons in Whitehall as various vested interests and bigotries were jealously guarded. The Germans' tactical vision was to bring them a series of striking victories in the war years and to cost the lives of many thousands of Allied soldiers.

By 1929, Guderian had become convinced of the need for the armoured division and successful exercises, using motorized troops to test his ideas, were held. Meanwhile, virtually all pretence being swept away, more development work on armoured projects was going ahead, although the rather thin camouflage of misleading terminology was used. Two years later he joined the staff of General Lutz, the Inspector of Motorized Troops. Here was a kindred spirit with whom he could organize further trials on the Panzer Division concept at Graffen-wohr and Juterburg. Despite a good deal of unobjective criticism from the "old and bold", the trials fired the imagination of many of the younger cavalry officers and of no less a person than the great von Hindenburg himself. (It is interesting to recall that this old man had

General Lutz. Guderian became his Chief of Staff in 1931 when he was appointed Inspector of Motorized Troops. "A clever man," wrote Guderian, "with great technical knowledge and brilliant powers of organization."

In 1934 full scale production of the Panzer I began.

said in February 1918 "I do not think that tanks are any use but as these have been made, they might as well be used."[1] One leopard at least was ready to change his spots!)

When the next milestone was reached in 1933, with the assumption of power by Hitler and the appointment of von Fritsch as Commander-in-Chief, the leading lights of the pro-armour faction were ready to press their case to the new management. Unfortunately, the new Chief of Staff, General Beck, did not share his chief's love of tanks but was an entrenched member of the old school. He believed in the tank only as an assault weapon, subservient to the needs of the infantry. Furthermore, he was opposed to the whole idea of armoured divisions. Despite his opposition, the enthusiasm of the Führer led to the establishment of an Armoured Troops Command under Lutz in 1934 with Guderian as Chief of Staff. In this year too, the first 150 Panzer I were built. The German Army had some tanks in service at last! Though built for training purposes, these very light tanks, armed only with machine guns, were to see considerable use on operations, largely because of the delays over the production of Panzer III and IV. Together with some early prototypes of Panzer II they were blooded in 1936, in the Spanish Civil War. Von Thoma, commander of the First Panzer Battalion, took a force of some 600 Germans to fight for General Franco. This first involvement not only gave the new arm a chance to test its tactical theories in battle but also an opportunity to develop the difficult art of working in

close co-operation with the Luftwaffe's new Stuka dive bombers. This was a deadly technique that was to have devastating results in the years to come. It was in Spain too that von Thoma worked on Guderian's concept of the offensive use of anti-tank guns. The realization of the rôle that anti-tank weapons must play in attack had a very significant effect upon German armoured tactics. It was a lesson that the Allies grasped far too late—to their cost. Just as the Russians had sent Zhukov to study under von Seeckt, so did they now send other future Marshals, including Koniev and Rokossovsky, to win their spurs on the Communist side.

Ever since Hitler had arrived on the scene, he had interested himself in the field of technical development and had inevitably come into contact with Guderian, whose considerable drive and expertise had caught his imagination. It was largely due to Hitler's support that the years 1934–35 were so productive. The specifications for Panzers II, III and IV were all approved at this time. Indeed 1935 saw Panzer II enter service and the first prototype of Panzer IV being built. All was by no means plain sailing. There were production problems to be overcome—machine tools had to be developed, there were difficulties over the manufacture of armour plate and delays over radios and optics. Guderian was insisting on high quality for these items—and, of course, he was right.

Exercises held in 1935 demonstrated once again the potentialities of the Panzer Division. On October 15 three were established and the Second given to Guderian. Their organization was really an improved version of the British Experimental Mechanized Force of 1927. There

[1] Fuller "Tanks in the Great War".

General Ritter von Thoma. As commander of the First Panzer Battalion he took a force of Germans to fight for General Franco in Spain in 1936.

and the composition and equipment of armoured troops. Although the case for armoured personnel carriers, self-propelled artillery of all types, and tracked supply vehicles was strongly pressed, the opposition was too strong and progress was desperately slow. The Wehrmacht was to pay the price many times over in Russia.

To spread the armoured gospel throughout the Army and industry, a series of important articles were published in technical and professional journals at this time. The most important was the one from which the title of this survey was extracted. It was a challenging piece of work which left no-one in any doubt about the aims of the armoured school of thought. Drawing the attention of the reactionaries to the weakness in protection and firepower of the current range of German tanks in comparison with those of the British and French, it emphasized the great advantages which lay with the side that was either impervious to enemy anti-tank weapons or was able to penetrate and outrange all the enemy's tanks. (The distinction here is significant, as it was not protection but lack of range and hitting power that was to prove such a failing of British tanks until Comet came into service in 1945).

"Only movement brings victory". This dogmatic and fundamental proposition is credited by Guderian to "our adversaries"[1] but it represents one of the cornerstones of his armoured faith. The article put it this way—"Everything is therefore dependent on this: to be able to move faster than has hitherto been done: to keep moving despite the enemy's defensive fire and thus to make it harder for him to build up fresh defensive positions: and finally to carry the attack deep into the enemy's

was a long way to go before the hard hitting formations of the war years were a reality, but a big step forward had been taken.

Even as a divisional commander, Guderian had considerable influence over Army policy, working closely with Lutz. Between 1935 and 1937, whilst the trials of Panzers III and IV were carried out, the new mark of Panzer II, with its improved suspension, and SdKfz 221 (the four-wheeled armoured car) were coming into service. First thoughts were also being given to Tiger. Nevertheless, a running fight continued within the German General Staff over the rôle of the tank in war

---

[1] Guderian "Panzer Leader", p. 40.

Panzer II Ausf.A which started to appear in 1937. The improved suspension, seen here, was first used on the previous model, Ausf.c.

The first Panzer III production model was completed in 1936. The model seen here in a peaceful river setting appeared after World War II had begun.

defences. . . . We believe that by attacking with tanks we can achieve a higher rate of movement than has been hitherto attainable, and—what is perhaps even more important—that we can keep moving once a break-through has been made." Then, putting their cards face upwards: "In an attack that is based on a successful tank action the 'architect of victory' is not the infantry but the tanks themselves, for if the tank attack fails then the whole operation is a failure, whereas if the tanks succeed, then victory follows."[1]

Emphasizing that firepower is the most important of the three basic characteristics of armour, the author stressed the need "for a short period of time, to dominate the enemy's defence in all its depth.", emphasizing the requirement for more panzer divisions to be available in reserve to exploit the initial attack and to achieve the breakthrough. Scorning the time-wasting of pre-liminary bombardments and underlining the attendant risk of thus losing surprise, the article finished with a strong advocacy of the tank as the principal arm, to be used in mass, closing with these words, "For to carry out great decisive operations it is not the mass of the infantry but the mass of the tanks that must be on the spot."[2]

Von Seeckt's teaching on the need for the flexible handling of reserves and for resolute leadership from the front already characterized the exercises being carried out by the armoured troops. When these two vital ingredients of victory are added to the philosophy delineated by the 1937 article and when the work done in Spain with the Stukas by von Thoma is remembered, it is easy to get a feel of what it was that brought such sweeping successes to the Panzer Divisions in Poland and France only two and three years later.

1 Guderian "Panzer Leader", p. 41–43.
2 Guderian "Panzer Leader", p. 46.

INITIATION 1938

1938 marks the next major event in the history of German armour—it was the year of the Anschluss and conse-quently the first appearance of the Panzer Divisions on the world scene, as they paraded their way through defenceless Austria. By now a Corps Commander, Guderian was put in charge of all armoured troops involved and stage-managed the Army's first major tactical move with its new formations.

The operation was not altogether the success for which Hitler had hoped—there was a high rate of unservice-ability amongst the tanks and the weakness of the repair and supply organization was all too apparent. These weaknesses had been highlighted in the previous year's training but, despite Guderian's warning, nothing had been done to rectify the situation. Nevertheless, his old division, 2nd Panzer, covered 420 miles in 48 hours. SS Panzer Regiment Leibstandarte "Adolf Hitler" under Sepp Dietrich motored 600 miles in the same period. Even today these figures would be something to boast about. Other factors on the credit side were the success of the movement plan, which confirmed Guderian's belief

An early model, Ausf.B, of the Panzer IV which appeared in 1937.

5

Schwerer Panzerspähwagen *SdKfz 231, the first of the eight-wheeled armoured cars, that came into service in 1938. It was armed with a 2cm gun and a machine-gun.*

that he could move two mechanized formations on the same route, and the general conviction that the tank units were developing along the right lines. Furthermore the psychological effects of this demonstration of Germany's new-found strength on the rest of Europe were profound. The possibility of war had suddenly achieved reality. The Führer had become a dominating figure in European politics, with a consequent boost to his already considerable stature in the Fatherland. The subsequent moves against the Sudetenland and Czechoslavakia were much more polished performances as far as the armour was concerned and served to increase the fears of the bystanders, underlining the threat that the new and highly mechanized Wehrmacht represented.

1938 was by no means a year of purely political progress. The inadequacy of the armament of Panzer III,

against which the armoured soldiers had long been railing, was at least recognized by the Ordnance Board and its upgunning to 50mm agreed. (However, in the first instance this was only to introduce the short KwK 39 L/42. Bitter experience in the Desert and in Russia and Hitler's personal intervention were to lead to a further upgunning, using the high velocity L/60, in 1941). Meanwhile work had been going forward in the less glamorous, but by no means less important, field of reconnaissance, resulting in the appearance of the first of the highly effective eight-wheeled armoured cars (SdKfz 231). On the organizational side, Hitler's personal involvement with the growth of the armoured force had resulted in the establishment of a single Headquarters for Mobile Troops with Guderian at its head. Despite Hitler's favours, the tangled web of frustration woven by the senior diehards within the General Staff did much to hamper Guderian's work, since his every action required their endorsement. To belittle him, he was given a mobilization appointment with a reserve corps of infantry formations, although, as we shall see, this was put right in time for him to play a significant part in the campaign against Poland in the following year.

For the motorized infantry, the first half-tracked armoured personnel carriers, for which Guderian had for so long been clamouring, were issued to 1st Panzer Division in 1939, just in time to be used on operations. The term Panzer Grenadier was not to be introduced until 1942, but these early vehicles marked the germ of the concept and the beginning of general recognition within the German Army of the great significance of truly mobile and protected infantry within the Panzer

Hitler taking the salute at a march past in the Ringstrasse, Vienna, after the Anschluss with Austria in 1938. The vehicles are SdKfz 221 armoured cars. These Leichter Panzerspähwagen *mounted a machine-gun only.*

Division. The 1937 article had, incidentally, contained this sentence: "We therefore demand that, in order to exploit our successes, the necessary supporting arms be made as mobile as we are." But it was to be a long hard grind before this ideal was achieved. Indeed, this situation was never reached for the logistic units, and the penalty was a heavy one.

The first half-track Schützenpanzerwagen *(armoured personnel carriers) were issued to troops in 1939. This SdKfz 251 (Mittlerer Schützenpanzerwagen) is seen during the Russian campaign in 1943.*

POLAND 1939

We have now reached the point at which the Panzer Divisions were to receive their first blooding in a short, sharp war against a heroic but poorly equipped enemy.

The six Panzer and four Light Divisions which formed

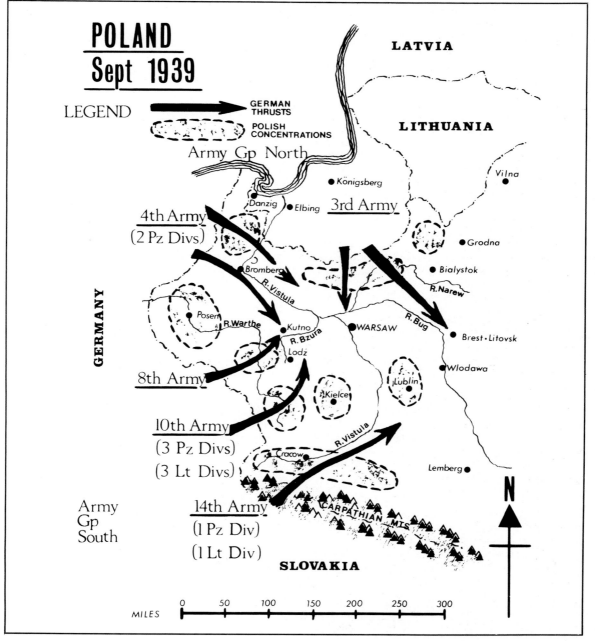

German infantry taking cover behind a Panzer II of a regimental headquarters (indicated by R on the turret side) on September 25, 1939 during the fighting for Warsaw.

the cutting edge of the German invasion of Poland in September 1939 were still only equipped with Panzer I and II. The Panzer Lehr Battalion, which had been specially incorporated into the order of battle, had the new Panzer III and IV. Both models were equipped with short-barrelled guns and so had indifferent anti-tank performances. However, as the thirteen battalions of Polish tanks were little better than reconnaissance vehicles, the shortcomings of the German machines were, perhaps, of little real significance. Panzer Lehr, a training unit, had been included in Guderian's XIX Corps at his request, as had the Reconnaissance Demonstration Battalion. This arrangement shows how determined he was to snatch every opportunity to gain experience for his armoured troops and to test out the latest equipment and tactical theories under battle conditions. Hitler visited him in Poland and cross-examined him about the performance of the tanks. As a result it was only a matter of days after the end of the campaign that Panzers III and IV were accepted as standard equipment for all tank battalions. Guderian took the opportunity of this visit to hammer home his views on the need for better guns and armour, though he pronounced himself satisfied with the speed of his current vehicles.

The boldness and the degree of control which characterized the German operations represent a complete breakthrough in tactical history. To take an example at regimental level—von Thoma, who commanded a Panzer Regiment at this time, has described the success of his operation to turn the flank of the Jublenka Pass. By making a night march of some fifty miles and by taking a route through thickly wooded and hilly country, he achieved complete surprise. On the larger scale, Guderian's lightning thrusts with XIX Corps, handling two Panzer and two Motorized Divisions as a single entity, and von Runstedt's equally swift encircling movements with his Army Group South, proved conclusively what rich advantages lay in the policy of forward control using first class communications. Both these commanders and also von Manstein, von Run-

stedt's brilliant Chief of Staff, took command of detailed situations themselves when necessary. Guderian worked from an armoured command vehicle, often from amongst the leading tanks.

THE "PHONEY WAR"

The period of the "phoney war" that followed provided a badly needed break for the Wehrmacht. Despite the scale of the recent victories, the Polish Eagle had left plenty of scars and the Army's equipment was badly knocked about. Although the organization of the Panzer Division had proved a success, that of the Light Divisions, which contained a full Reconnaissance Regiment but only a single tank battalion, had proved to be something of an anomaly. The decision was therefore taken to convert them to Panzer Divisions in time for the French campaign.

In 1935 the original Panzer Divisions had contained two Panzer Regiments, each of two battalions. These battalions had four light companies. By 1940 the Tank Battalion had been reduced to three companies, of which one had been classified as "medium" and equipped with Panzer IV. Because of the low muzzle velocity of Panzer IV's 75mm gun, its rôle was seen as that of a close support tank—a situation that Guderian had long pressed to have put right by upgunning. Meanwhile the infantry content of the division had been changed, so that there were now three battalions in the Motor Rifle Regiment instead of two. As before, the regiment included a motor-cycle battalion but a heavy infantry gun company was now added.

The task of converting the Light Divisions and of re-equipping the Panzer Divisions went slowly because of production troubles and the general state of muddle that seemed to prevail in the OKW. A by-product of this was the acquisition of some 334 Czech 35 and 38(t) tanks with which to fit out the former Light Divisions. In May 1940 nearly 1000 Panzer II and just over 500 Panzer I were still in general use with the existing Panzer Divisions.

Availability of Panzers III and IV was 349 and 278 respectively.

In the event, the Allied tank strength in France was little short of double that of the Germans and much of their equipment was as good or better. The French Char B and Somua S-35 were infinitely better protected than anything that the Germans possessed, as were the British Marks I and II Infantry tanks. However, the Mark I had only a single machine-gun as armament and was both slow and unreliable, being ridiculously underpowered. The Mark II (Matilda) was a different proposition, having a better gun in its 40mm than the German 37mm, to which it was impervious. Sadly for the Allies, only a handful of these stalwarts was available and even these were quickly disposed of at Arras by the 88mm anti-aircraft gun, being used for the first time in the anti-tank rôle. As for the French, their material advantages were lost through lack of an up-to-date tactical concept, lack of communications and so the lack of the ability to react with any flexibility to the enemy threat—defeat in detail was inevitable against tacticians of the class they were about to face. Like the British Infantry tanks, the French machines also lacked speed, a fact that greatly added to their tactical inflexibility. The Infantry tanks apart, the rest of the British contingent contained a high proportion of Mark VIB Light Tanks. These were quite unsuitable for anything but reconnaissance, though a few of the new Cruisers, carrying the same 40mm as Matilda, were also available. It would be wrong to place too much significance upon the British contribution, as it represented a small proportion only of the total Allied tank strength. However, we shall see that the only serious check to the German advance came from a counter-attack in which the bulk of the armour was British.

On February 7, 1940, a war game was played at Koblenz to study a new plan for the French operation which had been prepared by von Manstein. Although the term "Blitzkrieg" had not by then been coined, this was the concept that the plan envisaged. The diehards just could not or would not understand Guderian's proposal for a swift crossing of the Meuse at Sedan by

On April 9, 1940 Germany invaded Denmark and Norway. A Panzer I Ausf.A is seen here on the road to Kolding in Jutland, Denmark, on April 11.

Panzer I in southern Norway, April 1940. Norwegian resistance did not end until June 9.

mechanized formations, with a view to achieving the breakthrough at this point. It was described by General Halder (Chief of the General Staff) as "senseless". He and those like him would concede no more than that the Panzer Divisions would establish bridgeheads across the river. Here they would wait for the infantry formations to catch up.

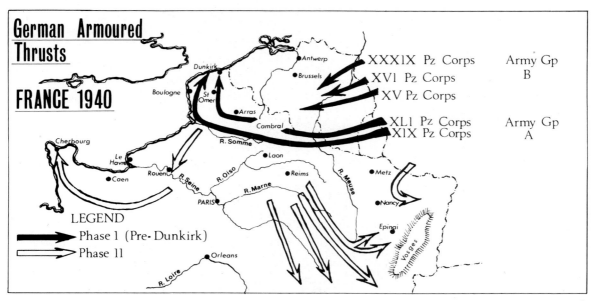

German Armoured Thrusts

FRANCE 1940

Dunkirk · Antwerp · Brussels · Boulogne · St Omer · Arras · Cambrai · Cherbourg · Le Havre · Caen · Rouen · R. Seine · R. Oise · Laon · Reims · R. Marne · R. Meuse · Metz · PARIS · Nancy · Epinal · Vosges · R. Loire · Orleans · R. Somme

XXXIX Pz Corps
XVI Pz Corps — Army Gp B
XV Pz Corps

XLI Pz Corps — Army Gp A
XIX Pz Corps

LEGEND
→ Phase 1 (Pre-Dunkirk)
⇒ Phase 11

9

General (later Field-Marshal) Erich von Manstein, who designed the plan of attack that was to sweep the Germans to victory in May 1940. In the opinion of many he was the greatest strategist on any side in World War II.

Seven days later, a similar study was held at General List's 12th Army Headquarters at Mayen. The outcome was the same. Even von Runstedt, with all his experience in Poland behind him, seemed unable to grasp the true potentialities of the armoured formations or the opportunities that really bold action might offer. It seemed that only Hitler, von Manstein and Guderian had any comprehension of the matter.

Despite his depression at the way things were going, Guderian remained convinced that once his divisions had broken through, they must be given the green light, with the Channel coast marking the end of the road. His divisional commanders were solidly behind him and the message was put down to every soldier under his command. In a situation in which no orders were forthcoming, their job was to push on by day and night to their objective.

As in September 1939, the German armoured troops were now ready to go into battle with complete confidence in their leaders, a clear understanding of the task, and a burning sense of purpose and pride in their own ability. It was these abstract factors that were to play so large a part in their victory and provide the drive and energy that were needed to keep up the non-stop pressure their tactical doctrine required.

BLITZKRIEG—FRANCE 1940

At first light on May 10, 1940 the German armies, which included ten Panzer Divisions and the SS Panzer Regiment "Leibstandarte Adolf Hitler", crossed the German frontier. The Campaign in the West had begun.

Panzer II held up by a blown bridge during the advance into Belgium, May 1940.

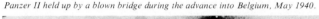

Guderian was still commanding his XIX Army Corps. Somehow he had kept the Armoured Reconnaissance Demonstration Battalion under command! XIX Corps formed part of Panzergruppe von Kleist for the first phase of the battle, but for the second Guderian was to command a Group of his own. He clashed with von Kleist from the outset. Whilst Guderian husbanded his tanks for the breakout and exploitation, von Kleist wasted many of his in assaults upon strongpoints for which the motorized infantry were far better suited.

Guderian's emphasis on concentration is typified by his pet catch phrase when talking about tactics— "Klotzen, nicht kleckern". This might be vulgarly translated today as "Thump 'em, don't pepper 'em". Again and again in the story of German armour we find a combination of concentration, surprise and the relentless maintenance of momentum at high speed producing the shock effect that is fundamental to success in the armoured battle.

Moving by day and night, Guderian's troops reached Sedan on the Meuse on May 13. 1st Panzer Division lost no time in hurling the 1st Rifle Regiment, under command of Lieutenant Colonel Balck, across the river. No less than 1000 Stukas supported the crossing. We shall hear more about this very gallant soldier who was to lead XLVIII Panzer Corps with such distinction in Russia and later to command Army Group G in the later days of the war in the West. General von Mellenthin, who served for many months as Balck's Chief of Staff, praises the high standard of all arms training which had been reached by 1st Rifle Regiment before the campaign began and which was to become a model for the future. This was something that neither the French nor the British had really begun to grasp—as the next few weeks would show.

There is no room to describe the campaign in detail. As Guderian had foreseen, the Germans swept all before them. Only at Arras did they suffer a solid, if momentary, check. Here a scratch British force of Mark I

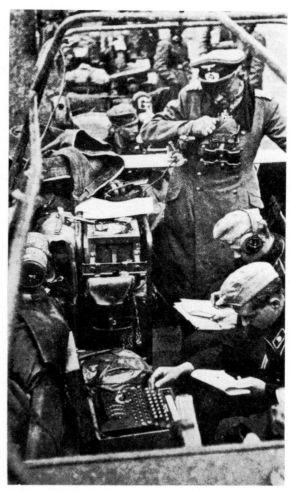

Guderian worked from an armoured command vehicle, often from amongst the leading tanks.

Panzer I, Ausf.A, about to cross a pontoon bridge during the campaign against France.

Leichter Panzerspähwagen *SdKfz 222* mounted a 2cm gun and a machine-gun in the turret which had a hinged wire grille as head cover. The grille opened in two parts, as seen here.

Schwerer Panzerspähwagen *SdKfz 232 on the way to Paris*. This armoured car was the same as the SdKfz 231 except that it had a medium range wireless with a frame aerial over the rear and turret.

and Matilda tanks from the 4th and 7th Royal Tank Regiments, flanked by some 70 French Somua, hurled themselves at SS Division Totenkopf and the flanks of General Erwin Rommel's 7th Panzer Division. But this gallant operation was lacking in artillery and air support and ground to a halt as Rommel himself took charge of operations to check it, using 88mm anti-aircraft guns in the anti-tank rôle to do so. Only these powerful weapons could pierce the thick armour of Matilda.

The armies swept on to the Channel coast and, in seventeen days and seventeen sleepless nights, the battle was won. The pressure had been kept up from the word "Go" and, not surprisingly, both men and machines were in great need of rest and repair. However, within days, the second phase of the campaign, to capture Paris and to complete the final defeat of the French, was on. It was even more successful than the first. Demonstrating great flexibility, using short verbal orders over the radio and travelling well forward in the spearhead of his Group, Guderian moved so fast that OKW would not believe his staff when they reported that they were on the Swiss frontier and their task completed. During this operation Guderian was visited by Dr Todt, responsible for armament production, to discuss the future tank production programme in the light of recent experience. These liaison visits at the highest level were quite normal and it is noticeable that they invariably had an effect on equipment policy within a very short time.

Despite their prodigious efforts and consequent fatigue, it is clear that the morale of the Panzer troops remained sky-high right up to the end of the campaign. One cannot help feeling that the quality of senior leadership within the fighting formations had a great deal to do with this. Commanders were known by the soldiers who would call out to them and cheer as they came past, reflecting the emphasis that Guderian and others had put upon the establishment of mutual trust between all ranks during training. He obviously had a very warm spot in his heart for the Reconnaissance Demonstration Battalion. On page 130 of "Panzer Leader" he writes: "I paid a short visit to the frontier and had a word with the leaders of the reconnaissance battalion. It was thanks to their tireless efforts that we had had such superb intelligence of the enemy." German recognition of the value of information as a weapon of

war was to be a continuing feature of panzer operations.

Describing the administrative measures taken to support the armour in France, von Thoma has told us how each division carried petrol for up to 200 Km and was re-supplied by airdrop (a technique unheard of by the Allies). Within divisional resources there were also nine days rations. Given a rate of advance of some 30 miles a day, including fighting, a Panzer Division needed only about three re-supplies of fuel within a seven day period and was self-sufficient for rations. This meant that the bulk of the available road transport could be devoted to the considerable tonnage of ammunition to be brought up daily. Of course things did not always go smoothly and Guderian describes at least one occasion when 2nd Panzer Division ran out of petrol through sheer inefficiency.

The administrative arrangements for these "blitzkriegs" and the problems of technical support they created were entirely different from those needed for a more protracted campaign. It may well be that many of the adminstrative mistakes made in Russia had their roots in the false lessons learned in France and Poland and in a failure to appreciate that lightning victory in Russia was really so remote a possibility, even for the Wehrmacht, that much longer term administrative support was essential. Whatever the reason, we shall see how great were the difficulties that the armoured troops encountered both in Russia and North Africa through lack of supplies and integral workshop facilities.

Despite glittering success, the German command and control in France was far from satisfactory. As in the past, prejudice and personal animosities were to cloud the issue and to lead to strife between the more senior commanders, particularly over orders to restrain the speed of advance. Interference by Hitler himself, culminating in the famous order to stop outside Dunkirk (thus, ironically, enabling the BEF to escape and Britain to carry on the fight) was a forewarning of a situation in which this fatal wrangling was to continue until the last days of the war, like a virus infection. Dominated by the evil genius of the Führer, it was to bring about a series of costly mistakes against which not even the brilliance of von Manstein was able to prevail. This is not the place to examine this particular aspect of German military history in depth, but it must be recog-

The most numerous of foreign tanks to be used by the Germans was the Czech TNHP which they designated the PzKpfw 38(t). Three of these are seen in the foreground of this mass of 7th Panzer Division vehicles halted during the last stages of the campaign in France, June 1940. The division was commanded by General Erwin Rommel.

After the fall of France a number of French tanks were taken into German service. This is a Hotchkiss H39 which has been modified by the installation of a wireless set and by a change in the cupola. The Germans designated it PzKpfw 39–H 735(f).

nized that it had profound effects upon the fortunes of German armour in the long run.

PREPARATION

The Battle of France over, Hitler began to look once again to the organization of the Army. Infatuated with the question of numbers, he decided to double the Panzer Divisions he could put into the field. This could only be achieved by halving the number of tanks currently on divisional establishments. The sheer folly of so dispersing his armour whilst doubling his overheads infuriated his Generals, but their protests fell on deaf ears. To compound his felony, Hitler also doubled the Motorized Infantry Divisions. The strain on industry was crippling. When he asked the Ordnance Office to raise tank production to 1000 a month, he was told that this was impossible

on grounds of cost and lack of industrial manpower.

It was at this time that the incident took place by which he was deceived over the upgunning of Panzer III—the Ordnance Office fitted the L/42 50mm in place of the L/60 high velocity gun that Hitler had ordered. The discovery of this deception in April 1941 created a distrust of the Ordnance staff in Hitler's mind which he never quite lost and must have seriously affected business connected with tank production for the rest of the war.

With the invasion of England in mind, Schnorkel versions of both Panzers III and IV were developed during 1940 as was an amphibious model of Panzer II. Some 50 of these latter were built but they never saw service. However the ingenious Schnorkel models were to be used in some river-crossing operations in Russia and the principle applied to the early models of Tiger Model E. That the Germans were clearly thinking at this

Panzer IV, Ausf.C, at St. Martin de Fresnay, France.

General Erwin Rommel, one of the most famous generals of World War II.

battles was small in terms of the vast conflict about to begin in Russia, which involved no less than 145 German divisions and nearly 2500 tanks, the circumstances under which they were fought were such that they provided unrivalled opportunities for the exercise of the principles of armoured warfare which the Germans had established over the years.

There have been many misconceptions over the desert campaign, not the least of which being that the Germans had a considerable advantage over the British in the quality and hitting power of their tanks. As von Mellenthin has pointed out, "the German tanks did not have any advantage in quality and in numbers we were always inferior."[1] To back this statement he gives figures of the relative positions before the "Crusader" battles in November 1941 in which the British fielded 748 tanks mounting 40mm or 37mm high velocity guns against 249 German machines of which 174 were Panzers III and IV, the balance being Panzer II—still carrying the 20mm only. The Germans were supported by 146 very inferior Italian tanks which had only a low velocity 47mm gun. The plain fact is that in the first year of the campaign the Germans completely outshone the British in tank tactics. Von Mellenthin ascribes their success to these factors:—

    Superior tactical methods

    The quality of their anti-tank weapons

    The systematic practice of the principle of co-operation by all arms.

As we consider some of the battles in detail we shall see that, of the first named factor, the facets which deserve most recognition were the German ability to achieve local superiority in tanks at the main point of attack, the skilful handling of their anti-tank guns in both attack and defence and, above all, the quality and professionalism of their leadership, from Rommel himself downwards. Finally, the Germans were past masters in the art of achieving tactical surprise, a fact that was often to prove decisive. Years of thought, hard training and the experience of two victorious campaigns were to pay a heavy dividend. One sovereign advantage the Germans did possess—a fleet of Stuka dive-bombers against which the British were unable to gain more than local air superiority until well on in the campaign and which gave Rommel a superb form of offensive air support against defended localities and columns of armour. By the same token, these aircraft were a powerful defensive weapon when needed.

Every Army has its Achilles heel—the Germans' was administration. We shall see time and again, that the inadequacies of the German system of supply were to bring them to the edge of disaster. Indeed, had the British not been so prolific in their forward stockpiling and then left those stocks intact to fall into German hands, the whole story might have been much shorter. Administrative problems were also to confound the best efforts of the armoured commanders in Russia—Guderian had foreseen all this, but despite the warnings of experience, no-one in the OKW really wanted to know.

The arrival of the Afrika Korps was timed to spread over several months. 5th Light Division arrived in Tripoli in February 1941 whilst 15th Panzer was not due until May. Although Rommel's orders were to wait until his force was assembled before beginning operations, he quickly realized that time was not on his side and that the

time of battles much further afield is demonstrated by the request generated by the Army for an air-cooled CI engine in a powerful armoured car for desert use. This demand was met in 1943 by the introduction of the SdKfz 234 series—too late for the desert war.

Meanwhile, in Germany, the Army was training hard to absorb the lessons of the past year and to prepare itself for the greatest trial of strength it had ever contemplated. The mind of the Führer was running away with him and 1941 was to mark not only the beginning of war on multiple fronts but also the beginning of the end, stemming as the end did from the folly of Operation Barbarossa —the invasion of Russia. Yet, as we shall see, German armour was to touch the heights before the final crash to annihilation came in 1945.

AFRICA—THE BIRTH OF A LEGEND

Whilst the German Army was training at home and in France, the Italians were taking a severe beating in the Western Desert at the hands of General Wavell. In view of the imminent collapse of Marshal Graziani's forces, two German divisions were selected to go to North Africa under the command of General Rommel to restore the situation. These were 5th Light (later redesignated 21st Panzer) and 15th Panzer Divisions. With the Italian motorized divisions already in the theatre under his command, Rommel was to launch a truly remarkable campaign with his Afrika Korps which not only turned the tables on the British but came within an ace of driving them out of Africa before the tide turned yet again and he was finally driven out of Tunisia himself in 1943. Many British lives and some hundreds of tanks had been lost by that time, but improved British generalship, substantial reinforcements of men and new equipment, and a greatly enhanced Desert Air Force all played their part in the German defeat. Though the scale of the Western Desert

[1] Von Mellenthin "Panzer Battles", p. 51.

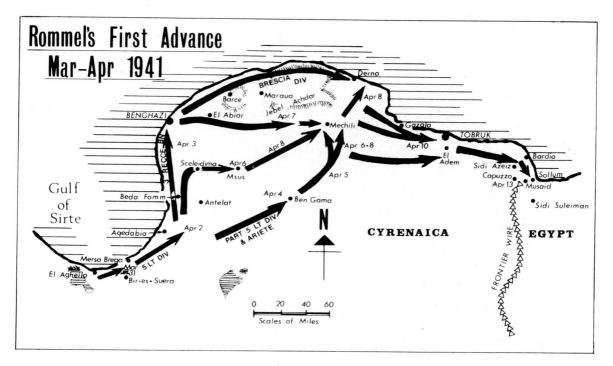

Rommel's First Advance Mar-Apr 1941

Gulf of Sirte

CYRENAICA

EGYPT

0 20 40 60
Scales of Miles

sooner he took control of all the Axis mobile troops in the theatre the better. Against all advice, he determined to get to grips with the British and immediately moved the front some 350 miles to the east, with 5th Light Division in the line, despite their lack of acclimatization. Without further ado he made contact with the British reconnaissance screen at El Agheila on February 24, attacking the Mersa Brega defile on March 31. In his memoirs[1] he describes the deception measures he put in hand, including the use of dummy tanks made of canvas mounted on Volkswagen. It is ironical that just such a ruse was to be used most effectively against him by Montgomery before the Second Battle of Alamein.

The story of Rommel's first dramatic desert victory is well known. Within days he had driven the British before him out of Cyrenaica, was investing the fortress of Tobruk and had troops over the wire in the area of Sollum. More important, he had inflicted heavy casualties on the British in terms of vehicles and stores and had put a number of senior commanders "in the bag". It was Rommel's dynamic leadership that kept his columns moving by day and night at a pace that they would have judged to be beyond them. But the story was repeated at lower levels—opportunities were seized and battlegroups led through tricky situations by the personal example of their commanders. It must be remembered that the German soldiers were fighting in the heat and dust of the desert for the first time, so much credit must also go to them. In June Rommel was to write to his wife[2] reporting a temperature of 107°F with the figure in the turrets of the tanks standing around 160°F. Whilst it was the same for both sides, the British had lived in the desert for long periods and had developed sensible methods of working under the severe conditions it imposed on both men and machines. These skills the Germans had to acquire by bitter experience.

Rommel's operations had inevitably put a great strain on his administration and upon the mechanical state of his vehicles. The sand had begun to cause excessive wear on the engines of the tanks and this, when added to the normal incidence of unserviceability, had brought his force almost to a halt. Reliance upon the repair facilities in Germany and the lack of a sound system of field repair in the forward areas were other contributory factors to his dilemma. Having fought a bitter battle against a mixed force of some 200 Matildas and Cruisers in Wavell's "Battle-axe" operations around Capuzzo and Sidi Omar, in which both sides took heavy casualties, he had almost reached the limit of his resources. These battles were significant for two reasons. Rommel had demonstrated his skill in the handling of his 88mm and high velocity 50mm anti-tank guns, moving them with the tanks and taking a heavy toll of the hitherto almost impervious Matildas. At the same time he had learned that, whatever might be wrong with his opponents' tactical skills, there was nothing lacking in the courage of the troops or the technical skill of the tank crews. One other highly significant thing had occurred during the summer; the Rommel "legend" had been born. This was to give the Axis a psychological advantage

The first of the two Panzer Divisions under Rommel's command (5th Light, later re-designated 21st Panzer) arrived in Tripoli in February 1941.

[1] Liddell Hart "Rommel Papers", p. 103.
[2] Liddell Hart "Rommel Papers", p. 140.

Sandstorm in the Libyan desert, April 1941. A Panzer II silhouetted in the foreground.

that lasted until Montgomery's deliberate counter to it had really taken effect through Rommel's defeat at the battle of Alam Halfa in September 1942. The more one studies the history of warfare the more one realises how significant such abstract factors can become. Rommel's personality and style of fighting made him into something of a hero in the eyes of his opponents and affected the whole character of the desert war—sometimes described as "the last war between gentlemen." Whilst both armies rested and re-equipped, a lull took place from June 1941 until the furious battles of Operation Crusader in November.

"BARBAROSSA"

During the same spring and summer, Hitler's invasion of Yugoslavia and Greece had been taking place, involving a number of Panzer Divisions which were also badly needed for his impending attack on Russia. In the event this fact was to delay the start of Operation Barbarossa, with fatal consequences. It seems hard to credit, but whilst preparations for this attack were in hand, Russian tank experts were being conducted round German industry to study tank production methods! Not that these seem to have been anything to boast about since

Field-Marshal Wilhelm List, German Commander-in-Chief in the Balkans, inspecting tank units in Bulgaria in April 1941. From here the invasion of Greece and the southern thrust against Jugoslavia was launched on April 6, by a force that included four Panzer Divisions.

the figures remained obstinately around 1000 machines a year, to Hitler's great impatience. The Wehrmacht's requirement in July 1941 was to be for nearly 8000 Panzer III for 36 divisions—but by then Barbarossa was on and all the demands of a massive campaign were being felt.

The strain on the German armaments industry was colossal. Up to the time that Panzer III was phased out in 1943, total production for this tank was 5,644, with a peak monthly figure of 213 being achieved in 1942. The chassis continued in service until the end of the war as a carriage for assault and SP guns and nearly fifteen and a half thousand such machines were produced. This was a significant tribute to the soundness of the original design.

Dawn, on Sunday June 22, 1941. After a short preliminary bombardment, tanks of 18th Panzer Division, using Schnorkel equipment designed for Operation Sea

The Wehrmacht advances into Greece.

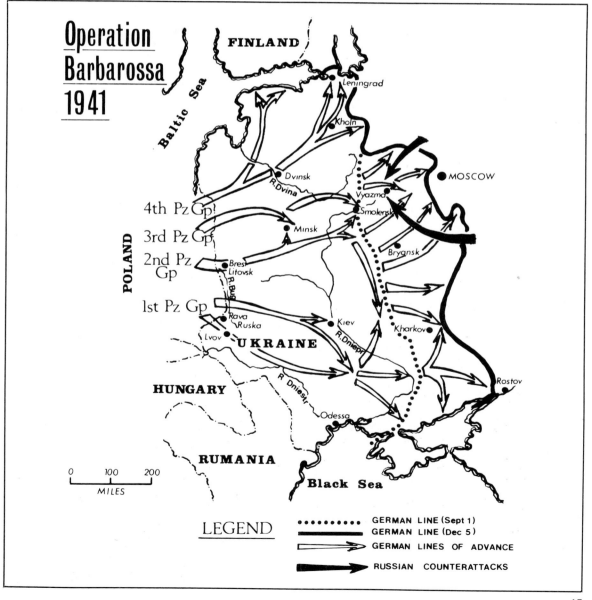

Operation Barbarossa 1941

FINLAND

Baltic Sea

POLAND

4th Pz Gp

3rd Pz Gp

2nd Pz Gp

1st Pz Gp

HUNGARY

RUMANIA

Leningrad

Kholn

Dvinsk

R. Dvina

MOSCOW

Vyazma

Smolensk

Minsk

Bryansk

Brest Litovsk

R. Bug

Rava Ruska

Lvov

UKRAINE

Kiev

R. Dniepr

Kharkov

R. Dniestr

Rostov

Odessa

Black Sea

| 0 | 100 | 200 |
MILES

LEGEND

• • • • • • • GERMAN LINE (Sept 1)
━━━━━━ GERMAN LINE (Dec 5)
⟹ GERMAN LINES OF ADVANCE
➡ RUSSIAN COUNTERATTACKS

Victory parade for the Panzers in Greece. Jugoslavia capitulated on April 17, Greece on April 24, 1941.

For the attack on Soviet Russia Field-Marshal von Bock (second from right) commanded Army Group Centre which included two panzer groups: Panzer Group 2, commanded by General Guderian, and Panzer Group 3, commanded by General Hoth. (B.L.Davis)

Lion, crossed the River Bug at Brest Litovsk. Operation Barbarossa was on.

Two Panzergruppe, led by Generals Hoth and Guderian, formed the spearhead of Army Group Centre (Field Marshal von Bock). The Army's mission was the destruction of the Russian Army located in West Russia "by deep penetration by armoured spearheads" (clearly someone was getting the message in OKW at last!). In this short study we have not the room to examine the story of this complex campaign in detail but only to highlight those aspects which affected the armoured troops.

The advance swept forward through Western Russia. Once again the Germans had proved the value of gaining complete tactical surprise. The broad tactical policy employed was that of a series of encircling movements by the armour with the "squeeze" being applied by the infantry formations. By July 11 the Dnepr had been crossed and substantial casualties inflicted upon the enemy. But the length of the lines of communication soon began to tell. Von Manstein, commanding the LVI Panzer Corps in the drive north towards Leningrad under Field Marshal von Leeb, has told how essential it was for formations to keep moving if they were not to be encircled by the enemy's reserves. He also describes an instance in which his own axis was cut by a single Russian KV1 which took no less than fifty German tanks to shift it, so strong was its armour and so much better was its gun than those of its opponents.

Despite the size of the invasion force (145 divisions and nearly 2,500 tanks, it will be remembered) the Germans were at a numerical and technical disadvantage. The latter was not fully appreciated until July, when the fast, well armoured and hard-hitting T34 was encountered in strength. As in the past, the excellence of the German leadership, their high training standards and, above all, their great tactical flexibility which so often enabled them to gain local numerical superiority at the critical point, went a long way towards making good their deficiencies. In contrast, the Russians were, initially, badly and inexpertly led. The training of their task crews was abysmal. Countless brave men threw away their lives in a welter of utter incompetence. But we shall see that this state of affairs was not to continue indefinitely.

As the battle moved eastwards, the Germans' difficulties began to increase. Fuel was a never-ending problem, the tanks were lacking proper maintenance and there were no workshops in the forward areas which could compete with the casualty rate. Spares were hard to come by and, as in the Western Desert, the dust of high summer was beginning to tear the tank engines to pieces. On August 4, Hitler visited von Bock's headquarters to discuss these matters and also to talk about the future conduct of the campaign. Both Hoth and Guderian were present.

Hitler announced that he had decided to make his main effort against Leningrad before launching the all-out assault on Moscow. This proposal ran so counter to the first principle of German armoured tactical doctrine—Maintenance of the Aim—that it brought a storm of protest from the Generals. No final decision was made. On the technical side, Hitler offered 300 new engines for the whole front but no replacement vehicles: these were needed for the equipment of new formations. Guderian then raised the problems arising from numerical inferiority. Hitler acknowledged that he had failed to give proper consideration to Guderian's prophecies of the mid-thirties and that had he done so he would never have embarked upon the campaign. However, despite these utterances, he was to disregard his Generals' views and on August 26 he produced orders for yet another disastrous diversion, giving priority to the seizure of the Crimea and switching valuable armoured effort to the south for this purpose.

So the weeks ticked by. Pushing slowly eastwards, Army Group Centre captured Kiev on September 20, taking more than 30,000 prisoners in the process. But then the autumn rains turned the dusty roads to quagmires. The German Army's progress dropped to a snail's pace. Resupply had often to be by air. Despite incessant demands from the fighting formations it was abundantly clear that winter would be upon them before any warm clothing, special equipment, or even anti-freeze for the vehicles was available. The price paid for this monstrous piece of maladminstration was terribly heavy. Since both the Luftwaffe and Waffen SS were well prepared for a winter campaign, it became abundantly clear that the blame lay with OKH. One can only assume that they had counted upon total victory before the winter set in and had failed to appreciate the effects of the delays which were the inevitable consequence of Hitler's constant meddling with the conduct of the war.

The impact of the Russian T34 was now being felt and was affecting morale. Guderian demanded that a special commission should visit the front to examine the

The Panzer Divisions advance into Russia, June 1941.

German motorized columns crowding the route into Russia.

Panzer II crossing a repaired bridge in Russia in the first weeks of Operation Barbarossa. The Germans had over 1,000 Panzer IIs when the Russian campaign began.

problems of tank warfare on the spot. The commission arrived in November and, as a result of its findings, two decisions were made. The first was to press on with the development of the 60-ton Tiger, now well advanced, and the second to design a lighter and faster tank of between 35 and 45 tons to be called Panther. The design was put to Hitler on January 23, 1942. This shows that the Germans knew how to cut corners when the need arose. Even more remarkable was the fact that the first production model was to appear in November of the same year. Despite many teething troubles, this was very competitive timing indeed by a tank building industry that was already bowed down under the strain of equipping new divisions, up-armouring and up-gunning existing models, and creating numerous SP variants. Whilst much of this work had to be done under the weight of Allied bombing, work was gradually moved to safer areas in Austria so that it could gain some degree of immunity. Later, the production of both Panther and Tiger B was to owe much to the use of slave labour in the Krupp and Daimler-Benz factories.

The autumn quagmires turned to concrete under the hammer blows of the November frosts. Whole formations were "frozen in" overnight. The suffering of the soldiers and the nightmares of resupply drove commanders to despair. Once again air supply was often the only possible course, with all the restrictions and difficulties this involved under such conditions. Whilst much of the transport of the infantry formations was

still horse-drawn, the Panzer Divisions too lacked suitable cross-country logistic vehicles, despite the pleas of the pre-war years.

By the time that Army Group Centre had finally pushed its way to the outskirts of Moscow, Panzergruppe Guderian, now renamed 2nd Panzer Army, was down to about 400 tanks. The cold was so intense that vehicles had to be started up every four hours and their transmission operated so that the strain on the metal of the transmission, made brittle by the cold, was eased. With oil in the sump like tar and the plates of vehicle batteries buckling, it is easy to realise how great that strain had become and to understand how breaks in final drives were occurring. The courage of the German soldiers at this time was unparalleled. By concentrating their battlegroups in villages, they gained some shelter from the elements and were able to sally out to attack Russian formations operating against them. To anyone who has fought under the conditions of even a severe European winter, the fact that the Germans managed to keep their tanks running at all in Russia and to keep up their offensive spirit is a source of wonder.

Between June 22 and November 30, 1941 the German Army lost 743,000 men—some 23 per cent of its strength. Thanks, very largely, to Hitler's interference, it had reached the limits of its human and technical resources. It was, of course, obvious that the time had come to call a halt and to make a tactical withdrawal, so that both men and machines could be refurbished and the necess-

Tanks of General Hoth's Panzer Group 3 entered Minsk, the capital of White Russia, on June 26, 1941—four days after the campaign started. On the left, a Panzer IV.

Panzer III crossing an anti-tank ditch in the Stalin Line, which was a permanent fortification of concrete bunkers on the old Russian frontier before the annexation of the Baltic states and the eastern part of Poland.

Street fighting in Russia. On the right a Sturmgeschütz III assault gun, on the left a Schwerer Panzerspähwagen SdKfz 231 six-wheeled armoured car.

ary preparations made to renew the attack in the better weather of the coming spring. But this was not to be. Hitler took personal command of the Army on December 19, 1941 and ordered a complete standfast. The merits and demerits of this decision have been argued elsewhere, sufficient be it to record that no less than 35 divisional commanders were relieved of their posts for protesting against this order, whilst Guderian, who had a blazing row with Hitler on December 20, was also removed on the 26th. Into the limbo he went, until his dramatic recall in February 1943. Hitler had gained a moral ascendancy over the Wehrmacht but it had cost him the flower of its field commanders.

Rommel in his "natural habitat"—the Desert—discussing operations with his staff. On the side of his command vehicle is the famous sign of the Afrika Korps, later elevated to the status of a Panzerarmee.

SIDI REZEGH TO GAZALA

Far away in North Africa, Rommel and his British opponents had entered into a fresh trial of strength. Nearly three times as many British tanks as German were poised in early November to begin Operation Crusader—designed to relieve the beleaguered fortress of Tobruk. At the same time, Rommel was preparing to assault the perimeter in an attempt to capture the port. His command had now acquired the title of Panzergruppe Afrika and was soon to be elevated to the status of a Panzerarmee.

On November 18, 1941 five British and six Axis divisions clashed in the general area south and south-east of Tobruk and around the airfield of Sidi Rezegh in particular. The British superiority in armour was substantial (750 tanks to 400) but they fell once again into the error of dispersing into groups of about 150 tanks each. These were attacked by the Germans in turn and, within a matter of hours, the imbalance had been redressed. As before, it was the 50mm and 88's that won the day, rather than the German tanks. Indeed, on November 23, General Cruewell, commanding the Afrika Korps, was sufficiently rash to copy the British tactic of the gallant charge up to the cannon's mouth, in an attack on the 5th South African Brigade. He lost 70

tanks out of 150 and the bulk of his motorised infantry.

The battle swung to and fro, both sides suffering heavy losses. Ignoring Cruewell's advice to clean up the tattered remnants of the defenders of Sidi Rezegh, Rommel swept off at the head of 21st Panzer Division towards Halfaya on the 24th in the hope of making a fresh breakthrough. But he ran out of the cover of his close air support and, once again, ran out of fuel; despite the considerable stocks he could have taken for the asking from the British dumps he had over-run.

Meanwhile, back in the Tobruk area, the New Zealanders, supported by the tanks of 1st Army Tank Brigade, had fought a brilliant night action at Belhammed and won a striking success at Ed Duda. As a result, the corridor to Tobruk was opened. On the 27th a sharp action at Bir el Chleta caused heavy casualties to both sides and nearly led to the loss of 15th Panzer Division. However, the British missed their chance and the division slipped through a gap to escape. Bad co-ordination and overdispersion had cost the British day. Rommel's sweep forward to the Sollum area had thrown the Eighth Army into considerable confusion. Cunningham, the Army Commander, was all for a

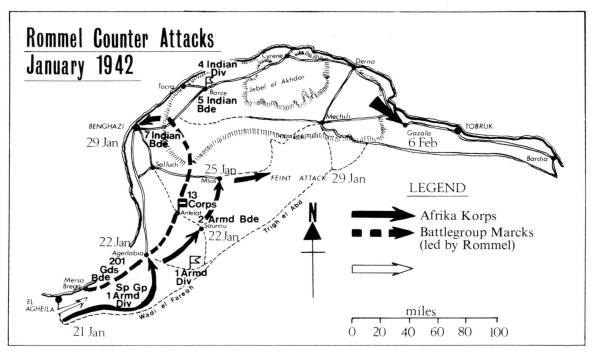

further withdrawal in order to consolidate his position. However, General Auchinleck, the C-in-C, stepped in to order the continuation of the offensive, replacing Cunningham with Ritchie. The result was to counter the shock effect of Rommel's move. By the time the RAF had struck him a series of resounding blows and inflicted serious loss upon his tanks, Rommel realised that only one course remained open to him—to withdraw to the safety of El Agheila and pull his battered force together.

After a brilliant withdrawal, he rallied the remnants of his Panzergruppe and set about the urgent business of re-equipment and reorganization. Some forty new tanks and a further four panzer companies arrived from Germany. Clearly, he was faring a good deal better for replacements than his fellows in Russia! Almost more valuable to him than the tanks, however, was the arrival of Luftflotte 2, which was to give him much needed air support in the battles to come.

Rommel decided that his best chance of success lay in obtaining complete tactical surprise. The Eighth Army had followed up his withdrawal and was holding nearly up to Mersa Brega with a force that consisted very largely of the untried 1st Armoured Division. Using a variant of his old ruse, Rommel put canvas covers over the tanks to disguise them and mustered his troops in complete secrecy. Not even the Italians knew what he was about. Then, on January 21, 1942, he attacked. Sweeping all before him, as before, he captured 96 tanks, 38 guns and 190 vehicles in the fight for Benghazi. Pressing on by day and night he threw the British right back to a hastily prepared defensive position at Gazala, which was reached on February 6. Cyrenaica was back in his hands but his troops and his equipment were at the end of their tether. There was nothing for it but to accept another pause until the momentous Gazala battles of May 1942— an encounter that has been described by von Mellenthin as "one of the greatest achievements in German annals."[1]

1942—A YEAR OF TECHNICAL CHANGE

On the technical side, 1942 was to prove a year of considerable change. Both the Germans and the Allies were to increase the quality of their tanks and, in particular, their hitting power.

At an important conference on January 23, during which he was shown the M.A.N. design for Panther, Hitler discussed the impressive anti-tank performance of the new hollow charge artillery ammunition. The tank experts were hard pressed to persuade him that the day of the tank was not drawing to a close. However, his proposals to concentrate more upon the production of self-propelled artillery than tanks were finally disposed of and he ordered that tank production should rise to 600 machines a month.

The Führer's mind was always seeking for some new and fantastic breakthrough in the weapons field. So it is not surprising that in March we find him giving orders to Krupps and Dr Porsche to design a tank of 100 tons, the prototype to be available in spring 1943. Later in the year we find that a firm of engineers, Grote and Hacker, were ordered to put an even more fantastic design in hand—this time for a 1,000 tonner!

April saw the appearance of the Porsche and Henschel

Tigers, for which Speer was able to forecast production, by October, of 60 Porsche and 25 Henschel machines, with a further 135 in all by the following March. At about this time the upgunned Panzer IV F2 was just arriving in North Africa, as were a number of Russian 7·62cm PaK 36(r) mounted on the Czech 38(t) chassis—known as Marder. Both models represented a substantial augmentation to the Germans' anti-tank resources. This was just as well for Rommel, as the new British 57mm (6-pdr.) anti-tank guns were being delivered to the Eighth Army, as were their first Grant tanks, mounting a 75mm gun in the hull sponson.

In May, Hitler approved the Panther design and an intensive drive to get it into mass production began. Simultaneously production of assault guns and Panzer III was stepped up. Hardly had these orders been given than a new programme to uparmour the front of Panzer IV and all assault guns to 80mm was put in hand, whilst investigations into the uparmouring of both Tiger and Panther were also begun. When one recalls all the other design studies and conversions that were going on at this time in the SP artillery field, the mind boggles at the problems facing the vehicle industry and the Ordnance Office. The general effect that this over-complication had on the provision of spares was soon to make itself felt in Russia. Nevertheless, the achievements of the design and production teams were prodigious and were certainly never rivalled in scale by the Allies (although the less complicated pattern of production followed by the Americans and British certainly had many significant advantages when it came to the business of the repair and replacement of casualties).

Despite the fact that Panzer III was fast outrunning its usefulness on the battlefield, Hitler ordered its up-gunning to the 75mm L/24 in August. In the same month the firm production order for Tiger went in. By this time, when, as we shall see later, Rommel was about to fight the battle of Alam Halfa, Panzerarmee Afrika had 27 Panzer IV F2. Even this small number was to make a considerable impact on the British tank crews, as they far outgunned even the new Grants.

The first Tigers went into action outside Leningrad in September. Once more the Führer's meddling had forced the Army into a course which was against all the best advice. The wet going in a forested area was entirely unsuitable for these large and cumbersome machines and the Russians were able to destroy them at will. Tiger production went ahead despite this disaster and a total of 1,350 Tigers was produced by August 1944. Slow and heavy it may have been, but the Tiger was a formidable machine to encounter and could stand tremendous punishment on its thick frontal armour. Its 88mm gun enabled it to engage all enemy tanks at very long ranges with devastating effect.

When the first production model of Panther came out in November it gave considerable mechanical trouble. However, this excellent tank was sorted out by the end of 1943 and proved to be a winner. Its KwK 75mm L/70 had tremendous hitting power, whilst its steeply sloping front glacis made it very difficult to attack effectively from head-on. Nearly 5,000 Panthers were made in all.

During June, Hitler had given verbal orders to his friend Dr Porsche to go ahead with his concept of the 100 tonner—now known as Maus, with a design weight of some 140 tons. In December he demanded that the pilot model should be ready by the summer of 1943

---

[1] Von Mellenthin "Panzer Battles", p. 90.

Prototype of Porsche's mammoth Mouse, undergoing trials with a 55-ton weight on the superstructure to simulate the turret. Maus *was Porsche's 185 ton answer to Hitler's demand for a super-heavy tank.*

The Henschel Tiger—TigerI, Ausf.H later Ausf.E—made its appearance in April 1942. This tank, with turret reversed, is negotiating a muddy slope.

The uparmoured Panzer IV Ausf.G had the long L/43 75mm gun, which was introduced in the previous, F2, model. In the end the Panzer IV turned out to be the most numerous German tank—the "workhorse" of the German armoured forces.

Panzer III was upgunned, as was Panzer IV. Upgunning of Panzer III to the L/60 5cm KwK 30 began in the course of the Ausführung (Model) J production run. The next version, Ausf.L, seen here in France in December 1942, was externally almost identical to its predecessor. The series terminated with Ausf.N, armed with the short KwK L/24 75mm gun, the previous main armament of the Panzer IV.

and that a production figure of five machines a month should be set. This figure was raised to ten in January. One gets the feeling that he was completely carried away by the sense of power that this endless tinkering with the equipment programme gave him. In the same month, despite all the orders given in 1942 about numbers and upgunning, production of Panzer III was discontinued, although the chassis was still to be used extensively for assault and SP guns. In contrast, the Panzer IV, with its L/48 75mm gun had become the principal tank of the German Army and a formidable feature of the battle-field. No less than 9,000 Panzer IV saw active service.

TRIUMPH AND TRAGEDY
IN RUSSIA, 1942

The Russian counter-offensive in the Moscow area died away at the end of December 1941, largely because of the Germans' determined stand on Hitler's orders and their ability to concentrate their dwindling tank strength against the numerous but ill-co-ordinated attacks of the badly trained Russian armoured formations. They owed much too to their skilled use of their tanks and anti-tank weapons, often in reverse slope positions, from which they massacred the enemy at short ranges and so off-set the advantage he held with his T34 and KV1. From January 1942 until the middle of May, the Soviet effort was concentrated on an all-out effort to recapture the important industrial centres of the Donetz Basin. Despite the use of over 1,000 tanks in many of their successive assaults, they were utterly defeated by their highly skilled opponents—not because the Germans were better equipped, for, as we know, they were not, but because the Russians had not by then begun to grasp the first principles of tank warfare and were convinced that sheer weight of metal must prevail.

The Panther had initial mechanical difficulties, but when these were corrected it proved itself to be one of the most formidable tanks in the business.

German resistance to the Russian counter-offensive at the end of 1941 owed much of its success to the skilled use of tank destroyers, like this Sturmgeschütz III, *in reverse slope positions.*

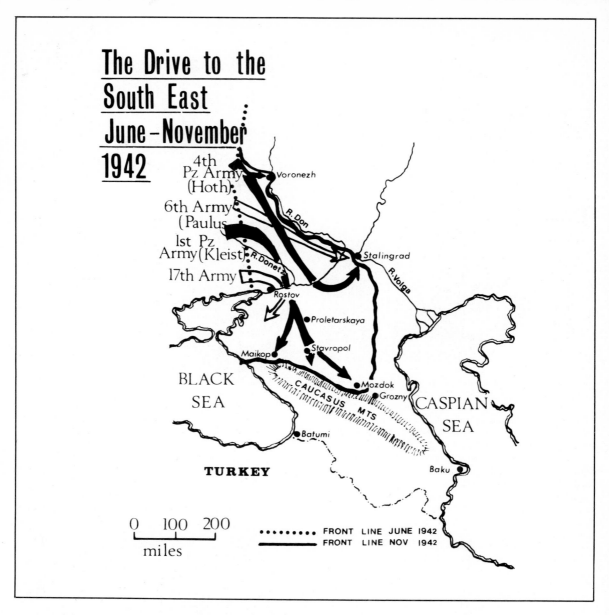

The Drive to the South East June-November 1942

4th Pz Army (Hoth)

6th Army (Paulus)

1st Pz Army (Kleist)

17th Army

Voronezh

R. Don

R. Donetz

Stalingrad

R. Volga

Rostov

Proletarskaya

Maikop

Stavropol

Mozdok

Grozny

CAUCASUS MTS

BLACK SEA

CASPIAN SEA

Batumi

Baku

TURKEY

0   100   200
miles

●●●●●●●● FRONT LINE JUNE 1942
━━━━━━━ FRONT LINE NOV 1942

By early summer the German Army was ready to resume the offensive in the centre. Operations in the far south to capture the Crimea were already under way.

Army Group Weichs, which had 4th Panzer Army (Colonel General Hoth) under command, was tasked to break Marshal Timoshenko's defences in the Kursk sector and subsequently to destroy his Army Group against the line of the River Don. This preliminary operation was to provide a springboard for further advances towards Stalingrad and the oil-rich lands of the Caucasus. Hoth, with two Panzer corps and some 800 tanks, was to spearhead the attack. Having achieved the breakthrough, he was to swing right-handed and advance on Stalingrad as Paulus's 6th Army extended along the Don behind him.

The operation, launched on June 28, was a complete success. 4th Panzer Army advanced 120 miles in ten days, battling as it went. This was a classic armoured operation on a big scale. Hoth's orders were clear cut and were not

changed. All the available offensive air support was assigned to him, to the exclusion of the slower moving infantry formations. Similarly, a generous allocation of reconnaissance aircraft was put under direct command of his Army. The going was ideal. Huge rolling open plains allowed complete freedom of manoeuvre. The tanks pressed resolutely on, regardless of what was happening on their flanks or of what they had left behind them. These matters were for the follow-up formations and the inherent risks involved were accepted in the interests of maintaining the Army Group aim. Finally, as so often in the past, every General Officer and every subordinate commander was right forward, exerting his personal influence in the very forefront of the battle.

Hardly had 4th Panzer Army reached Voronezh on July 5 than Hoth was re-directed south to support the crossing of the lower Don by Field Marshal von Kleist's 1st Panzer Army, now beginning its advance to the Caucasus. Here was a typical example of the sort of

Colonel General Hoth, commander of 4th Panzer Army.

Field Marshal von Kleist, seen here (right) greeting the commander of Hungarian forces fighting as Germany's allies on the Eastern Front, was in command of 1st Panzer Army that advanced to the Caucasus. In 1940 von Kleist commanded a Panzer Group in the campaign against France and the Low Countries.

ill-informed interference by the Führer's Headquarters which so often drove German commanders in the field to despair. Von Kleist had no need for this support and the additional strain on the routes which the presence of 4th Panzer Army imposed merely slowed up the whole operation. As he remarked at the time, had 4th Panzer Army only been directed onto Stalingrad, the city would have been in German hands by the end of July "without a fight". The whole course of the campaign would then have been altered—indeed, the very outcome might well have been different. In the event, Hoth was directed onto Stalingrad—but too late. At the end of July he was ordered to fight his way north from the lower Don towards Stalingrad, which Paulus's 6th Army was now approaching. By the time he arrived in mid-August the city could no longer be taken "without a fight". It would now have to be stormed. Large numbers of valuable tanks were lost in the subsequent close quarter fighting in the urban area; the lessons of Warsaw had been forgotten.

Meanwhile, 1st Panzer Army made fast time down towards the Caucasus, covering some 200 miles in 11 days. But the troops were becoming exhausted, the tanks

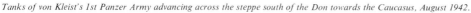

Tanks of von Kleist's 1st Panzer Army advancing across the steppe south of the Don towards the Caucasus, August 1942.

were in grave need of maintenance and fuel had become desperately short. The Army fell prey to a scrappy form of guerilla fighting involving local resistance fighters and the remnants of Russian formations along its supply routes. Von Kleist's lot was made no easier by the removal of his offensive air support to go to Stalingrad. As it reached the Caucasus mountains, the advance gradually dragged to a halt.

In the Stalingrad region, things were to go from bad to worse. In November, a violent Russian counter-offensive fought without regard to human or tank casualties, isolated the city, now held by 6th Army. Despite desperate attempts, in which many Russian tanks were destroyed, 4th Panzer Army, reinforced by LVII Panzer Corps from 1st Panzer Army, was unable to make the breakthrough to relieve Paulus.

CHANGES IN ORGANIZATION

During 1942 the organization of the Panzer Division underwent some significant changes. The dramatic success of the 88mm anti-aircraft gun in the anti-tank rôle led to the introduction of an 88mm battalion into the division. Because of the problems of tank production, the number of tank battalions in each division was reduced to two and the third re-equipped with SP anti-tank guns (Panzerjäger). In consequence, divisions often had as few as 70 or 80 tanks and seldom more than 100. At long last the half-tracked APC (SdKfz 251/1) was produced for one battalion of infantry in each Wehrmacht Panzer Division although SS formations were to receive enough for two. At the same time the designation "Panzergrenadier" was introduced and was generally adopted for all infantry units in Panzer Divisions. The term was later to apply to mechanized infantry divisions also.

The way in which SS formations received preferential treatment over the issue of equipment caused much understandable jealousy. For example, some SS Panzer Divisions had their own organic Tiger units, whilst the Wehrmacht's Tigers were Army troops in independent units. So strong did the rivalry between the two factions become that golden tactical opportunities were to be lost in North-West Europe in 1944 and 1945 through the inequitable issue of fuel and the alleged refusal of some formations to help out their hard-pressed comrades in arms.

GAZALA AND THE FALL OF TOBRUK, 1942

We left the Panzerarmee Afrika facing the British in front of Gazala in the spring of 1942. On May 26, with 333 German and 228 Italian tanks, Rommel advanced by night round the southern extremity of the Gazala position against nearly 900 British tanks, including 167 Grants. The Eighth Army had by now re-equipped with 57mm anti-tank guns and these were well dug in behind extensive minefields. Rommel did enjoy one substantial advantage—the advent of Luftflotte 2 had given him a numerical superiority in the air of 2·5 to 1.

Once again, the British threw away the advantage that their tank strength gave them by over-dispersion and their failure to operate their motorized infantry in sufficiently close co-operation with their armour; this despite Auchinleck's injunction to Ritchie on the subject—"I consider it of the highest importance that you should not break up the organization of either of the armoured divisions. They have been trained to fight as divisions, I hope, and fight as divisions they should." But Ritchie knew best and split them up, with disastrous results.

It goes without saying that, despite the poor overall direction of the British tactical battle, the troops fought magnificently and, in consequence, very heavy casualties were inflicted upon both sides. However, the fundamental difference between them remained. The British, masters of the static defensive battle, possessed neither the ability to regroup nor the flexibility of their opponents. In consequence, opportunity after opportunity to crush the Germans was lost.

Throughout the Gazala battle and those that followed, Rommel was in his element. On May 29 he led the supply echelons of 15th Panzer Division through gaps in the minefields which were inadequately covered by fire; thus saving the Afrika Korps, which was out of fuel and ammunition. On the 30th he led the leading platoon of 21st Panzer Division in a tremendous tussle against the 150 Brigade Box, where the Matildas of 44 RTR covered themselves with glory.

The ding-dong struggle rolled back and forth. No quarter was given or sought. By June 15, after several days hard slogging around the Knightsbridge Box, both sides were nearing exhaustion. Rommel was in his usual precarious logistic state. A fierce fight on the Tobruk-El Adem line resulted in the destruction of several British

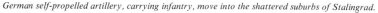

German self-propelled artillery, carrying infantry, move into the shattered suburbs of Stalingrad.

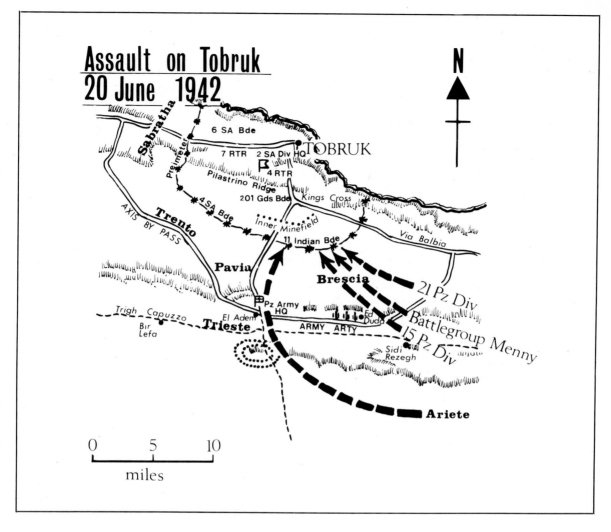

Assault on Tobruk 20 June 1942

brigades, as Rommel dealt each a concentrated blow. As a result, he was able to acquire vast stocks of British fuel and rations and so restore his administrative balance. Ritchie simply could not get the hang of this desert fighting, despite Auchinleck's plea that he should bring "maximum force into play in the El Adem area. . . . We must emulate the enemy's speed in thought and action. . . ."

On June 20 the Germans broke through the Tobruk perimeter. General Nehring, Commander of the Afrika Korps, and von Bismarck, Commander of 21st Panzer Division, led the assault, the latter riding in a motorcycle sidecar alongside the leading tanks. Rommel, not to be outdone, personally commanded an attack on a 3·7 anti-aircraft battery that was having a devastating effect upon his tanks. On this occasion the 3·7 was shown to rival the 88mm as an anti-tank weapon. But for the stubbornness of the senior Gunners in Cairo, this weapon could have been used with telling success against the Afrika Korps from the earliest days of the campaign. The whole story of the desert war might then have been changed.

Despite the capture of 30,000 prisoners in Tobruk, Rommel was now getting towards the end of his resources. His victory was greeted with great acclaim in Berlin and on the 21st he was promoted Field Marshal. Flushed with success, he fell into his previous error of over-reaching himself. Despite the warnings of Field Marshal Kesselring and of his own loyal staff, he determined to sweep through to the Delta, believing that the British were in a worse plight than he. A resounding victory at Mersa Matruh, giving him a further 8,000 prisoners, seemed to prove his point. However, as he battled forward to the area of the Eighth Army's next defensive position at El Alamein, his strength fell day by day and he outran his air cover. By July 4 the Afrika Korps was down to less than 40 tanks and the soldiers were utterly exhausted. Auchinleck had taken over personal command of the Eighth Army and the British position had stabilized. Somehow, Rommel rallied his troops to resist a series of determined attacks which continued throughout July. It was a real battle of attrition which came very close to sounding the death knell of the Panzerarmee. Had the British armour only been handled better the result could well have been the final eclipse of all Rommel's hopes. As it was, the end of the month saw both armies at a standstill. Auchinleck had saved the day in what the British call First Alamein— but the Germans were still in the fight, despite the sorry state of their Italian allies.

In the Gazala battle very heavy casualties were inflicted on both sides.

THE END IN AFRICA

For the British the next four months were to see them make their first steps towards final victory. For the Germans they were to herald a series of defeats, leading to final collapse.

The arrival of a mass of new equipment in the Delta for the Eighth Army together with a number of fresh divisions from the United Kingdom restored the Army's capacity to carry on the fight and to take the offensive. Furthermore, important changes in command took place. In the middle of August General Alexander replaced Auchinleck and General Montgomery took over command of Eighth Army.

Meanwhile the Royal Navy and the Desert Air Force were having a devastating effect upon the German logistic system, so that even the daily maintenance of the Afrika Korps was a struggle. A battered and weary Panzerarmee, with sickness rife in its ranks after two and a half years hard slogging up and down the Desert and with its equipment suffering badly from lack of spares and replacements, had to face, in Montgomery, a General who had a revitalised force at his disposal and was possessed of the will and ability to win.

Rommel was anxious to withdraw back into Cyrenaica so that he could refurbish and regroup his resources as best he might. But permission to abandon the Alamein position was refused. He therefore decided to take what he saw as the only alternative course—to make a final and determined bid to break through to the Nile. His decision, which was taken in the face of his staff's advice, was largely influenced by a promise from Field Marshal Kesselring to provide him with the petrol he needed.

Both Rommel and Montgomery had appreciated the tactical significance of the Alam Halfa Ridge—a long feature covering the eastern approach to the Alamein position. Even as Rommel waited for the moon to be right for a night operation, Montgomery prepared to defend it.

On August 31, 1942, under a full moon, the Panzerarmee broke into the minefields in the south near Qaret el Himeimat. Of the 200 German tanks available 27 were Panzer IV F2, the new "Mark IV Special" with its long 75mm gun. The going was softer than expected and a number of unidentified minefields were encountered. As a result, surprise was lost and the rate of advance slowed down severely. When daylight came the Axis troops were advancing slowly towards the Ridge where a mixed force of British Grants, Crusaders and 37mm Stuarts lay in wait.

As the range closed a fierce fire-fight ensued in which the new Mark IV's and Rommels supporting Stukas played an important part. But the attack was held. By evening the Panzerarmee was halted and almost out of petrol—the sinking of a precious tanker in Tobruk by the Royal Navy had done much to see to that.

Throughout September 2 the Desert Air Force and the British guns hammered away so that by the 3rd the Axis troops were in full retreat, having suffered heavy losses of men and material. By the morning of the 6th Rommel had regrouped on the western edge of the great mine barrier, managing to retain control of the gaps in the south through which he had passed. The weeks that followed saw the Germans spread thinly along the Alamein position, interspersed with their Italian allies. Nowhere were they able to form a sizeable counter-attack force. Rommel's health forced him to return home on sick leave whilst his troops waited grimly but without hope to face Montgomery's inevitable onslaught.

When the blow fell on October 23 the result was almost inevitable. Despite heroic resistance, the Germans were ground down by the sheer weight of the artillery fire and air attacks which characterized the next ten days. Montgomery had deliberately bided his time until he was thoroughly ready. 300 of the new Sherman tanks had arrived in his armoured formations and the troops had been retrained.

Rommel returned to command in the battle but even his ability was no substitute for the imbalance in strength with which he had to contend. The British paid a heavy price in tanks and men for their victory but it did not compare in relative terms with the cost to the Germans and Italians. So fierce had been the bombardment that virtually all their anti-tank guns were destroyed—enabling the British tanks, as they broke out, to engage those of the Axis at long range and pick them off.

Thanks to a combination of his own skill and Montgomery's caution and greatly aided by a sudden storm of torrential rain, Rommel managed to disengage on the night of November 7 and fall back to Sollum, leaving 450 out of his original 600 tanks on the battlefield.

The writing was now on the wall. Though still a very sick man, Rommel fought a brilliant withdrawal along the coast into Tunisia, with Montgomery hard on his heels. It is interesting to find that in the battle of Medenine Rommel lost no less than 50 tanks without inflicting a single loss on his opponents. This was mainly due to the fact that the British had now introduced yet another anti-tank gun, the 17-pdr. (76·2mm), to supplement the 57mm and Montgomery had clearly learned how to handle it.

On November 8, 1942 the Allies invaded North Africa and the Axis forces were caught between two

The new "Mark IV Specials"—as the British called them—though few in number played an important part in the fierce fire-fight at Alam Halfa. They were armed with the long 7,5cm KwK 40 L/43.

fires. Despite the introduction of a handful of Tiger tanks and the effectiveness of Panzer IV F2, particularly against the inexperienced troops under General Eisenhower, capitulation was inevitable. Hundreds of battle-tried and highly skilled tank-crewmen went into captivity. Their loss was a serious blow for the Wehrmacht. By May 13, 1943 the fight for North Africa was over and an historic era in the development of armoured warfare had ended.

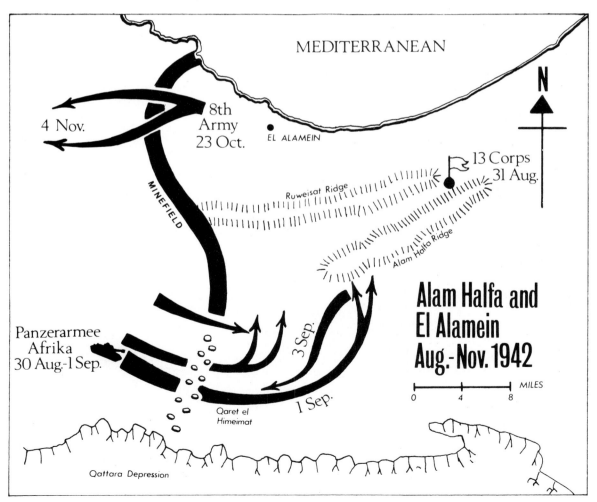

MEDITERRANEAN

N

4 Nov.

8th
Army
23 Oct.

EL ALAMEIN

13 Corps
31 Aug.

Ruweisat Ridge

MINEFIELD

Alam Halfa Ridge

Panzerarmee
Afrika
30 Aug-1 Sep.

3 Sep.

1 Sep.

Qaret el
Himeimat

**Alam Halfa and
El Alamein
Aug.-Nov. 1942**

MILES

0   4   8

Qattara Depression

1943—THE TURNING POINT

1943 was to mark the turning point of the war for the Germans. The magnitude of the disasters at Stalingrad in February and of Operation Citadel in the Kursk Salient in July ensured that all hopes of final victory had disappeared.

Even as F.M. Paulus's 6th Army was making its last heroic stand, at a cost of some 140,000 dead and 90,000 prisoners, huge Russian forces were sweeping von Kleist's 1st Panzer Army out of the Caucasus. The Germans continued to strike blow after blow at the flood-tide that was overwhelming their whole front, but their numbers were dwindling steadily and their resources were almost spent. Faith in the High Command had gone. Only the quality of their leadership, their patriotism and high sense of military dedication kept the armies going.

In the midst of all these difficulties, von Manstein, now commanding Army Group Don, somehow per-suaded Hitler to allow him to make a limited tactical withdrawal in order to regroup 1st and 4th Panzer Armies. This done, he launched a brilliant counter-stroke against a force eight times the size of his own. By concentrating his 350 tanks, he achieved a seven to one majority at the Schwerpunkt of his attack and broke clean through to the Donetz, shattering the opposition and inflicting enormous casualties. Surprise and clear-cut directives, giving freedom for tactical judgement and the relief of responsibility for the flanks, enabled commanders to concentrate on the crucial business of leading their formations and of maintaining the aim of the operation. Had the weather only held for a little longer, there is no telling what the scale of von Manstein's success might have been. But the thaw set in and General Mud took over from General Winter. The whole battle-field became a morass in which both sides were left wallowing and all further fighting became impossible.

The British first encountered the Tiger in Tunisia in February 1943. Having had news of the tanks' arrival through a prison camp "leak" they were prepared for them. This Tiger was knocked out at Kournine.

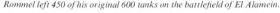

Rommel left 450 of his original 600 tanks on the battlefield of El Alamein.

General Winter in command. Panzer III with German infantry near Rostov in February 1943.

General Mud takes over from General Winter.

GUDERIAN RECALLED

Back in Germany a remarkable situation had arisen. Early in February, the higher echelons of the OKW had at last realized that they had lost the confidence of the field armies and that the once magnificent armoured force was at its last gasp. Commanders were calling for a man with great experience of armour and of command in battle to resurrect their panzer formations. In a spell of unusual lucidity and, possibly, of near despair, Hitler put his pride in his pocket, realizing that only Guderian could meet this heavy challenge. He sent for him on February 17 and offered to reinstate him in the Army as Inspector General of Armoured Troops. It was a huge and daunting task, embracing every aspect of the organization, training and equipment of armoured units and formations. At Guderian's insistence, he was given the status of an Army Commander and directly subordinated to Hitler himself. (An almost entirely similar situation had arisen earlier in England when

General Hobart, whom Guderian so admired, had been brought back by Churchill and offered the chance to put British armour on its feet. Hobart insisted that whoever did so would need a seat on the Army Council—but even the exigencies of war failed to break down the conventionalism of Whitehall and he had to decline the job, taking over a new armoured division instead.)

Guderian's remit was wide and he was even given powers over the Waffen SS and Luftwaffe armoured formations on matters of training and organization. Armed with this directive, Guderian made a rapid appreciation and presented his findings to Hitler and the assembled General Staff on March 9. So desperate was the overall situation that he had as his aim for 1943 the provision of "a certain number of Panzer Divisions with complete combat efficiency, capable of making limited objective attacks."[1] The qualification is highly signifi-

---

[1] Guderian "Panzer Leader", p. 295.

In February 1943 Guderian was recalled by Hitler and appointed Inspector-General of Armoured Troops.

cant. For 1944 he sought to create divisions capable of large scale operations, each equipped with some 400 tanks and supporting arms in proportion. Far better, he urged, to have a few, well balanced, strong divisions than many only partly equipped.

What a contrast these proposals made to the policies of the High Command since 1940, which had so emasculated divisions in order to pander to Hitler's insane love of large numbers of formations, entirely ignoring the appalling waste of manpower and misuse of precious equipment that inevitably ensued; quite apart from the fact that it cut clean across the tactical requirement for the concentration of armour and for the balance that had been demanded by all their expert advisers since Panzer Divisions were first established.

Whilst stressing the need to improve the reliability of Panther, Guderian emphasized the importance of keeping up the production rate of the well-tried Panzer IV, provided that it did not affect that of Tiger and Panther. In this he was wise. We have already seen that, in spite of newer models, Panzer IV was to remain the German Army's workhorse for the rest of the war. With the recent disastrous introduction of Tiger clearly in mind, he demanded that future new equipment should be introduced into battle properly—in sufficient numbers and at the right time, under the right conditions. He proposed better crew training (including participa-

tion in the final assembly of their tanks), the provision of adequate scales of training ammunition and equipment and of sufficient time to train, without the customary interference of making units under training move from one area to another. Only carefully selected and experienced commanders were acceptable to him and new formations were to be built on cadres of battle-experienced troops, specially withdrawn from the field for this purpose. Reconnaissance units were to be resurrected and a new reconnaissance vehicle, based on existing assemblies, provided. (Here spoke his own experience in Poland and France. In Russia, reconnaissance units had almost disappeared). As so often before, he made the case for more armoured half-tracks for the Panzer grenadiers, stressing the importance of their rôle; he called for more self-propelled artillery and SP anti-tank guns in the Panzer Division and finally proposed that secondary theatres should be made to manage with second class equipment if need be.

It was a tour de force and, for a man who had been eating his heart out in despair for over a year, a performance of such quality that only a superb professional could have produced it in the circumstances. No-one today would challenge any of his proposals and they were received with enthusiasm by his audience, who saw with relief that here, at last, was the man who would shoulder their burdens and assume the responsibilities that they had so shamefully mishandled. Despite the success of his presentation, Guderian found himself once more locked in combat with the Gunners, who objected to his plans for the control of SP anti-tank guns and assault guns, which they felt must remain with the artillery. On this point alone, Guderian was over-ruled, only for Hitler to acknowledge nine months later that he had made a mistake. By then the die was cast and it was too late.

Months of furious activity followed, during which near miracles of reorganization and re-equipment were achieved. The new Panzerjäger 38(t) "Hetzer" came into widespread use, spaced armour was provided for the few remaining Panzer III and for Panzer IV, to defeat the Russians' hollow charged ammunition, whilst the frontal armour of both Panther and Panzer IV was increased to 100mm.

Porsche's Tiger (known as Elefant) was now coming into service. Lacking a coaxial machine-gun for close-quarter fighting, it was really an SP anti-tank gun rather than a tank. Guderian condemned it as such. However, some 90 of these cumbersome machines were produced and had to be used. They were formed into two battalions and used in Operation Citadel in Model's 9th Army. Their limitations were quickly exposed and the majority were knocked out early in the battle. For the very reasons that he had rejected Elefant, Guderian also rejected the wooden mock-up of Porsche's Maus. Turreted though it was, this monster, whose all-up weight now looked as if it would approach 200 tons, was to carry no machine-guns for close-range fighting. Two of these giants reached the trial stage, but they never came into service.

Meanwhile, Panzer IV production was continuing at an average of about 200 a month, Panther production was approaching that figure, and Tiger production brought the overall monthly tank output up to about 500. In view of the weight of the Allied aerial attacks on industrial centres and the multifarious other vehicles and SP guns being produced simultaneously, these figures were

Porsche's Panzerjaeger Tiger, originally called Ferdinand (after Porsche) and then re-named Elefant. It was simply a conversion of the original Porsche Tiger tank design to a self-propelled anti-tank weapon. It fought in Operation Citadel, on other parts of the Eastern front, and then in Italy. This vehicle has the additional protection in front of the gun mantlet which was a retrospective modification made after experience in the field.

remarkable. In part they were the result of foresight, which had led to the establishment of factories in the heart of Austria, out of range of the bombers. Panther was still giving a lot of trouble. Guderian was far from happy about its transmission and suspension, whilst its optics, too, were unsatisfactory. Hitler was desperate to get his new toy into action, against all advice.

KURSK

Ever since the end of von Manstein's counterstroke earlier in the year, the Germans had been containing a large pocket of Russians in the salient opposite Kursk. Von Manstein was eager to mount a fresh attack to eliminate it before the enemy had time to consolidate but, although he agreed the need, Hitler would not agree the timing. He was determined to get Panther into battle and the operation was to wait until Panthers were available in strength. Guderian, bearing in mind his limited aims for 1943, was never keen on becoming involved at Kursk and begged Hitler to call the whole idea off. He knew that the Army simply could not afford the price in tanks and trained soldiers that would have to be paid. Whilst Hitler admitted that he had misgivings, he allowed himself to be persuaded by Keitel and Zeitzler, his senior advisers, and announced that the plan would go forward as soon as Panther was ready. June came and von Manstein himself approached the Führer to press for cancellation. The Russians had made extensive defensive preparations, surprise was lost, and the Wehrmacht was faced with a battle on ground of the enemy's choosing with no room to manoeuvre. The defensive minefields that the Russians had prepared were now many miles deep and countless strongpoints had been constructed. Hitler was implacable. On July 4 Hoth's 4th Panzer Army of 18 divisions (including 10 armoured) attacked from the south whilst Model with 9th Army, also of 18 divisions (seven of them armoured), attacked simultaneously from the north. It was the greatest armoured battle

of all time—described by General Strawson as "Alam Halfa blown up 1,000 times."[1]

A tremendous slogging match ensued. Torrential rain turned much of the southern flank into a bog. The going was terribly slow. In the north, 9th Army bogged down after six miles. 4th Panzer Army battled resolutely on, knocking out some 2,000 tanks and a similar number of guns, whilst taking 32,000 prisoners. But it was like hitting a sponge. The German losses were very heavy. Finally, on July 13, Hitler called off the operation when he heard that the Allies had landed in Sicily; a curious excuse for his own utter failure as Commander in Chief to appreciate the price his Army was paying for his stubbornness. The Russians had by this time built up the Red Army to mammoth proportions and were able

[1] Strawson "Hitler as Military Commander", p. 176.

Von Manstein, seen here (centre) inspecting the positions of a Panzergrenadier Regiment in June 1943, pressed Hitler to cancel Operation Citadel. Previously he had been eager to mount an attack that would eliminate the Kursk salient. (B.L.Davis)

Operation Citadel—the Battle of Kursk—begins. On July 4, 1943, thirty-six German divisions, including 17 Panzer Divisions, began a pincer movement against the Kursk salient.

to replace their casualties as fast as they were incurred. Even as they mounted their counter-attack in the salient, they launched two simultaneous assaults between Bryansk and Orel, making deep penetrations. They had seized the initiative and the Germans were never to recover it.

The Red Army facing the Germans at Kursk was a very different proposition to the brave but ill-trained and un-co-ordinated horde that faced them in 1941. The salient had been brilliantly prepared for defence. A complex pattern of well camouflaged strongpoints, based upon groups of anti-tank guns protected by mine-fields and sited to a depth of over 12 miles had been organised across the front. Known to the Germans as "Pakfronts", these strongpoints called for a new tactical concept to deal with them. Up to 10 guns would open up on a single tank at short range. The Russian fire discipline was exemplary. Very often the first indication of the existence of one of these concealed positions was the destruction of a leading tank by fire or the explosion of a mine beneath its tracks. A single German corps would sometimes lift as many as 40,000 mines in one day.

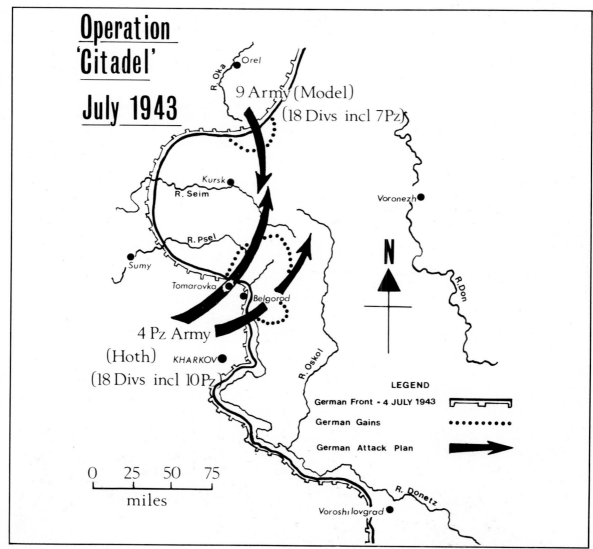

The Battle of Kursk was the greatest armoured battle of all time.

TACTICAL TECHNIQUES

The Panzer Divisions developed a formation known as a "Panzerkeil". This was a wedge, spearheaded by heavy tanks to bludgeon a path into the position, with medium and light tanks echeloned off to the flanks. This technique was elaborated to the "Panzerglocke", a bell-shape, with armoured engineers following up the leading Tigers or Panthers. As before, medium tanks covered the flanks. A command group came close behind the engineers to control both the tanks and the supporting bombers. Light tanks filled the mouth of the bell, ready to develop the pursuit if need be.

Although regarded with some trepidation, attacks were made with marked success at night—but only when the going and weather were suitable, the standard of training of the troops was sufficiently high, and a daylight reconnaissance had been possible. In addition it was found to be essential for clearly defined features to exist, such as a road or track, to mark the axis of the advance. When available, direction-finding equipment was also employed. Since the whole formation moved closed-up it is easy to understand the need for a high standard of training. Losses at night were usually slight, so the dividend was a handsome one.

In general, success against "Pakfronts" depended upon:

a. Adequate reconnaissance
b. Good ground-to-air communications
c. A high state of tank gunnery
d. Maintenance of momentum, with the tanks halting only to fire
e. The correct positioning of Forward Observers for all supporting weapons
f. The practice of holding reserves of fuel and ammunition, carried in armoured vehicles, close behind the fighting echelons
g. The skilful use of white and coloured tank smoke for screening and marking.

In his book "Panzer Battles", von Mellenthin asserts that the flower of the German Army fell at Kursk but that "the fierce resolution of the fighting troops remained unshaken."[1] That this was so is borne out by the series of successful actions fought by elements of General Balck's XLVIII Panzer Corps (part of 4th Panzer Army) over the coming months. On August 20, a battle-group of some 20 tanks, a Panzergrenadier battalion and a reconnaissance company, together with a handful of guns, all under the command of Colonel von Natzmer, the 1a of Panzergrenadier Division Gross Deutschland, pushed back an entire Russian armoured corps and an

---

[1] Von Mellenthin "Panzer Battles", p. 230.

A German armoured column moves up to the battle-front in Operation Citadel as Stukas return to base. Nothing could break the Russian defence, and on July 13 the offensive was called off as the Russian counter-offensive in its turn took over command of the battlefield.

The Jagdpanther with its 88mm gun had an outstanding success in battle, especially in North-West Europe.

infantry division at Akhtyrka. Tactical surprise and skilful handling of the tanks won the day.

In the months that followed, Balck's inspiring leadership and innate tactical skill met with success after success. In November, a major attack by his Corps in the Kiev Salient, involving some six Panzer Divisions, destroyed over 150 tanks, 320 assorted artillery pieces and 3,000 men.

TECHNICAL ACHIEVEMENT

Meanwhile, back in Germany, Guderian was hard at work. Amidst much speculation over Hitler's fantastic ideas on super-heavy tanks, the Gunners made a bid to get production of Panzer IV stopped, in order to divert industrial effort to the manufacture of self-propelled guns. After hard battling, this stupid proposition was foiled by Guderian. The loss of the Panzer IV production would have been disastrous to his strenuous efforts to rebuild the Army's armoured strength. Panther was by no means cured of its ills and Panzer IV was still the principal tank in service. At this time a superb armoured car, the Puma (SdKfz 234/2), powered by a diesel engine and mounting a high velocity 50mm KwK L/60 gun in its turret, had become available. Originally intended for desert use, it had now appeared too late.

On October 20, the pilot model of the Jagdpanther was shown to Hitler. In January 1944 it was in production! This magnificent SP anti-tank gun was to have outstanding success in battle and to pose many problems for the armoured units of the Allies in the struggle for North-West Europe. On October 24, four days later, the wooden mock-ups of Tiger B (often called the King Tiger) and Jagdtiger (on the same chassis as Tiger B) were also demonstrated. It was to be only two months from this date that the first production model of Tiger B came off the stocks. Technical achievements of this magnitude are hard to believe even today. When one considers the circumstances under which they occurred, the facts become even more incredible. During the same winter, the first trials of the running gear for Maus were taking place—clearly it took far more than Guderian's rejection of the concept to dissuade Hitler or his friend Dr Porsche!

FIGHTING WITHDRAWAL

In September 1943, Italy had capitulated and, as in Russia, the Germans were fighting a desperate but offensive rearguard action there with considerable skill. Another winter came and went on the Eastern Front, with all that this meant in terms of logistic difficulty and human suffering for the armour. The soldiers fought on with grim determination. Although the Red Army was by now becoming increasingly well trained and equipped, the German commanders were continuing to use their tanks with telling effect when the opportunity offered. In May 1944 von Manteuffel's Gross Deutschland Division counter-attacked a massive breakthrough at Jassy, just inside the Rumanian frontier. At the cost of only 11 tanks to himself, von Manteuffel hit the Russians so hard that only 60 Russian tanks escaped. This was his first encounter with the Joseph Stalin heavy tank and it made a great impression on him. It was proof against the 88mm at 2,200 metres and this range had to be halved to ensure a knock-out. Yet the fact remains that the Germans' superiority in tactical handling and greater flexibility continued to give them local successes. Talking to Liddell Hart after the war about this engagement, von Manteuffel remarked "In a tank battle, if you stand still you are lost".[1]

Barely a month later, on June 6, the Allies invaded Normandy. The last phase of the battle for the defence of the Fatherland had begun. With three campaigns on their hands, every tank the Germans could muster was needed in the field.

JUNE 1944—NORMANDY

Of the sixty German divisions in the West in June 1944 ten were armoured. Despite the casualties suffered on the Eastern Front and the incessant drain these imposed upon German resources of tank crews and vehicles, the three divisions of 1 SS Panzer Corps (21st Panzer, Panzer Lehr and 12th SS Panzer (Hitler Jugend)) which were covering the invasion area were in good order, well equipped and had high morale. Furthermore, in accordance with Guderian's policy, their commanders were battle-tried and of good quality. The Corps Commander was Sepp Dietrich and the Army Group Commander Erwin Rommel. The remaining seven panzer divisions were in Panzergruppe West under the direct control of

[1] Liddell Hart "The Other Side of the Hill".

Field Marshal von Runstedt, the Commander-in-Chief West.

By this time both Tiger E and Panther were available in some strength. A few Tiger B were also to be found on this front. As the campaign developed, growing numbers of Jagdpanther strengthened the Germans' tank destroying capability. Given a free hand, von Runstedt and Rommel should have inflicted heavy punishment on the Allies, despite the fact that they disagreed on the method to be employed. But the control from Berlin was so tight and the latitude allowed to commanders in the field so limited that every tried principle of armoured warfare went by the board, with divisions being committed piecemeal and ultimately destroyed in detail in many cases. Nevertheless, the tremendous hitting power of the German tanks and the character of the close bocage country, which cut fighting ranges to a few hundred yards at the most, cost the invaders dear. However, it was now the Allies turn to enjoy absolute air superiority. The effect this had upon the movement of

reinforcing divisions was devastating, both in terms of delay and of casualties. Troops on the battlefield were under constant air attack from fighters throughout the hours of daylight and frequently bombed at night.

On July 17 Rommel's car was attacked from the air and the Field Marshal was severely wounded. So ended the fighting career of one of Germany's outstanding "panzer leaders" and one who had made a major contribution to the development of mobile warfare. On the next day, a curiously inept attack by three British armoured divisions east of Caen, known as "Operation Goodwood", was heavily defeated by a smallish force of well deployed tanks and anti-tank guns sited on the dominating Bourguebus ridge. Over 300 British tanks were destroyed. Whilst this operation achieved one of its primary aims, in that it drew the bulk of the German armour onto the Caen "hinge", enabling the US 1st Army to break out of the bridgehead on the west, its conduct ran counter to every tried principle and a heavy price had to be paid in consequence. Despite the protests

Winter on the Eastern Front.

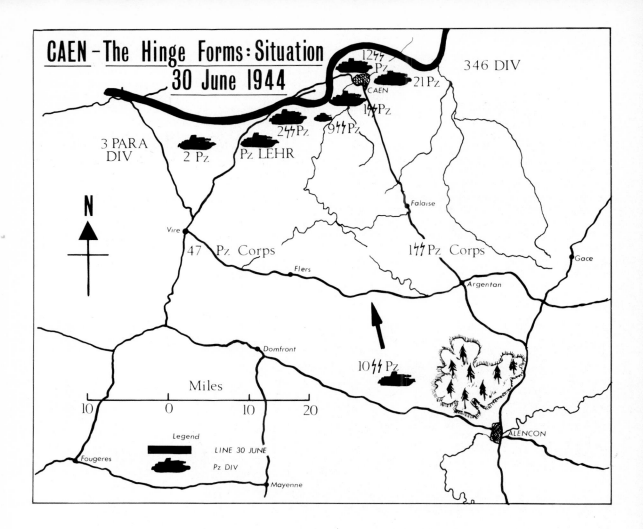

CAEN – The Hinge Forms: Situation 30 June 1944

346 DIV

12ᛋᛋPz

CAEN

21Pz

1ᛋᛋPz

3 PARA DIV

2ᛋᛋPz

9ᛋᛋPz

2 Pz

Pz LEHR

Falaise

N

Vire

47 Pz Corps

Flers

1ᛋᛋPz Corps

Gace

Argentan

Domfront

10ᛋᛋPz

ALENCON

Miles

10   0   10   20

Legend

LINE 30 JUNE

Pz DIV

Fougeres

Mayenne

of General Roberts of 11th Armoured Division, the tanks were largely shorn of their infantry and had to advance on a one squadron front in the wake of a pulverizing aerial bombardment. Under devastating anti-tank fire, the advance came to a halt. As the day wore on the German position was reinforced and deepened and, with darkness, the divisions had to limp off the battlefield to reorganize. The initial effect of the bombing had been stunning. Tiger tanks were turned upside down by the blast, but the Germans fought on, demonstrating once again the strength of their fighting spirit.

The victory was short-lived. Within weeks the disastrous defeats of Falaise and of Hitler's ill-judged counter-stroke towards Avranches reduced the German armoured formations to near annihilation. Only scattered remnants escaped in the great retreat across the Seine. No further major armoured engagement was to be fought in the West until the Führer's last desperate gamble in the Ardennes in December.

As part of the aftermath of the assassination attempt on Hitler on July 20, Guderian, still struggling to keep the battered armoured force in being, was appointed Chief of the General Staff—an ironical development in the face of his earlier disgrace and fall from favour. Whatever conclusions may be drawn from this apparent

capitulation to the will of a man whom he had almost openly derided, no-one can deny the scale of the achievements of this highly professional and dedicated soldier during a period of more than 20 years devotion to the cause of armour and his country.

JUNE 1944—THE RUSSIANS ADVANCE

Even as the battle of the Normandy bridgehead was raging, the Russians were breaking through on the Central Front. Their main attack was launched on June 22 with 146 infantry divisions and 43 tank brigades. In their efforts to stem the tide, the Germans lost 25 divisions. Some 80,000 men were taken prisoner. Despite the measure of this disaster, the high professional skill of their commanders never left them—nor did their determination to fight on. Between August 5 and 9 General Balck, now commanding 4th Panzer Army, mounted a telling counterstroke against two Russian bridgeheads across the Vistula in the general area of Baranov. Realizing the need to conserve his limited manpower, he made maximum use of concentrated artillery fire and massed assault guns to support a force of only six tank battalions. Demonstrating, once again, his ability to regroup at will and so to bring superior force to bear at a given point, deliberately reducing his strength

By the time of the Allied landings in Normandy the Panther's teething troubles were long since over and this most formidable tank was available in some strength.

elsewhere to dangerous proportions, Balck inflicted so heavy a defeat on the Russians that the advance was halted and disaster averted.

The great bulk of the German armour was now committed in the East. Nevertheless, well handled groups of tanks and SP guns were to impose very serious delays upon the Allies' advance through France, Belgium and Holland.

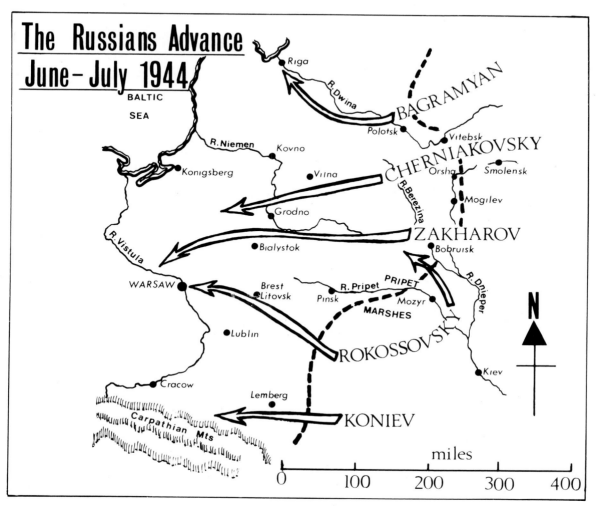

The Russians Advance June – July 1944

BALTIC SEA

Riga

R. Dwina

BAGRAMYAN

Polotsk

Vitebsk

CHERNIAKOVSKY

R. Niemen

Kovno

Vilna

Orsha

Smolensk

Konigsberg

R. Berezina

Mogilev

Grodno

ZAKHAROV

R. Vistula

Bialystok

Bobruisk

WARSAW

Brest Litovsk

R. Pripet

PRIPET

Pinsk

Mozyr

R. Dnieper

MARSHES

N

Lublin

ROKOSSOVSKY

Kiev

Cracow

Lemberg

Carpathian Mts

KONIEV

miles

0   100   200   300   400

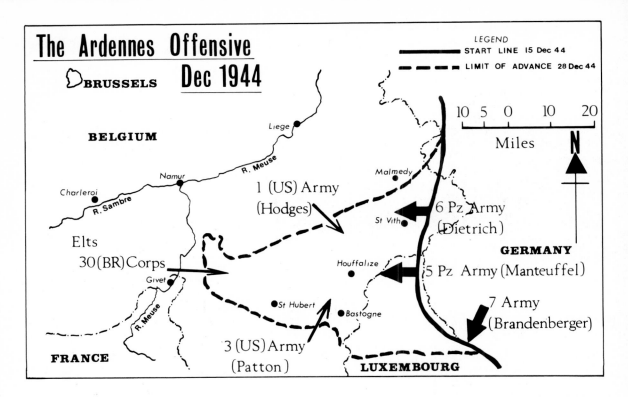

HITLER'S LAST THROW—
THE ARDENNES

Although defeat was staring him in the face, Hitler determined to make a final effort in the West to split Eisenhower's forces and so buy some time. Recalling von Runstedt, who had been disgraced after the early set-backs in Normandy, and gathering together every tank and every soldier he could raise, Hitler formed a force of ten well-equipped Panzer Divisions and some twenty infantry divisions to attack the Americans' positions in the Ardennes on December 16. Surprise, aided by bad weather, paid off dramatically for the first few hours. However, the terrain, the determination of some of the American units and an uncharacteristic German failure to exploit areas of success, all combined with the setting of an over-ambitious aim, ensured that von Runstedt failed to reach his first major objective, the River Meuse, on time. After some of the hardest fighting of the war, the front was stabilized. By January 2 the battle was lost, at a terrible cost to the German Army. Whilst the Offensive reduced the Allies' effective fighting strength by ten per cent and resulted in the loss of some thousands of tanks and other vehicles, the almost bottomless well of American industry was able to make good all the material damage in two weeks. For the Germans, the loss of some 130,000 men killed and wounded was an almost irreparable blow. 6th SS Panzer Army alone had lost 37,000 men and between 300 and 400 tanks. 5th Panzer Army, under von Manteuffel, lost over 200.

Remarkably, German production was still at full pressure. Speer, the Minister in charge, has claimed that in 1944 he turned out sufficient tanks to equip 40 Panzer Divisions. Half-track production reached 7,800 that year and Panthers, now much improved in reliability, were appearing at a rate of 330 a month. All this, despite the fact that Allied air action was accounting for 30% of production. It was not equipment that the Army needed but trained soldiers and trained tank crews in particular. By May 1945 the entire armoured force had disintegrated, most of it crushed under the Russian steamroller.

CONCLUSIONS

The story of German armour is a remarkable one. Years of study by dedicated professionals, superb leadership on the battlefield, sound training and high tactical skill, combined with a forceful and imaginative equipment policy, had produced some notable achievements. Good though their equipment was, it was above all the Germans' ability to achieve surprise, their great flexibility, enabling them to produce numerical superiority at the "Schwerpunkt", and the fighting spirit and determination of their soldiers, which were the telling factors in many of their successes. Balanced forces, exceptional skill and understanding in the handling of anti-tank weapons in attack and defence, and a highly developed system of ground to air communications, also played major parts. On the debit side, the forces of reaction in the High Command, which resolutely refused to grasp the true significance of the rôle of large armoured formations in mobile warfare, combined with Hitler's maniacal insistence upon centralized control and his inability to cease interfering with his field commanders' operations, made ultimate defeat almost inevitable. Having said this of Hitler, one has to acknowledge the part he played in pushing forward the armoured equipment programme, which might have taken a very different form, with priorities quite other than those that Guderian fought so hard to establish. In comparison with the inherent weakness of the High Command system, the shortcomings of the Germans logistics are of lesser significance, though they undoubtedly led to the loss of many opportunities. It is perhaps easy to be over-critical on this score. The difficulties were enormous. The fact that the Army kept going under the conditions it faced in Russia from the outset, and on virtually all fronts from the middle of 1942, was, in itself, a considerable achievement which deserves special study.

It is now well over 25 years since the final defeat of the Third Reich. The nature of warfare has changed out of all recognition, not least because we can no longer expect to have time to build up existing field formations at the outbreak of war. The cost of modern technology seriously inhibits the size of standing armies and the the advent of the tactical nuclear weapon has created considerable confusion of thought. Yet the basic rules governing the successful conduct of tactics at the lower level remain. Despite the risks of training to win a war already fought, we must recognize that there is still much to be learned from the German armoured experience of the years 1919 to 1945.

General Hasso von Manteuffel, commander of 5th Panzer Army. He previously commanded the "Gross Deutschland" Panzer Division.

General Balck, one of the greatest armoured commanders of World War II, whose career included command of 11th Panzer Division, 48 Panzer Corps, 4th Panzer Army (all on the Eastern Front), and Army Group G in the West.

An 88 and a Sturmgeschuetz in position to meet a Russian attack in September 1944.

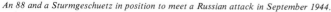

ORIGINAL PANZER DIVISIONAL SIGNS

1st Panzer

2nd Panzer

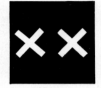
3rd Panzer

4th Panzer

5th Panzer

6th Panzer

7th Panzer

8th Panzer

9th Panzer

10th Panzer

PANZER DIVISIONAL SIGNS FROM LATE 1940

After their victory in France in 1940 the Germans doubled the number of their panzer divisions for the next campaign. Signs of the old divisions were changed and the new signs shown here were introduced. Panzer divisions from 21 onwards were formed after 1940. The Gross Deutschland was officially a panzer grenadier division but with its full tank regiment and armoured reconnaissance unit under command it was actually a panzer division.

1st Panzer

2nd Panzer

3rd Panzer

4th Panzer

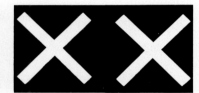
6th Panzer

5th Panzer

7th Panzer

8th Panzer

9th Panzer

10th Panzer

11th Panzer

12th Panzer

Gross Deutschland

13th Panzer

14th Panzer

15th Panzer

16th Panzer

17th Panzer

18th Panzer

19th Panzer

20th Panzer

21st Panzer

22nd Panzer

23rd Panzer

24th Panzer

25th Panzer

Afrika Korps

116th Panzer

Afrika Korps
(variation)

1st Panzer
(variation)

4th Panzer (1943)

7th Panzer
(1943–44)

19th Panzer
(1943–44)

23rd Panzer
(variation)

26th Panzer

Panzer Lehr

Kurmark

Feldherrnhalle 2

Hermann Goering

12th Panzer
(variation)

SS PANZER DIVISIONAL SIGNS

1st SS Panzer
Leibstandarte
Adolf Hitler

2nd SS Panzer
Das Reich

3rd SS Panzer
Totenkopf

5th SS Panzer
Wiking

9th SS Panzer
Hohenstanfen

9th SS Panzer
(variation after Arnhem
1944 – red windmill)

10th SS Panzer
Frundsberg

12th SS Panzer
Hitler Jugend

Achtung Panzer. *Over the hill into battle.*

The Panzer Divisions (1939-1945)

A Short Record of Their Individual Histories Compiled by

DUNCAN CROW *from various authorities*

The first three Panzer Divisions were formed in October 1935.

1st Panzer Division

FORMED in October 1935 at Weimar. Its original establishment was Panzer Brigade 1 (Panzer Regiments 1 and 2, each with two battalions), Motorised Rifle Brigade 1 (Rifle Regiment 1, with two battalions, and Motorcycle Battalion 1), Aufklärung Abteilung 4, Artillerie Regiment 73 (two battalions), and divisional units numbered 37. e.g. Nachrichten Abteilung 37.

The division fought in Poland, September 1939, and in Flanders-France, May-June 1940. In the first part of the latter campaign it attacked Dunkerque.

In October 1940 the division provided Panzer Regiment 2 and cadres for the formation of 16th Panzer Division.

The division fought in Russia, north and centre[1], from the beginning of the campaign in June 1941 until the end of 1942. Early in 1943 it was moved to France, then to the Balkans in June, and in July and August it was in Greece. In November 1943 it returned to Russia (northern Ukraine) and fought in the counter-offensive west of Kiev. In September 1944 it was sent to the Carpathians and took part in the Debrecen counter-attack during the loss of Transylvania. From then until the end of the war the division fought in Hungary and eastern Austria, surrendering in the eastern Austrian Alps area.

Its final full establishment was:

Panzer Aufklärung Abteilung 1

Panzer Regiment 1 (two battalions)
Panzergrenadier Regiment 1 (two battalions)
Panzergrenadier Regiment 113 (two battalions)
Artillerie Regiment 73 (three battalions)
Heeres Flak Abteilung 299
Panzerjaeger Abteilung 37
Nachrichten Abteilung 37
Panzer Pioniere Bataillon 37

Plus divisional HQ, divisional HQ Abteilung, and divisional services.[2]

2nd Panzer Division

Formed in October 1935 at Würzburg. Its original establishment was Panzer Brigade 2 (Panzer Regiments 3 and 4, each with two battalions), Motorised Rifle Brigade 2 (Rifle Regiment 2, with two battalions, and Motorcycle Battalion 2), Aufklärung Abteilung 5, Artillerie Regiment 74 (two battalions), and divisional units numbered 38.

After the Anschluss in March 1938 the division was moved to Vienna. It fought in Poland, September 1939, and then in Flanders-France, May-June 1940. In August 1940 it was moved back to Germany, and in September provided Panzer Regiment 4 and cadres for the formation of 13th Panzer Division.

[1] The German campaign against Russia—Operation Barbarossa—was carried out by Army Groups North, Centre, and South.

[2] Casualties and equipment shortages meant that the actual strengths of Panzer Divisions were rarely up to full establishment—especially was this the case towards the end of World War II.

From September 1940 to February 1941 the division was stationed in Poland. It was then transferred to the Balkans and fought in Greece (April 1941). From Greece it went to France and then, after the opening of the Russian campaign, to Army Group Centre for the drive on Moscow. From the nearby forests it had a brief glimpse of the distant Kremlin.

The division fought in Russia, centre, throughout 1942 and 1943 at Smolensk, Orel, and Kiev. In January 1944 it was moved to Amiens, France, for a re-fit. It fought in Normandy and in the withdrawal across France (June-September 1944), in the Ardennes offensive (December 1944), and in the Rhine battle. It was at Plauen, where it had recently been moved to, when the war ended in May 1945.

Its final full establishment was:
  Panzer Aufklärung Abteilung 2
  Panzer Regiment 3 (two battalions)
  Panzergrenadier Regiment 2 (two battalions)
  Panzergrenadier Regiment 304 (two battalions)
  Artillerie Regiment 74 (three battalions)
  Heeres Flak Abteilung 273
  Panzerjaeger Abteilung 38
  Nachrichten Abteilung 38
  Panzer Pioniere Bataillon 38
Plus divisional HQ, divisional HQ Abteilung, and divisional services.

3rd Panzer Division
Formed in October 1935 in Berlin. Its original establishment was Panzer Brigade 3 "Berlin" (Panzer Regiments 5 "Wünsdorf" and 6 "Neuruppin", each with two battalions), Motorised Rifle Brigade 3 "Eberswalde" (Rifle Regiment 3 "Eberswalde", with two battalions, and Motorcycle Battalion 3 "Freienwalde"), Aufklärung Abteilung 3, Artillerie Regiment 75 "Eberswalde" (two battalions), and divisional units numbered 39.

The division fought in Poland, September 1939, and in Flanders-France, May-June 1940. It then returned to

Panzer IV, Ausf.C, of 2nd Panzer Division.

Germany and provided Panzer Regiment 5 and cadres for the formation of 5th Light Motorised (later 21st Panzer) Division.

From the beginning of the Russian campaign in June 1941 until February 1942 the division fought in Russia, centre, and was then transferred to the south. In the summer of 1943 it was heavily engaged in the Kharkov area and in September moved to the Dnepr bend. Throughout 1944 the division fought in the Ukraine and in Poland. In January 1945 it was moved to Hungary where it fought until April when it was transferred to Austria. It surrendered to the Americans in Styria.

Its final full establishment was:
  Panzer Aufklärung Abteilung 3
  Panzer Regiment 6 (two battalions)
  Panzergrenadier Regiment 3 (two battalions)
  Panzergrenadier Regiment 394 (two battalions)
  Artillerie Regiment 75 (three battalions)
  Heeres Flak Abteilung 314
  Panzerjaeger Abteilung 39
  Nachrichten Abteilung 39
  Panzer Pioniere Bataillon 39
Plus divisional HQ, divisional HQ Abteilung, and divisional services.

A motorised column passing a Panzer II on a road in southern Norway, April 1940. No Panzer divisions were sent to Norway, but individual tank units played a significant part in the campaign.

StuG III caught in the toils of a Russian winter. Self-propelled artillery was an important element in the Panzer Division. (Axel Duckert)

The next two Panzer Divisions, the 4th and 5th, were formed in 1938. Another, the 10th, was formed early in 1939. Six Panzer Divisions, the 1st to 5th inclusive and the 10th, were thus formed before the beginning of World War II on September 1, 1939. All six took part in the Polish campaign of September 1939.

4th Panzer Division

Formed in 1938 at Würzburg. Its original establishment was Panzer Brigade 7 (Panzer Regiments 35 and 36, each with two battalions), Motorised Rifle Brigade 4 (Rifle Regiments 12 and 33, each with two battalions, and Motorcycle Battalion 4), Aufklärung Abteilung 7, Artillerie Regiment 103, and divisional units numbered 84.

The division fought in Poland, September 1939, and in Flanders-France, May-June 1940. In October 1940 the division provided Panzer Regiment 36 and cadres for the formation of 14th Panzer Division.

From the beginning of the Russian campaign in June 1941 the division fought continuously in Russia, centre. It took part in the northern pincer of the Kursk offensive in July 1943, and when this failed played an important part in the defensive fighting in the Gomel area. When the Russian advances began again in the summer of 1944 the division fell back towards Latvia. Early in 1945 it moved into Germany where its remnants later surrendered to the Americans.

Its final full establishment was:
> Panzer Aufklärung Abteilung 4
> Panzer Regiment 35 (two battalions)
> Panzergrenadier Regiment 12 (two battalions)
> Panzergrenadier Regiment 33 (two battalions)
> Artillerie Regiment 103 (three battalions)
> Heeres Flak Abteilung 290
> Panzerjaeger Abteilung 49
> Nachrichten Abteilung 79
> Panzer Pioniere Bataillon 79

Plus divisional HQ, divisional HQ Abteilung, and divisional services.

5th Panzer Division

Formed in November 1938 at Oppeln. Its original establishment was Panzer Brigade 8 (Panzer Regiments 15 and 31, each with two battalions), Motorised Rifle Brigade 5 (Rifle Regiments 13 and 14, each with two battalions, and Motorcycle Battalion 5), Aufklärung Abteilung 8,

Artillerie Regiment 116 (two battalions), Panzer Abwehr Abteilung 53 (from March 1940, Panzerjaeger Abteilung 53), Nachrichten Abteilung 77, and Panzer Pioniere Bataillon 89.

The division fought in Poland, September 1939, and then in Flanders-France, May-June 1940. In October 1940 it provided Panzer Regiment 15 and cadres for the formation of 11th Panzer Division.

The division fought in the Balkans, driving north from Bulgaria to Nis in Jugoslavia and then fighting in Greece in April 1941. In June 1941 it fought in Russia, centre, from the opening of the campaign, first in the drive on Moscow and then in the Rzhev-Gzhatsk area to the west of the capital. The division fought at Orel during the Battle of Kursk and suffered heavily. Early in 1944 it fought in the area west of the middle Dnepr. Later in the year it moved back into Latvia and Kurland.

At the beginning of 1945, before the opening of the Russian offensive, the division was in East Prussia. It finally surrendered to the Russians after a fierce defence of the Hela peninsula north of Danzig.

Its final establishment was:
> Panzer Aufklärung Abteilung 5
> Panzer Regiment 31 (two battalions)
> Panzergrenadier Regiment 13 (two battalions)
> Panzergrenadier Regiment 14 (two battalions)
> Artillerie Regiment 116 (three battalions)
> Heeres Flak Abteilung 228
> Panzerjaeger Abteilung 53
> Nachrichten Abteilung 77
> Panzer Pioniere Bataillon 89

Plus divisional HQ, divisional HQ Abteilung, and divisional services.

After the Polish campaign four more Panzer Divisions (the 6th, 7th, 8th, and 9th) were formed by the conversion of the four Light Divisions which had all fought in Poland.

6th Panzer Division

Formed in October 1939 at Wuppertal from the 1st Light Division with three tank battalions (Panzer Regiment 11, with two battalions, and Panzer Abteilung 65), Rifle Brigade 6 (Rifle Regiment 4, with three battalions, and Motorcycle Battalion 6), Aufklärung Abteilung 57, Artillerie Regiment 76 (two battalions), and divisional units numbered 57, except Panzer Abwehr Abteilung 41 (from March 1940, Panzerjaeger Abteilung 41) and Nachrichten Abteilung 82.

The division fought in Flanders and France, May-June 1940, and was then posted to East Prussia. From June 1941 it fought in Russia, first in the Leningrad area and then in the central part of the front where it suffered heavy losses, to the extent that for some weeks it fought on foot because it had lost every single vehicle and at one time was reduced almost to company strength.

In May 1942 the remnants of the division were moved to France for rest and re-fitting. In December it returned to Russia, this time to the south, taking part in Fourth Panzer Army's attempt to break through to 6th Army in Stalingrad, and was then engaged in the Kharkov area until July 1943 when it took part in the Belgorod offensive (the southern pincer of the Battle of Kursk). In January 1944 it moved to Hungary and later fought in the defence of Budapest. In March 1945 it withdrew into Austria and surrendered to the Russians at Brno in Czechoslovakia in May.

Motor-cycle troops of 6th Panzer Division. In the background three Panzer 35(t).

Its final full establishment was:
  Panzer Aufklärung Abteilung 6
  Panzer Regiment 11 (two battalions)
  Panzergrenadier Regiment 4 (two battalions)
  Panzergrenadier Regiment 114 (two battalions)
  Artillerie Regiment 76 (three battalions)
  Heeres Flak Abteilung 298
  Panzerjaeger Abteilung 41
  Nachrichten Abteilung 82
  Panzer Pioniere Bataillon 57
Plus divisional HQ, divisional HQ Abteilung, and divisional services.

7th Panzer Division

Formed in October 1939 with three tank battalions (Panzer Regiment 25, with two battalions, and Panzer Abteilung 66), Rifle Brigade 7 (Rifle Regiments 6 and 7, each with two battalions, and Motorcycle Battalion 7), Aufklärung Abteilung 58, Artillerie Regiment 78 (two battalions), and divisional units numbered 58, except Panzer Abwehr Abteilung 42 (from March 1940, Panzerjaeger Abteilung 42) and Nachrichten Abteilung 83.

The division fought in Flanders and France, May-June 1940. In February 1941 it returned to Germany and in

7th Panzer Division halted during its sweep across northern France to Cherbourg in June 1940. The division at this time was commanded by General Erwin Rommel. The tank on the extreme left is a Panzer 38(t).

47

Tanks of 8th Panzer Division negotiating a water hazard, Russia, 1941. Panzer IIs in the background.

July was sent to Russia, centre. It fought in Russia until June 1942 when it was sent back to France and took part in the occupation of the southern part of the country in November.

In December 1942 the division returned to Russia, this time to the south, and fought in the Belgorod offensive (the southern pincer of the Battle of Kursk), and at Kharkov in August 1943. In August 1944 it was moved to the Baltic States and fought in Kurland and at Memel until November. When the Russian offensive was renewed it gradually withdrew to the west, surrendering to British troops at Schwerin in May 1945.

Its final full establishment was:

    Panzer Aufklärung Abteilung 7
    Panzer Regiment 25 (two battalions)
    Panzergrenadier Regiment 6 (two battalions)
    Panzergrenadier Regiment 7 (two battalions)
    Artillerie Regiment 78 (three battalions)
    Heeres Flak Abteilung 296
    Panzerjaeger Abteilung 42
    Nachrichten Abteilung 83
    Panzer Pioniere Bataillon 58

Plus divisional HQ, divisional HQ Abteilung, and divisional services.

8th Panzer Division

Formed in October 1939 from the 3rd Light Division with three tank battalions (Panzer Regiment 10, with two battalions, and Panzer Abteilung 67), Rifle Brigade 8 (Rifle Regiment 8, with three battalions, and Motorcycle Battalion 8), Aufklärung Abteilung 59, Artillerie Regiment 80 (two battalions), and divisional units numbered 59, except Panzer Abwehr Abteilung 43 (from March

1940, Panzerjaeger Abteilung 43) and Nachrichten Abteilung 84.

The division fought in Flanders and France, May-June 1940. In April 1941 it motored into northern Jugoslavia to Zagreb. In July it went to Russia, north, taking part in the beginning of the siege of Leningrad. From March to November 1942 it fought at Cholm. From April to August 1943 it was engaged in the Orel area, taking part in the northern pincer of the Battle of Kursk and the subsequent withdrawal in face of the Russian counteroffensive. In October it suffered severely in the withdrawal from Kiev. Until September 1944 it fought in Russia, south, then moved to the Carpathian Mountains and from there to the defence of Budapest. The division withdrew into Moravia and surrendered to the Russians at Brno in May 1945.

Its final full establishment was:

    Panzer Aufklärung Abteilung 8
    Panzer Regiment 10 (one battalion)
    Panzergrenadier Regiment 8 (two battalions)
    Panzergrenadier Regiment 28 (two battalions)
    Artillerie Regiment 80 (three battalions)
    Heeres Flak Abteilung 286
    Panzerjaeger Abteilung 42
    Nachrichten Abteilung 84
    Panzer Pioniere Bataillon 59

Plus divisional HQ, divisional HQ Abteilung, and divisional services.

9th Panzer Division

Formed in January 1940 from the 4th Light Division with Panzer Regiment 33 (two battalions), Rifle Brigade 9 (Rifle Regiments 10 and 11, each with two battalions,

After being badly battered in Russia the remnants of 9th Panzer Division were moved to the south of France to be re-formed.

and Motorcycle Battalion 59), Aufklärung Abteilung 9, Artillerie Regiment 102 (two battalions), and divisional units numbered 60, except Panzer Abwehr Abteilung 50 (from March 1940, Panzerjaeger Abteilung 50), Nachrichten Abteilung 85, and Pioniere Bataillon 86. In parenthesis it may be noted that Panzer Regiment 33 was composed of members of the former Austrian Army tank battalion that, after the Anschluss in 1938, was incorporated into the German Wehrmacht as Panzer Abteilung 33. In March 1943 Panzer Regiment 33 was officially given the name Prinz Eugen Panzer Regiment.

In May 1940 the 9th fought in Holland, the only panzer division to do so. From Breda (Holland) it drove south to Antwerp, Brussels and Mons, and then to Arras, from where it went north to Dunkerque. In the second part of the campaign it had a hard time near Amiens and then thrust south to Lyons.

From September to December 1940 the division was in Poland and was then sent to the Balkans. On April 6, 1941 it struck south-west from the western frontier of Bulgaria towards Skopje in Jugoslavia.

After the Balkans campaign the division was sent to Russia, south, in July, and in October was moved to Russia, centre. It took part in the Battle of Kursk and was then closely committed in the Dnepr bend. After being badly cut up in Russia, south, the remnants of the division in March 1944 were moved to the Nîmes area in the south of France where they were combined with the 155th Reserve Panzer Division to re-form the 9th Panzer Division.

The division fought in the Normandy and Falaise battles, and in September 1944 was fighting in the Aachen area. In December it took part in the Ardennes

offensive. The division was surrounded in the Ruhr and captured in the "Ruhr Pocket" in April 1945.

Its final full establishment was:

Panzer Aufklärung Abteilung 9
Panzer Regiment 33 (one battalion)
Panzer Abteilung 51 (from March 1, 1944)
Panzergrenadier Regiment 10 (two battalions)
Panzergrenadier Regiment 11 (two battalions)
Artillerie Regiment 102 (three battalions)
Heeres Flak Abteilung 287
Panzerjaeger Abteilung 50
Nachrichten Abteilung 85
Panzer Pioniere Bataillon 86

Plus divisional HQ, divisional HQ Abteilung, and divisional services.

10th Panzer Division

Formed in April 1939 in Prague with Panzer Brigade 4 (Panzer Regiments 7 and 8, each with two battalions), Rifle Brigade 10 (Rifle Regiments 69 and 86, each with two battalions), Aufklärung Abteilung 90, Artillerie Regiment (two battalions) and other divisional units numbered 90, except Pioniere Bataillon 49.

The division fought in Poland in 1939 and then in the Flanders-France campaign in May-June 1940. In the first part of the campaign it captured Calais.

Later in 1940 it provided Panzer Regiment 8 and cadres for the new 15th Panzer Division.

In July 1941 the division went to Russia, centre, until April 1942, when it was sent to France for re-fitting. It repulsed the Canadian armoured raid on Dieppe on August 19, 1942.

In December 1942 the division was sent to Tunisia,

Panzer IV, Ausf.B, moving along a flooded road in Belgium, May 1940. Ten Panzer Divisions took part in the campaign in the West against France.

where it was destroyed in May 1943 and never re-formed.

Its final full establishment was:

Panzer Aufklärung Abteilung 10
Panzer Regiment 7 (two battalions)
Panzergrenadier Brigade 10 (Panzergrenadier Regiments 69 and 86, each with two battalions)
Artillerie Regiment 90 (three battalions)
Heeres Flak Abteilung 302
Panzerjaeger Abteilung 90
Nachrichten Abteilung 90
Panzer Pioniere Bataillon 49

The next ten Panzer Divisions, the 11th to 20th inclusive, were all formed in August or October 1940, as was an eleventh, the 23rd.

11th Panzer Division

Formed in August 1940 from the 11th Rifle Brigade with the 15th Panzer Regiment and cadres from the 5th Panzer Division. Its original establishment was Panzer Regiment 15 (two battalions), Rifle Brigade 11 (Rifle Regiments 110 and 111, each with two battalions, and Motorcycle Battalion 61), Aufklärung Abteilung 231, Artillerie Regiment 119 (three battalions), Nachrichten Abteilung 341, Pioniere Abteilung 209, and other divisional units numbered 61.

The division took part in the Balkan campaign from

Among the foreign tanks taken into German service were two Czech types: the TNHP (seen on the extreme left of the 7th Panzer Division picture), and the LTM–35 (seen here in Russia). The TNHP was designated Panzer 38(t) by the Germans, and the LTM–35 was designated Panzer 35(t). (t) =tschechisch =Czechoslovakian.

January to April 1941, driving north from Bulgaria through Nis to Belgrade and being credited with the capture of the Jugoslav capital on April 12.

In July 1941 the division went to Russia, fighting first in the south, then in the centre until June 1942, then in the south again. It took part in the Belgorod offensive (the southern German pincer in the Battle of Kursk) in July 1943, and was then heavily engaged in the Krivoy Rog area in the Dnepr bend. Early in 1944 the division suffered severely in the Korsun encirclement south of Kiev and in June its remnants were sent to France for rest and re-fit.

The division next fought in southern France against the advancing United States Seventh and French First Armies after the Riviera landings in August 1944. It withdrew to Alsace, defended the Belfort Gap in September, and then moved north to the Saar. It fought at Remagen in March 1945 and, at the end of the war, surrendered to the Americans in Bavaria.

Its final full establishment was:

Panzer Aufklärung Abteilung 11
Panzer Regiment 15 (three battalions)
Panzergrenadier Regiment 110 (two battalions)
Panzergrenadier Regiment 111 (two battalions)
Artillerie Regiment 119 (three battalions)
Heeres Flak Abteilung 277
Panzerjaeger Abteilung 61
Nachrichten Abteilung 89
Panzer Pioniere Bataillon 209

Plus divisional HQ, divisional HQ Abteilung, and divisional services. The 11th was known as the Gespenst [Ghost] Division.

12th Panzer Division

Formed in October 1940 in Germany from the 2nd Infantry Division (Motorised) with Panzer Regiment 29 (three battalions), Rifle Brigade 12 (Rifle Regiments 5 and 25, and Motorcycle Battalion 22), Aufklärung Abteilung 2, Artillerie Regiment (three battalions) and other divisional units numbered 2, except Pioniere Battalion 32.

The division fought in Russia, centre, from July 1941; then moved in September to Army Group North where it took part in the siege of Leningrad until November 1942 when it moved back to Army Group Centre. From March to August 1943 it was on the Orel front and subsequently took part in the defence of the middle Dnepr. In February 1944 the division returned to the north and in August retired to Kurland where it was captured by the Russians in 1945.

Its final full establishment was:

Panzer Aufklärung Abteilung 12
Panzer Regiment 29 (two battalions)
Panzergrenadier Regiment 5 (two battalions)
Panzergrenadier Regiment 25 (two battalions)
Artillerie Regiment 2 (three battalions)
Heeres Flak Abteilung 303
Panzerjaeger Abteilung 2
Nachrichten Abteilung 2
Panzer Pioniere Bataillon 32

Plus divisional HQ, divisional HQ Abteilung, and divisional services.

13th Panzer Division

Formed in October 1940 in Rumania where it served as a training unit until June 1941. Its original establishment was Panzer Regiment 4 (two battalions) from 2nd Panzer Division, Rifle Brigade 13 (Rifle Regiments 66 and 93, each with two battalions, and Motorcycle Battalion 43), Aufklärung Abteilung 13, Artillerie Regiment (three battalions) and other divisional units numbered 13, except Pioniere Bataillon 4.

In June 1941 the division moved from Rumania to Russia, south, where it took part in the capture of Kiev. From October 1942 to January 1943 it was in the Caucasus, and from February to August in the Kuban. From October 1943 to January 1944 the division fought around Krivoy Rog in the Dnepr bend.

At this period the division's establishment was:

    Panzer Aufklärung Abteilung 13
    Panzer Regiment 4 (two battalions)
    Panzergrenadier Regiment 66 (two battalions)
    Panzergrenadier Regiment 93 (two battalions)
    Artillerie Regiment 13 (three battalions)
    Heeres Flak Abteilung 271
    Panzerjaeger Abteilung 13
    Nachrichten Abteilung 13
    Panzer Pioniere Bataillon 4

Plus divisional HQ, divisional HQ Abteilung, and divisional services.

In May 1944 Panzergrenadier Regiment 1030 "Feldherrnhalle" was added to the division but was destroyed in the southern Ukraine soon afterwards. The division itself retired to Germany for re-fitting in September and in October was sent to Hungary. In January 1945 it was destroyed in the defence of Budapest but was immediately re-constituted as Panzer Division "Feldherrnhalle 2".

Panzer Division Feldherrnhalle 2

Formed at the beginning of 1945 with elements of the destroyed 13th Panzer Division and the destroyed Panzergrenadier Division 60 "Feldherrnhalle", both of which were decimated in the fighting at Budapest. From

Another foreign tank taken into German service was the French Hotchkiss H39. This particular tank, with German modifications, is preserved in the Établissement du Matériel de Gien. (Collection Pitaud).

Hungary the division fought its way back to Austria where it was at the end of the war.

  Its final establishment was:

    Panzer Aufklärung Abteilung Feldherrnhalle 2
    Panzer Regiment Feldherrnhalle 2
    Panzergrenadier Regiment Feldherrnhalle 2
    Panzerfüsilier Regiment Feldherrnhalle 2
    Panzer Artillerie Regiment Feldherrnhalle 2
    Panzer Sturmgeschütz Brigade Feldherrnhalle 2
    Heeres Flak Abteilung Feldherrnhalle 2
    Panzerjaeger Abteilung Feldherrnhalle 2
    Nachrichten Abteilung Feldherrnhalle 2
    Panzer Pioniere Bataillon Feldherrnhalle 2

14th Panzer Division

Formed in August 1940 from the 4th Infantry Division with Panzer Regiment 36 (two battalions) from 4th Panzer Division, Rifle Brigade 14 (Rifle Regiments 103 and 108, each with two battalions, and Motorcycle Battalion 64), Aufklärung Abteilung 4, Artillerie Regiment (three battalions) and other divisional units numbered 4, except Nachrichten Abteilung 40 and Pioniere Bataillon 13.

Some of the French Chars B1 bis which were captured by the Germans were converted into flamethrowers and were designated Pz Kpfw B1 bis (f) Flamm. The fuel was carried in the armoured box at the rear. The close-up shows the flame gun in place of the normal armament. This particular tank was re-captured by the Allies near Deventer, Holland, in April 1945. (Major-General N. W. Duncan)

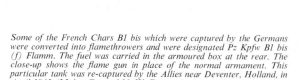

In March 1941 the division was transferred from Germany to Hungary to take part in the Balkans campaign. In April it motored into northern Jugoslavia heading for Belgrade. In May and June it was in Germany re-fitting for the Russian campaign.

From July 1941 to December 1942 the division fought in Russia, south, and was surrounded and destroyed at Stalingrad with 6th Army and Panzer Divisions 16 and 24.

The division was re-formed in Brittany, April-October 1943, and was then sent to Russia in November to the Dnepr bend. It was re-fitted in the Ukraine in June 1944, moved to Kurland in August, and was captured there by the Russians in April 1945.

Its final full establishment was:

> Panzer Aufklärung Abteilung 14
> Panzer Regiment 36 (three battalions)
> Panzergrenadier Regiment 103 (two battalions)
> Panzergrenadier Regiment 108 (two battalions)
> Artillerie Regiment 4 (three battalions)
> Heeres Flak Abteilung 276
> Panzerjaeger Abteilung 4
> Nachrichten Abteilung 4
> Panzer Pioniere Bataillon 13

Plus divisional HQ, divisional HQ Abteilung, and divisional services.

15th Panzer Division

Formed in August 1940 from the 33rd Infantry Division with Panzer Regiment 8 (two battalions) from 10th Panzer Division, Rifle Regiments 104 and 115, each with two battalions, Motorcycle Battalion 15, Aufklärung Abteilung 115, Artillerie Regiment (three battalions) and other divisional units numbered 33.

In April 1941 the division went to Libya as part of Afrikakorps and fought throughout the rest of the campaign along the North African littoral, surrendering with the rest of the Axis forces in Tunisia on May 12, 1943.

Its final full establishment was:

> Panzer Aufklärung Abteilung 15[1]
> Panzer Regiment 8 (two battalions)
> Panzergrenadier Regiment 104 (two battalions)
> Panzergrenadier Regiment 115 (two battalions)
> Artillerie Regiment 33 (three battalions)
> Heeres Flak Abteilung 315
> Panzerjaeger Abteilung 33
> Nachrichten Abteilung 33
> Panzer Pioniere Bataillon 33

Plus divisional HQ, divisional HQ Abteilung, and divisional services.

In July 1943 in Sicily it was re-formed as the 15th Panzergrenadier Division.

16th Panzer Division

Formed in August 1940 with Panzer Regiment 2 (two battalions) from 1st Panzer Division, Rifle Brigade 16 (Rifle Regiments 64 and 79, each with two battalions, and Motorcycle Battalion 16), Aufklärung Abteilung 16, Artillerie Regiment (three battalions) and other divisional units numbered 16.

After being held in reserve during the Balkans campaign the division was sent to Russia, south, where it was continuously engaged until its encirclement and destruction at Stalingrad with 6th Army and Panzer Divisions 14 and 24.

The division was re-formed in France in March 1943. During the negotiations which culminated in Italy leaving the Axis and capitulating to the Allies it was sent to northern Italy and then to Taranto. In September it was moved hastily to Salerno just before the Allied landings and had hard fighting both there and in the Naples area.

In November 1943 the division returned to Russia to take part in the German offensive west of Kiev. It suffered heavy losses and withdrew to the Baranow area (on the River Vistula north-east of Cracow). In October 1944 it was re-fitted at Kielce and in January 1945 took part in the fighting against the Russian attack from the Baranow bridgehead. In April it had withdrawn to Brno in Czechoslovakia where part of the division surrendered to the Russians and part to the Americans.

Its final full establishment was:

> Panzer Aufklärung Abteilung 16
> Panzer Regiment 2 (two battalions)
> Panzergrenadier Regiment 64 (two battalions)
> Panzergrenadier Regiment 79 (two battalions)
> Panzer Artillerie Regiment 16 (three battalions)
> Heeres Flak Abteilung 274
> Panzerjaeger Abteilung 4
> Nachrichten Abteilung 16
> Panzer Pioniere Bataillon 16

Plus divisional HQ, divisional HQ Abteilung, and divisional services.

17th Panzer Division

Formed in October 1940 with Panzer Regiment 17 (two battalions), Rifle Brigade 17 (Rifle Regiments 40 and 63, each with two battalions, and Motorcycle Battalion 17), Aufklärung Abteilung 17, Artillerie Regiment (three battalions) and other divisional units numbered 27.

The division fought in Russia, centre, from June 1941 to November 1942, and then in the south where it took part in Fourth Panzer Army's attempt to relieve 6th Army in Stalingrad. In summer 1943 it was in the Donets and Dnepr bend sectors. From March 1944 it was in the withdrawal across northern Ukraine. In January 1945 it was fighting in the Baranow bridgehead area. In April it was overrun by the Russians.

Its final full establishment was:

> Panzer Aufklärung Abteilung 17
> Panzer Regiment 17 (two battalions)
> Panzergrenadier Regiment 40 (two battalions)
> Panzergrenadier Regiment 63 (two battalions)
> Panzer Artillerie Regiment 27 (three battalions)
> Heeres Flak Abteilung 297
> Panzerjaeger Abteilung 27
> Nachrichten Abteilung 27
> Panzer Pioniere Bataillon 27

Plus divisional HQ, divisional HQ Abteilung, and divisional services.

18th Panzer Division

Formed in October 1940 with Panzer Regiment 18 (two battalions), Rifle Brigade 18 (Rifle Regiments 52 and 101, each with two battalions, and Motorcycle Battalion 18), Aufklärung Abteilung 18, Artillerie

---

[1] In his *Panzer Battles 1939–1945* Major-General F. W. Von Mellenthin refers to this unit throughout the Libyan campaign as 33rd Recce.

StuG III driving into the blazing waste of a Russian town.

Regiment (three battalions) and other divisional units numbered 88.

The division fought in Russia, centre, from June 1941 to June 1942, then in the south, then in the centre again. In October and November 1943 it was in action west of Kiev, where it suffered heavily in the German counter-offensive. In consequence of its losses it was re-organised as the 18th Artillery Division.

Its final full establishment as a panzer division was:

    Panzer Aufklärung Abteilung 18
    Panzer Regiment 18 (two battalions)
    Panzergrenadier Regiment 52 (two battalions)
    Panzergrenadier Regiment 101 (two battalions)
    Panzer Artillerie Regiment 88 (three battalions)
    Heeres Flak Abteilung 280
    Panzerjaeger Abteilung 88
    Nachrichten Abteilung 88
    Panzer Pioniere Bataillon 88

Plus divisional HQ, divisional HQ Abteilung, and divisional services.

19th Panzer Division

Formed in October 1940 with Panzer Regiment 27 (two battalions), Rifle Brigade 19 (Rifle Regiments 73 and 74, each with two battalions, and Motorcycle Battalion 19), Aufklärung Abteilung 19, Artillerie Regiment (three battalions) and other divisional units numbered 19.

The division fought in Russia, centre, from June 1941 to April 1943, when it was transferred to the south. In July 1943 it was in the Belgorod offensive (the southern pincer of the Battle of Kursk) where it suffered heavy losses. In March 1944 it was in the withdrawal across northern Ukraine. From July until the end of the year it was in East Prussia and was then moved to Radom, south of Warsaw. In January and February 1945 it fought against the Russian break-out from the Baranow bridgehead, withdrawing towards Breslau. In February it moved south to Silezice in Bohemia and was there when the war ended.

Its final full establishment was:

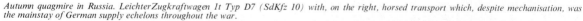

Autumn quagmire in Russia. LeichterZugkraftwagen 1t Typ D7 (SdKfz 10) with, on the right, horsed transport which, despite mechanisation, was the mainstay of German supply echelons throughout the war.

Panzer Aufklärung Abteilung 19
Panzer Regiment 27 (two battalions)
Panzergrenadier Regiment 73 (two battalions)
Panzergrenadier Regiment 74 (two battalions)
Panzer Artillerie Regiment 19 (three battalions)
Heeres Flak Abteilung 272
Panzerjaeger Abteilung 19
Nachrichten Abteilung 19
Panzer Pioniere Bataillon 19

Plus divisional HQ, divisional HQ Abteilung, and divisional services.

20th Panzer Division

Formed in October 1940 with Panzer Regiment 21 (two battalions), Rifle Brigade 20 (Rifle Regiments 59 and 112, each with two battalions, and Motorcycle Battalion 20), Aufklärung Abteilung 92, Artillerie Regiment (three battalions) and other divisional units numbered 92.

The division fought in Russia, centre, from the beginning of the campaign, taking part in the initial drive on Moscow and continuing to be engaged thereafter. In July 1943 it was in the Orel offensive (the northern pincer of the Battle of Kursk). In the summer of 1944 it fought against the Russian offensive, suffered heavily, was transferred to Rumania in August, and was there engaged in fierce fighting. In November 1944 it was moved to East Prussia, and then in December it was moved south to Hungary. The division was overrun in May 1945 in the central sector of the Eastern front.

Its final full establishment was:
Panzer Aufklärung Abteilung 20
Panzer Regiment 21 (two battalions)
Panzergrenadier Regiment 59 (two battalions)

Panzergrenadier Regiment 112 (two battalions)
Panzer Artillerie Regiment 92 (three battalions)
Panzerjaeger Abteilung 92
Nachrichten Abteilung 92
Panzer Pioniere Bataillon 92

Plus divisional HQ, divisional HQ Abteilung, and divisional services.

21st Panzer Division

Formed in February 1941 from 5th Light Motorised Division with Panzer Regiment 5 and cadres from 3rd Panzer Division.

The division went to Libya as part of Afrikakorps in February 1941 and fought throughout the rest of the campaign along the North African littoral. After the Second Battle of El Alamein in October-November 1942 the division, having taken part in the battle, provided the rear-guard during the withdrawal to Tripoli and Tunisia. It surrendered with the rest of the Axis troops in Tunisia in May 1943.

Its final establishment was:
Panzer Regiment 22 (two battalions)
Rifle Regiment 125 (two battalions)
Rifle Regiment 192 (two battalions)
Motorcycle Battalion 21
Aufklärung Abteilung 200[1]
Artillerie Regiment 155 (three battalions)
Other divisional units numbered 200, except
Pioniere Bataillon 220

---

[1] In his *Panzer Battles 1939–1945* Major-General F. W. Von Mellenthin refers to this unit throughout the Libyan campaign as 3rd Recce.

Panzer III of the Afrikakorps in Tripoli. Like the Desert Rats (the British 7th Armoured Division) the 15th and 21st Panzer Divisions became one of the undying legends of World War II.

Burning oilfields met the German advance into the Caucasus. Leichter Schützenpanzerwagen (SdKfz 250) advance beside a pall of smoke, with their Panzer Grenadier crews.

In July 1943 the division was re-formed in Normandy from occupation troops with the following establishment:

    Panzer Aufklärung Abteilung 21
    Panzer Regiment 22 (two battalions)
    Panzergrenadier Regiment 125 (two battalions)
    Panzergrenadier Regiment 192 (two battalions)
    Panzer Artillerie Regiment 155 (three battalions)
    Panzerjaeger Abteilung 200
    Nachrichten Abteilung 200
    Panzer Pioniere Bataillon 220

Plus divisional HQ, divisional HQ Abteilung, and divisional services. Heeres Flak Abteilung 305 was added to the division later.

Although scheduled for posting to the Eastern front the division's orders were cancelled and it remained in France where it fought against the Allied landings in Normandy in June 1944 and was engaged in the subsequent withdrawal from France. After re-fitting in Germany it returned to the Western front from September to December in the Saar and northern Alsace. In January 1945 it finally moved to the Eastern front, centre, where it was overrun by the Russians at the end of the war.

22nd Panzer Division

Formed in 1941. The division was sent to Russia, south, in March 1942 and fought in the Crimea. It then fought in the Don bend near Stalingrad and was almost destroyed there in November 1942 when the Russian offensive began.

Its final full establishment was:

    Panzer Aufklärung Abteilung 140
    Panzer Regiment 204 (two battalions)
    Panzergrenadier Regiment 129 (two battalions)
    Panzergrenadier Regiment 140 (two battalions)
    Panzer Artillerie Regiment (three battalions)
    Heeres Flak Abteilung 289
    Panzerjaeger Abteilung 140

    Nachrichten Abteilung 140
    Panzer Pioniere Bataillon 140

Plus divisional HQ, divisional HQ Abteilung, and divisional services.

The division was subsequently disbanded. Panzergrenadier Regiment 129 was posted to 15th Panzergrenadier Division, formerly 15th Panzer Division.

23rd Panzer Division

Formed in October 1940 in France, with Panzer Regiment 23 (two battalions), Rifle Brigade 23 (Rifle Regiments 126 and 128, each with two battalions, and Motorcycle Battalion 23), Aufklärung Abteilung 128, Artillerie Regiment (three battalions) and other divisional units numbered 128.

The division's formation was not completed until October 1941. In March 1942 it was sent to Russia and took part in defeating the Russian offensive against Kharkov in May. In December it took part in Fourth Panzer Army's attempt to break through to 6th Army in Stalingrad. At the end of 1943 it was in the Dnepr bend fighting and suffered severe losses in the withdrawal westwards. It moved to Poland for re-fitting and fought there in September 1944. In October it was moved to Hungary and fought at Debrecen. It then moved north to the Baranow bridgehead and was there when the Russians launched their attack in January 1945. It was overrun by the Russians at the end of the war.

Its final full establishment was:

    Panzer Aufklärung Abteilung 23
    Panzer Regiment 23 (two battalions)
    Panzergrenadier Regiment 126 (two battalions)
    Panzergrenadier Regiment 128 (two battalions)
    Panzer Artillerie Regiment 128 (three battalions)
    Heeres Flak Abteilung 278
    Panzerjaeger Abteilung 128
    Nachrichten Abteilung 128
    Panzer Pioniere Bataillon 128

Plus divisional HQ, divisional HQ Abteilung, and divisional services.

In their retreat from the Caucasus the Germans had to abandon much of their equipment, including these Pz Kpfw IV F2—the first Panzer IVs to be armed with the long-barrelled KwK 40 L/43 7,5cm gun. They were known to the British as "Mark IV Specials".

Stalingrad. Three Panzer Divisions were lost here with Field Marshal Paulus's 6th Army.

24th Panzer Division

Formed in February 1942 from the 1st Cavalry Division, with Panzer Regiment 24 (two battalions), Rifle Brigade 24 (Rifle Regiments 21 and 26, each with two battalions, and Motorcycle Battalion 24), Aufklärung Abteilung 86, Artillerie Regiment 89 (three battalions), and divisional units numbered 40.

The division fought in Russia, where it had previously fought as the 1st Cavalry Division. It was destroyed at Stalingrad in January 1943, re-formed in Normandy in March-April, and sent to Italy in August. In October it returned to Russia, south, where it suffered heavily west of Kiev in November.

The division suffered heavily again in March 1944 during the general withdrawal from the Dnepr bend. In July it was in southern Poland, and in October it was in Hungary where it took part in the Debrecen counter-attack. From December 1944 to January 1945 it was in Slovakia from where it was sent to west Prussia. It withdrew into Schleswig-Holstein where it surrendered to the British in May 1945.

Its final full establishment was:

      Panzer Aufklärung Abteilung 24
      Panzer Regiment 24 (two battalions)
      Panzergrenadier Regiment 21 (two battalions)
      Panzergrenadier Regiment 26 (two battalions)
      Panzer Artillerie Regiment 89 (three battalions)
      Heeres Flak Abteilung 283
      Panzerjaeger Abteilung 40
      Nachrichten Abteilung 86
      Panzer Pioniere Bataillon 40

Plus divisional HQ, divisional HQ Abteilung, and divisional services.

25th Panzer Division

Formed in February 1942 from occupation troops in Norway. It was moved to southern France in August

1943 and then to Russia, south, in October. This latter move was against the advice of the Inspector-General of Armoured Troops (Colonel-General Guderian) who considered that the division was not yet ready for action. "This unfortunate division," as Guderian called it in his memoirs, was committed to action near Kiev in November. It suffered heavy losses in the withdrawal across northern Ukraine in March 1944, and in April it was sent to Denmark to be re-formed.

In September 1944 the division returned to the Eastern front, this time to the central sector, where it fought in the Vistula area. Throughout January 1945 it was engaged in the defence of Warsaw, and it then withdrew into Germany where it was over-run by the Russians in May.

Its final full establishment was:

    Panzer Aufklärung Abteilung 87
    Panzer Regiment 9 (two battalions)
    Panzergrenadier Regiment 146 (two battalions)
    Panzergrenadier Regiment 147 (two battalions)
    Panzer Artillerie Regiment 91 (three battalions)
    Heeres Flak Abteilung 284
    Panzerjaeger Abteilung 87
    Nachrichten Abteilung 87
    Panzer Pioniere Bataillon 87

Plus divisional HQ, divisional HQ Abteilung, and divisional services.

26th Panzer Division

Formed in October 1942 in Brittany by the conversion of the 23rd Infantry Division, with Panzer Regiment 26 (two battalions), Rifle Brigade 26 (Rifle Regiments 9 and 67, each with two battalions, and Motorcycle Battalion 26), Aufklärung Abteilung 26, Artillerie Regiment (three battalions) and other divisional units numbered 93.

The division was sent to Italy after the fall of Mussolini in July 1943 and fought there until the end of the war, surrendering near Bologna in May 1945.

Its final full establishment was:

    Panzer Aufklärung Abteilung 26
    Panzer Regiment 26 (two battalions)
    Panzergrenadier Regiment 9 (two battalions)
    Panzergrenadier Regiment 67 (two battalions)
    Verstärktes Grenadier Regiment (two battalions)[1]
    Panzer Artillerie Regiment 93 (three battalions)
    Heeres Flak Abteilung 304
    Panzerjaeger Abteilung 93
    Nachrichten Abteilung 93
    Panzer Pioniere Bataillon 93

Plus divisional HQ, divisional HQ Abteilung, and divisional services.

27th Panzer Division

Began to form in France in 1942, but was sent to Russia, south, in September before its formation was complete. The division was destroyed early in 1943 and was not re-formed.

116th Panzer Division

Formed in April 1944 by the conversion of the 16th Panzergrenadier Division. The division fought in Normandy from June 1944 until the withdrawal from France at the end of August. It was moved to Düsseldorf in September for re-fitting and was then transferred to the Köln sector in November. In December it fought in the southern sector of the Ardennes offensive, where it suffered heavy losses.

In January 1945 the division was moved to the Kleve sector on the Rhine. In April it was surrounded by the Americans in the "Ruhr Pocket", where it surrendered.

Its final full establishment was:

    Panzer Aufklärung Abteilung 116
    Panzer Regiment 16 (two battalions)
    Panzergrenadier Regiment 60 (two battalions)
    Panzergrenadier Regiment 156 (two battalions)
    Panzer Artillerie Regiment 146 (three battalions)
    Heeres Flak Abteilung 281
    Panzerjaeger Abteilung 228
    Nachrichten Abteilung 228
    Panzer Pioniere Bataillon 675

Plus divisional HQ, divisional HQ Abteilung, and divisional services.

Panzer Lehr Division[2]

Formed in November 1943 from the demonstration units of various training schools. Concentrated in eastern France in February 1944, the embryonic division was then transferred to Budapest in April. Here it incorporated Infanterie Lehr Regiment 901 which had been operating in the Balkans. In May the division returned to France—to the Orleans area.

When the Allied invasion of Normandy began in June 1944, the division was one of the main obstacles to the Anglo-American break-out from the bridgehead. It took a leading part in the Normandy battle and suffered heavily in the process.

After the withdrawal from France the division was sent to the Saar, and from there to Paderborn. After re-fitting as part of Sixth SS Panzer Army it returned to the Saar in November, was moved to the Eifel in December, and took part in the Ardennes offensive. It was eventually trapped in the "Ruhr Pocket" and surrendered to the Americans in April 1945.

Its final full establishment was:

    Panzer Aufklärung Abteilung 130
    Panzer Regiment 130 (two battalions)
    Panzergrenadier Regiment 901 (two battalions)
    Panzergrenadier Regiment 902 (two battalions)
    Panzer Artillerie Regiment 146 (three battalions)
    Heeres Flak Abteilung 311
    Panzerjaeger Abteilung 130
    Nachrichten Abteilung 130
    Panzer Pioniere Bataillon 130

Plus divisional HQ, divisional HQ Abteilung, and divisional services.

---

[1] Like the Allies, the Germans discovered that armoured divisions in Italy, because of the nature of the terrain and the fighting, needed extra infantry. (See Duncan Crow, *British and Commonwealth Armoured Formations (1919–1946)*, Profile Publications Ltd., 1971, page 36).

[2] One authority says that the division was sometimes referred to as 130th Panzer Lehr Division. The compiler, who came across the division frequently in the North-West Europe campaign, did not, however, meet with this designation.

King Tigers (Tiger B) in a French wood during the Battle of Normandy.

Panzer Division "Gross Deutschland"

Formed as Panzer Grenadier Division "Gross Deutschland" in May 1942 from the crack motorised Infanterie Regiment "Gross Deutschland" which had fought in Poland, September 1939, and in the campaign against France, May-June 1940. "Gross Deutschland" took part in the Russian campaign from the outset, fighting in the central sector until June 1942 when it was moved to the south for three months before returning to the centre. In November 1942 it went to the south again when the Russian winter offensive began, and in February and March 1943 it was engaged in the re-capture of Kharkov and Belgorod. At the beginning of the Battle of Kursk in July 1943 "Gross Deutschland" was in 48 Panzer Corps, Fourth Panzer Army—the southern pincer. It was then transferred to the centre when the Russians began their offensive in the Orel sector later that month; after a short period it returned to 48 Panzer Corps in the south.

During the winter of 1943–44 "Gross Deutschland" was heavily engaged in the withdrawal to the Dnepr bend. In May 1944 it was moved to Bessarabia as the Russian attack reached the Dniestr and Rumania. In July it moved once again to the centre as the Russians pushed into Poland, and the following month it moved further north to Latvia and Lithuania to help in the defence of East Prussia. It fell back to Memel where it fought a rearguard action until the end of November. In December, survivors who had escaped from Memel re-formed west of Koenigsberg in East Prussia and from then until the end of March when they were overrun they fought the Russians at the Frisches Haff, the long bay at the south-east of the Gulf of Danzig.

"Gross Deutschland" was the Wehrmacht's most favoured Panzer Division. Its establishment was larger than that of an ordinary Panzer Division, larger even than that of the SS Panzer Divisions, which themselves were more favoured than the Wehrmacht divisions. Its units in 1944 were:

Panzer Aufklärung Abteilung "Gross Deutschland"
Panzer Regiment "Gross Deutschland" (three battalions)
Panzer Grenadier Regiment "Gross Deutschland" (three battalions)
Panzer Füsiliere Regiment "Gross Deutschland" (three battalions)
Panzer Artillerie Regiment "Gross Deutschland" (three battalions)
Heeres Flak Abteilung "Gross Deutschland"
Panzerjaeger Abteilung "Gross Deutschland"

Panzer Sturmgeschütz Brigade "Gross Deutschland"
Panzer Nachrichten Abteilung "Gross Deutschland"
Panzer Pioniere Bataillon "Gross Deutschland"

Plus divisional HQ, divisional HQ Abteilung, and divisional services. Not only did "Gross Deutschland" have a larger establishment than an ordinary Panzer Division but its actual strength kept closer to this than did the actual strengths of the run-of-the-mill Panzer Divisions which became more and more attenuated, especially in the number of tanks they had, as the war entered its later stages.

In January 1945 "Gross Deutschland" was put in control of the "Gross Deutschland Verbände" which consisted of most of the Wehrmacht's crack troops including Panzer Grenadier Division "Brandenburg", Führer Grenadier Division, Führer Begleit Division, and Panzer Division "Kurmark".

Both the Führer Begleit (Escort) and the Führer Grenadier Divisions were upgraded to divisional status from brigades in January 1945. The Führer Begleit Brigade (originally Battalion) was a motorised escort for Hitler's GHQ. To gain experience part of it saw action in Russia, north, on two occasions, but for most of the war until the end of November 1944 it was at the Führer's GHQ. In November 1944, less elements retained on guard duty, it was sent to the west to take part in the Ardennes offensive. In February, after it had been upgraded to a division, it was sent with the Führer Grenadier Division to the Oder front south-east of Berlin. It was surrounded at Spremberg near Cottbus and was virtually annihilated when breaking out on April 21, 1945. The division had a Panzer Regiment with two battalions, a Panzer Grenadier Regiment, an Infantry Battalion "for special use", an artillery Abteilung, and a Flak regiment.

The Führer Grenadier Brigade was formed as a special bodyguard after the attempt on Hitler's life on July 20, 1944. After seeing action against the Russian breakthrough at Gumbinnen in East Prussia from October to December 1944 it was sent west to take part in the Ardennes offensive. In February, now with divisional status, it was sent to Stargard east of Stettin and took part in the defence of Pomerania. At the beginning of April after fighting at Kustrin east of Berlin it was transferred to Vienna and ended the war in Austria. The division had a Panzer Regiment, a Panzer Grenadier Regiment, a motorised Panzer Grenadier Battalion, a Panzer Fusilier Battalion, an Infantry Battalion "for special use", a Panzer Sturmgeschütz Brigade, a Panzer Artillery Regiment, and a Flak Abteilung.

Panzer Division "Kurmark"

Formed in January 1945 at Cottbus south of Berlin from Kampfgruppe Langkeit its organisation was:

Panzer Aufklärung Abteilung "Kurmark"
Panzer Regiment "Kurmark" (two battalions)
Panzer Grenadier Regiment "Kurmark" (two battalions)
Panzer Artillerie Regiment "Kurmark" (two battalions)
Panzer Nachrichten Abteilung "Kurmark"
Panzer Pioniere Bataillon "Kurmark"

Plus divisional HQ, divisional HQ Abteilung, and divisional services.

The new division first went into action on the Oder front at the beginning of February. It remained on that front until the end of April when it broke out of Russian encirclement at Halbe, between Berlin and Cottbus, and crossed the Elbe to surrender to the Americans.

In the last stages of the war a number of scratch Panzer Divisions were formed, or were in the process of being formed when the war ended. Apart from Panzer Divisions "Kurmark" and "Feldherrnhalle 2" already mentioned, these included Panzer Divisions "Clausewitz", "Donau", "Schlesien", "Thüringen", and "Westfalen" formed in 1945 from instruction schools, training units, and reserve formations; "Kurland" formed from elements of 14th Panzer Division and motorised units in the area; "Holstein" formed from the 233rd Reserve Panzer Division; and "Münchenburg" formed from SS units.

One Panzer Division was a Luftwaffe formation, although it came under Army control after General Guderian became Inspector-General Armoured Forces in February 1943. This was

Fallschirm Panzer Division "Hermann Goering"
The "Hermann Goering" Panzer Division, composed entirely of volunteers, had its origins in the elite pre-war Luftwaffe Jaeger Regiment "Hermann Goering". In 1942 this became the "Hermann Goering" Brigade whose role was the training of paratroopers and air landing units. Early in 1943 it became first a Panzer Grenadier Division and then a Panzer Division. It was equipped in Belgium, then moved to southern France, and from there was sent to Tunisia where it was destroyed in the North African campaign which ended in May 1943.

The division was quickly re-formed in southern Italy and Sicily and played a prominent part in the Sicilian campaign in July and August 1943. It was withdrawn to Italy and in January 1944 was given the title Fallschirm

Panzer Division "Hermann Goering", although the Fallschirm (Parachute) designation was purely honorary. The division became heavily engaged in containing the Anzio bridgehead from January onwards until the Allied break-out. In July it was transferred to Russia, centre, to help in trying to counter the Russian summer offensive. In August it fought at Warsaw and then in October withdrew north to East Prussia. Here it provided the cadre for Fallschirm Panzer Corps "Hermann Goering" consisting of a Panzer Division and a Panzer Grenadier Division. The Corps was engaged at Elbing, near Danzig, and broke out of Russian encirclement with heavy losses.

The establishment of Fallschirm Panzer Division "Hermann Goering" was:

Panzer Aufklärung Abteilung "Hermann Goering"

Panzer Regiment "Hermann Goering" (three battalions)

Panzer Grenadier Regiment "Hermann Goering" 1 (two battalions)

Panzer Grenadier Regiment "Hermann Goering" 2 (two battalions)[1]

Panzer Artillerie Regiment "Hermann Goering" (four battalions)

Flak Regiment "Hermann Goering"

Panzer Nachrichten Abteilung "Hermann Goering"

Panzer Pioniere Bataillon "Hermann Goering"

Ersatz Bataillon "Hermann Goering"

---

[1] In each Panzer Grenadier Regiment the first battalion had three Panzer Grenadier companies, a heavy Panzer Grenadier company, and a light anti-tank company; the second battalion had three Panzer Grenadier companies, a heavy Panzer Grenadier company, a heavy anti-tank company, and two light infantry howitzer companies. The thirteenth company in the regiment was an infantry howitzer company, and the fourteenth was an anti-tank company.

Panthers (Ausf.A) of the "Gross Deutschland" Division counter-attacking near Memel, November 1944.

There were seven Panzer Divisions in the Waffen-SS. Three were formed in 1942 as Panzer Grenadier Divisions, the other four in 1943. In October 1943 all seven became Panzer Divisions.

1st SS Panzer Division "Leibstandarte SS Adolf Hitler"

Hitler's bodyguard regiment, SS Leibstandarte Adolf Hitler, was officially constituted and given its title on the National Socialist Party Day in 1933. The L.A.H. fought in Poland, September 1939, and in Flanders-France, May-June 1940. In July 1942 in France it was formed into SS Panzer Grenadier Division "Leibstandarte Adolf Hitler" with Infanterie Regiments L.A.H. 1 and 2 (from December 1942 re-designated Panzer Grenadier Regiments L.A.H. 1 and 2) each with three battalions, Panzer Regiment L.A.H. with two battalions, Aufklärung Abteilung L.A.H., Artillerie Regiment L.A.H. (three battalions), Flak Abteilung L.A.H. (five batteries), Sturmgeschütz Abteilung L.A.H. (three batteries), Panzerjaeger Abteilung L.A.H. (three companies), Nachrichten Abteilung L.A.H., Pioniere Bataillon L.A.H., and Versorgungs Einheiten L.A.H.

On October 22, 1943 the division became 1st SS Panzer Division "Leibstandarte SS Adolf Hitler". Its establishment was:

> SS Panzer Aufklärung Abteilung 1
> SS Panzer Regiment 1 (two battalions)
> SS Panzer Grenadier Regiment 1 L.A.H. (three
>   battalions)
> SS Panzer Grenadier Regiment 2 L.A.H. (three
>   battalions)
> SS Panzer Artillerie Regiment 1 (four battalions)
> SS Flak Abteilung 1 (five batteries)
> SS Sturmgeschütz Abteilung 1 (three batteries)
> SS Panzerjaeger Abteilung 1 (three companies)
> SS Panzer Nachrichten Abteilung 1
> SS Panzer Pioniere Bataillon 1
> SS Versorgungs Einheiten 1
> SS Werfer Abteilung 1 (from September 1944)
> SS Feldersatz Bataillon 1 (from October 1944)

Plus divisional HQ, divisional HQ Abteilung, and divisional services other than the Versorgungs Einheiten.

From its formation as SS Panzer Grenadier Division L.A.H. in July 1942 until February 1943 the division remained in Normandy. It then went to Russia, south, and was part of the southern pincer in the Battle of Kursk at Belgorod in July 1943. In August it was transferred to northern Italy where it remained until the end of October when it returned to Russia, south, and fought at Zhitomir in the Ukraine and at Vinnitsa and Tscherkassy. In April 1944 it was at Tarnopol in the western Ukraine and the following month it was sent to Belgium where it was re-fitted.

In June 1944 the division joined the Normandy battle, where it fought chiefly in the Caen sector. After the withdrawal from France it fell back to the Eifel, was re-fitted in Westphalia in November, and returned to the Eifel. The division fought in the Ardennes offensive and for this operation it was allotted the 150th Panzer Brigade. In February 1945 it was moved to Hungary and ended the war in Austria.

2nd SS Panzer Division "Das Reich"

At the outbreak of the war in September 1939 the SS-Verfügungstruppen consisted of three infantry regiments, each of three battalions. These were: Standarte 1 "Deutschland", Standarte 2 "Germania", and Standarte 3 "Der Führer". The three Standarten were formed into the SS-VT Division in April 1940, and later that year, without "Germania" (see 5th SS Panzer Division "Wiking") this designation was changed to SS Division Reich and then to SS Division "Das Reich". The division was motorised.

In November 1942 the reorganised and re-equipped SS Division (Motorised) "Das Reich" which had been fighting in Russia, centre, was designated SS Panzer Grenadier Division "Das Reich" (2nd SS Division). This reorganisation took place in Normandy to which the division had been sent from Russia in June. It returned to Russia early in 1943 and fought at Kharkov, Belgorod, the Dnepr bend, Zhitomir, and Vinnitsa, before returning once again to France in April 1944, this time to the Toulouse area. By now it had been re-designated, on October 22, 1943, as 2nd SS Panzer Division "Das Reich".

The division was moved up to Normandy after the Allied landings. It went into action against First U.S. Army early in July 1944. After the defeat in France the division withdrew to the Eifel area and then, after being re-equipped, took part in the Ardennes offensive. With the rest of Sixth SS Panzer Army it was moved east to Hungary in January 1945 and ended the war near Linz, where it surrendered to the Americans.

The division's establishment was:

> Aufklärung Abteilung SS Panzer Division "Das
>   Reich"
> Panzer Regiment 2 SS Panzer Division "Das
>   Reich" (two battalions)
> SS Panzer Grenadier Regiment 3 "Deutschland"
>   (three battalions)
> SS Panzer Grenadier Regiment 4 "Der Führer"
>   (three battalions)
> Artillerie Regiment SS Panzer Division "Das
>   Reich" (four battalions)
> Flak Abteilung SS Panzer Division "Das Reich"
> Sturmgeschutz Abteilung SS Panzer Division
>   "Das Reich"
> Panzer Jaeger Abteilung SS Panzer Division "Das
>   Reich"
> Nachrichten Abteilung SS Panzer Division "Das
>   Reich"
> Pioniere Bataillon SS Panzer Division "Das
>   Reich"

Plus divisional HQ, divisional HQ Abteilung, and divisional services. In 1943 Panzer Grenadier Regiment SS "Langemark" (two battalions) was attached to the division.

3rd SS Panzer Division "Totenkopf"

In October 1939 after the Polish campaign the first three SS "Totenkopf" regiments were formed into the SS Division Totenkopf (motorised). In November 1942 in southern France, after serving in Russia, this became the SS Panzer Grenadier Division "Totenkopf" and then on October 22, 1943 it was re-designated 3rd SS Panzer Division "Totenkopf". By this time the division was in the Dnepr bend, having returned to Russia, south, in February 1943, to fight at Kharkov in March and Belgorod in the Battle of Kursk in July. It remained on the Eastern front until the end of the war, fighting in the southern Ukraine until July 1944 when it was moved to Bialystok, north-east of Warsaw. In January 1945 it was transferred from the Eastern front, centre, to Hungary, and from there fell back through Vienna to Linz where it surrendered to the Americans in May 1945.

The division's establishment was:

Aufklärung Abteilung SS Panzer Division "Totenkopf"

Panzer Regiment 3 SS Panzer Division "Totenkopf" (two battalions)

SS Panzer Grenadier Regiment 5 "Thule" (three battalions)

SS Panzer Grenadier Regiment 6 "Theodor Eicke" (three battalions)

Artillerie Regiment SS Panzer Division "Totenkopf" (four battalions)

Flak Abteilung SS Panzer Division "Totenkopf"

Sturmgeschütz Abteilung SS Panzer Division "Totenkopf"

Panzer Jaeger Abteilung SS Panzer Division "Totenkopf"

Nachrichten Abteilung SS Panzer Division "Totenkopf"

Pioniere Bataillon SS Panzer Division "Totenkopf"

Plus divisional HQ, divisional HQ Abteilung, and divisional services. In 1942, when it was the SS Division "Totenkopf", "Freikorps Danmark" served in the division.

5th SS Panzer Division "Wiking"

Late in 1940 SS Regiment "Germania" together with SS Regiment "Nordland" (raised from Danish and Norwegian Nazi sympathisers), SS Regiment "Westland" (raised from the Netherlands and Belgium), and the 5th SS Artillery Regiment, formed the "Germania" SS Division. Soon afterwards this title was changed to "Wiking" SS Division. The division fought in Russia.

In November 1942 in the Caucasus the division was re-formed into SS Panzer Grenadier Division "Wiking". It fought on the Manych with Fourth Panzer Army at the beginning of 1943 and then with First Panzer Army in the Kharkov area from February to August, falling back to the Dnepr bend. On October 22, 1943 it was re-designated 5th SS Panzer Division "Wiking".

From January to March 1944 the division continued to fight in Russia, south. It was then moved to Russia, centre, to Kovel east of Lublin. From May to July it was back in Germany, re-fitting at Heidelager, and then returned to the Eastern front, centre. In January 1945 it was moved south to Hungary and it ended the war at Graz, Austria.

The division's establishment was:

Aufklärung Abteilung 5 SS Panzer Division "Wiking"

SS Panzer Abteilung "Wiking" (two battalions)

SS Panzer Grenadier Regiment 9 "Germania" (three battalions)

SS Panzer Grenadier Regiment 10 "Westland" (three battalions)

Artillerie Regiment 5 SS Panzer Division "Wiking" (four battalions)

Flak Abteilung 5 SS Panzer Division "Wiking"

Panzer Jaeger Abteilung 5 SS Panzer Division "Wiking"

Nachrichten Abteilung 5 SS Panzer Division "Wiking"

Pioniere Bataillon 5 SS Panzer Division "Wiking"

Feldersatz Bataillon 5 SS Panzer Division "Wiking"

Versorgungs Einheiten

Plus divisional HQ, divisional HQ Abteilung, and divisional services other than the Versorgungs Einheiten.

9th SS Panzer Division "Hohenstaufen"

Formed in the winter 1942–43 in Berlin as the 9th SS Panzer Grenadier Division it was sent to Ypres in Belgium to complete its formation. On October 22, 1943 the division was re-designated 9th SS Panzer Division "Hohenstaufen".

Its establishment was:

SS Panzer Aufklärung Abteilung 9

SS Panzer Regiment 9 (two battalions)

SS Panzer Grenadier Regiment 19 (three battalions)

SS Panzer Grenadier Regiment 20 (three battalions)

SS Panzer Artillerie Regiment 9 (four battalions)

SS Flak Abteilung 9

SS Sturmgeschütz Abteilung 9

SS Panzer Jaeger Abteilung 9

SS Nachrichten Abteilung 9

SS Pioniere Bataillon 9

Plus divisional HQ, divisional HQ Abteilung, and divisional services.

The division was formed at the same time as the 10th SS Panzer Division "Frundsberg" and with it formed II SS Panzer Corps. In March 1944 it was moved from Ypres to southern France and from there, almost immediately, with 10th SS Panzer Division to the Ukraine to meet a crisis that had developed there. It fought in the Tarnopol sector and then in June was abruptly ordered west, again with 10th SS Panzer Division, to take part in the Normandy battle. II SS Panzer Corps came into action in Normandy during the afternoon of June 29.

After the Normandy defeat the division was re-fitted in the Netherlands and was at Arnhem when the Allied airborne landings took place. It played a major part in defeating that operation. It then took part in the Ardennes offensive as part of Sixth SS Panzer Army, was moved to Hungary in February still as part of that army with the 1st, 2nd and 12th SS Panzer Divisions, and ended the war in Austria.

10th SS Panzer Division "Frundsberg"

Formed in the winter 1942–43 in the south of France as the 10th SS Panzer Grenadier Division. In June 1943 its designation was changed to 10th SS Division "Karl der Grosse", and then, on October 3, on Hitler's order, to SS Panzer Division Frundsberg. Finally, on October 22, it was re-designated 10th SS Panzer Division "Frundsberg". Its two Panzer Grenadier Regiments were changed from 1 and 2 (Frundsberg) to SS Panzer Grenadier Regiments 21 and 22, each with three battalions. The rest of the division's establishment was SS Kradschützen Regiment 10 (two battalions), SS Panzer Regiment 10 "Langemark" (two battalions), SS Panzer Artillerie Regiment 10 (four battalions), SS Flak Abteilung 10, SS Sturmgeschütz Abteilung 10 SS Panzer Jaeger Abteilung 10, SS Nachrichten Abteilung 10, SS Pioniere Bataillon 10, and divisional HQ, divisional HQ Abteilung, and divisional services.

After the completion of its formation the division

moved to northern France in November 1943. It stayed there until March 1944, when it was moved with 9th SS Panzer Division to the Ukraine. It fought at Tarnopol and Lvov and was then ordered to France on June 12, with 9th SS Panzer Division, to join in the Normandy battle. It came into action on June 29 against the British 8 Corps bridgehead across the River Odon.

The division was re-fitted in the Netherlands and was in the Arnhem area when the Allied Operation "Market Garden" took place on September 17; it was sent to defend Nijmegen. In December it took part in the Ardennes offensive, was subsequently moved to Pomerania, and after hard fighting there, on the Oder, and in Lausitz, it surrendered to the Russians in Saxony at the end of the war.

12th SS Panzer Division "Hitlerjugend"

Formed as a Panzer Grenadier Division on July 20, 1943 at Antwerp from cadres of Leibstandarte Adolf Hitler and personnel of the Hitlerjugend Leadership schools. The division was to form I SS Panzer Corps with Leibstandarte Adolf Hitler. On October 21 Hitler ordered that the Corps was to consist of two Panzer

Divisions; consequently, the following day, the division was re-designated 12th SS Panzer Division "Hitlerjugend". Its two Panzer Grenadier Regiments had their designations changed from 1 and 2 (Hitlerjugend) to SS Panzer Grenadier Regiments 25 and 26, each with three battalions. The rest of the division's establishment was SS Panzer Aufklärung Abteilung 12, SS Panzer Regiment 12 (two battalions), SS Panzer Artillerie Regiment 12 (three battalions), SS Panzer Flak Abteilung 12, SS Werfer Abteilung 12, SS Panzer Jaeger Abteilung 12, SS Panzer Nachrichten Abteilung 12, SS Panzer Pioniere Bataillon 12, and divisional HQ, divisional HQ Abteilung, and divisional services.

The division first went into action on June 7, 1944 in the Caen area in Normandy. It provided the backbone to the defence against First Canadian Army during the Battle of Falaise, and then fell back to the Eifel. It was re-fitted at Bremen, took part in the Ardennes offensive, and was then moved to Hungary as part of Sixth SS Panzer Army with three other SS Panzer Divisions— 1st, 2nd and 9th—a move which began on January 20, 1945. At the end of the war the division was in Austria where it surrendered with the rest of what was left of Sixth SS Panzer Army.

GLOSSARY
Abteilung—Company, Detachment
Artillerie—Artillery
Aufklärung—Reconnaissance
Bataillon—Battalion
Flak (Flugabwehrkanone)—Anti-Aircraft Gun
Heeres—Army
Nachrichten—Signals
Panzer—Armour(ed), Tank
Panzerjaeger—Tank Destroyer (lit. Hunter)
Pioniere—Engineers
Sturmgeschütz—Assault Gun
Werfer—(Rocket) projector

Field-Marshal Rudolf Gerd von Rundstedt, Commander-in-Chief West. He had previously commanded Army Group South against Poland in 1939, Army Group A (which had the decisive role) against France in 1940, and Army Group South against Russia in 1941–42.

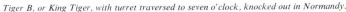

Tiger B, or King Tiger, with turret traversed to seven o'clock, knocked out in Normandy.

PANZER DIVISION

	Officers	Other Ranks	Rifles or Carbines	Pistols	Sub-MGs	LMGs	Heavy MGs	81-mm Mortars	120-mm Mortars	Flame Throwers	20-mm Anti-Aircraft Guns	20-mm Anti-Tank Guns	28/20-mm Anti-Tank Guns	37-mm Anti-Aircraft Guns	75-mm Anti-Tank Guns (Towed)	75-mm Anti-Tank Guns (Self-Propelled)	75-mm Tank Guns (L/43 or L/48)	75-mm Tank Guns (L/70)	88-mm Anti-Aircraft Guns	75-mm Infantry Howitzers (Self-Propelled)	150-mm Infantry Howitzers (Self-Propelled)	105-mm Gun Howitzers (Towed)	105-mm Howitzers (Self-Propelled)	150-mm Howitzers (Towed)	150-mm Howitzers (Self-Propelled)	PzKpfw IV	PzKpfw V Panther	Motor Vehicles	Motor-cycles
(a) Div. H.Q.	32	109	95	44	3																							32	8
(b) Div. H.Q. Abteilung	3	216	138	65	19	16	2	2																				31	28
(c) Panzer Aufklärung Abteilung	27	915	434	300	206	147	4	10		6	4	35				3												199	22
(d) Panzer Regiment	69	1,592	822	704	228	252										13	52	51								52	51	313	53
(e) Panzer Grenadier Regiment¹	64	2,230	1,373	595	336	224	24	14	8	24	6									12	6							406	81
(f) Panzer Grenadier Regiment²	61	2,197	1,449	574	235	144	26	14	8	18	25										6							380	83
(g) Artillery Regiment	69	1,580	1,217	343	203	92					12											12	12	12	6			407	31
(h) Heeres Flak Abteilung	22	742	673	69	47	18					9			8					8									171	16
(i) Panzerjaeger Abteilung	20	493	271	142	100	47					18				12	31												135	17
(j) Nachrichten Abteilung	16	499	444	69	51	35																						114	14
(k) Panzer Pioniere Bataillon	24	861	562	247	102	96	6	6		20																		174	42
(l) Div. Services	64	1,821	1,708	165	13	86						3	3															323	85
	471	13,255	9,186	3,317	1,543	1,157	64	46	16	68	74	38	3	8	12	47	52	51	8	12	12	12	12	12	6	52	51	2,685*	480

13,726

¹ Armoured.
² Motorised.

*including 357 armoured vehicles

SS PANZER DIVISION

	Officers	Other Ranks	Rifles or Carbines	Pistols	Sub-MGs	LMGs	Heavy MGs	81-mm Mortars	120-mm Mortars	Flame Throwers	150- or 210-mm Rocket Projectors	20-mm Anti-Aircraft Guns	20-mm Anti-Tank Guns	28/20-mm Anti-Tank Guns	37-mm Anti-Aircraft Guns	75-mm Anti-Tank Guns (Towed)	75-mm Anti-Tank Guns (Self-Propelled)	75-mm Tank Guns (L/43 or L/48)	75-mm Tank Guns (L/70)	88-mm Anti-Aircraft Guns	75-mm Infantry Howitzers (Self-Propelled)	150-mm Infantry Howitzers (Self-Propelled)	105-mm Gun Howitzers (Towed)	105-mm Gun Howitzers (Self-Propelled)	150-mm Howitzers (Towed)	150-mm Howitzers (Self-Propelled)	170-mm Guns (Self-Propelled)	PzKpfw IV	PzKpfw V Panther	Motor Vehicles	Motor-cycles
(a) Div. H.Q.	32	109	95	44	3																									32	8
(b) Div. H.Q. Abteilung	3	216	138	65	19	16	2	2																						31	28
(c) Panzer Aufklärung Abteilung	27	915	434	300	206	147	4	10		6		4	35				3													193	22
(d) Panzer Regiment	70	1,701	816	719	245	296						6					13	64	62									64	62	313	53
(e) Panzer Grenadier Regiment	89	3,153	1,957	852	443	284	38	20	12	24		43									12	6								527	88
(f) Panzer Grenadier Regiment	89	3,153	1,957	852	443	284	38	20	12	24		43									12	6								527	88
(g) Panzer Artillerie Regiment	89	2,078	1,636	409	255	109																	12	12	12	6	12			534	40
(h) Flak Abteilung	22	802	729	73	47	22						18			8					12										181	16
(i) Sturmgeschütz Abteilung	15	329	294	80	70	22	12										22													100	11
(j) Panzerjaeger Abteilung	20	493	271	142	100	47										12	31													135	17
(k) Panzer Nachrichten Abteilung	16	499	444	69	51	35																								114	14
(l) Panzer Pioniere Bataillon	26	958	654	254	102	99	6	6		20																				212	52
(m) Werfer Abteilung	14	459	380	40	53	18					18																			107	8
(n) Div. Services	64	1,821	1,708	165	13	86							3	3																323	85
	576	16,686	11,513	4,064	2,050	1,465	100	58	24	74	18	114	38	3	8	12	69	64	62	12	24	12	12	12	12	6	12	64	62	3,329*	530

17,262

*including 359 armoured vehicles

63

Index